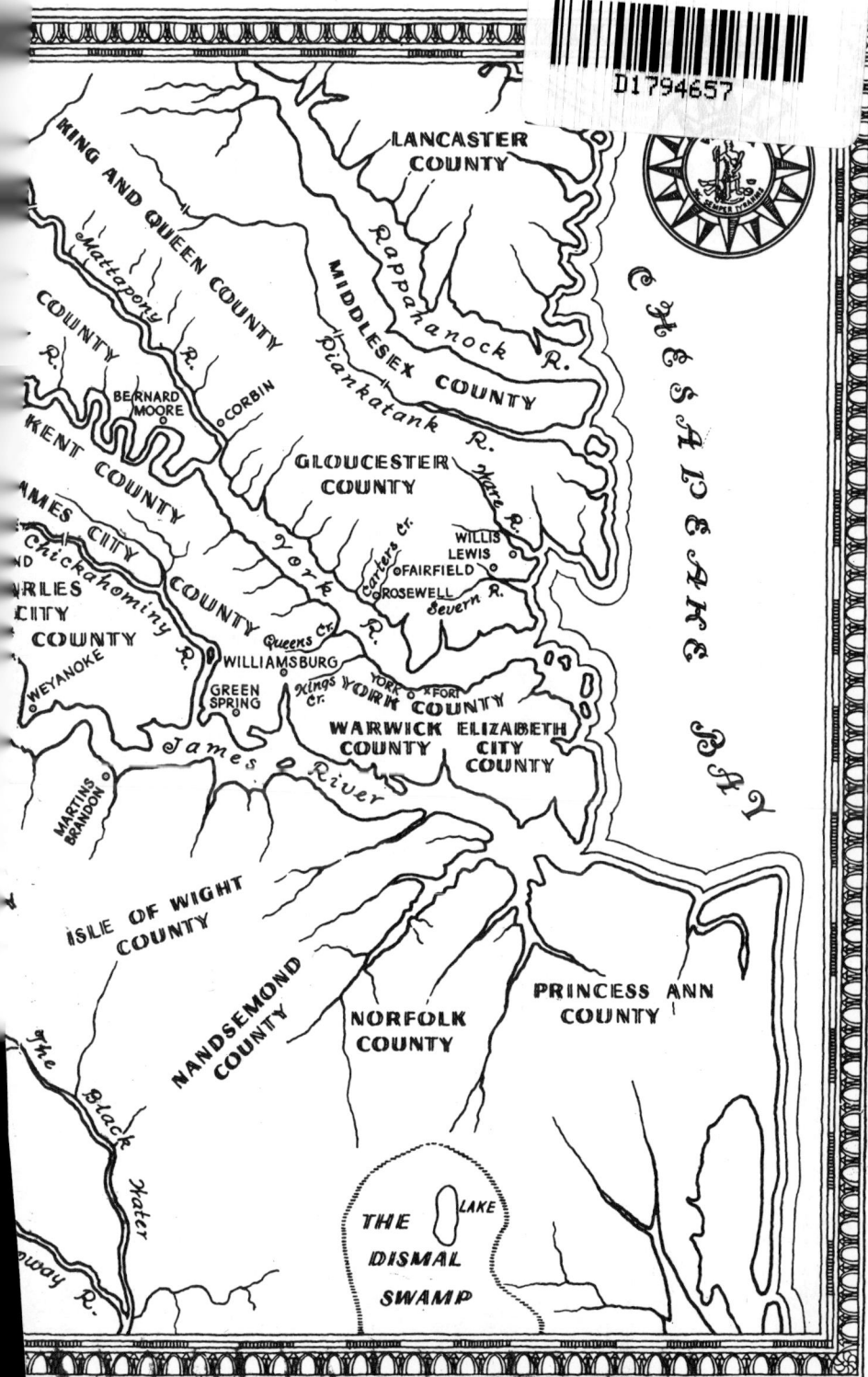

JEFFERSON

THE ROAD TO GLORY

1743–1776

JEFFERSON AT THE SIGNING OF THE DECLARATION OF INDEPENDENCE. By John Trumbull. (*Courtesy of Yale University Art Gallery*)

JEFFERSON THE ROAD TO GLORY

1743 to 1776

by

Marie Kimball

GREENWOOD PRESS, PUBLISHERS
WESTPORT, CONNECTICUT

Library of Congress Cataloging in Publication Data

Kimball, Marie Goebel, 1889-1955.
   Jefferson, the road to glory, 1743-1776.

  Reprint of the ed. published by Coward-McCann, New York.
   Includes bibliographical references and index.
   1. Jefferson, Thomas, Pres. U.S., 1743-1826.
2. Presidents--United States--Biography. I. Title.
E332.K5 1977   973.4'6'0924 [B]   76-52415
ISBN 0-8371-9444-X

COPYRIGHT, 1943, BY COWARD-MCCANN, INC.

Originally published in 1943 by Coward-McCann, Inc., New York

Reprinted in 1977 by Greenwood Press, Inc.

Library of Congress catalog card number 76-52415

ISBN 0-8371-9444-X

Printed in the United States of America

*TO THE MEMORY OF A GREAT SCHOLAR,
AND MY FATHER,
JULIUS GOEBEL*

AUTHOR'S NOTE

The author wishes to express her deep appreciation of the kindness and generosity of the various institutions whose manuscripts and books she has been privileged freely to use. They are the Manuscript Division of the Library of Congress, the Massachusetts Historical Society, the Virginia Historical Society, the Historical Society of Pennsylvania, the Division of Manuscripts of the New York Public Library, the Alderman Library of the University of Virginia, the Library of Yale University, the Henry E. Huntington Library, the Library of the University of California, the State Library, Richmond, Virginia, and the Library Company of Philadelphia.

She wishes particularly to thank Fiske Kimball. He has patiently discussed all phases of the book with her. He has given her the benefit of his wisdom, and he has made her fight, bleed, and die for her opinions.

Contents

	Aristocrat or Backwoodsman?	3
I.	Who Were the Jeffersons?	7
II.	An Eight O'clock Scholar	26
III.	The Class of 1762	39
IV.	Love Is Young	64
V.	"Old Coke"	73
VI.	A Taste for Literature	100
VII.	Young Blood	130
VIII.	The House on a Mountain	147
IX.	True Love	166
X.	Impulse to Revolution	187
XI.	The Four Freedoms	209
XII.	The Rights of British America	229
XIII.	The Gentleman from Virginia	251
XIV.	The Road to Glory	277
	Notes	307
	Index	337

Illustrations

Thomas Jefferson, by John Trumbull	*frontispiece*
Excavations at Shadwell	20
The College of William and Mary	40
Governor Francis Fauquier	50
The Governor's Palace, Williamsburg	56
George Wythe, after Trumbull	74
Jefferson's Early Handwriting	84
The Plantations along the Southwest Mountains	140
View from Monticello toward the Blue Ridge	150
The South Outchamber at Monticello	154
Jefferson's Design for Monticello, 1771-1772	160
Letter of Martha Wayles Jefferson	170
The Capitol, Williamsburg	190
Jefferson's College Plan for Lord Dunmore	232
Jefferson, by Mather Brown, 1786	254
The Declaration of Independence, by Trumbull	302

JEFFERSON

THE ROAD TO GLORY

1743-1776

Aristocrat or Backwoodsman?

THOMAS JEFFERSON has not ordinarily been regarded as the scion of one of the great Virginia families. Indeed, owing to his own casual attitude toward the question of ancestry, little attention has been paid to his antecedents, beyond his parentage. Largely on the basis of his statement that his father was the third or fourth settler in that "part of the country in which I live," and that his father's "education had been quite neglected," Peter Jefferson has been pictured as an ignorant backwoodsman. Strangely and inexplicably, according to this view, he had married a member of the great and wealthy Randolph clan, much his superior in the social scale. This delicately reared woman he took into the wilderness, to a house that was little more than a cabin, with only the roughest and rudest of accommodations. From this curious union sprang the man who, as the son of this father, has been revered as the champion of the lowly, yet, as the son of this mother, has been execrated as faithless to his class.

Jefferson's biographers have hitherto quite overlooked the fact that the family was one of substance and position in the seventeenth century, indeed, that they had intermarried with the Randolphs at an early period. They have likewise failed to observe that the Randolphs and other great Virginia families, as well as the Jeffersons, participated in a gradual immigration upstream and westward from the Tidewater in search of virgin soil. It was a normal procedure for the rich Virginia planter to move from his exhausted fields to his more fertile and more distant lands. Thus Isham Randolph, son of William of Turkey Island and maternal grandfather of Thomas Jefferson, went from the Tidewater to Dungeness, his plantation some 35 miles above the falls of the James

River. His daughter Jane, who married Peter Jefferson, settled with her husband about the same number of miles to the west on the Rivanna, a tributary of the James. These families necessarily at first lived in small outbuildings, or outchambers, as Jefferson was later to call them, until the great house could be built. Even Jefferson did this, in 1772, when he brought his young wife to Monticello, the new house on his paternal acres.

Jefferson has had the misfortune to be first portrayed by his enemies. John Marshall's "Life of Washington," published in 1804-1807, gave the earliest of these hostile pictures. It was, in essence, a party document, systematically belittling and deprecating the victorious leader of the opposing party. In 1809 Henry Lee, then in prison for debt, wrote his "Memoirs of the War in the Southern Department." It bristles with embittered hostility to Jefferson, to whose triumphant elevation to the presidency Lee attributed his own ruin. Henry Adams, in his "History of the United States," which covers the administrations of Jefferson and Madison, could not wholly forget his own ancestral loyalties. More recently Albert J. Beveridge's "Life of Marshall" revived the prejudices of its hero. Although Beveridge subsequently came to understand and admire Jefferson, he did not live to repair his injustice. These are the books which, fundamentally, have determined the prevailing attitude toward Jefferson, even to this day.

Jefferson's own biographers have, alas, been no such figures as his detractors. The first, George Tucker, who published his "Life of Thomas Jefferson" in 1837, has little to say to us today. Essentially, there has been but one biography of importance, that of Henry S. Randall, published in 1858. Although its style, now flowery, now hortatory, always adulatory, dates the book and makes it difficult reading, it is a storehouse of information. At the time Randall wrote, Jefferson's papers and accounts were still intact in the hands of his descendants at Edgehill. Randall made full and able use of them in his three volumes. His book thus became a mine of material for secondary, journalistic lives. So fully did Randall present these family papers that, with few exceptions, most subsequent biographers scarcely looked anywhere else. The majority of more recent biographies are little more than a paraphrase and condensation of Randall. Indeed, whole sentences, if not whole passages, may often be recognized. Again and again, particularly for the early years, the biographers have merely written with Randall open before them, without adding anything of their own.

Randall devoted but 164 of his two thousand pages to Jefferson's early life, including the writing of the Declaration. Subsequent biographers, following in the footsteps of their master, have not done much more. In about a hundred pages, sometimes a little more, sometimes a little less, they have hurried over these years in their haste to reach those which were crowded with public duties and honors, while Jefferson was Secretary of State and President. The period immediately following the writing of the Declaration, the period of Jefferson's greatest service to his "country," as he called Virginia, in which he reformed the archaic and often inhuman laws and institutions of the state, has, to be sure, been given some attention. The tragic years of his governorship, with a dying wife at his side, when he wisely devoted all the strength of Virginia, in men and materiél, to the common cause, instead of employing it merely for the defense of the state, have left him branded in the public eye as a coward. No person has ever accused Samuel Adams or John Hancock of cowardice in fleeing from Lexington when warned by Paul Revere that the British were coming. Thanks to the calumnies of a discredited English journalist nearly a century and a half ago, Jefferson is to this day charged with unmanly conduct in having left Monticello after Jack Jouett rode up the mountain to warn him that Tarleton's dragoons were near.

Since Randall's day, many new sources have been made available. The journals of the various public bodies with which Jefferson was connected have become readily accessible, the letters and public papers of many of the men who worked with him in forming the United States have been published or placed at the disposal of the scholar. Jefferson's own letters, his account books, his memorandum books of various kinds have gradually, and to a great extent, come into public hands.

So far these sources have not been employed to shed much

light on Jefferson's early years. From them now emerges the picture of an eager, thoughtful youth, who would "fly to his studies," as his best friend remarked, but who, at the same time, "panted after the fine arts," made music several hours a day, danced away the evenings, or spent them with a crony at backgammon and chess. The influences, social and educational, the background of family and friends which created the man that was Jefferson, spring to life. The picture of the aloof and solitary man, fond of old slippers and plain clothes, bent upon practicing the democracy he was preaching, gives way to that of a gay young blade in a scarlet coat, a devoted lover, an adoring husband, a model paterfamilias, who, in his country's hour of need, revealed himself a great philosopher and an inspired public servant.

I. Who were the Jeffersons?

THERE WAS enchantment in the summer air. The lush fragrance of abundant honeysuckle drifted down the mountainsides and hovered over the green and smiling valley that lay at their feet. The warm sun brought out the rich and pungent odor of the forest, to which no man had yet put an axe. It was a symphony of "mountains distant and near, smooth and shaggy, single and in ridges, a little river hiding itself among the hills so as to shew in lagoons only," as the most distinguished citizen of the region was later to write. There was no sign of habitation, no house, no barns, no mill, no road, no path, only the narrow, threadlike trail made by the silent feet of the red men. Along this came riding a tall, sandy-haired man, mounted on a handsome mare. He was drinking in the perfume of the valley with long, deep breaths, and his eyes were shining with the wonder and delight of the prospect before him.

The year was 1734 and the young rider—he was twenty-six years old at the time—was Peter Jefferson, destined to become the father of Thomas Jefferson. He had ridden over from his plantation on Fine Creek, a few miles above the falls of the James, to the western part of the newly formed county of Goochland, in Virginia, where the distant ridges of the Blue Mountains jutted into the horizon. In this region William Randolph of Tuckahoe, his neighbor and most intimate friend, had already patented many hundreds of acres, and the talk of the two men was ever full of the miracle of this beautiful land, of the richness and fertility of a soil still virgin. On this summer day Peter Jefferson was frankly looking for new worlds to conquer. He was a keen and ambitious man, fully aware that the Tidewater was being worn out by too intensive cultivation with a crop that took all from the land and gave nothing in return. Like many of his neighbors, he was eager to extend his holdings and expand his fortune. This verdant countryside, where there were as yet but few settlers, was to him his promised land. The region was at this time no longer the actual frontier, for the Indians had retreated beyond the mountains, but rather, as William Byrd expressed it, "a retired part of the country."

Although the Jeffersons had hitherto not been among the large landholders of Virginia, or one of the most prominent families, they had been established and respected for several generations. Indeed, Thomas Jefferson's grandfather and great-grandfather held various public offices in the colony. The name appears in the very early records. A "Mr. Jefferson" is mentioned as one of the two delegates of Flower de Hundred in the Virginia Assembly of 1619, the first legislative body called in the New World.[1] John Jefferson, a blacksmith, is listed as living in Elizabeth City County in 1623, but it has never been proven that he was related to the family from whom the President was descended. There was a Robert Jefferson to whom, in 1666,[2] were granted 92 acres of land in Gloucester County, but his identity is likewise nebulous.

The first man of the name who was unquestionably an ancestor was a Thomas Jefferson residing in Henrico County in the late seventeenth century. The date of his birth is not known. We do know, however, that he was a surveyor, an important functionary at that period, as well as one of the more colorful and prominent citizens. His name occurs more than fifty times in the extant records of the period as a juror, a witness to wills, an appraiser, a surveyor, a recipient of bounty for killing wolves, or in some other capacity,[3] something that has hitherto been quite overlooked. The earliest mention of him is in the will of Christopher Branch of Kingsland, Henrico County, dated June 20, 1678, of which he was one of the executors.[4] Thomas Jefferson's plantation was in the so-called Curles section of the James, where the river begins its snakelike peregrinations, near that of Sir Thomas Dale and Sir Thomas Yardley's Flower de Hundred, which lends not a little color to the idea that he was related to the "Mr. Jefferson" of

1619. In this vicinity, on one side of the river or the other, also lived the Randolphs, the Ishams, the Eppes, Fields, Branches, Cockes, and Blands, all families likewise prominent in the history of Virginia.

This Thomas Jefferson, the great-grandfather of the President, died in 1697. An "Inventory of all and singular goods and chattels" was filed on October 1, 1698.[5] Exclusive of negroes, corn, and tobacco, which usually accounted for a large part of a man's fortune, the estate amounted to £97 16s 16½d, a not inconsiderable sum at this time. Thus Thomas Osborne, a close friend who, in 1625, had settled at "Coxendale" in Henrico, not far from Jefferson, left a will—to which Jefferson was a witness—that was proved in 1692.[6] His estate was valued at £125, and he was esteemed a man rather better off than the average.

The estate left by Thomas Jefferson was much what might have been left by any prosperous planter of those days.[7] He divided his possessions into three parts, which he left to his widow, his son, Thomas, and his daughter, Martha. Each of the three legatees received a "feather bed, Bolster and Pillow, a Rugg & blankett." There were the usual bed curtains, "vallens," hide and bed cords, two couches, three chests with lock and key, the inevitable trunk in which the finest garments were kept—this time of black leather—the canvas "sheetes," diaper tablecloths, towels, and napkins, three "rusha leather chaires," five "rush bottom chairs," a considerable amount of silver, pewter, and kitchen utensils, and, among other things, a looking glass, ivory comb and brush, a "hatt" brush, and a "silver dram cup. Buttons & shoe buckels."

Thomas Jefferson, Jun'r, or Captain Jefferson, as he was known —the son of the preceding Thomas—was born about 1677.[8] He was also a man of position in the community In 1714 he became a justice of the peace,[9] and in 1718 and 1719 he acted as a sheriff of Henrico County.[10] The office of sheriff was a dignified one in the seventeenth and early eighteenth centuries. The incumbent saw that the orders of the court were executed, he summoned the voters to election, and collected the taxes, fines, and fees. In 1723, Captain Jefferson built a church in Bristol parish which, until its destruction in the nineteenth century, was known as "Jefferson's church." [11] As his title indicates, he was a captain of the militia. This is substantiated by William Byrd, who wrote in his diary on September 23, 1711, "about 11 we went to church with Will Kennon's troop to wait on me and there we found Captain Jefferson's, Captain Bolling's, Captain Eppes' and Captain Worsham's troops and companies which made a good appearance." [12] On October 2 Byrd again remarks that "about 11 we took horse and rode to Captain Jefferson's where the militia of that side of the river was drawn up. I reviewed them a little and because they were not all come I went to Captain Jefferson's house where we drank some persico and then returned into the field where I caused the troops to be exercised by each captain and they performed but indifferently for which I reproved them. . . . When all was over we went to dine with Captain Jefferson and I ate some roast beef." [13]

In 1698 Jefferson married Mary Field. The "Lycence" was granted on April 13 of that year. She was the daughter of Major Peter Field of New Kent County and of Judith, his wife, widow of Henry Randolph.[14] It was an early connection of the two families that was destined to extend to President Jefferson's own children and beyond. Captain Jefferson and his wife started in their married life at Osborne's in Henrico, subsequently Chesterfield County, and owned the lands which later became the glebe of the parish, according to the autobiography of their famous grandson.[15] Osborne's was not the name of his plantation but of the locality where he lived, a dozen miles from Bermuda Hundred. Like so many other settlements on the James, it took its name from the man who owned the wharf or warehouse at a given point, in this case Thomas Osborne. At first only a few houses clustered about the wharf. Gradually a custom house and a store were added, and presently there emerged a full-fledged community of a dozen or so souls.

At a court held at Varina, Henrico County, on December 1, 1699, a property of 167 acres on the south side of the James, called Mount-My-Lady in the deed, passed from Robert Hancock to Thomas Jefferson.[16] It was the site of the famous Mt. Malado, a retreat for the sick, built by Sir Thomas Dale at the time of the establishment of Henrico in 1611, and appears on Fry and Jefferson's map of 1752 as Mt. Malawdy. Young Jefferson continued to increase his holdings, and various small grants of land in Henrico were made to him, often in conjunction with others, from 1704 to 1718. Like most of his Tidewater neighbors, however, his thoughts early turned to the fresh and untouched lands lying farther up the James beyond the falls, and in 1718 he, with three other men, patented 1500 acres "lying and being at a place called Fine Creek."[17] This lay in the western part of Henrico that was to become Goochland County in 1727, and formed the nucleus of his son Peter's inheritance. Jefferson was among the first to acquire land in this region, preceding even the land-hungry Randolphs by several years. In 1720 he seems to have met with misfortune, for on December 8 of that year a "petition of Thomas Jefferson setting forth his great loss sustained by fire and praying relief thereon" was presented to the Assembly. The Committee of Claims considered it, among others, and made several allowances, but we are not told whether Jefferson received anything.[18]

Captain Jefferson's name occurs frequently in the Henrico records, usually in connection with the sale, purchase, or escheating of land. He appears to have been a man of enterprising temperament. A sidelight on his means, which were sufficient for him to race a horse, something not possible for a "common fellow," is revealed in a suit brought at Varina on April 1, 1698. Jefferson's mare, Bony, was matched against a horse named Watt, "said horse and mare to Run at the race-place commonly called ye Ware." The wager was £5, a considerable sum for the period. "The aforesaid Mare, with her Rider who weighed about one hundred and thirty, Did Leap off, and outrunning the aforesaid horse, came in first."[19] The rider of the defeated horse, Watt, was loath to pay and suit was brought, in which Mr. Jefferson came out the victor.

The life of Thomas Jefferson, Junior, was not to be a long one. An entry in the family Bible states that he died in the fifty-third year of his age.[20] He left two sons and three daughters. The name Thomas had been carried on and given to his eldest son, born on September 24, 1700, but he died when only twenty-three years old, "being on a voyage on Board the Williamsburg, Capt. Isham Randolph commander to Virginia."[21] Two years later, on March 15, 1725, Captain Jefferson made his will, which was not proved until six years later.[22] To Field, the eldest living son, born in 1702, was given "a mourning ring of the value of twenty shillings." Under the system of entail then prevailing in Virginia he doubtless inherited the property at Osborne's.[23] Peter, the third son, was made chief beneficiary of his father's will. "Upon my son, Peter Jefferson, and his Heirs forever," were bestowed "my land on Fine Creek and ye Maniken Creek," the will reads. "I also give unto my son, Peter, and to his Heirs forever, two Negro's Farding and Pompey. I also give unto my son Peter my chest and wearing cloaths with the cloth and trimming that is in the chest, my cane, my six silver spoons which I bought of Turpin, Two Horses named Norman and Squirrell, my Trooping Arms and Gunn I had of Joseph Wilkinson, Two Feather Beds, Ruggs and Blankets, one suit of curtains and Vallains, a Diaper Table Cloth and six napkins ... the Couch standing in the Hall and the Two Tables standing there, six Leather chairs, Half my stock of cattle, sheep, and Hogs." The remainder of the property was divided between his three daughters, Mary, Martha, and Judith Farrar.

Peter Jefferson had been born on February 29, 1708, and was thus twenty-two years old when his father died. On the basis of Thomas Jefferson's observation in his autobiography, that his "father's education had been quite neglected," it has been customary to regard Peter Jefferson as a countryman of negligible intellectual attainments, as well as of scant property. His formal education may very well have been haphazard but, as his son remarks, "he read much and improved himself." Too much emphasis cannot be laid on Jefferson's remarks concerning his father's schooling as he wrote in his seventy-seventh year of a man already 63 years dead. Peter Jefferson's training was doubtless not inferior to that of most planters of his day, when schooling was difficult to obtain in the colonies and when only the wealthiest young men were sent to England to study. In the inventory of his property, filed after his death on August 17, 1757, we find 42 books listed, betraying a variety of interests and indicating that Peter

WHO WERE THE JEFFERSONS? 13

Jefferson was far from being an uneducated man.[24] Among these books are "Rapin's History of England in 2 vols.," along with "2 vol. of the continuation thereof, Solomon's State tryals, Ogilvie's Description of America, 1 quarto Bible with Book of Common Prayer, Nelson's Office of a Justice, Scrivener's Guide, 2 vol., The present State of Great Britain, The London and Country Brewer, Trent's Dictionary, Frank's Astronomy, A Secret History of Queen Anne's Ministers, Switzer's [illegible], Virginia Justice, Anson's Voyage round the World, A large Prayer Booke, Bishop of Sador and Man's Instruction for Indians, Three Old books, Spect^r IX volumes, Tattler 5 vols, Guard^n 2 vols, Addis^n Works, 3 vols, Map of the 4 Quarters of the World, Map of the City of London, Do of Virginia, Four old maps."

Peter Jefferson's library compares not unfavorably with those of his friends and contemporaries. His closest friend, Joshua Fry, a former professor at William and Mary, who was considered a learned man and who might well have been expected to leave a handsome library, disposed of only "1 Parcell of Books in y^e out Room £4.17.6 Ditto, ditto in the back room 26 sh. Ditto, ditto the out shed, 8 sh. 6 d = £5.12."[25] John Harvie, another friend, who died 12 years after Peter Jefferson, had 189 titles, "a parcel of French and Latin books," and "a number of Books about the country in different hands, titles unknown."[26] The Reverend James Maury, with whom Thomas Jefferson, the future President, later studied, was probably possessed of the largest library of anyone in the upland community. On his death, in 1770, there are found 400 volumes and 44 pamphlets.[27] Davis Stockton, another Albemarle resident, had two books worth five shillings, John Farrar had three, and Charles Smith, who died in 1761, owned "One Bible and Testament and one Sermon Book." Such books represented the "library" of the ordinary man. Clearly, Peter Jefferson, in reading as well as in property, belonged not with men such as these, but with those of the upper class.

The lands on Fine Creek and Manakin Creek, two streams falling into the James a few miles above the falls at Richmond, were, thus, Peter Jefferson's chief inheritance. The land is flat and was, at that time, new and fertile, ideally adapted for growing tobacco.

Time and abuse have dealt cruelly with it. Today it is a picture of desolation, barren, and covered with a forest of scrub trees. An abandoned mill nestles under some tall oaks on Fine Creek, but it is improbable that this one had anything to do with Peter Jefferson. The last remaining link to his name is a small settlement some miles from the creek still known as "Jefferson."

It has not been definitely established just when Peter Jefferson settled on Fine Creek. We can assume that it was before 1731, however, for in that year he was made one of the magistrates of the new county of Goochland in which his property lay. Six years later he was appointed sheriff.[28] In his account book for 1728, under the heading "Dr. Mr. Thomas Jefferson in Acc't with Peter," we find noted "To building a house at Fine Creek, £3-10, To building 2 Tob° Houses at D° £3."[29] This "house" may very well have been the small building which the law demanded should be erected in order to "seat" the new plantation, before full title was given.[30] Obviously no "great house" could be constructed for £3-10 even at that time. Peter Jefferson's accounts for these early years, which might tell us so much, are, alas, so fragmentary that it is impossible to learn much from them. Dealing mostly with such casual items as "1731, Oct. 19. To expenses in Wmsburgh on a Tryall with Chambone, £1-2," or with cash paid for a mare, for some corn, or for hauling tobacco, they are far from being the all-revealing chronicle of daily doings left by his famous son.

At the time Peter Jefferson probably built at Fine Creek, few of the great plantation houses we regard as characteristic of colonial Virginia had yet been constructed. At the majority, if not all, the well-known plantations, the first building of the group to be erected and occupied was not the mansion house but one of its outbuildings —by itself of no exceptional character. The houses of this time, even those of prosperous planters, were of no great size or pretensions. The typical house was of wood, with end chimneys. Most of them were still one room deep, with but two rooms on a floor; it was rare to have a full second story. Tuckahoe, the Randolph house across the James, which was begun in 1725, certainly consisted at first of only the end of the H which it came to constitute. Peter Jefferson's house, then, we have every reason to assume, was a small, preliminary structure or, at most, the story and a half house characteristic of this period.

Near neighbors of the Jeffersons, as neighbors went in those days, likewise living in the so-called Curles section of the James, but on the north side of the river, were the Randolphs. The Randolphs were a family of considerable distinction in England during the seventeenth century. The first to emigrate to America, in 1674, was William, who settled at Turkey Island on the James River, about 25 miles below Richmond. In 1680 he had married Mary, the daughter of Colonel Henry Isham of Bermuda Hundred, the plantation almost opposite his own, on the south side of the James. Their third son, Isham, born in December 1655, following the trend of the day to go up the river to new land, established himself at Dungeness on the north side of the James, some thirty miles above Richmond and about ten from Fine Creek.[31] His house, as well as the two succeeding ones, all long since gone, stood in a grove of lofty trees, on a bluff overlooking the fertile fields that lie in the valley of the James. A long avenue of ancient cedars leads from the river road to the plantation which, although deserted, still bears its old name. It was a large estate, some three thousand acres, and a hundred slaves are said to have been employed about the place.

Isham Randolph, Thomas Jefferson's maternal grandfather, was a man of considerable consequence in the colony. He was Colonial Agent from Virginia in London for some years during his early life. After returning to Virginia he became a member of the House of Burgesses and in 1738 was made Adjutant General of the Colony, "being well known and universally acceptable," as the Journal of the Council states.[32] In 1740 he was appointed colonel of the Goochland militia. He was a man of education and cultivation. It may well have been partly from him that his grandson inherited his lifelong interest in the natural sciences. In London Isham Randolph had made the acquaintance of Peter Collinson, the distinguished naturalist and well-known correspondent of Linnaeus. Collinson was likewise a correspondent of John Bartram, the Philadelphia botanist. When the latter proposed to journey to Virginia, in 1737, to study the flora of the country, Collinson sent him a sketch of his friend along with a piece of advice. "When thee proceeds home," he writes, "I know no person who will make thee more welcome than Isham Randolph. He lives thirty or forty miles above the falls of James River, in Goochland, above the other settlements. Now I take his house to be a very suitable place to make a settlement at, for to take several days' excursions all round, and to return to his house at night.... One thing I must desire of thee, and do insist that thee must oblige me therein: that thou make up that drugget cloth, to go to Virginia in, and not appear to disgrace thyself or me: for though I should not esteem thee the less to come to me in what dress thou wilt, yet these Virginians are a very gentle, well-dressed people, and look perhaps more at a man's outside than at his inside. For these and other reasons, pray go very clean, neat, and handsomely dressed to Virginia." [33]

The connection formed between Bartram and Isham Randolph, and the sharing of interests, was continued by the latter's grandson, Thomas Jefferson, with the John Bartram and William Bartram of his day, in interchanges of seeds and information.

In 1717, while Isham Randolph was in London, he met and married Jane Rogers, daughter of Charles Rogers and Jane Lilburn.[34] Three years later the eldest of their eleven children was born and named Jane, for her mother. It was she who, at the age of nineteen, became the wife of Peter Jefferson and the mother of Thomas Jefferson. At the time of his marriage Peter Jefferson was thirty-one years of age and a very eligible young man. He was the intimate friend and boon companion of William Randolph of Tuckahoe, cousin of his future wife, and it may well have been through this connection that he met young Jane Randolph. They were married in October 1739. Their marriage bond, signed by "Pet Jefferson and Arthur Hopkins" and dated October 3, 1739, is the most prized of all the documents in lovely, sleepy Goochland County Court House.

Jane Randolph brought her husband a marriage portion of £200 sterling, the same amount as Peter was later to leave to each of his own daughters. It was not paid, however, until Isham Randolph's death in 1742. Young Peter Jefferson was possessed of much more

WHO WERE THE JEFFERSONS?

property than has hitherto been realized, some 5000 acres which he himself had patented, in addition to what he had inherited, and an interest in 50,000 acres lying toward the Blue Ridge Mountains for which he and six others sought a patent in 1737. It was a period at which large tracts were readily acquired by suitable persons; when not the lowly and outcast sought a few acres toward the west, but when people of substance increased their property by patenting new lands up the river or in outlying counties. This is very clearly brought out by a decision of the Council at a meeting held on May 5, 1741, when the petition of Alexander Stinson for 1200 acres in Goochland was rejected "as the petitioner is not known to any of this Board and therefore thought too much for so obscure a person."[35] Peter Jefferson was perfectly aware of this and was not slow to take advantage of it. In company with William Randolph, Thomas Turpin, his brother-in-law, and others, he patented large tracts, and he was later active with John Lewis, the emigrant from Pennsylvania, Joshua Fry, Thomas Walker, John Harvie, and others in the formation of the Loyal Land Company. From the land books, deed books and surveyor's books of the various counties, insofar as they are still extant, from the Legislative Journals of the Council of Colonial Virginia, and from Thomas Jefferson's own farm book, in which he gives a roll of his lands in 1794 with the date of their first acquisition, it is now possible to reconstruct a picture of Peter Jefferson's holdings from 1730, when he acquired his first 322 acres of land, until his death in 1757.[36]

From these sources also we learn that not only was he a far greater landholder and speculator in land than has hitherto been known, but that in the twenty years following the patenting of the first thousand acres which became Monticello, he added about three thousand acres in adjoining farms.[37] To assist him in the management of these, he employed a steward and five overseers,[38] something hitherto scarcely appreciated. This effectively disposes of the idea advanced by certain writers that Peter Jefferson belonged to "the overseer class."

Of interest here is primarily the land on which Peter Jefferson made his home and where his son was to be born. On July 14, 1735, he patented one thousand acres on the south side of the

Rivanna River, land which was subsequently to become Thomas Jefferson's beloved Monticello. The following year Peter Jefferson and his convivial friend, William Randolph, concluded their famous agreement whereby the former acquired part of the Shadwell tract. The document reads: "The indenture made this eighteenth day of May in the year of our Lord Christ MDCCXXXVI between William Randolph Junr of the County of Goochland Gent. of the one part and Peter Jefferson of the said County Gent. of the other part Witnesseth that the said William Randolph for and in consideration of Henry Wetherburn's biggest bowl of Arrack punch to him delivered at and before the sealing and delivery of these presents the receipt whereof the said W. R. doth hereby acknowledge hath granted etc., unto the said Peter Jefferson and to his heirs & assigns one certain tract or parcell of land 200 acres on the north side of the Northanna in the parish of St. James Goochland, 18 May, 1736." [39] In 1741 Jefferson bought the two hundred adjoining acres from Randolph, and it was on this property that he is said to have established himself.

Just how long after securing his land Peter Jefferson settled there, we do not know. Jefferson observes in his "Autobiography" that his father was "the third or fourth settler about the year 1737." Whether he merely "seated" the plantation at this time, and made the necessary clearing and planting, leaving the place in charge of tenants or servants, or whether he started on his dwelling house, we have no way of telling. We do know, however, that before the spring of 1743 he had brought to it his wife and two little daughters, Jane and Mary. He named the place Shadwell, after the parish in London where Jane Randolph had been born. His house stood in a clearing on a slight rise of ground, embowered in glowing, flowering trees, redbud and dogwood, against a background of tender green poplars, chestnuts, walnut, sycamores, and locusts, interspersed with the deep green of cedars and firs. He may have thought of these low hills only as land to be cleared, but he saw the vision of the Blue Ridge beyond, and this vision he transmitted to his son.

The Three Notch'd Road passed near Shadwell on its way to Secretary's Ford, not far distant, and kept the Jefferson family from feeling too much out of the world. Indians often passed by on their way to Williamsburg, but they were not hostile Indians and Peter Jefferson was their friend. Many years later his son was to write of the pleasant relationship that existed between the red men and the Jefferson family. They were, he observed, "a people with whom, in the early part of my life, I was very familiar, and acquired impressions of attachment and commiseration for them which have never been obliterated. Before the Revolution they were in the habit of coming often and in great numbers to the seat of government, where I was very much with them. I knew much of the great Ontasseté, the warrior and orator of the Cherokees; he was always the guest of my father, on his journeys to and from Williamsburg. I was in his camp when he made his great farewell oration to his people, the evening before his departure for England. The moon was in full splendor, and to her he seemed to address himself in his prayers for his own safety on the voyage, and that of his people during his absence; his sounding voice, distinct articulation, animated action, and the solemn silence of his people at their several fires, filled me with awe and veneration, although I did not understand a word he uttered." [40]

Despite its remoteness and scarcity of population this section was by no means the frontier. The real Virginia frontier, with its defenses of block houses, stockades, and forts, was at this time a good hundred miles to the west of Shadwell, in what is now Highland County and West Virginia. From certain records we learn that in 1745, two years after Jefferson's birth, there were, in what are now the limits of Albemarle County, 106 white inhabitants, 177 Negroes, and 1 Indian. Within a year the white population had increased to 160, and the Negro to 200.[41] On the basis of calculations in Jefferson's "Notes on Virginia," it has been figured out that there were in 1745, in the whole county, which included what is now Buckingham, parts of Appomattox and Campbell, as well as Amherst, Nelson, and Fluvanna Counties, 4250 souls.[42]

This great and unwieldy county was subdivided by an act of the Assembly in September 1744, to take effect on December 31 of the same year. The dividing line was to be the Point of Fork of the James River, and the land lying to the west of that became the new county of Albemarle. The first county court was to meet in January of that year, although it was not until February that it actually convened, and Peter Jefferson was appointed one of the justices, along with Joshua Fry and four others. On March 28, 1745,[43] he was made a lieutenant colonel of the militia. In 1755 he received the accolade of being named county lieutenant,[44] an office which combined the functions of commander in chief of the militia with that of patron saint to the community. One year before this he had been chosen to represent Albemarle in the House of Burgesses, where he served on several committees, chiefly the one for the courts of justice.[45] As one of the outstanding citizens of the county, he replaced Benjamin Cocke as a vestryman of the parish of St. James, Northam, in 1747.[46]

It has hitherto been assumed that Peter Jefferson built the usual Virginia farmhouse of the period and region, a story and a half in height, with four main rooms, garret chambers, and brick chimneys against each end. Randall, Jefferson's early biographer, depending on family tradition nearly three generations later, says this was the case.[47] In 1851 he saw there only "a cavity, nearly filled by the plough ... bits of broken bricks and plaster, and remnants of chimney-stones, fire-cracked and vitrified, which lay in and about it." All ideas of Jefferson's birthplace have meanwhile rested solely on this passage. The remains seen by Randall were by no means necessarily those of any of the earliest plantation buildings, antedating the fire which destroyed the Shadwell house in 1770. The property was leased in 1800 to Craven Peyton and we find allusions to construction there at that period.[48] When this subsequent house was destroyed is not known. Following this the land was long abandoned to cultivation. The site is now occupied again by the numerous buildings of a plantation group dating from the years following 1870.

The accounts of Peter Jefferson and the ground itself have more to tell us. The former are very fragmentary for the early years, as we have seen, and there are no entries for building at Shadwell at this time. Such work as was undertaken may well have been done by his servants or slaves. In 1753, however, much building was executed for Jefferson by one John Biswell. Log tobacco houses

THE EXCAVATIONS AT SHADWELL

WHO WERE THE JEFFERSONS?

were built on Chapel Ridge and at New Quarter. Biswell spent 42 days working on the mill, and Jupiter and Samson 20 days each. There are many other items for which no place is stated and which would thus seem to have been on the home plantation. "By 517 yards of Lathes @ 3 farthings per yard. £3-12-," writes Jefferson. "By mill fraim & plank, as he says 1954 foot, £3-12-, By his 16th part of Lime Stone House buildings, £1-6-, By 42 days work on the Mill @ 2/6—£5-5-, By 20 days Jupiter and Samson on D° @ 1/3, £2-10-, By Hewing sills & posts for Porches, 112 foot @ 5 fa, £-5-7 By Shelter over the Oven 7/6, By moving the stable & finishing a Porch -3-, By getting & nailing on 400 Sap Shingles on 3 small Houses, £1-10- By getting door Cases & Steps for Cellar, £-2-6 By sawing 175 foot scantling for Dormons [dormers] £-7-10, By Lyning Stable 2/ mending Hen House, 3/ £-5-, By hewing Sills for Dwelling House, 1 - -." [49]

This last item is most important. It tells us that a dwelling house, of frame construction, was being built, or at least enlarged, in 1753. In 1754 occurs another entry of interest, "By covering a house, £-15-." Quite possibly, as was almost universally customary in Virginia, Peter Jefferson and his family had lived first in some minor outbuilding, pending the erection of the ultimate "dwelling house" or mansion house, in this case delayed by the long residence of the family at Tuckahoe. Thus the actual birthplace of Thomas Jefferson may well have been in what ultimately became one of the outbuildings of the plantation group. Even in 1758, after Peter Jefferson's death, there was an item of glass for half a dozen windows, paid by his executor, John Harvie, indicating that the proprietor of Shadwell continued to add to his buildings to the last days of his life.

In the summer of 1941 excavations were undertaken on the site. They revealed that the buildings of the Shadwell of Peter Jefferson's day were indeed numerous, as is suggested by Biswell's account. They extended in a long line east and west on the summit of the low, gentle ridge between the Rivanna and the Southwest Mountains, the placing characteristic of the first houses of the district.[50] It is not certain that the foundations of the house where Jefferson was actually born have been found, or that further remains do not lie beneath the large house of today. It seems not unlikely, however, that one stone cellar, 15 feet square inside, which was probably beneath some principal room, marks the position of the mansion house, whatever its final size may have been. These cellar walls have been robbed of their stone to a depth of several feet below ground. Today there remain no foundations of any chimneys, which might have gone less deep than this. The lower part of the stone steps, however, still descends from the north, the house facing exactly south. Belief that this was the earliest of the surviving foundations is confirmed by the fact that all others found were of brick, whereas this was of stone. Although the soil of the site is of red clay with scarcely a pebble, stone was available on the near-by mountain slope, even before the first brick could be burned.

It was not long, however, before brick were made, for twenty feet east of the stone cellar is a foundation of massive brickwork. It is that of a building running north and south at right angles to the uniform front line of the group. The top of the surviving wall is but little below the surface, and here the absence of any chimney is more significant. It would surely have been bonded to the wall and thus some trace should survive. Clearly this was an outbuilding, perhaps a dairy without need of heat. This foundation is obviously an early one, for some of the brick are of the exceptional, irregular thickness found also in the ruins of Viewmont, the house of Joshua Fry, Peter Jefferson's friend and neighbor. This Shadwell outbuilding, too, had a cellar with floor of even, beaten clay. Steps down, on the eastern side, were also of brick, but had once had the stout wooden nosings commonly used in old Tidewater examples. Here and there a thick, square tile served for bond or coping. Unlike the stone foundation, this one was entirely filled with the debris of brick walls collapsed and leveled off, and of many charred fragments of wood—mute evidence of the fate which was to overtake Shadwell. If a similar outbuilding balanced the mansion house to the west, its position would be just below a wing of the modern building, as yet unexcavated.

Further eastward along the ridge are two square hearths, one with a well-preserved central concavity and no trace of any chimney rising above. This is probably the remains of a bake house or smoke house, doubtless of wood, as there is no surrounding foundation. It may well have been the very "shelter over the oven" which Biswell built in 1753.

Thus the plantation group of Peter Jefferson, as it stood prior to its destruction, attained an extent very different from the simple pioneer house commonly supposed. It was not the cabin of a frontiersman but a gentleman's seat, aiming at regularity of plan, with the detached, balanced wings and long chain of outbuildings so characteristic of Virginia.

Peter Jefferson was more than a planter and a speculator in land. Following in the footsteps of his grandfather, he became a surveyor. It was a profession thoroughly in keeping with the hardy and enterprising spirit that was his, a profession that attracted many eminent men in the colony, such as William Byrd and, later, George Washington. Commissioned by the governor, on nomination of the county court, the surveyor laid out the boundaries of the patented public lands in order that grants and deeds might be obtained. Both the surveyor and assistant surveyor were obliged to "enter in to bond with two sufficient surities, to our Sovereign Lord the King," to the extent of £500 current money.[51] Several men were, of course, engaged in these enterprises, and Peter Jefferson was associated with various well-known surveyors of the day, such as Thomas Turpin, Thomas Brooke, the younger, and, above all, the celebrated Joshua Fry. In 1749 Fry and Jefferson were commissioned to continue the boundary line between Virginia and North Carolina, which had been begun by William Byrd in 1728. The two men plunged through the primeval wilderness from Peter's Creek to Steep Rock Creek, a distance of some ninety miles, to achieve this, and to acquire a lasting reputation.

Joshua Fry, a man renowned as an educator as well as a soldier, came to Albemarle at about the same time as Peter Jefferson, and the two men were soon on terms of intimate friendship. Fry is known to have been born in Somerset about 1700 and to have been educated at Oxford, where he entered Wadham College in 1718. He seems to have come to Virginia in 1720, as he appears as a vestryman and magistrate of Essex County in that year.[52] In 1729 he was appointed master of the grammar school at William and Mary College and in 1732 was made professor of natural philosophy and mathematics.[53] Fry, however, had visions of realms other that that of teaching; the spirit of adventure that led him to the New World prompted greater undertakings. He resigned his professorship in 1737 and, as a friend wrote at the time, "retired to the back settlement to raise a fortune for his family." At the first court held in Albemarle he was made one of the magistrates as well as county lieutenant. He likewise qualified as surveyor.[54] Peter Jefferson was later appointed assistant surveyor. From this time on the two men were constantly associated.

By 1744 Fry was living at Viewmont, a house situated on a lonely ridge some 13 miles from Shadwell. It was a good half day's journey in those times, yet they managed to enjoy each other's company. It was doubtless of Fry that Thomas Jefferson spoke in recalling a custom of his parent. "My father had a devoted friend, to whose house he would go, dine, spend the night, dine with him on the second day, and return to Shadwell in the evening," he writes. "His friend, in the course of a day or two, returned the visit, and spent the same length of time at his house. This occurred once every week; and thus, you see, they were together four days out of the seven." [55]

John Harvie, who was later to become a guardian of young Thomas, was another friend and neighbor of Peter Jefferson. He was a Scotsman who had emigrated to Virginia in 1730. About the time William Randolph was granted the 2400 acres later known as Edgehill, Harvie bought of Joshua Graves 2500 acres lying east of the Randolph property and extending as far as the present Keswick Station. Here he built the story and a half house typical of the period and called it Belmont.[56] He was a well-educated man and one of the six men originally to practice at the Albemarle bar.

A few miles distant, at Castle Hill, lived another great friend who was likewise to become guardian of young Thomas Jefferson. This was the famous Dr. Thomas Walker, a man of many gifts. He was known as a physician, merchant, commissary to the militia, burgess, land speculator, and, above all, explorer. An inventory of his library, hitherto unobserved, reveals the catholicity of his tastes and interests. Hippocrates, Cato, Shakespeare, Swift, Richardson, a Universal History in twenty volumes, an abridgement of Virginia laws, and many medical books were among those on his shelves.[57] Although he had been born in King and Queen County, through his marriage with Mildred Thornton, the widow of Nicholas Meriwether, he came into possession of some eleven thousand acres in Albemarle known as Castle Hill, one of the first grants made in that part of the county in 1727. The land lies on the eastern side of the Southwest Mountains, and Walker was already settled there when John, his eldest son, was born in 1744. Jack Walker and Thomas Jefferson grew up together and became the closest of friends.

This, then, was the little group of comrades and friends who controlled the destiny of the new county and its citizens. They were united not only by their interest in the common good, but by their love of the new country that had drawn them all thither. Then, as today, it was a setting of lavish natural beauty in which they lived. The rolling hills, the exotic stretches of plowed, red clay fields, the distant blue of the mountains smiling their enchantment over the scene, were in striking contrast to the plains of the land from which they had come.

II. An Eight O'clock Scholar

Not long after the Jefferson family had moved to their new home their eldest son was born. It was on April 13, 1743 (April 2, Old Style) as the hills were turning green and the redbud and first dogwood were beginning to unfold their blossoms on the mountains that rose before Shadwell. The child was christened Thomas, as his grandfather and great-grandfather had been before him. A year and a half later Elizabeth, a third sister, was born. In this year the placid family life at Shadwell was suddenly interrupted—an interruption that was destined to last for seven long years. In 1745, William Randolph, the young proprietor of Tuckahoe and Peter Jefferson's oldest and dearest friend, died very suddenly, when only thirty-three years old. With his death his three daughters, Judith, Mary, and Priscilla, and an infant son, Thomas Mann Randolph, born in 1741, were orphaned. Their mother, Maria Judith Page, of Rosewell, had died not long before her husband.

In his will, of which Peter Jefferson was one of the executors, William Randolph directed that, "Whereas I have appointed by my will that my Dear only Son Thomas Mann Randolph should have a private education given him at Tuckahoe, my will is that my Dear and loving friend Mr. Peter Jefferson do move down with his family to my Tuckahoe house and remain there till my son comes of age with whom my dear son and his sisters shall live."[1] It was a most unusual request, but Peter Jefferson honored the wish of his friend. Packing their clothes, bundling up the four children—according to his family, Thomas Jefferson often said his earliest memory was of being handed to a servant who was on horseback, and being carried thus on a pillow—and taking along with their personal servants, the Jefferson family set off on the long trip to Tuckahoe. It was only about fifty miles, but in those days of horses and coaches and roads that were scarcely more than mud tracks, the journey lasted two and even three days. Once at their destination, the Jeffersons settled down and remained at Tuckahoe, if not until Peter's charge was of age, at least for seven of the seventeen years requested.

William Randolph had inherited Tuckahoe on his father's death, about 1730.[2] Subsequently he seems to have enlarged it from its small beginnings, and the house assumed much of the character we know today. Thus it was described by Lieutenant Anburey: "His house seems to be built solely to answer the purposes of hospitality.... It is in the form of an H and has the appearance of two houses, joined by a large saloon; each wing has two stories, and four large rooms on a floor; in one the family reside, and the other is reserved solely for visitors; the saloon that unites them is of considerable magnitude and on each side are doors; the ceiling is lofty, and to these they principally retire in summer, being but little incommoded by the sun, and by the doors of each of the houses, and those of the saloon being open, there is a constant circulation of air; they are furnished with four sophas, two on each side, besides chairs, and in the center there is generally a chandelier; these saloons answer the two purposes of a cool retreat from the scorching and sultry heat of the climate, and of an occasional ball room. The outhouses are detached at some distance, that the house may be open to air on all sides."[3]

Tuckahoe was thus ideally arranged for the two families it now housed, and it can have been no hardship for Mrs. Jefferson, at least, to move into and care for her cousin's house. Here she had been a familiar during her girlhood. Her own children, too, were to enjoy the educational advantages provided for the Randolph children. When, in his "Autobiography," Thomas Jefferson states that his father placed him "at the English school at 5 years of age," he is undoubtedly referring to the school conducted at Tuckahoe. A small, white frame building, shaded by great trees, and containing but one high room with coved ceiling, served as the schoolhouse. Here lessons were heard and here young Thomas

Jefferson, in company with his cousins, learned his a b c's. William Randolph had been very specific in his will about the education he wished his son, Thomas Mann, to enjoy. It was stipulated that he was not to be sent to William and Mary College, and, under no circumstances, to England. The executors were directed to employ a private tutor, a custom not uncommon among the wealthier families. The tutor in this case, as in most others, conducted what amounted to a small private school, for the children of friends or neighbors were usually asked to join the children of the household. William Randolph was careful not to leave his daughters, Judith and Mary, out of the scheme and stipulated that they were likewise to be educated according to their "quality and circumstances." It is not unreasonable to suppose that the little Jefferson daughters, Jane, Mary, and even Elizabeth, sat at the feet of the same master.

Peter Jefferson gave most minute attention to the Randolph business affairs, and the plantation was conducted as though it were his own. His account books of this period are filled with details relating to it. Thus we learn the names of the different quarters or farms of which the plantation was composed, in this case seven: Tuckahoe, Lower Quarter, three farms on Fine Creek, one on Dover Creek, and another on the Rappahannock—also the name of the overseer of each, the quantity of tobacco produced, the amount of tobacco that went to each overseer and the amount he was paid.[4] All other details are as carefully noted; when and how much corn was bought or sold, the purchase of a stallion or a mare, the amount paid James Bartley for smith's work, and so on. It is a tribute to Peter Jefferson's executive ability, as well as to his stamina, that he was able to manage his own lands on Fine Creek and at Shadwell, along with the Randolph property, and still carry on his duties as a surveyor.

The years at Tuckahoe were not devoted solely to plantation affairs. Peter Jefferson's accounts show that he was also active as a surveyor at this time. From November 1744 to December 1745, for example, he received for his services in this field, £20 6s 8d, amounting to thirty thousand pounds of tobacco, according to his own statement.[5] Beginning in September 1746, he was engaged with Joshua Fry and others in an undertaking of the first importance. This was surveying the line from the head springs of the Rappahannock to those of the Potomac, thus defining the western limit of the Northern Neck, and, thereby, the grant to Lord Fairfax. Thomas Lewis, one of the men concerned in the enterprise, has left a journal, picturing the incredible hardships and heartbreaking difficulties of such an adventure and the final dénouement at Tuckahoe. After three months in the wilderness it was agreed "that we should meet at Colo. Jefferson's the first day of January (1747) in Order to make out what plans of the Northern Neck were wanting." Lewis left his home, which was in the vicinity of Staunton, on December 30 ("the snow very deep") in order to meet according to appointment. He reached Colonel Fry's the following day and on "3rd got to Colo Jeffersons about 12 Oclock. The Surveyors Mr. Brook & Capt Winslow not yet come." The surveyors were a long time reaching Tuckahoe. From the eighth to the thirteenth Mr. Lewis records "continued waiting for the Surveyors to no purpose." Finally, on the fourteenth, he "concluded to goe to them in Essex to know their Resolution and accordingly Set off." His destination was about fifty miles to the northeast of Tuckahoe. On the twenty-fourth, only a little more than three weeks behind schedule, all four surveyors finally assembled at Tuckahoe and "Began our plans of the Northern Neck But as we wanted paper and Several other Materials were obliged to send to Williamsburg to Mr. parks for them. Continued Close at Work till Sunday the 8th of February on wc. we all Rode down to Richmond Church where we heard the Revernd mr. Stith preach. The Gentlemen of the Town Treated us to a handsome Dinner etc at mr. Coules Ordinary. We Returned home & the next Day began afresh, & so continued to Saturday February ye 21th." The following day the surveyors "took Leave of Colo. Jefferson & Family" and two days later Mr. Lewis "crossing the mountain got home. Having Finished a troublsom & Difficult affar." [6]

At this period Jefferson and Fry undertook another task which was to perpetuate their names, the drawing of their famous map of Virginia. As early as 1737 Fry, Robert Brooke, and William Mayo, all prominent surveyors, had proposed to the Virginia Assembly "to make an exact survey of the Colony, and print and publish a map thereof in which shall be laid down the bays, navigable rivers, with surroundings, counties, parishes, towns and gentlemen's seats, with whatever is useful or remarkable." [7] Nothing came of this at the time. At a meeting of the burgesses on September 7, 1744, the proposal was renewed and referred to the Committee of Propositions and Grievances,[8] which was the last that was heard of it. Meanwhile Fry and Jefferson concluded to proceed with a similar scheme. In 1751 there appeared a map "of the most inhabited part of Virginia containing the whole province of Maryland with parts of Pensilvania, New Jersey & North Carolina. Drawn by Joshua Fry and Peter Jefferson in 1751." It was engraved and published by Thomas Jeffrys in London. The only reference to the map in Peter Jefferson's few remaining papers is the laconic statement in his accounts, under date of April 11, 1752, "By drawing 1 map of Virginia, 1½ pistoles." [9]

After the return of the Jefferson family to Shadwell, in 1752, Thomas, then nine years old, was sent to the so-called Latin School of the Reverend William Douglas, where he was to study Greek, Latin, and French. It was not unusual, in colonial Virginia, for a young minister, as the most educated man in the community, to interlard his parochial duties with the more profitable and quite as necessary functions of teacher. The subjects of instruction offered might embrace almost all forms of human knowledge, if we may judge from an advertisement of a young clergyman appearing in the *Virginia Gazette*. He "proposes to teach Ladies & Gentlemen the French, Latin, Greek and English languages, Book-keeping by double entry, Algebra, Geometry, Measuring, Surveying, Mechanicks, Fortification, Gunnery, Navigation, and the use of the Globes and Maps, after a natural, easy and concise Method, without Burthen to the Memory." [10]

The Reverend Mr. Douglas, who had been born in Scotland, came to the colony in 1748 or 1749 and was, for a while, a tutor in the family of Colonel Monroe in Westmoreland County, the father of the future President. In 1750 he went back to England, was ordained, and returned with his wife and daughter to settle in Goochland County. Here, for the next 27 years, he had charge of the parish of St. James, Northam. For 19 years he likewise preached at Manakin Town in King William Parish and for four years expounded the words of the Lord to a charge in Buckingham County.

Dover Church, where Douglas preached in Goochland and where the glebe was situated, was the first church built in that county.[11] It was situated on Dover Creek, the next creek upstream beyond Tuckahoe, a distance of about five miles. The church, a barnlike structure some 50 by 24 feet, had been established in 1720 and completed in 1724, but until the arrival of Mr. Douglas had had no regular preacher. The advent of the reverend gentleman as the permanent pastor of the parish of St. James, Northam, where Peter Jefferson was a vestryman, created quite a stir in Goochland County. He came fresh from the Old World, with the reputation of a man of learning. He appears to have had a considerable library as his books were valued at £150 in the inventory of his estate.[12]

It seemed a suitable place to which to send young Thomas Jefferson to school, the more so as he would be within a few miles of his Randolph cousins. Whether he returned to live at Tuckahoe, or whether he boarded with Douglas, is not clear. From Peter Jefferson's account book we learn that he paid the Reverend Mr. Douglas £16 sterling a year for his son's education. He also notes "by Books for my Son £1/10/6."[13] At that, he probably paid dearly, for, late in life, Jefferson wrote of the intellectual accomplishments of his old mentor: "My teacher Mr. Douglas, a clergyman from Scotland, was but a superficial Latinist, less instructed in Greek, but with the rudiments of these languages he taught me French."[14] The picture is not that of a stimulating or inspiring teacher; the young scholar probably learned in spite of, rather than because of, his efforts.

Thomas Jefferson continued his studies with the well-meaning Mr. Douglas until the summer of 1757, when a tragedy of the first magnitude befell the Jefferson family. Peter Jefferson fell ill. Thomas Walker, his friend and physician, visited him professionally on June 25. In July he was called three times, in August, eleven times. On the seventeenth of that month Peter Jefferson died, in the prime of life. He left eight children, the youngest of whom was not yet two years old. Two others had died at birth. How catastrophic was the loss of the father for the eldest son, then just emerging from childhood, we learn from a letter, written many years later, revealing the bewilderment in which he groped: "When I recollect that at fourteen years of age, the whole care and direction of myself was thrown on myself entirely, without a relation or friend qualified to advise or guide me, and recollect the various sorts of bad company with which I associated from time to time, I am astonished I did not turn off with some of them and become as worthless to society as they were." [15]

Peter Jefferson died a rich man. He left a detailed will providing for the future of his wife and children.[16] The house and plantation of Shadwell were left to his wife for her natural life, together with one-sixth of the slaves, and the "Household stuff." Certain Negroes and their natural increase were given to each of the six daughters, along with £200 each payable on their marriage, or one year after they had reached twenty-one years of age. To Thomas, as the eldest son, were left both privileges and duties. The will reads: "I give and bequeath to my son Thomas my mulatto fellow Tawny, my books, mathematical instruments, and my cherry tree desk and bookcase.... I give and bequeath all my slaves not herein otherwise disposed of, to be equally divided between my two sons, Thomas and Randolph, at such time as my son Thomas shall attain the age of 21 years, each of my said sons to have and to hold the slaves allotted to them in such Division to them and their heirs forever, but subject nevertheless to this condition, that the estate bequeathed to my son Thomas as to clear profits thereof be and remain equally liable with my other estates to provide for the maintenance and support of my family, the education of my younger children, and the payment of my daughters' Portions.

"Item, I give and bequeath to my son Thomas either my lands on the Rivanna River and its branches, or my lands on the Fluvanna in Albemarle County, which I purchased from John and Noble Ladds, together with all my other Lands adjacent thereto which I have taken up by virtue of an order of Council, which of the two he shall choose, he being to make his election within one year after he shall attain the age of 21 years...."

The son Randolph, at this time only two years old, was given a similar choice of the two parcels of land, although owing to his youth it was an academic question. It was provided that the one who selected the property on the Fluvanna should get the lands Peter Jefferson held on the Hardware River. He directed, furthermore, that the family should live and be maintained, and the children be educated out of the profits of the estate. To his wife went one-third of the cattle, hogs, and sheep on any and all of his lands, along with two work horses. The balance of the livestock was to be disposed of according to the discretion of the executors "for the support and maintenance of my Family and for the benefit of my two sons equally, and for no other purpose whatsoever." He concludes: "I give and bequeath to my son Thomas all the residue of my estate whether real or personal of what kind whatsoever." The executors and guardians were the Honorable Peter Randolph, Mrs. Jefferson's cousin, Thomas Turpin the elder, Peter Jefferson's brother-in-law, Dr. Thomas Walker, and John Harvie, friends and business associates.

Aside from his lands, his books, and his maps, which have already been mentioned, Peter Jefferson died possessed of much more personal property than has ever been suspected. A detailed inventory was fortunately filed with his will and leaves us in no doubt as to his manner of life or earthly possessions.[17] It is noteworthy that he owned two desks, at a time and in a community where desks were not the most common pieces of household furniture, and two bookcases, one of cherry, which he left his son, the other of walnut. There were three large walnut tables, two five feet long, one four feet, and six other tables, twenty chairs, two dressing tables and two dressing glasses, a large mirror, five beds with their furniture, and a chest of drawers. Much of this furniture, eight tables, three dressing tables, and fourteen chairs, was made in 1750, while the Jeffersons were in residence at Tuckahoe, as Peter Jefferson's account book testifies.[18] There was also considerable silver, including a coffeepot, teapot, and milk pot, a silver punch ladle, teaspoons, salts, sugar tongs and strainer—in other words, the household equipment of a man of substantial means. A comparison of Peter Jefferson's estate with that of Thomas Lee of Stratford, one of the richest planters in the colony, whose inventory was filed in 1758, one year after Jefferson's, is not at all unfavorable to the former. Lee, with a house more than twice the size of Shadwell, owned eleven tables as against Jefferson's nine, fifty-five chairs, two desks, eight beds, two chests, and two couches.[19]

With the death of Peter Jefferson, Thomas's schooldays with the Reverend Mr. Douglas came to an end. After spending 12 years of his life in the Tidewater, he returned for the first time since babyhood to stay in the Piedmont. His guardians determined to send him to study with one of the most scholarly and prominent clergymen of the colony, the Reverend James Maury. He was pastor of the parish of Fredericksville, which, according to acts of 1744 and 1757, embraced sections of Hanover, Albemarle, and Louisa Counties.[20] This gentleman, whom Jefferson has described in his "Autobiography" as "a correct classical scholar," [21] was a man of very different abilities and background from Douglas. He came of a Huguenot family which had fled France after the Edict of Nantes and settled in England. Members of the Maury family emigrated to Virginia very early in the eighteenth century and made their home in the Tidewater.

James Maury, the son of Matthew Maury and Mary Anne Fontaine of "Fontainebleau," King William County, was born in 1718 and attended William and Mary College. In February 1742, he went to England for Holy Orders and in June of the same year received the King's Bounty for Virginia.[22] He was ordained in London, and in July 1742 was appointed an usher of the grammar school of the College of William and Mary.[23] His real vocation was the Church, however, and in 1754 he was made rector of Fredericksville parish. Here he continued for 15 years, until his death on June 9, 1769. He married Mary Walker, daughter of James Walker of King and Queen County, and was the progenitor of a large family.

A few years before Maury's arrival to take charge of his parish, a church had been built on the eastern side of the Southwest Mountains to replace the rough cabin which had hitherto served as a place of worship.[24] It was called Belvoir Church, but was commonly known as Walker's, from its nearness to Thomas Walker's estate. Although a glebe of four hundred acres was provided for him, with a parsonage and outbuildings, it is said that Maury preferred to live on his own plantation which was situated near by, on the border of Albemarle and Louisa Counties, about five miles from the present town of Gordonsville.[25] Here, in the shadow of Peter's Mountain, he supplemented his income by conducting a school for boys. A schoolhouse built of logs stood for many years in the yard of Edgeworth, as his plantation came to be known, and the spot was subsequently marked by a hedge of cedars.[26] From the accounts of John Harvie, one of the executors of Peter Jefferson's estate, we learn that in 1759 there was paid to the "Reverend James Maury for board and schooling of Thomas Jefferson £22," and that in October of the same year a Mr. Ingles was paid £7 10s for "teaching five children to dance." This undoubtedly included the youthful Thomas, as the three younger children were not yet old enough. From the same source we also learn that from August 24 to December, 1759, Thomas received £3 for pocket money, that books to the extent of £5 3s 10d were imported "per the Caesar for Mr. Thomas Jefferson," and that in March 1759 he attained to the dignity of a seal—"By Family expenses for a seal to Thos Jefferson, £1/7." [27]

A letter of the Reverend Mr. Maury dated "Fredericksville Parish, Louisa County, August 9, 1755," pictures none too cheerfully life in their outlying province, only a dozen miles from Shadwell, at about the time of Jefferson's schooldays: "I am planted about two miles to the northeast of Walker's under the South West Mountain in Louisa, close by one of the headsprings of the main northern branch of Pamunkey, which runs through my grounds— a very wholesome, fertile and pleasant situation.... Our people are loaded with debts and taxes. Money is much scarcer than it has been for many years. Our spring crops of wheat and barley, oats and rye have been ruined by an early drought. Our Indian corn, the main support of man and beast in this part of the world, has been so much hurt by a later drought, that I fear scarce enough will be made for the sustenance of our people, exclusive of our stock, great numbers of which must in all probability perish this winter. Some of our neighboring colonies have likewise suffered in the same manner and cannot assist us. So fertile, too, are our lands that there is no such thing as a magazine for grain in all British America which, as it has never known the want of bread, has never made any provision against it." [28]

Like most of his contemporaries, Maury indulged in a little land speculation. His brother-in-law, Peter Fontaine, pastor at Westover, wrote of these activities: "James has got a parish amongst the mountains and is concerned with the Ohio Company, who have an entry on Halifax ... of 800,000 acres of land. His wife's uncle, Col. Walker, is the chief person in this scheme. They have it quite free for some years, and sell it to settlers as £3 the hundred acres. They have about thirty settlements upon it, if the French and their Indians have not routed them lately." [29] He is also known early to have patented ten thousand acres in Augusta County "to begin on the Allegheny on the north side of the dividing line between Carolina and Virginia and to continue up the river for complement." [30]

When the Reverend James Maury died on August 24, 1769, the long obituary which was printed in the *Virginia Gazette* stated that "it might have been hard to say whether he was more admired as a learned man or reverenced as a good man." However that may be, Maury will go down in history not as a teacher or a saint but as the protagonist of the celebrated "Parson's cause," or "Twopenny Act," which first introduced Patrick Henry to an applauding world.[31] The pay for parsons had been set by the General Assembly in 1748 at 16,000 pounds of tobacco a year. This act had been given the royal approval and could not be repealed without the same consent. Ten years later the General Assembly passed another act making the salaries payable in money at two pence per pound of tobacco. Governor Fauquier, whose sympathies were not with the clergy, approved the act instead of vetoing it, as had been expected. There were years of grumbling and discontent in the various parishes, and several ministers sued. In 1763 Maury brought suit for damages in Hanover County. Patrick Henry, who had been admitted to the bar three years before on reading "Coke upon Littleton" and scanning the Virginia laws, and who was practically unknown at the time, appeared for the defendants. His speech was of such an impassioned nature and so radical in tone— he denied the right of the King to disallow acts of the colonial legislature—that within five minutes the jury returned a verdict for one penny damages, and Henry became a popular idol. Maury had lost his suit, but he was forever to shine in reflected glory.

There can be no doubt that the world of the spirit, the world of books and learning, was first opened to the young Jefferson during this time. At the Reverend Mr. Maury's he came in contact with a library such as he had never before known, and it is inevitable that his own passion for books was stimulated by it. It is a source of regret that no catalogue or list of Maury's books has been preserved. The inventory that was filed with his will merely makes mention of "1 Book Press with 400 volumes of Books, 44 Pamphlets." [32] In his will Maury directed that his son, James, and his four daughters choose six books each from the library, and it was left to the executors to determine whether or not it should be sold.

Maury's interests embraced not only languages, literature, history, and religion, but, as we shall see, natural philosophy as well. It may very likely have been he who first aroused his youthful charge's curiosity in this field. How intense was Maury's interest in the subject we gather from a letter written by Peter Fontaine in 1754, in which he speaks of his brother-in-law: "His last letter to me consists of three sheets, wrote on all sides, with a box containing a piece of antedeluvian mud, petrified with the perfect print of a cockle shell upon it, taken from the top of one of the Great Mountains [as the Blue Ridge was then called], and a piece of sea-coal as good as any in Whitehaven, taken out of a broken bank." [33] Such shells as are described in Maury's hands may well have given the stimulus to the observations embodied in a famous passage, some years later, in Jefferson's "Notes on Virginia." [34]

Although Maury was one of the most cultivated men of his day —even his slaves gloried in such classical names as Cato, Clio, Ajax, Aggy, and Memnon—and although the school he conducted was very well known, no one of his pupils was moved to leave an account of it, or of schooldays there. Late in life, when writing to James Maury, the son of his teacher, Jefferson makes a lone reference to those days: "All my old friends are nearly gone. Of those in my neighborhood, Mr. Divers and Mr. Lindsay alone remain. If you could make it a *partie quarrée,* it would be a comfort indeed. We would beguile our lingering hours with talking over our youthful exploits, our hunts on Peter's Mountain, with a long train of et cetera in addition.... Reviewing the course of a long and sufficiently successful life, I find in no portion of it happier moments than these were." [35]

It is unfortunate for us that Jefferson did not enlarge upon the "long train of et cetera" for we know all too little of his boyhood and youth. That he improved himself, the sequel leaves us in no doubt. When not engaged in his studies, he rode and hunted as did all the youth of Virginia at that time and since. Surrounded by the vast open fields of the Tidewater or the forests of the Piedmont, with their countless varieties of trees and flowering shrubs, it was inevitable that he should learn to prize solitude and to read the secrets of nature. No better indication of the attentive ear and eye which observed all and forgot nothing is to be found than in Jefferson's "Garden Book" or his celebrated "Notes on Virginia." Both abound in knowledge and observations that reflect a boyhood spent not only in communion with nature but in an understanding of it in its manifold forms.

III. The Class of 1762

AFTER TWO years of study with the Reverend Mr. Maury, young Jefferson was seized with the restlessness that is likely to descend upon most boys of sixteen. As he approached his seventeenth birthday he doubtless felt that he was entering upon man's estate and experienced a growing impatience with the schoolroom. Maturity was achieved at an earlier age in the eighteenth century than it is in the twentieth. Was not a famous contemporary, George Washington, a full-fledged surveyor at sixteen years of age and commander of the Virginia forces when only twenty-three? The subject of his further education, however, seems to have been uppermost in Jefferson's mind. Following a gay Christmas holiday spent at Colonel Dandridge's in Hanover County, where he first made the acquaintance of Patrick Henry and "passed perhaps a fortnight together at the revelries of the neighborhood and season,"[1] Jefferson repaired to "Chatsworth," on the James, the seat of his cousin and guardian, Peter Randolph. Here a long discussion was held concerning his prospects and his future. Heartened by a talk with a man of the world, Jefferson summoned all his courage and on January 14, 1760, wrote to John Harvie, another of his guardians and the manager of his business affairs. It is an eager, straightforward letter in which he amassed all available arguments, and it is his first letter of which the text is known.

"Sir," it reads, "I was at Colo. Peter Randolph's about a fortnight ago & my Schooling falling into Discourse, he said he thought it would be to my advantage to go to the college, & was desirous I should go, as indeed I am myself for several reasons. In the first place as long as I stay at the Mountains the Loss of one fourth of my Time is inevitable, by company's coming here & detaining me from school. And likewise my Absence will in a great Measure put a stop to so much Company, & by that Means lessen the expenses of the Estate in House-Keeping. And on the other Hand by going to the College I shall get more universal Acquaintance, which may hereafter be serviceable to me; & I suppose I can pursue my Studies in the Greek & Latin as well there as here, & likewise learn something of the Mathematics. I shall be glad of your opinion." [2]

The college which young Jefferson so ardently longed to attend was, of course, the College of William and Mary, in Williamsburg. It was already a venerable institution, having been founded in 1693. Like most European universities of the period, of which it was a colonial adaptation, it had an ecclesiastical origin and background. Some years before Jefferson entered the college, however, the stern theological trend had been modified to a degree. In 1727 the Board of Visitors had inaugurated a system according to which there were to be four schools "within the College Precincts": the grammar school, which instructed young boys up to fifteen years of age, the philosophy school, the divinity school, which was postgraduate, and the Indian school. The philosophy school, which corresponded roughly to our college, had two masters, the professor of natural philosophy and mathematics, who taught "Physicks, Metaphysicks and Mathematicks," and the professor of moral philosophy, who expounded "Rhetorick, Logick and Ethicks," including natural and civil law.[3] The study of law and medicine was, at this time, pursued by apprenticeship to some well-known lawyer or physician, and not included in the college curriculum.

"That the youth of the college may the more cheerfully apply themselves to these studies," we read in the Statutes of the College, "and endeavor to rise to the academic degrees, we do, according to the form and institution of the two famous universities in England, allot four years before they attain to the degree of Batchelor, and seven years before they attain the degree of Master of Arts." [4]

Owing to the many fires which, since the earliest days, have

THE COLLEGE OF WILLIAM AND MARY. (*Photograph by F. S. Lincoln*)

devastated and destroyed portions of the college, the records have been but imperfectly preserved. It is thus impossible to know exactly all the lectures the young Jefferson attended and precisely what subjects he chose to pursue. From the Statutes of the College, however, we may gain some idea of the training he received. Thus we read of the philosophy school: "For as much as we see now daily a further progress in philosophy, than could be made by Aristotle's logick and physick, which reigned so long alone in the schools and shut out all other; therefore we leave it to the President and Masters, by the advice of the Chancellor, to teach what systems of logick, physicks, ethicks and mathematicks, they think fit in their schools. Further we judge it requisite that besides disputations, the studious youth be exercised in declamation and themes on various subjects, but not any taken out of the Bible. Those we leave to the Divinity School." [5]

The "studious youth" had a further opportunity of displaying his knowledge in the examinations at the beginning, not the end, of each of the three terms into which the college year was divided. These were held in public halls and the examiners were the President, Masters and Ministers of the College "and any other learned men that please to afford their company at these examinations." [6] Further examinations were to "be undergone concerning their progress in the study of philosophy before they are promoted to the Divinity School. And let no blockhead or lazy fellow in his studies be elected" [7]—advice which might well be taken to heart today.

The government of the college was in the hands of the president and the six masters, namely the two professors of divinity, the two professors of philosophy, the master of the grammar school, and the master of the Indian school. They met whenever there was business to conduct, rather than at stated intervals. From the "Journal of the Meetings of the President and Masters of William and Mary College," we learn that at the time of Jefferson's matriculation the Reverend Thomas Dawson was president, but he died the following year and was succeeded by the Reverend William Yates. Emanuel Jones was the master of the Indian school, and William Webb was appointed, in 1761, to succeed the convivial Welsh poet, the Reverend Goronwy Owen, as master of the grammar school. William Small was, during this period, professor of natural philosophy and mathematics.[8]

William and Mary had, at this time, what might be called almost a monastic character as far as the professors were concerned. They were not supposed to marry but were required to live in the college. When two of them took unto themselves a wife each and set up housekeeping in the town, they were severely reprimanded and more or less read out of meeting.[9] The students of Jefferson's day presented the same problem that students have always presented to the authorities, and attempts to govern them seem to have met with the usual dubious success. Racing, gaming, and drinking were as popular with the sport-loving sons of the Virginia planters as they were frowned upon by their mentors. A few years before Jefferson entered the college, president and masters took matters firmly in hand and passed the following regulations:

"1. Ordered that no scholar belonging to any school in the College, of what age, rank, or quality, soever, do keep any race horse at ye College, in ye town—or any where in the neighborhood—y^t they be not in any way concerned in making races, or in backing or abetting, those made by others, and y^t all race horses kept in ye neighborhood of ye College, & belonging to any of ye scholars, be immediately dispatched and sent off & never again brought back, and all this under pain of ye severest animadversion and punishment.

"2. Ordered, y^t no scholar belonging to ye College of w^t age, rank, or quality, soever or wheresoever residing, within or without ye College, do presume to appear playing or betting, at ye billiard or other gaming tables, or be any way concerned in keeping or fighting cocks under pain of ye like severe animadversion or punishment.

"3. Ordered y^t no scholar belonging to ye College do frequent, or be seen, in ye ordinaries, in or about ye town except they be sent for by their relatives, or other near friends.

"4. And for ye more effectual prevention of these & the like irregularities, It is ordered y^t no scholar of w^t age, rank or quality soever residing within ye bounds of ye College, do presume to go out of ye said bounds particularly towards the mill pond with out ye express Leave of his respective master, or tutor, first had & obtained. . . .

"5. Ordered, y^t no scholar do bring or cause to be brought any cards or dice, or other implement of gaming—y^t ye having cards or dice in possession, within ye bounds of ye College, shall be deemed and adjudged a conviction ipso facto of ye crime of gaming." [10]

These regulations, written in a clear hand, were posted in every school of the college.

It was also decreed that "Special care likewise must be taken of their morals, that none of the scholars presume to tell a lie or curse or swear, or talk or do any thing obscene, or quarrel and fight, or play at cards or dice, or set in to drinking or do any thing else that is contrary to good manners. . . . The master shall chuse some of the most trusty scholars for public observators, to give him an account of all such transgressions, and according to the heinousness of the crime, let the discipline be used without respect of persons." [11]

Despite the strictness of the rules and the presence of the "public observators," escapades were not unknown. John Walker of Castle Hill, Jefferson's boyhood friend and companion, involved himself and two others in a scrape that caused their temporary expulsion. In the Journal of the Meetings of the President and Masters of the College for October 6, 1763, we read: "Resol: That you John Walker, James McClurg & Walter Jones (on account of your injurious behavior on Tuesday night last to a family in town) are ordered to betake yourselves immediately to your friends in the country with such letters etc. as shall be delivered to you by the Society for them; and that you do not presume to appear in college, or the town (after tomorrow) until the 10th day of Novr next when you are to return, and make such further submission as the society shall think proper; otherwise you will be looked upon as expelled from college." [12]

The next day Jefferson wrote John Page: "Affairs at W. and M. are in the greatest confusion. Walker, McClurg and Wat Jones are expelled pro *tempore* or, as Horrox softens it, rusticated for a month. Lewis Burwell, Warner Lewis and one Thompson have fled to escape flagellation." [13] Serious as the offense may have seemed at the time, Walker managed to survive it and live to occupy various posts of distinction later in life.

Such was the college to which young Jefferson came with his hopes high on March 25, 1760. It was cooler than usual for this time of the year, as a quite unprecedented snow flurry had surprised Williamsburg but a few days before. The temperature was only 49, although by afternoon it had risen to 56.[14] Puffy white clouds drifted across the blue of the sky and a gentle wind blew from the southeast. The season was backward. Daffodils and the delicate white narcissi, for which Williamsburg has always been famous, lifted their timid heads. Dogwood and redbud were waiting to burst into bloom, and the heavy pink petals of the peach trees were drifting slowly to the ground.

From one of the three Bursar's books which survive, we learn that Jefferson remained at William and Mary until April 25, 1762.[15] The board bill of £13 a year which he paid the college reveals that he left on this day. He lived in the college and was not one of those scholars who resided in the town "so near the College that from thence the College bells can be heard, and the public hours of study be duly observed." The Bursar's books likewise tell us who were Jefferson's fellow students during the period he attended the college—there were less than a hundred students at this time [16]—and during the following years when he was studying law with George Wythe in Williamsburg.

His associates represented the flower of the colony. Almost every one was destined to occupy high office in Virginia or in the new nation that was to be born when they had reached maturity. Of all his college mates Jefferson singled out John Page, son of Mann Page of Rosewell, a princely estate in Gloucester County, as his particular friend. Theirs was a true and lasting friendship. Common interests and tastes did not dissolve as the years went on, and the two men corresponded at frequent intervals for half a century. Page may have lacked much of Jefferson's determination and sternness of character, yet his inherited position and his sterling abilities led him to participate in all the important movements of his time and brought him almost every high office—burgess, member of the Governor's council, Lieutenant Governor, delegate to Congress, and, finally, Governor of Virginia, in 1802.

Page has left us an account of his days as a student at Williamsburg and his associates there. Brief as is the reference to Jefferson, it is important as showing how early in life his characteristic traits were established. The elder Page put his son to board with the president of the college. "Father had feed [him] handsomely," Page writes, "to be my private tutor, and he, finding me far better graduated in Latin than many boys much older than myself, was proud to introduce his pupil to the particular attention first of Governor Dinwiddie, an old Scotch gentleman, who was fond of appearing a patron of learning, and secondly to Governor Fauquier, to whose much greater learning and judgement my ever to be beloved Professor, Mr. Small, had held me up as worthy of his attention. I had finished my regular course of studies in the Philosophy Schools, after having gone through the Grammar School, before the death of Governor Fauquier.... Before I had the benefit of a Philosophical Education at College, with Mr. Jefferson, Mr. Walker, Dabney Carr and others, under the illustrious Professor of Mathematics, Wm. Small, Esq°, afterwards well known as the great Dr. Small, of Birmingham, the darling friend of Darwin, History and particularly Military and Naval history, attracted my attention.... I never thought, however, that I had made any great proficiency in any study, for I was too sociable, and fond of the conversation of my friends, to study as Mr. Jefferson did, who could tear himself away from his dearest friends, and fly to his studies." [17]

Second only to Page in Jefferson's affections during their college days, and subsequently his most intimate friend, was Dabney Carr. He was the son of John Carr and Barbara Overton of Bear Castle, Elk Run, Louisa County. Jefferson and Carr were born in the same year and were boyhood friends. Family tradition has it that the two used to study together beneath a favorite oak on the southwestern slope of Monticello. It was agreed between them that whoever should be the first to die would be buried beneath this tree.[18] After finishing his education at William and

Mary, Carr studied law and began practicing "at the same bars as Patrick Henry, and, although he had not yet reached the meridian of life, he was considered by far the most formidable rival in forensic eloquence that Mr. Henry had ever yet had to encounter. He had the advantage of a person at once dignified and engaging, and the manner and action of an accomplished gentleman." [19] In the spring of 1773, as a new member of the House of Burgesses representing Louisa (although he seems to have lived in Goochland where his will was filed) Carr was chosen to move the resolutions establishing intercolonial committees of correspondence. This he did in a speech that made history. "With what delight," writes Wirt, "the house of burgesses hailed this new champion, and felicitated themselves on such an accession to their cause, it is easy to imagine." [20] Carr was appointed a member of the first committee, but within thirty-five days of making this speech, on May 16, 1773, he died. He was buried at Shadwell, but Jefferson, who had been away from home at the time of his friend's sudden death, had his body moved to the spot on which they had agreed as boys. In Jefferson's garden book, under date of May 22, 1773, we find a notation indicating that the graveyard he had planned years before was on this day begun as a resting place for his friend: "2 hands grubbed the graveyard 80 feet square = 1-7 of an acre in $3\frac{1}{2}$ hours, so that one would have done it in 7 hours, and would grub an acre in 49 hours = 4 days." [21]

At thirty, Dabney Carr died a well-to-do man. Aside from a house, described as "elegantly furnished," his personal estate was appraised at £1067 4s 2d. His library, which comprised over two hundred volumes, must have been a delight to the two friends. There were about 75 books on law, 30 dealing with history, 28 volumes on theology and religion, and about 80 of general literature, including Latin and English.[22]

The high estimate Jefferson placed upon his friend's character and abilities was never more poignantly expressed than in a letter he wrote Dabney Carr, Jr., many years later. "His character," he says, "was of a high order. A spotless integrity, sound judgement, handsome imagination, enriched by education and reading, quick and clear in his conceptions, of correct and ready elocution, impressing every hearer with the sincerity of the heart from which it flowed. His firmness was inflexible in what he thought was right; but when no moral principle stood in the way, never had a man more the milk of human kindness, of indulgence, of softness, of pleasantry of conversation and conduct. The number of his friends, and the warmth of their affection, were proofs of his worth, and of their estimate of it." [23]

John Walker was in college at the same time and another student who was almost a neighbor was William Fleming, whose home was Mount Pleasant in Goochland, on the south side of the James, nearly opposite Dungeness, the home of Jefferson's maternal grandparents. After studying law, he settled in Cumberland County and became a burgess. Later he was to be prominent in the revolutionary movement, as well as a distinguished judge.[24]

Other college mates were Benjamin Harrison of Brandon, that most beautiful of plantations on the James, who served in the House of Delegates for many years, Francis Willis of White Hall on the Ware River, later congressman from Georgia, Lewis Burwell, subsequently burgess from Gloucester, Thomas Nelson, "his father Mr. Secretary," Francis Eppes, whose son, John Wayles, was to marry Jefferson's younger daughter, Edward Bland, Archibald Bolling, William Broadnax, and several members of the Armistead family of Gloucester County.

The two men who contributed most to the development of the youthful Jefferson during his Williamsburg period were, without question, William Small and George Wythe. In his "Autobiography," Jefferson, in describing his years at William and Mary, paid tribute to them, in the following words:

"It was my great good fortune, and what probably fixed the destinies of my life, that Dr. Wm. Small of Scotland was then professor of Mathematics, a man profound in the most useful branches of science, with a happy talent of communication correct and gentlemanly manners, & an enlarged & liberal mind. He, most happily for me, became soon attached to me & made me his daily companion when not engaged in the school; and from his conversation I got my first views of the expansion of science & of the system of things in which we are placed. Fortunately the philosophical chair became vacant soon after my arrival at college, and he was appointed to fill it *per interim:* and he was the first who ever gave in that college regular lectures in Ethics, Rhetoric & Belles lettres. He returned to Europe in 1762,[25] having previously filled up the measure of his goodness to me, by procuring for me, from his most intimate friend, G. Wythe, a reception as a student of law, under his direction, and introduced me to the acquaintance and familiar table of Governor Fauquier, the ablest man who had ever filled that office. With him, and at his table, Dr. Small & Mr. Wythe, his *amici omnium horarum,* & myself, formed a *partie quarrée,* & to the habitual conversations on these occasions I owed much instruction.—Mr. Wythe continued to be my faithful and beloved Mentor in youth, and my most affectionate friend through life." [26]

Little is known of William Small, the extraordinary man who exercised so profound an influence on his students and particularly on Jefferson and his whole career. Of his life in England it has been recorded that he was the friend of the famous Scotsman, James Watt, and of Erasmus Darwin, a distinguished scientist and progenitor of Charles Darwin. He appeared in Williamsburg as professor at the college in 1758 with no fanfare, and he returned to England six years later to live and work at Birmingham, where he died in 1775. Brief as was his connection with William and Mary, he kept the interests of the college at heart, and it was to him that the governing body turned in 1767 to buy an elaborate physical apparatus that was the wonder of the New World. In the time he spent at the College of William and Mary, Small did more to liberalize the institution than any man before him. Not only did he make a drastic departure from the didactic pedagogical methods of the day, in abandoning the ancient memory lessons and introducing the modern lecture system, but he advanced thoughts and ideas undreamed of by the young men of the colony and wholly foreign to the trend of their thinking.

It has been well said of him that he "was the enemy of all the narrow dogmatism of the old philosophy. As a friend and adviser of Watt, Dr. Small ministered at the birth of invention, and as the tutor of Jefferson he was sponsor to the birth of freedom." [27]

A letter dealing with a vacant mastership at William and Mary, written by Stephen Hawtry in 1765, after Small's return to Europe, gives us one of the few pictures we have of the man and his reaction to the institution of learning which he graced for so short a time:

Brick Court 26th March
1765

DEAR NED:

Since you left London, I called at The Virginia Coffee House to endeavour to find out Mr. Small, but could learn no Tidings of him, therefore left a note for him desiring him to let me know where I might see him, in consequence of this he called on me a few days since and gave me what particulars he knew relating to the College. He is a polite, well-bred man and said he should be glad to give you any information in his power in regard to the College....

Your salary is £150 sterling, paid as regularly as if at the Bank of England. Every boy pays a pistole entrance money & 20 s sterling per annum, out of which you pay the first usher (there being two) 5 s. Though I said that every boy pays this sum, it would be speaking more properly to say they ought to pay it, for they are very irregular in their payments of that, and unless you look sharp after it and insist upon your right you may stand a chance of not receiving above 1/4th.

You have two rooms—by no means elegant, tho equal in goodness to any in the College—unfurnished, and will salute your eyes on your entrance with bare plaister walls. However, Mr. Small assures me they are what the rest of the Professors have, and are very well satisfied with the homeliness of their appearance, tho' at first sight rather disgusting. He thinks you will not chuse to lay out any money on them.

You may buy furniture there, all except bedding and blankets, which you must carry over; chairs and tables rather cheaper than in England. He says his furniture consists of 6 chairs, a table, grate bed and bedstead, and that is as much as you will want.

He says you must have one suit of handsome, full-dressed silk cloaths to wear on the King's birthday at the Governor's, the only time you will have to appear *fine* in the whole year, but then it is expected that all English gentlemen attend and pay their respects. . . . As to the rest of your wearing apparel, you may dress as you please, for the fashions don't change, and you may wear the same coat 3 years. . . .

You will have much confinement. They break up (in summer) for a month, and twice in the year besides, for a fortnight each time. . . . Shoes and Stockings are very dear articles. Thread stockings are worn chiefly. . . . If you want to know anything further write me word, tho' I don't believe I have omitted anything. . . . [28]

The year of Small's arrival, 1758, also marked the coming of another man of unusual talents and abilities, the new royal Governor, Francis Fauquier. He was at this time in his early fifties, a person of great cultivation and distinction of manner. To these qualities were added a deep devotion to scientific pursuits and a fine appreciation of music and literature as well. "With some allowances," Burk, the historian of Virginia, remarks, he "was everything that could have been wished for by Virginia under a royal government. Generous, liberal, elegant in his manners and acquirements, his example left an impression of taste, refinement and erudition on the character of the colony, which eminently contributed to its present high reputation in the arts." [29] He became a very popular figure, and during the ten years of his governorship Williamsburg flowered as it had never before, intellectually as well as socially. His presence was a stimulus to the colony and about him he gathered men of similar inclinations and kindred spirit. It was inevitable that he and William Small, who shared so many of his tastes, should be drawn together, and to this circle was added the eminent jurist, George Wythe, and a slender youth of twenty, Thomas Jefferson. Years later, in 1815, Jefferson wrote Girardin how Wythe and Small had procured for him "the attentions of Governor Fauquier, the ablest man who ever filled the chair of government there. They were inseparable friends, and at their frequent dinners with the Governor (after his family had returned to Eng-

FRANCIS FAUQUIER, F.R.S., H.M. LIEUTENANT-GOVERNOR AND COMMANDER-IN-CHIEF OF VIRGINIA, 1758-1768. (*From the miniature in possession of his family*)

land), he admitted me always, to make it a *partie quarrae*. At these dinners I have heard more good sense, more rational and philosophical conversation, than in all my life besides. They were truly Attic societies. The Governor was musical also, and a good performer, and associated me with two or three other amateurs in his weekly concerts." [30]

The Attic atmosphere—and it must, indeed, have seemed nothing less to this unworldly young man—was marked by only one flaw, the Governor's inordinate passion for gambling. In a single night he is said to have lost at cards his entire patrimony. "He found among the people of his new government," says Burk, "a character compounded of the same elements as his own, and he found little difficulty in rendering fashionable a practice which had, before his arrival, prevailed to an alarming extent. During the recess of the courts of judicature and assemblies, he visited the most distinguished landholders in the Colonies, and the rage for playing deep, reckless of time, health, or money, spread like a contagion among a class proverbial for their hospitality, their politeness and fondness for expense. In everything beside, Fauquier was the ornament and delight of Virginia." [31] Fortunately the young Jefferson remained untouched by this vice. He played cards, to be sure, as any young man of fashion would do, but not with the spirit of a gambler, "avarice being a passion alien to his breast," as William Byrd remarked of his own son. Jefferson's account books, which begin with his twenty-fourth year, show occasional trifling losses when he played with friends. On the whole, however, he was content with his studies, with the philosophical conversations and the sounds of music echoing through the Governor's palace.

The town of Williamsburg, from which the students were to be protected and which attracted them with the ruthless infallibility of a magnet, was the outstanding one of the colony, as well as the seat of government. "It is a town well stocked with rich stores of all sorts of goods," the Reverend Hugh Jones wrote as early as 1720, "and well furnished with the best provision and liquors. Here dwell several very good families and more reside here in their own houses at public times. They live in the same neat manner, dress after the same modes, and behave themselves exactly as the gentry in London." [32] Bishop Meade even goes so far as to say: "Williamsburg was once the miniature copy of the Court of St. James, somewhat aping the manners of that royal palace, while the old church and its graveyard, and the College chapel were, *si licet cum magnis componere parva*, the Westminster Abbey and the St. Paul's of London, where the great ones were interred." [33]

Williamsburg was little more than a village, yet it offered such metropolitan diversions as were to be found otherwise only in New York, Philadelphia, or Boston. Here were situated not merely the buildings of the College of William and Mary, which Jefferson none too charitably described as "rude, misshapen piles, which, but that they have roofs, would be taken for brick-kilns," but the Capitol, where the House of Burgesses met, "a light and airy structure... on the whole the most pleasing piece of architecture we have," and the Governor's palace, "not handsome without, but it is spacious and commodious within, is prettily situated, and with the grounds annexed to it, is capable of being made an elegant seat. There are no other public buildings but churches and courthouses, in which no attempts are made at elegance. Indeed, it would not be easy to execute such an attempt, as a workman could scarcely be found capable of drawing an order." [34]

We are fortunate in having a description of the appearance of the town the very year that Jefferson entered the college.[35] "It consists of about two hundred houses," an English traveler writes, "does not contain more than one thousand souls, whites and negroes; and is far from being a place of any consequence. It is regularly laid out in parallel streets, intersected by others at right angles; has a handsome square in the center, through which runs the principal street, one of the most spacious in North America, three quarters of a mile in length, and above a hundred feet wide. At the opposite ends of this street are two public buildings, the college and the capitol: and although the houses are of wood, covered with shingles, and but indifferently built, the whole makes a handsome appearance. There are few public edifices that deserve to be taken note of; those which I have mentioned are the principal, and they are far from being magnificent. The Governor's palace, indeed, is tolerably good, one of the best upon the continent; but the church, the prison, and the other buildings, are all of them extremely indifferent. The streets are not paved, and are consequently very dusty, the soil hereabout consisting chiefly of sand: however, the situation of Williamsburg has one advantage which few or no places in these lower parts have, that of being free from mosquitoes. Upon the whole, it is an agreeable residence; there are ten or twelve gentlemen's families, constantly residing in it, besides merchants and tradesmen: and at the time of the assemblies, and general courts, it is crowded with the gentry of the country: on those occasions there are balls and other amusements; but as soon as business is finished, they return to their plantations and the town is in a manner deserted."

Although Williamsburg obviously fell short of the standards of a man with a European background, especially as far as its architecture was concerned, it offered endless opportunities and diversions to the planter who came to take his seat in the House of Burgesses or to attend to other business. It opened a world of wonder to the youth who had spent his entire life in the depths of the country, offering him much he had longed for and had never known. There was intellectual companionship, which he craved, there were books and bookstores to satisfy his longing for books. There was the college library, greater than any library he had ever known. Some years before Governor Spotswood had presented it with his fine collection of books and maps. Here young Jefferson came upon the "Description des châteaux et parcs de Versailles, de Trianon et de Marly, par M. Piganiol de la Force," and it is interesting to speculate on the influence this work may have had upon his eager mind, both in regard to architecture and gardening.

Music was Jefferson's first and lasting love, as he himself said, and he is known to have played the violin with much ability.

"If there is a gratification which I envy any people in this world," he wrote a friend in France, "it is to your country its music. This is the favorite passion of my soul, and fortune has cast my lot in a country where it is in a state of deplorable barbarism." [36] Nevertheless, in Williamsburg he was able to enjoy more of it than he had heretofore. "I hear from every house a constant tuting may be listened to from one instrument or another," wrote Landon Carter, rather savagely, in his diary. Various musicians had settled in the town, and it is possible that Jefferson studied with one of them. A Mr. Singleton had come to Williamsburg in 1752 and put the following advertisement in the *Virginia Gazette:* "Mr. Singleton takes this opp. of informing gentlemen & others, That he proposes to Teach the Violin in this city, and places adjacent, at a pistole each per month, and a pistole Entrance, provided a sufficient no. of scholars can be engaged (not less than six in any one place). He will give attendance at York, Hampton, & Norfolk, on the aforesaid terms." [37]

The same year Peter Pelham, Jr., an Englishman, arrived in Williamsburg to assist in the installation of a new organ in Bruton Church. The General Assembly decided to employ him as an organist at a salary of £25 a year. This not being sufficient for his needs, he was later made keeper of the jail, with an additional £40 salary, and the privilege of living in his bailiwick. Here he resided for many years, giving music lessons and providing the music at all theatrical performances.[38] In his account book Jefferson notes that on May 5, 1769, he "pd Pelham for playing on organ 2/6." Then there was Mr. Charles Leonard, "a native of Cologne, Germany, and well known in Virginia for his excellent but capricious performances on the violin," [39] who was active during Jefferson's time in Williamsburg, and there was at least the memory and the splendid musical legacy left by Cuthbert Ogle. He died five years before Jefferson came to the college, but his library of music, probably the largest in America at that period, which had been left to his son, was available.[40] The musician with whom, apparently, Jefferson came most closely in contact was one Alberti, who is mentioned in the account books as early as

March 1769. He is a somewhat obscure figure, but according to Jefferson's own account, some years later, "Alberti came over with a troop of players and afterwards taught at Williamsburg. Subsequently I got him to come up here (Monticello) and took lessons for several years. I suppose that during at least a dozen years of my life, I played no less than three hours a day." [41]

During his Williamsburg days Jefferson was constantly entering the purchase of "fiddle strings" in his account book and on May 28, 1768, he noted that he had paid "Dr. Pasteur for violin £5." [42] At the end of his life he still owned two instruments—beside a small one which he had carried about with him on his journeys—which he claimed "would fetch in London any price." One was a Cremona, as Jefferson stated, the other had belonged to John Randolph and Jefferson had come into possession of it somewhat after the half facetious manner his father had acquired property by means of Henry Wetherburn's biggest bowl of Arrack punch. In Jefferson's account book for 1775, under the date of August 17, he notes: "Delivered to Carter Braxton an order on the treasurer in favor of J. Randolph, Atty. General, for £13, the purchase money for his violin. This dissolves our bargain recorded in the General Court, and revokes a legacy of £100 Sterling to him now standing in my will, which was made in consequence of that bargain." [43] The bargain to which Jefferson refers was made in 1771. It reads:

Oct. 11th, 1771

It is agreed between John Randolph, Esqr. of the City of Williamsburg, and Thomas Jefferson, of the county of Albemarle, that in case the said John shall survive the said Thomas, that the Exr^{'s}. or Adminirs of the said Thomas shall deliver to the said John 800 pounds sterling of the books of the said Thomas, to be chosen by the said John, or if not books sufficient, the deficiency to be made up in money: And in case the said Thomas should survive the said John, that the Executors of the said John shall deliver to the said Thomas the violin which the said John brought with him into Virginia, together with all his music composed for the violin, or in lieu thereof, if destroyed by any accident, 60 pounds sterling worth of books of the said John, to be chosen by the said Thomas. In witness whereof the said John and Thomas have hereunto subscribed their names and affixed their seals the day and year above written.

JOHN RANDOLPH (L.S.)
TH JEFFERSON (L.S.)

Sealed and delivered in presence of
G. Wythe
Thos. Everand
P. Henry, Jr.
Richard Starke
Wm Johnson
Ja. Steptoe

Virginia s.s.

At a general court held at the capitol on the 12th day of April, 1771, this agreement was acknowledged by John Randolph and Thomas Jefferson, parties thereto, and ordered to be recorded.

Teste
BEN. WALLER, c.c.cur.[44]

On receipt of the "purchase money," in 1775, Randolph wrote to Jefferson: "I have received ten guineas of the Treasurer, & have left the violin with Mr. Cocke of Wmsburg. I wish I had had a case for it.

"Tho we *may politically* differ in sentiments, yet I see no reason why *privately* we may not cherish the same esteem for each other which formerly I believe subsisted between us. Should any coolness happen between us, I'll take care not to be the first mover of it. We both of us seem to be steering opposite courses; the success of either lies in the womb of time. But whether it falls to my share or not, be assured that I wish you all health and happiness." [45]

Jefferson was eager to add an organ to his other musical instruments, although it is not recorded that he succeeded in this ambition. Robert Carter, the Councillor, had had one made in London and installed in his handsome Williamsburg house, facing the Palace Green. In 1778 Jefferson enquired of Carter whether he would be willing to sell it. Carter had been an

THE GOVERNOR'S PALACE, WILLIAMSBURG. (*Photograph by F. S. Lincoln*)

intimate friend of Governor Fauquier and had been associated with him and Jefferson in the weekly concerts at the Palace. His organ seems to have been as dear to him as the violin was to Jefferson and he politely declined to part with it, saying that he had two daughters who practiced "upon keyed instruments." [46]

Later, when established at Monticello, Jefferson devised a unique scheme for gratifying his musical tastes. "The bounds of an American fortune," he wrote a friend in 1778, "will not admit the indulgence of a domestic band of musicians, yet I have thought that a passion for music might be reconciled with that economy which we are obliged to observe. I retain among my domestic servants, a gardener, a weaver, a cabinet-maker, and a stone-cutter, to which I would add a *vigneron*. In a country where, like yours, music is cultivated and practiced by every class of men, I suppose there might be persons of these trades who could perform on the French horn, clarinet, or hautboy, and bassoon, so that one might have a band ... without enlarging the domestic expense. A certainty of employment for half a dozen years, and at the end of that time, to find them, if they chose, a conveyance to their own country, might induce them to come here on reasonable wages." [47] This plan, alas, was destined never to be fully realized but to go the way of so many dreams.

A list of the volumes of music which Jefferson owned is contained in the comprehensive catalogue of his library which he made in 1782. There are books of instruction for the violin, the harpsichord and German flute. Two pages of the catalogue are devoted to vocal music, two to instrumental. Among the masters whom Jefferson enjoyed and whose works are still living for us today, are Handel, Purcell, Corelli, Vivaldi and Boccherini. During his sojourn in Europe Jefferson apparently was to become acquainted with the music of Haydn and to add his sonatas, his concertos and cantatas to the collection.

Two music stands, one for violin, another, unique in character and very likely after Jefferson's own design, for use in playing quartets, along with a music rack, have come down to us as mute evidence of his love of this art. Of his splendid musical library only a few fragments remain. There is a volume of duets for two violins and another of "solos for a violin with a thorough Bass for the Harpsichord or Violoncello, by Arcangelo Corelli." Then there is a volume of songs and duets, in Italian, by Maria Cosway, which she presented to him during their Paris idyll. Cupid enchanting a lion, somewhat characteristic of their relationship, forms the frontispiece, likewise from the gifted pen of Mrs. Cosway. Of unusual interest is the music copied in Jefferson's own hand at a very early period. There are several songs, "Thou Soft Flowing Avon," with its banal words: "Thou soft flowing Avon by whose silver stream, of things more than mortal thy Shakespear did dream;" "The Adieu," "Love and Opportunity," the words carefully written out in the delicate script of Jefferson's youth. There is likewise an "Air" for the clavichord or forte-piano composed by a man with the romantic name of Herring, a quartet "Fin ch'an dal vino," and an arrangement of a selection from Don Giovanni. Indicative of his musical taste at this period is a small sheet of paper, apparently sent an agent, with the following notation: "On this paper is noted the beginning of the several compositions of Campioni which are in the possession of Thomas Jefferson. He would be glad to have everything else he has composed of Solos, Duets or Trios. Printed copies would be preferred, but if not to be had, he would have them in MS."

In Jefferson's own hand is also a "Fingerboard for Spanish guitar," with notes on how to play the instrument. Although this might possibly have been made for Mrs. Jefferson, as her husband notes on August 31, 1776, paying £3 14s for guitar strings, this is doubtful, for she was no beginner in music at the time of her marriage. It is much more likely that it was prepared in 1815 for his little granddaughter, Virginia Randolph. Years later in writing her reminiscences of Jefferson she says: "I had for a long time a great desire to have a guitar. A lady of our Neighborhood was going to the West, and wished to part with her guitar, but she asked so high a price that I never in my dreams aspired to its possession. One morning, on going down to breakfast, I saw the guitar. It had been sent up by Mrs. —— for us to look at, and grandpapa told me that if I would promise to learn to play on it I should have it. I shall never forget my ecstasies. I was but fourteen years old, and the first wish of my heart was unexpectedly gratified." [48]

A large part of Jefferson's musical library descended to one of his great-granddaughters and came to a most untimely end. One winter morning, some years ago, she found that a Negro house boy had burned almost the entire collection in making the parlor fire. He had kept the old newspapers given him for that purpose and substituted, one by one, the precious pages of Jefferson's music which lay on a near-by shelf. A few volumes, too sturdy to burn readily, withstood his efforts. They were chiefly those purchased for Jefferson's daughter, Martha, during the days she was studying music at a convent in Paris. Her name, in the delicate script of the eighteenth century, is written across the top, "Mademoiselle Jefferson, Panthemont, Paris." There are still the "Stabat Mater par Pergolesi," the "Sonates pour le Clavecin par M. Schobert," a wistful "Receuil de Petits Airs," and a number of other selections.

Second only to his love of music was Jefferson's fondness for the theater, which he was now able to indulge. From the beginning of the eighteenth century Williamsburg had been a center for this sort of thing. The first theater in America was built there—the contract for the building was drawn in 1716—and companies from London came to regale the students and the planters. At times when there was no regular theatrical troupe a group of the "young gentlemen of the College," known as the "Players of the College of William and Mary" along with the "Virginia Company of Comedies" composed of the "gentlemen and ladies of this country," displayed their talents.[49] A few years before Jefferson's arrival a new theater was built by subscription on Waller Street, near the Capitol. This is doubtless the one Jefferson frequented. Here companies from New York and the famous Hallams from London produced such plays as "The Tragical History of King Richard III," "A Play call'd The Merchant of Venice (written by Shakespeare)," and farces and comedies long since forgotten. At times itinerant players capable of all sorts of tricks came to amuse the Williamsburgers. Then there were "a man and his wife and with them two children who perform the agility of body, by various sorts of postures, tumbling and sword dancing, no greater perfection than has been known in these parts for many years, if ever." [50]

Aside from music and the theater, Williamsburg had less serious diversions to offer. There was the life of the taverns, with their semipublic entertainments, the fairs in April and December, racing, gaming, and cock fighting, in short, all the pleasantly and mildly wicked amusements of a metropolitan center. Love of the horse, of fox hunting, and of racing had characterized the Virginian from the earliest times. As we have seen, Jefferson's own grandfather was the proud owner of the race horse, Bony. The Reverend Hugh Jones well remarked, "the common planters leading easy lives don't much admire labour, or any manly exercise except horse racing." [51] Races were held twice a year at Williamsburg and lasted about a week. People from all over the colony swarmed to them. There was a racecourse at the west end of the town with two, three, or four mile heats. A generous purse, raised, as a rule, by subscription, of £100 each for the first day's races and £50 each for the succeeding days, added to the interest. There was no closed season for cock fighting. It was not an outlawed sport, as it is today, but one that had a large following. The *Virginia Gazette* could be relied upon to announce one whenever arranged. Thus advertised for April 4, 1768, was "a match of cocks, between Brunswick and Sussex Gentlemen to show 30 cocks a side, for 5 s a battle and 50 s the odd. At night there will be a ball for the Ladies and Gentlemen." On another occasion it informed the citizens "a cock match will be fought on the 7th day of April next, at the Ordinary, formerly Sayre's Ordinary, near Hobs Hole, in Essex County, for sixty pistoles." [52] The youthful Washington recorded in his diary in January 1752: "A great Main of cocks fought in Yorktown between Gloucester and York for 5 pistoles each battle and 100 ye odd. I left it with Colo. Lewis before it was decided." [53]

The diversions *par excellence* in Williamsburg, as in any social capital, were the balls given during the fall and winter months. They were held at frequent intervals while the General Assembly was in session, and one of these was the background of young

Jefferson's first love affair. These balls were held most often, perhaps, at the Raleigh Tavern, although occasionally at the Capitol or in private houses, and the populace eagerly looked for such announcements in the *Virginia Gazette* as: "For the Ladies and Gentlemen there will be a ball at Henry Wetherburne's on Tuesday Evening next, the 10th instant and on every Tuesday during the sitting of the General Assembly. Tickets half a pistole." [54]

The Raleigh Tavern was the most famous one in Virginia. For years it was the social center of Williamsburg, and Jefferson and his aides subsequently made it a political center in the days immediately preceding the Revolution. It was a large, wooden structure, two stories in height, with eight dormer windows on every side. It was situated on the Duke of Gloucester Street between the Palace Green and the Capitol. A bust of Sir Walter Raleigh, executed in lead, was placed over the door, and gave the tavern its name. The large assembly room on the ground floor called the "Apollo," presumably after a similar room in the Devil's Tavern, London, where Raleigh and Ben Jonson are reputed to have met, was the scene of the balls, as well as of large dinners and other festivities. It was a long room with a great marble fireplace. The overmantel was illumined by the words: *Hilaritas Sapientiae et bonae Vitae proles*. The tavern had been built in 1735 and was, in Jefferson's day, already quite a venerable institution. Although the genial Henry Wetherburn, its most famous host and the man who had been involved in the bargain made between Jefferson's father and William Randolph, had been superseded, the popularity of the place continued undimmed.

A Virginia ball of this period was an institution peculiar unto itself. Dancing was not the only diversion offered. Various objects might be raffled, and there was very likely to be "a cake." In John Blair's diary for the year 1751, there are numerous references to this custom. Thus on January 8, he notes, "Dined at Col. Burwell's and stayed all night and danced and drew 14th cake. January 11th, Had dance and a cake at Mr. Cocke's." [55] We are fortunate in having a description of such a ball by an English traveler, Nicholas Cresswell, explaining the mysterious function of "the cake." "Last night I went to the Ball," he writes. "It seems this is one of their annual balls supported in the following manner: A large, rich cake is provided and cut into small pieces and handed round to the company, who at the same time draw a ticket out of a Hat with something merry wrote on it. He that draws the King has the honour of treating the company with a ball the next year, which generally costs him six or seven Pounds. The Lady that draws the Queen has the trouble of making the cake. Here was about 37 ladies dressed and powdered to the life, some of them very handsome and as much vanity as is necessary. All of them fond of dancing but I do not think they perform it with the greatest elegance. Betwixt the country dances they have what I call everlasting jigs. A couple gets up and begins to dance a jig (to some Negro tune) others comes and cuts them out, and these dances always last as long as the fiddler can play. This is sociable but I think it looks more like a Bacchanalian dance than one in a polite assembly. Old men, young wives with young children in the lap, widows, maids and girls come promiscuously to these assemblies, which generally continue until morning. A cold supper, punch, wines, coffee and chocolate, but no tea. The men chiefly Scotch and Irish. I went home about two o'clock, but part of the company stayed, got drunk and had a fight." [56]

Jefferson was liberally to sample this gay life of Williamsburg before some stern inner impulse bade him call a halt and caused him to evolve a system of strict personal conduct from which he was never to deviate. In writing to his grandson and namesake, Thomas Jefferson Randolph, many years later, he tells of the temptations that beckoned to him in these days and of what enabled him to resist and overcome them. "I had the good fortune," he says, "to become acquainted very early with some characters of high standing, and to feel the incessant wish that I could ever become what they were. Under temptations and difficulties, I would ask myself what would Dr. Small, Mr. Wythe, Peyton Randolph do in this situation? What course in it will assure me their approbation? I am certain that this mode of deciding on my conduct, tended more to correctness than any reasoning power I possessed. Knowing the even and dignified line they pursued, I could never doubt for a moment which of two courses would be in character for them. Whereas, seeking the same object through a process of moral reasoning, and with the jaundiced eye of youth, I should often have erred. From the circumstances of my position, I was often thrown into the society of horse racers, card players, fox hunters, scientific and professional men, and of dignified men; and many a time have I asked myself, in the enthusiastic moment of the death of a fox, the victory of a favorite horse, the issue of a question eloquently argued at the bar, or in the great council of the nation, well which of these kinds of reputation should I prefer? That of a horse jockey? a fox hunter? an orator? Be assured, my dear Jefferson, that these little returns into ourselves, this self-catechising habit, is not trifling nor useless, but leads to the prudent selection and steady pursuit of what is right." [57]

IV. Love is Young

It was inevitable that the young Jefferson should fall victim to a romantic passion during his Williamsburg days. What young man of nineteen does not cherish a tender heart? Many of his biographers have taken pains to point out, on vague hearsay, that, as a youth, he was far from handsome, being tall and angular, with a skin so fair that it freckled too readily, and hair variously described as red or sandy. Yet there can be no question that Jefferson was a leader among the young people at Williamsburg. He was wealthy, he was a superb horseman—in an age when athletic distinction was held as far above mental prowess as it is today—he was what we call a good sport, and he was more than a little of a ladies' man. In his early letters we find him sending frequent messages through friends to Miss Alice Corbin, Miss Sukey Potter, and other young women of his acquaintance. "Tell them," he writes, "that though the heavy earthy part of me, my body, be absent, the better half of me, my soul, is ever with them." [1]

The story of Jefferson's romance is told in the letters he wrote his friend John Page, whom, he said, he loved as a brother.[2] To him he unburdened his heart. With a single exception, they are the earliest letters we have from Jefferson's pen. Seven in number, they were written during his nineteenth to twenty-first years, when either he or Page was absent from Williamsburg. Not a little jejune, they are typical of a youth of that age—moody, at times almost melancholy, uncertain of the course the future will take, full of dreams and vague ideals, and, naturally, a vast preoccupation with the fair sex. Thus on Christmas Day, 1762, he addressed a letter to Page redolent with the gloominess and mock heroics of a *Sturm und Drang* hero. "This very day, to others the day of greatest mirth and jollity, sees me overwhelmed with more and greater misfortunes than have befallen a descendant of Adam these thousand years past, I am sure; and perhaps, after excepting Job, since the creation of the world.... Is there such a thing as happiness in this world?" he asks, and the answer is a strong "No."

The Christmas Day on which Jefferson wrote these words found him visiting at Fairfield, the ancient seat of the Burwell family. Young Lewis Burwell, the fourth of that name in Virginia, one of Jefferson's classmates at William and Mary, had inherited the place on the death of his father, ten years before. It was doubtless with him that Thomas was spending the holidays. The plantation lay on Carter's Creek, about two miles above Rosewell. The house was one of the earliest of the great houses of Virginia; it had been built in 1692, as the iron figures on one of its gables testified. With its clustered chimneys and thick walls, penetrated by few and very small windows, it was reminiscent of an earlier period and had an antique appearance, in contrast to the newer Georgian houses, even at the time of Jefferson's visit. The place had, apparently, already reached a certain state of decay, as we gather from his indulgently humorous description of the woes of a night there:

"I am sure if there is such a thing as a Devil in this world, he must have been here last night and have had some hand in contriving what happened to me. Do you think the cursed rats (at his instigation I suppose) did not eat up my pocket-book, which was in my pocket, within a foot of my head? And not contented with plenty for the present, they carried away my jemmy-worked silk garters, and half a dozen new minuets I had just got, to serve, I suppose, as provision for the winter.... You know it rained last night, or if you do not know it, I am sure I do. When I went to bed, I laid my watch in the usual place, and going to take her up after I arose this morning, I found her in the same place, it's true! but *Quantum mutatus ab illo!* all afloat in water, let in at a leak in the roof of the house, and as silent and still as the rats that had eat my pocket-book. Now, you know, if chance had had anything to do in this matter, there were a thousand other spots where it might have chanced to leak as well as this one, which was perpendicularly over my watch. But I'll tell you; it's my opinion that the Devil came and bored the hole over it on purpose. Well, as I was saying, my poor watch had lost her speech. I should not have cared much for this, but something worse attended it; the subtle particles of the water with which the case was filled had, by their penetration, so overcome the cohesion of the particles of the paper, of which my dear picture and watch paper were composed, that in attempting to take them out to dry them, Good God! *Mens horret referre!* My cursed fingers gave them such a rent, as I fear I never shall get over. This, cried I, was the last stroke Satan had in reserve for me: he knew I cared not for anything else he could do to me, and was determined to try this last most fatal expedient. '*Multis fortunae vulneribus percussus, huic uni me imparem sensi, et penitus succubui!*' ... However, whatever misfortunes may attend the picture or lover, my hearty prayers shall be that all the health and happiness which heaven can send may be the portion of the original, and that so much goodness may ever meet with what may be most agreeable in this world, as I am sure it must in the next. And now, although the picture may be defaced, there is so lively an image of her imprinted in my mind, that I shall think of her too often, I fear, for my peace of mind; and too often, I am sure, to get through old Coke this winter." [3]

The "dear picture" which Jefferson carried in his watch, along with the watch paper [4] made by the fair hands of the subject, was that of Rebecca Burwell, the sister of his host and the Belinda of his early letters. She was, as the Virginians say, "widely and prominently connected." Her father, Lewis Burwell, 3d, had long sat in the House of Burgesses, been a member of the Council—subsequently its president—and, finally, acting Governor of Virginia before the arrival of Dinwiddie in 1751. He died in 1752. His wife, Mary Willis of Gloucester, had preceded him, thus leaving the son and three daughters orphaned. Rebecca, the youngest of the sisters, was but ten years old. Her aunt, Elizabeth Burwell, had married the wealthy William Nelson of Yorktown,[5] and Rebecca was taken into their family as a daughter. Nelson was likewise, for many years, a member of the council and often its presiding officer. This brought the family frequently to Williamsburg where the younger members joined in the gaieties of the circle to which Jefferson belonged, and it may very well have been here that he met his Belinda.

She was at this time a young girl of sixteen. We have, alas, no description of her. We do not know whether she was fair or dark, diminutive or of grander proportions. All we know of her, except her lover's frequent reference to her "goodness," are a few words written many years later by a pious daughter: "her character, in the opinion of her giddy companions, was stamped with enthusiasm."[6] Doubtless she was possessed of her full share of youthful beauty and charm. The quaint word "enthusiasm" may well have described that most prized of feminine attributes, vivacity, without which no beauty can be truly beautiful and a plain woman may be transformed.

There can be no question of Jefferson's attachment to Rebecca Burwell, or that he toyed with the idea of marriage. Nevertheless there was a certain reluctance in the young lover's attitude, an innate aversion to settling down before he had had a chance to travel and see more of the world than that enchanting section known as Virginia. It was a time when, once married, one stayed married, and started the serious business of raising a family. There were no trips to Europe or to New York for the busy matron, and seldom for her husband. With rare exceptions, traveling was something undertaken before matrimony. This, then, was Jefferson's first battle between the heart and the head, and, as on the famous occasion many years later which he immortalized in his "Dialogue of the Head and Heart," the heart was not to win. To Page, who acted as his "attorney" and, one cannot help feeling, the advocate of Belinda, Jefferson wrote from Shadwell on January 20, 1763:

"How does R. B. do? Had I better stay here and do nothing, or go down and do less? or, in other words, had I better stay here while

I am here, or go down that I may have the pleasure of sailing up the river again in a full-rigged flat? Inclination tells me to go, receive my sentence, and be no longer in suspense; but reason says, if you go, and your attempt proves unsuccessful, you will be ten times more wretched than ever.... Have you any inclination to travel, Page? because if you have, I shall be glad of your company. For you must know that as soon as the Rebecca (the name I intend to give the vessel above mentioned) is completely finished, I intend to hoist sail and away. I shall visit particularly England, Holland, France, Spain, Italy (where I would buy me a good fiddle) and Egypt, and return through the British provinces to the Northward, home. This, to be sure, would take us two or three years, and if we should not both be cured of love in that time, I think the devil would be in it." [7]

Two months passed before this letter was finally dispatched; the leisurely temper of the times and of the country discouraged haste. In the meantime Jefferson added two postscripts,[8] hitherto unpublished, showing that his heart was still in the Tidewater. On February 12 he wrote:

"I was disappointed in sending the above at the time I expected. I think I have a right to add a postscript half as long as the letter at least. In a letter from Jack Walker received since writing the above, he assures me the small pox is in town, so you may scratch out that sentence of my letter wherein I mentioned coming to Williamsburg so soon. I have heard that poor Nancy wandered from home not long since in the night, and that it was supposed to be occasioned by a fit of hystericks. However if she did and what you told me about the West-Indian and her was true, I ascribe it to a different cause, and would not draw my bet with J. Edmunds for a bottle of claret. [Next sentence illegible.] The small pox being in town will open an inexhaustible fund of news for you to write me. Miss Willis is to be married next week to Dangerfield. Why can't you and I be married too, Page, when and to whom we would choose? Do you think it would cause any such mighty disorders among the planets? Or do you imagine it would be attended with such very bad consequences in this bit of a world, this clod of dirt, which I insist, is the vilest of the whole system? Nobody knows how much I wish to be with you, *sed non ita fato datum?* Remember me to Brown, to Willis, to W. Armistead, and to every body else. When is Brown to be married? Is their no probability of either you or Willis paying the infant of arrack we betted? I shall begin to curse you very soon if you do not write to me. You cannot complain that you want opportunities since you need only put a letter in the post office at any time and I shall soon get it. I verily believe that I shall die soon and yet I can see no other reason for it but that I am tired of living. At this moment when I am writing I am scarcely sensible that I exist."

Finally, on March 11, an occasion was found to send the letter and, with a few added lines about the "story of Nancy," it was off.

Not quite satisfied with the progress of affairs, the wily Page introduces the idea of a rival—doubtless Jacquelin Ambler—and Jefferson replies in July 1763:

"The rival you mention I know not whether to think formidable or not, as there has been so great an opening for him during my absence. I say *has been,* because I expect there is one no longer. Since you have undertaken to act as my attorney, you advise me to go immediately and lay siege *in form.* You certainly did not think, at the time you wrote this, of that paragraph in my letter wherein I mentioned to you my resolution of going to Britain. And to begin an affair of that kind now, and carry it on so long a time in form, is by no means a proper plan. No, no, Page; whatever assurances I may give her in private of my esteem for her, or whatever assurances I may ask in return from her, depend on it—they must be kept in private. Necessity will oblige me to proceed in a method which is not generally thought fair, that of treating with a ward before obtaining the approbation of her guardian. I say necessity will oblige me to it, because I never can bear to remain in suspense so long a time. If I am to succeed, the sooner I know it, the less uneasiness I shall have to go through. If I am to meet with disappointment, the sooner I know it, the more of life I shall have to wear it off: and if I do meet with one, I hope in God, and verily believe, it will be the last. . . . If Belinda will not accept of my service, it shall never be offered another. That she may, I pray most sincerely; but that she will, she never gave me reason to hope. . . . I should be scared to death at making her so unreasonable a proposal as that of waiting until I return from Britain, unless she could first be prepared for it. I am afraid it will make my chance of succeeding considerably worse. But the event at last must be this, that if she consents, I shall be happy; if she does not, I must *endeavour* to be as much so as possible. . . ." ·

Surely these were not the words of an eager and determined lover!

Thoughts of Rebecca continued to haunt the young student of law, however, and in the fall of 1763 he wrote William Fleming, one of his cronies: "From a crowd of disagreeable companions, among whom I have spent three or four of the most tedious hours of my life, I retire into Gunn's bed-chamber to converse in black and white with an absent friend. Dear Will, I have thought of the cleverest plan of life that can be imagined. You exchange lands for Edgehill, or I mine for Fairfield, you marry S——y P——r [Sukey Potter], I marry R—— B——, join and get a pole chair and a pair of keen horses, practise the law in the same courts, and drive about to all the dances in the country together." [9]

In October of the same year Jefferson returned to Williamsburg, which he took pleasure in calling "Devilsburg." On the evening of the sixth a ball was held in the Apollo room of the Raleigh Tavern, and there Jefferson saw his beloved again after his long absence at Shadwell. Her sweet ways, her endearing charm, must have swept him completely off his feet, for he was led to attempt the declaration which had trembled on his lips these many months. The following day he wrote Page the outcome: "In the most melancholy fit that ever any poor soul was, I sit down to write to you. Last night, as merry as agreeable company and dancing with Belinda in the Apollo could make me, I never could have thought the succeeding sun would have seen me so wretched as I now am! I was prepared to say a great deal: I had dressed up in my own mind, such thoughts as occurred to me, in as moving language as I knew how, and expected to have performed in a tolerably creditable manner. But, good God! When I had an opportunity of venting them, a few broken sentences, uttered in great disorder, and interrupted with pauses of uncommon length, were the too visible marks of my strange confusion! The whole confab I will tell you, word for word, if I can, when I see you, which God send may be soon." [10]

Despite this evening, which seemed so catastrophic to the young lover, the affair continued to simmer along, with the ups and downs inherent in such a situation. Once again, the following January, Jefferson wrote his counselor, Page, and rehearsed the situation, after an interview in which he had more fully and ably set forth his intention and his position. "The contents of your letter have not a little alarmed me;" he says, and once more we suspect the mention of a rival by his correspondent, "and really, upon seriously weighing them with what has formerly passed between —— and myself, I am somewhat at a loss what to conclude; your *"semper saltat, semper ridet, semper loquitur, semper solicitat,"* etc. appear a little suspicious; but Good God! it is impossible! I told you our confab in the Apollo; but I believe I never told you that we had on another occasion. I then opened my mind more freely and more fully. I mentioned the necessity of my going to England, and the delay which would consequently be occasioned by that. I said in what manner I should conduct myself till then, and explained my reasons, which appears to give that satisfaction I could have wished; in short, I managed in such a manner that I was tolerable easy myself, without doing anything which could give Belinda's [11] friends the least umbrage, were the whole that passed to be repeated to them. I asked no question which would admit of a categorical answer; but I assured Belinda that such questions would one day be asked—in short were I to have another interview with him,[12] I could say nothing now which I did not say then. . . . After the proof I have given of my sincerity, he can be under no apprehension of a change of my sentiments; and were I to do as my friends advise me, I would give no better security than he has at present. He is satisfied that I shall make him an offer, and if he intends to accept of it, he will disregard those made by others; my fate depends on Belinda's present resolutions, by them I must stand or fall—if they are not favorable to me, it is out of my power to say anything to make them so which I have not already said; so that a visit could not possibly be of the least weight, and it is, I am sure, what he does not in the least expect." [13]

Rebecca Burwell may well have felt that Jefferson's declaration savored too much of the head rather than of the heart; such careful and painstaking planning of the future was scarcely in line with the passionate declaration a Virginia belle had the right to expect. Whether or not she hoped for the visit Jefferson mentions, she did not receive one. He adhered to his resolution and did not see her for the next six months. Meanwhile Miss Burwell had proceeded on the well-known feminine principle that a bird in the hand is worth two in the bush. It is not surprising, therefore, to find Jefferson writing, in March 1764, the same William Fleming to whom he had made such gay proposals but a few months before: "With regard to the scheme which I proposed to you some time since, I am sorry to tell you it is totally frustrated by Miss R. B.'s marriage with Jacquelin Ambler, which the people here tell me they daily expect: I say the people here tell me so, for (can you believe it?) I have been so abominably indolent as not to have seen her since last October, wherefore I cannot affirm I knew it from herself, though I am as well satisfied it is true as if she had told me. Well, the Lord bless her, I say! ... Many and great are the comforts of a single state, and neither of the reasons you urge can have any influence with an inhabitant and a young inhabitant too of Wmsburgh." [14]

The news was, indeed, all too true. Miss Rebecca Burwell duly made Mr. Jacquelin Ambler, who was to distinguish himself as the future Treasurer of Virginia, "the happiest of mortals," according to one of her friends, and the young Jefferson turned with a heart far from heavy to bury himself in the study of the law.

V. "Old Coke"

IN APRIL 1762, Jefferson left the College of William and Mary to study law under the wise and able guidance of George Wythe. Seldom has there been a happier or more lasting relation between disciple and master than existed between Jefferson and "the beloved mentor" of his youth. Throughout a long life Jefferson never tired of paying tribute to this remarkable man and, indeed, he owed Wythe a great deal. The words with which he pictures him ring with a sincerity and warmth that spring from the heart. "No man ever left behind him a character more venerated than George Wythe," Jefferson writes. "His virtue was of the purest tint; his integrity inflexible, and his justice exact; of warm patriotism, and, devoted as he was to liberty, and the natural and equal rights of man, he might truly be called the Cato of his country, without the avarice of the Roman; for a more disinterested person never lived. Temperance and regularity in all his habits gave him general good health, and his unaffected modesty and suavity of manners endeared him to everyone. He was of easy elocution, his language chaste, methodical in the arrangement of his matter, learned and logical in the use of it, and of great urbanity in debate; not quick of apprehension, but, with a little time, profound in penetration, and sound in conclusion. In philosophy he was firm, and neither troubling, nor perhaps trusting, anyone with his religious creed, he left the world to the conclusion, that that religion must be good which could produce a life of such exemplary virtue.... Such was George Wythe, the honor of his own and the model of future times." [1]

Jefferson was far from being the only one on whom Wythe's

extraordinary talents made a deep impression. Of all the people he met on his tour in America, Andrew Burnaby, the young English traveler, singled out Wythe as worthy of particular mention: "In Virginia," he writes, "I have had the pleasure to know several gentlemen adorned with many virtues and accomplishments.... Amongst others, I cannot resist the inclination of mentioning George Wythe, Esqre, who, to a perfect knowledge of the Greek language, which was taught him by his mother in the back woods, and of the ancient, particularly the Platonic philosophy, had joined such a profound reverence for the Supreme Being, such respect for the divine laws, such philanthropy for mankind, such simplicity of manners, and such inflexible rectitude and integrity of principle, as would have dignified a Roman senator, even in the most virtuous times of the republic." [2]

In appearance, if we are to judge by Trumbull's portrait in "The Declaration of Independence," Wythe possessed the thoughtful aspect of the philosopher. An engraving made in his old age reveals a certain similarity to Voltaire, as made familiar by Houdon. Jefferson, seeing Wythe through the eyes of affection, observed that "his stature was of middle size, well formed and proportioned, and the features of his face were manly, comely and engaging." [3] Henry Clay, who, as a boy of sixteen, became Wythe's clerk in 1793 and thus knew him from a different angle, says: "Mr. Wythe's personal appearance and personal habits were plain, simple and unostentatious. His countenance was full of blandness and benevolence and I think he made, in the salutation of others, the most graceful bow I have ever witnessed." [4] Like many men whose physique is not too impressive, he was meticulous in his dress and, if not a trifle vain, at least eager to make the most of his appearance and his station. Thus he writes his agents in London to send him "a robe such as is worn by the clerk in the house of commons, but better than the one I had before from Mr. Child, which indeed was scandalous." [5] He also ordered "a dark wig...two pair of black Manchester velvet breeches and a suit of very fine light cloath fit for our hot summers with a silk waistcoat and a pair of silk breeches besides." [6]

George Wythe's career had been unique. Beginning as a small

GEORGE WYTHE. From the portrait by J. F. Weir, after Trumbull. (*Courtesy of the National Musem, Independence Hall*)

country lawyer in an outlying district of Virginia, he rose to be a distinguished jurist, a signer of the Declaration of Independence, a member of the first Continental Congress, the first professor of law at the College of William and Mary, and the Chancellor of Virginia. This remarkable man was born in 1726 or 1727 of a well-to-do family that had been settled in Elizabeth City County since 1680. Although his early education had been somewhat haphazard—his mother is credited with having taught him Latin as well as Greek—and although it is not certain that he ever had any formal schooling, he was to become one of the most learned men in Virginia. Not only had he read widely in English and Roman law, but his knowledge of the classics and liberal sciences was equally profound. The first part of his life had been somewhat disorganized, probably because of the early death of his father and the inheritance of the family fortune by his eldest brother. Wythe was sent to Prince George County to study law with an uncle, Stephen Dewey, and was admitted to the bar at twenty years of age. Subsequently he became associated with a certain John Lewis in Spotsylvania and spent the next eight years there "indulging in the amusements and dissipations of society." He had returned to Williamsburg by 1754, and buried himself in the study of law and ancient languages. "He also acquired by his own reading," as Jefferson observed, "a good knowledge of mathematics, and of natural and moral philosophy."

When Peyton Randolph went to England in 1754, Wythe acted as Attorney General for the colony. The following year his elder brother died and the struggling young lawyer, resigned to the fate of a younger son, found himself in affluent circumstances —an event that was ultimately to prove tragic for him. From 1754 until the outbreak of the Revolution, he sat in the House of Burgesses, representing Williamsburg, the College, or Elizabeth City County. At the same time he carried on an extensive legal practice. He soon became the first at the bar, Jefferson tells us, "taking into consideration his superior learning, correct elocution, and logical style of reasoning; for in pleading he never indulged himself with an useless or declamatory thought or word; and became as distinguished by correctness and purity of conduct in his profession, as he was by his industry and fidelity to those who employed him." [7]

Wythe had been drawn into the brilliant circle that gathered about Governor Fauquier on his arrival in Virginia in 1758, and from that moment he may be said to have blossomed. Here, as we have seen, he came in contact with the young Jefferson and henceforth "he directed my studies in the law, led me into business, and continued, until death, my most affectionate friend." [8]

In 1779, when Jefferson, as Governor of Virginia, was to institute long-needed reforms at the College of William and Mary, it was Wythe he appointed to the "Professorship of Law and Police." This was only six years after John Vardill had been made professor of natural law at King's College in New York, and twenty years after the establishment of the Vinerian chair of English law at Oxford. There is no doubt that Wythe was a born teacher and enjoyed the contact with young minds. His students wrote of him with the greatest enthusiasm. Richard Henry Lee urged his brother Ludwell to complete his law studies under Mr. Wythe saying: "He discharges (his) duty with a wonderful ability, both as to theory and practice." [9] John Coalter, another student, subsequently a judge of the supreme court of Virginia, speaks of "the exalted and tried abilities of the gentleman" that "promise the apt and diligent student a certain and noble source of inspiration." [10]

John Brown, a young disciple and one of Kentucky's future senators, has left us a vivid description of Wythe's abilities and methods, which were far from being a mere dry paraphrase of Blackstone, the text he used. He seems to have been the first man in this country to use the moot court in connection with his teaching. From 1770-1776 there flourished in New York a club of young lawyers where matters currently before the Supreme Court and other questions were debated, but this had no connection with King's College. "Mr. Wythe," writes Brown, "ever attentive to his pupils, founded two institutions for that purpose, the first is a moot court, held monthly or oftener in the place formerly occupied by the General Court in the Capitol. Mr. Wythe and the other professors sit as judges. Our audience consists of the most respectable of the citizens, before whom we plead causes given out by Mr. Wythe. Lawyer like, I assure you. He has formed us into a legislative body consisting of about forty members. Mr. Wythe is Speaker to the House and takes all possible pains to instruct us in the rules of Parliament. We meet every Saturday and take under our consideration the Bills drawn up by the Committee appointed to revise them, then we debate and alter (I will not say amend) with the greatest freedom.... These exercises serve not only as the best amusement after severe studies, but are very useful and attended with many important advantages." [11]

In 1790, when Wythe was made sole Chancellor of Virginia, he resigned his professorship and removed to Richmond. The spirit of the teacher was too deeply ingrained in him to be disregarded, however, and he formed a small law school in his new place of residence. At his unfortunate death, in 1806, by poisoning at the hands of an avaricious grandnephew, the lectures which he had delivered during his many years of teaching came by will to Jefferson. As it was the desire of Wythe's friends and admirers to see them published, John Tyler, then Governor of Virginia, wrote Jefferson in 1810 asking whether he would not look over the manuscript and make such corrections and improvements as Wythe had intended. "They are highly worthy of publication...," Tyler observes. "It is a pity they should be lost to society and such a monument of his memory be neglected. Judge Roan has read them ... and is highly pleased with them, thinks they will be very valuable, there being so much of his own sound reasoning upon great principles, and not a mere servile copy of Blackstone, & other British commentators—a good many of his own thoughts on our constitutions and the necessary changes they have begotten, with that spirit of freedom which always marked his opinions.... It will afford a lasting evidence to the world, among much other, of your remembrance of the man who was always dear to you and his country. I do not see why an American Aristides should not be known to future ages. Had he been a vain egoist his sentiments would have been often seen on paper; and perhaps he erred in this respect, as the good and the great should always leave their precepts and opinions for the benefit of mankind...."[12]

This project did not come to realization for the manuscript never reached Jefferson. It was passed from one man to another, from Mr. Duval, who was one of the executors of Wythe's will and who "always had access to Mr. Wythe's library," as Tyler remarks, to Mr. William Crane and ultimately to a Mr. Ritchie, after which it disappeared and has, as yet, not come to light.

Such was the man under whose tutelage Jefferson placed himself in the spring of 1762, immediately on leaving William and Mary. At the end of December of that year he returned to Shadwell and remained for nine months. This time seems to have been spent in reading the fundamentals of the law, an occupation not without its dull moments, even for him. In a letter he wrote John Page from Fairfield, on his way home, he remarks that he fears he will think of Belinda too often for his peace of mind, "too often, I am sure, to get through old Coke [13] this winter; for God knows I have not seen him since I packed him up in my trunk in Williamsburg. Well, Page, I do wish the Devil had old Coke, for I am sure I never was so tired of an old dull scoundrel in my life. What! are there so few inquietudes tacked to this momentary life of ours, that we must need be loading ourselves with a thousand more? Or, as brother Job says (who, by-the-bye, I think began to whine a little under his afflictions), 'Are not my days few? Cease then, that I may take comfort a little before I go whence I shall not return, even to the land of darkness, and the shadow of death.' But the old fellows say we must read to gain knowledge, and gain knowledge to make us happy and admired. *Mere jargon.*"[14]

Despite an occasional rebelliousness, only natural in a youth of nineteen, Jefferson persisted in his reading of "old Coke," and acquired an admiration for him which the years could not dim and fashions in law books could not change. Half a century later, in deploring the tendency of "our merchants, priests and lawyers to adhere to England and Monarchy in preference to their own country and its constitution," he wrote: "With lawyers it is a new thing. They have in the mother country been generally the firmest supporters of the free principles of their constitution. But there too they have changed. I ascribe much of this to the substitution of Blackstone for my Lord Coke, as an elementary work. In truth, Blackstone and Hume have made tories of all England, and are making tories of those young Americans whose native feelings of independence do not place them above the wily sophistries of a Hume or a Blackstone." [15]

Jefferson was to be well rewarded for supporting the youthful tedium with "old Coke" by the discovery of a kindred spirit. For it was Coke who had challenged the royal prerogative in the realm of Britain as Jefferson was later to do, with the same arguments, for the rights of freeborn Englishmen in the dominions beyond the seas.

As a student of law, Jefferson subjected himself to a merciless, self-imposed discipline. We see this reflected in letters written at various times in his life to young friends about to embrace the profession. These letters are of great interest as not only do we learn from them the habits and methods of study he had worked out with conspicuous care, but we also gain a knowledge of the writers and thinkers who influenced the development of the young Jefferson's ideas. They likewise reveal the variety of other subjects that came under his observation as he read along in the law. The most informative of them was written during this period "for the use of a young friend whose course of reading was confided to me; and it formed a basis for the studies of others subsequently placed under my direction, but curtailed for each in proportion to his previous acquirements and future views." [16] The "young friend" was a man only a few years Jefferson's junior, Bernard Moore, of Chelsea, King William County. His sister, Betsy, had married John Walker, and the young people were, naturally, thrown together a great deal. Among the "others" who followed the precepts laid down were two men destined to be President of the United States, James Madison and James Monroe. In 1814 Jefferson sent John Minor a copy of his letter to Moore "not for its merit, for it betrays sufficiently its juvenile date; but because you have asked it." It was sent without change "except as to the books recommended to be read; later publications enabling me in some of the departments of science to substitute better, for the less perfect publications which we then possessed." [17]

"Before you enter on the study of the law," Jefferson writes his friend, "a sufficient groundwork must be laid. For this purpose an acquaintance with the Latin and French languages is absolutely necessary.... Mathematics and natural philosophy are so useful in the most familiar occurrences of life, and are so peculiarly engaging and delightful as would induce every person to wish an acquaintance with them. Besides this, the faculties of the mind, like the members of the body, are strengthened and improved by exercise. Mathematical reasonings and deductions are therefore a fine preparation for investigating the abstruse speculations of the law." Jefferson then gives a list of books he considers fundamental for the study of mathematics, astronomy, geography, and natural philosophy. "This foundation being laid," he continues, "you may enter regularly on the study of the laws, taking with it such of its kindred sciences as will contribute to eminence in its attainment. The principal of these are physics, ethics, religion, natural law, belles lettres, criticism, rhetoric and oratory. The carrying on several studies is attended with advantage. Variety relieves the mind as well as the eye...."

Remarking that "a great inequality is observable in the vigor of the mind at different periods of the day," Jefferson suggests that the student should divide his day into five parts. From rising, which was usually at dawn, until eight o'clock "employ yourself in physical studies. Ethics, religion, natural and sectarian, and natural law." A list of suitable books follows, grouped under the heads of agriculture, chemistry, anatomy, zoology, botany, ethics and natural religion, religion and natural law. Of greatest interest, probably, are the philosophers. Under the heading "ethics and natural religion," are recommended, among others, Locke's "Essay," Locke's "Conduct of the Mind in the Search after Truth," Stewart's "Philosophy of the Human Mind," Condorcet's "Progrès de l'Esprit Humain," Cicero's "Offices," Hutchinson's "Introduction to Moral Philosophy," Lord Kames' "Natural Religion." The required reading for religion includes the Bible, with certain commentaries on the New Testament, the Sermons of Sterne, Massillon, and Bourdaloue, and for natural law, Vattel's "Droits des Gens," Rayneval's "Institutions du Droit de la Nature et des Gens."

The second period, from eight until twelve o'clock noon, is to be devoted to the reading of law. Jefferson's observations on this are of particular interest to us in connection with his own study of the subject. "The general course of this reading," he remarks, "may be formed on the following grounds. Lord Coke has given us the first views of the whole body of law worthy now of being studied; for so much of the admirable work of Bracton is now obsolete that the student should turn to it occasionally only. When tracing the history of particular portions of the law, Coke's Institutes are a perfect digest of the law in his day. After this new laws were added by the Legislature, and new developments of the old law by the judges, until they had become so voluminous as to require a new digest. This was ably executed by Matthew Bacon.... The same process of new laws and new decisions on the old laws going on, called at length for the same operation again, and produced the inimitable commentaries of Blackstone. In the department of chancery, a similar progress has taken place. Lord Kaims [18] has given us the first digest of the principles of that branch of our jurisprudence...."

A list of "required" books is appended. These include, for common law, Coke's "Institutes"; "Select Cases from the Subsequent Reporters to the Time of Matthew Bacon"; Bacon's "Abridgment"; "Select Cases from the Subsequent Reporters to the Present Time"; "Select Tracts on Law," among which those of Baron Gilbert are all of the first merit; "The Virginia Laws"; "Reports" on them. Chancery: Lord Kames' "Principles of Equity"; "Select Cases from the Chancery Reporters to the Time of Matthew Bacon"; "The Abridgment of Cases in Equity"; "Select Cases from the Subsequent Reporters to the Present Day"; Fonblanque's "Treatise of Equity." Blackstone's "Commentaries," "as the last perfect digest of both branches of law."

A bit of advice follows this somewhat formidable array. "In reading the Reporters, enter in a common-place book every case of value, condensed into the narrowest compress possible, which will admit of presenting distinctly the principles of the case. This operation is doubly useful, insomuch as it obliges the student to seek out the pith of the case, and habituates him to a condensation of thought, and to an acquisition of the most valuable of talents, that of never using two words where one will do."

The third period of the day, from twelve to one, is given over to reading politics. The books recommended include, among others, Locke "On Government," Sidney "On Government," Priestley's "First Principles of Government," "Review of Montesquieu's Spirit of Laws," De Lolme, "Sur la constitution d'Angleterre," Hatsell's "Precedents of the House of Commons," "Select Parliamentary Debates of England and Ireland," Chipman's "Sketches of the Principles of Government," Say's "Economie Politique," Malthus on "The Principles of Population."

Mercifully and vaguely labeled "In the Afternoon," the fourth period is to be devoted to the reading of history in its various branches. For ancient is recommended, among others, the Greek and Latin originals, and Gibbon's "Decline of the Roman Empire." Modern calls for "Histoire moderne de Millot," Russell's "History of Modern Europe," Robertson's "Charles V." English history, "the original historians, to wit 'The History of Edward II,' by E. F., Habington's 'Edward IV,'" etc., and finally, for American history, Robertson's "History of America," Burk's "History of Virginia," and others.

From "Dark to Bedtime" the mind is to be improved "by belles lettres, criticism, rhetoric, and oratory." Under the latter head Jefferson observes, "This portion of time (borrowing some of the afternoon when the days are long and the nights short) is to be applied also to acquiring the art of writing and speaking correctly.... Criticise the style of any book whatsoever, committing the criticism to writing. Translate into the different styles, *to wit*, the elevated, the middling and the familiar.... Undertake, at first, short compositions as themes, letters, etc., paying great attention to the elegance and correctness of your language." [19] The diligent student is then advised to read the "Orations" of Demosthenes and Cicero, model his own on these, and try them out on a willing and long-suffering friend.

If this is a fair picture of young Jefferson's day at this period of intense study and concentration—and we have no reason to doubt it—it is small wonder that he emerged from this training one of the most cultivated and widely read men in the colonies. How serious were his interests, how unappeasable his thirst for knowledge is evident. As he remarked, years later, when sending some early papers to a friend, "They were written at a time of life when I was bold in the pursuit of knowledge, never fearing to follow truth and reason to whatever results they led and bearding every authority which stood in their way." [20] No words ever rang with greater truth or more aptly described the young Jefferson than his own phrase, "I was bold in the pursuit of knowledge." There were few realms of human endeavor which he did not try to penetrate and to master—and few repulsed him.

Except for certain later books which superseded the "less perfect publications which we then possessed," we may assume that Jefferson's library as a student contained the volumes he recommended to Bernard Moore. Unfortunately no list or catalogue of his books at this period has been preserved. Such a paper, if it existed, was destroyed along with the majority of his notes and books in the fire that razed Shadwell in February 1770. We have only the meager knowledge, as far as law books are concerned, supplied by a list of purchases he made at the bookshop kept by the publisher of the *Virginia Gazette*.[21] In the account book kept by the shop, which is a day-by-day record of the sales of books and writing materials, subscriptions to the *Gazette* and advertisements in it, we learn that on February 14, 1764, Jefferson bought "Practice, King's Bench, 2 vols. Do Common Pleas, 2 vols., (author not given), Harrison's Chancery Practice, 2 vols." On the twentieth he acquired an "Attorney's Pocket Companion" and on October 3 he had bound Rastall's "Collection of Statutes." The following April he purchased "Virginia Laws since the Revisal," in June, "Act of Parliament," and in October 1765, "Grounds and Rudiments of Law."

In preparation for his appearance before the bar he also bought "Sheridan on Elocution," and he doubtless followed his own advice in testing his skill as an orator on friends. The question has often been raised why a man of Jefferson's attainments was not conspicuous as a public speaker. James Madison and William Wirt, who knew Jefferson, declared that his voice became husky if raised too long above an ordinary conversational tone.[22] Whether or not this was the case, Jefferson's gifts very obviously lay in his pen rather than in oratory. It would have been difficult for anyone at that time to have challenged the eloquence of Patrick Henry. Probably the most impartial estimate of Jefferson's abilities in this direction are the words of his brilliant contemporary and associate, Edmund Randolph. In his "Essay on the Revolutionary History of Virginia" Randolph says of Jefferson: "Indefatigable and methodical, Jefferson spoke with ease, perspicuity and elegance. His style in writing was more impassioned, and although often incorrect, was too glowing not to be acquitted as venial departures from rigid rules. Without being an overwhelming orator, he was an impressive speaker who fixed the attention. On two signal arguments before the general court, in which Mr. Henry and himself were coadjutors, each characterized himself. Mr. Jefferson drew copiously from the depths of the law, Mr. Henry from the recesses of the human heart." [23]

During these formative years, while he was studying with Wythe, Jefferson, as he himself tells us, "was in the habit of abridging and commonplacing what I read meriting it, and sometimes mixing my own reflections on the subject." [24] This custom of putting his thoughts down on paper remained uninterrupted until a few days before his death when his faltering hand penned the three faint words "free, Th. Jefferson." [25] It resulted in two documents which are of the utmost importance for the study of the formation of his ideas. These are two commonplace books, one of a legal nature, the other purely literary. In the former he wrote down, as he came upon them in his reading, the ideas on law, and subsequently on theories of government, that most impressed him and that he wished forever to lock in his mind. The second commonplace book, begun at about the same time, is devoted to literary extracts from the Greek, Latin, and English. A third one, dealing with problems in equity, is of less importance in his development. These three books, along with three pocket ac-

[handwriting sample]

1762   *(Courtesy of a private collector)*

[handwriting sample]

1763   *(Courtesy of Yale University)*

[handwriting sample]

1764   *(Courtesy of Yale University)*

[handwriting sample]

1765   *(Courtesy of the Library of Congress)*

[handwriting sample]

1766   *(Courtesy of the New York Public Library)*

[handwriting sample]

1767   *(Courtesy of the Library of Congress)*

JEFFERSON'S EARLY HANDWRITING

count books and Mercer's "Exact Abridgement of all the Public Acts of Assembly of Virginia in Force and Use, January 1, 1758," which contains some notes made while Jefferson was studying it, were among the few papers that survived the fire.[26]

No study of the commonplace books, which have so much to tell, can be undertaken without a careful analysis of the development of Jefferson's handwriting. This, along with a study of the paper on which they are written and its watermarks, taken in conjunction with certain early book bills, enables us to fix the dates, more exactly than has hitherto been possible, of Jefferson's reading at this time, whether of the law or literature. It furnishes, likewise, the most accurate clue we have yet had to the formation and growth of Jefferson's thought during this important period.

The paper which Jefferson used in his legal commonplace book, judging by the watermarks, is unlike any used in known examples of his letters or drawings from 1769 onwards. The pages of the greater part of the manuscript, however, bear a watermark identical with that of the paper on which Jefferson entered the notes of cases in 1768 and 1769 [27] which were published in 1829 as "Report of Cases Determined in the General Court of Virginia from 1730-40 and 1768-72." As the period during which Jefferson used a certain paper averages about three years,[28] we can assume that he acquired this paper not before 1765-1766 and that the early entries in the commonplace book date from this time. Page 155 is written on a different paper from that of the rest of the book. As it bears notes on a volume published in 1781, it was obviously incorporated later. It must be borne in mind, in this discussion, that Jefferson used loose sheets of paper, usually folded once, for making these notes, and later had them bound.

Jefferson's early handwriting exhibits definite characteristics in each year. Like many very young people, he seems to have taken a certain pleasure in modifying the style of his writing from time to time. Thus Goethe wrote, on reading over the letters he had written his father and sister while a student at Leipzig, "I was shocked at the incredible carelessness of my handwriting which extended from October, 1765, to the middle of the following January. Suddenly, in the middle of March, a firm and regular hand made its appearance, the sort I was accustomed to use in competition for prizes. My amazement resolved itself into thanks to good, old Gellert who, as I well recall, besought us, in his sincere way, to try to improve our writing rather than our style in the essays we wrote for him." [29]

One feature of Jefferson's early writing is the variation in the use of the letter "s." Apparently, he early made an attempt to uproot the long "s" characteristic of a previous style, and adopt the more modern short "s," such as we use today. When he set out to make a fair copy, or to make a journal entry, as in his fee book, or garden book, he would remember to use the short "s" and the handwriting is very regular, in what might be called a copybook style. When he wrote informally, as in letters to his friends or in making notes, the long "s" continued to appear for a considerable time. Even as late as 1771 one slipped into his account book in the word "burgessing."

The earliest extant, dated example of Jefferson's handwriting is the letter he wrote John Page from Fairfield on December 25, 1762.[30] It reveals a sloping, rather cramped hand with the letters of the words fairly close together. The initial "s" is sometimes long, sometimes short, double "s" and "s" in the middle of a word are invariably long. The stem of the "d" extends upward and back with a good deal of a flourish. In this letter he has abandoned the archaic capitalization of nouns which characterizes the earliest entries in the literary commonplace book. The second example, of January 20 to March 11, 1763, naturally does not show much variation, but by January 19, 1764, the hand is much more regular, the letters more widely spaced, and there is a certain tendency toward a more vertical character. In this example the initial "s," as well as the double "s" and "s" in the middle of the word, are long. The stem of the "d" has lost its flourish, indeed the "d" has taken on quite a different form. These two characteristics of the writing of this year enable us to date the early notes in Jefferson's copy of Mercer's "Abridgement," published in 1759, as of 1764, as are also certain quotations from Pope's "Homer" and Pope's "Iliad" in the literary commonplace book.[31] The next dated example is the letter Jefferson wrote John Page from Annapolis on May 25, 1766. Here the writing has taken on many of the characteristics that distinguish his mature hand in the size, shape, and spacing of the letters. The initial "s" is sometimes long, sometimes short, although the long is preferred, and the "s" in the double "s" and in the middle of a word are long. Except for a very occasional flourish, the "d" is entirely reformed. By August 1767, when the first of Jefferson's known pocket account books begins, the long "s" is completely dropped and the handwriting has attained most of the traits that mark it thenceforth.

There are three specimens of Jefferson's handwriting which, by a process of elimination, must fall in the year 1765. The character of the writing is more vertical than that which preceded it in 1763 and 1764, more regular, and the letters more clearly formed, than in the Page letter of 1766 or the account book of 1767 and 1768. The form of the "th" is peculiar to the several examples that seem to fall in this period. In all three the initial "s" is invariably short, the "s" in the middle of the word, or double "s," usually long. These three specimens are the document on marriage, quoted elsewhere, a fair copy of a law of 1727, headed "Concerning the Poor and Vagabond," [32] and the four selections from the poet Mark Akenside, in the literary commonplace book. The paper of the legal document bears a "Pro Patria" watermark, and we know that on May 18, 1764, Jefferson bought two quires of "Pro Patria paper" from the *Virginia Gazette* shop. We cannot, of course, be certain that this is the same. We know, also, that Akenside was one of the poets whose works Jefferson owned by 1764, as he had the volume bound at the same shop on October 18 of that year.

On the basis of this analysis of the handwriting and the paper we are justified in inferring that the first 174 entries in the legal commonplace book were made in 1766. The books from which excerpts were copied during this period were such as a law student would be using: Andrews' "Reports of Cases Origined before the King's Bench..., 1737-1740"; Coke's "The Third Part of the Institutes of the Laws of England"; Salkeld's "Reports on the Cases in the King's Bench, 1689-1712"; and Raymond's "Reports of Cases argued and adjudged in the Courts of the King's Bench and Common Pleas."

Beginning with May 1766, and until August 12, 1767, when the long "s" disappears entirely from the entries in his account book for that year, Jefferson, as we have seen, had so far reformed his writing that the initial "s" was always short, although the double "s" remained long. There are no items entered in the legal commonplace book that show the peculiarities of writing of this period. Selections which do so, however—from Ovid, Horace, Pope's translation of Homer, and Milton's "Paradise Lost"—make their appearance in the literary commonplace book. This is not surprising, as it corresponds in part to the time Jefferson was making his first journey outside of Virginia, visiting Annapolis, Philadelphia, and New York. It was a tour of some months' duration, and his legal studies were, of course, interrupted. It would not have been unnatural for him, however, to carry with him a few favorite poets, pondering their thoughts as he rode along, and inscribing selections during the long evenings at lodging houses in towns where he had no friends.

To the period following August 1767 belong the entries Nos. 175 to 695 in the legal commonplace book. The characteristics of the writing change sharply here. Except for one appearance in No. 176 and again in No. 180, the long "s" is completely dropped, and the hand is identical with that of the account book of that year. Although his student days were over, Jefferson carried on his practice of making extracts from Salkeld's "Reports," as well as from the other reports already mentioned. To these he added passages from Peere Williams's "Reports of Cases argued and determined in the High Court of Chancery," Lord Kames' "Historical Tracts," John Dalrymple's "Essay Towards a General History of Feudal Property in Great Britain," Matthew Hale's "History of the Common Law," Croke's "King's Bench Reports, Tempore Elizabeth," and Lord Kames' "Principles of Natural Religion."

Side by side with his commonplace book of the common law, Jefferson kept one for equity.[33] The writing in the first part of this, although smaller and more cramped, has many of the characteristics of the document on marriage and the selections from Akenside. The first nine pages occasionally contain the long "s," both initial and in the middle of words. We may thus infer that the book was begun in 1765, although completed later. Jefferson first extracted certain special cases from William Salkeld's "Reports of Cases in the King's Bench," then digested Thomas Vernon's "Reports of Cases Decided in Chancery." Peere Williams's "Reports of cases argued and determined in the High Court of Chancery" subsequently came under his scrutiny. That Jefferson's entries were made simultaneously in these two commonplace books dealing with the law is well shown in the instance of these last excerpts. The five entries (Nos. 550-554) from Peere Williams, in what we have called the legal commonplace book, are in the very regular half-printed writing he had lately adopted (with No. 452) and which lasted for a brief period (ending with No. 554). This same type of handwriting commences in the equity commonplace book precisely with the extracts from Peere Williams there (No. 619) and ends with the table at No. 1131 in which he summarizes the "Powers of a Court of Equity." Then follow, in each book, excerpts from Lord Kames, in one case from his "Historical Tracts," in the other from his "Principles of Equity." The latter Jefferson extracted at great length. Notes on other cases in chancery follow.

After the usual and necessary examinations, Jefferson was admitted to the bar of the general court in the early days of 1767.[34] This court, which consisted of the Governor and Council, sat in Williamsburg for 24 days each April and October. Before it were tried civil, criminal, and appellate cases. Five members formed a quorum. By a law enacted in March 1761, "to prevent frivolous suits in the general court, and trifling and vexatious appeals from the county courts and other inferior courts," a lawyer practicing in the general court was forbidden to "prosecute or defend a cause" in the county courts, under penalty of a fine of £20 for each violation.[35] This seems to have been more honored in the breach than in the observance, for Jefferson, like others, practiced in both courts. In certain of his memorandum books written in Virginia almanacs, as was sometimes his custom, he has marked the days on which the general court met, as well as the court of oyer and terminer in Williamsburg, and the county courts of Albemarle and Augusta.[36] From his fee book we learn that during the five years he practiced as a lawyer he had cases in no less than 53 of the 57 counties which at that time constituted the colony of Virginia.[37] The cases which he handled were largely such as would arise in an agrarian community. They dealt, to a great extent, with the problems involved in the ownership of land, its boundaries, partitions, sale, and inheritance. There were, of course, also cases arising out of the institution of slavery.

In the methodical manner that was growing on him, Jefferson proceeded to keep a careful record of his cases, in a fee book as well as in a register of cases. The first of his cases in the latter volume, inscribed no doubt with pride, in the delicate hand of his youth, is dated February 12, 1767. "Gabriel Jones (Augusta) v. Andrew Lewis (Augusta)," we read, "enter caveat for 100 acres of land near Warm Spring, Augusta. See state of case—Mar. 20 recd of Jones £3—Apr. 13 pd. L. Savage for tax and sum. 8/3—1768 June 18 took out N. S. & pd. Walthoe 5/19."[38] Cases came in rather rapidly for a young lawyer. During his first year of practice he was employed in 68, in his second, 115. In 1769 there were 198; in 1770, 221; 1771, 237; 1772, 154; 1773, 127; 1774, 29;[39] when, as Jefferson remarked, the functions of the courts were suspended. These represent only the cases in the General Court. There seems to be no complete list of his other cases, but certain of his account books contain supplementary ones. Thus from the account book for 1771 we learn that he was employed in 430 cases in all in that year. In 1772, there were 347.

In the course of time Jefferson was retained as counsel by many of the outstanding men of Virginia. Such names as Theodoric Bland, Richard Bland, Lord Fairfax, Lewis Burwell, William Byrd, Benjamin Harrison, Carter Henry Harrison, Edward Lee, Richard Henry Lee, Francis Willis, Senior and Junior, along with others equally distinguished, appear in his lists of clients.[40] Others were situated in North Carolina, Scotland, and "Gr. Britain." Very shortly after starting to practice he was associated in the trial of cases with the leading lawyers of the colony, Wythe,

Pendleton, Peyton Randolph, and George Mason.[41] As early as October 1767, he was retained by the Receiver General, Colonel Corbin, as associate counsel with the Attorney General in a suit brought by former Governor Dinwiddie against one of the Lees.[42]

When Robert Carter Nicholas, one of the leading lawyers of Virginia and Treasurer of the colony, withdrew from practice in April 1771, he sought to put his affairs in Jefferson's hands. In Jefferson's register of cases we find the following note under the date of October 31, 1771: "Robert Carter Nicholas, having retired from the bar, put his business in to my hands, to be finished, about April last. Finding myself, however, under the necessity of declining it, I make no entries of cases, nor charge anything, but what I actually received." [43]

At the end of his first year of practice, the young lawyer summarized his financial status. "Profits of the year 1767," we read in his fee book, "cash rec'd, £43-4-0-¾ + cash due £250-0-5 = Total profits £293-4-5-¾." Naïvely, perhaps, he seems to have assumed all debts would be paid. Two years later his cash receipts had jumped to £147 2s 11½d, legal fees due £223 8s ½d, total profits, as he still hopefully considered them, £370 11s 0d. At the end of six years, when he made an inclusive summary, his total receipts amounted to £797 10s 5¾d, legal fees due, £1321 16s 6½d, total profits, £2119 7s ¼d.[44]

The fees which a lawyer was permitted to charge were fixed by law. Those which might be asked by a man practicing before the general court were higher than those allowed an attorney in the county or inferior courts, but in neither case could a man grow rich without a great deal of hard work and a large number of clients. In an "Act for Regulating the Practice of Attorneys," passed by the burgesses in March 1761, it was decreed that "Lawyers practicing in the general court may demand or receive for an opinion or advice, where no suit is or shall be brought & prosecuted or defended by the attorney giving such advice, but not otherwise, £1/1s/6, and in any suit at common law, other than the actions hereinafter mentioned, fifty shillings; in all chancery suits, or real mixed or personal actions, where the title or bounds of lands shall or may come in question, five pounds." [45]

No man could make a fortune on this basis. Indeed, in view of the prevailing habit of a leisurely settlement of debts, it was difficult even to make a fair living. On May 20, 1773, Jefferson joined with Edmund Pendleton, John Randolph, James Mercer, Patrick Henry, and Gustavus Scott in inserting an advertisement in the *Virginia Gazette*. "On serious consideration of the present state of our practice in the General Court we find it can no longer be continued on the same terms. The fees allowed by law, if regularly paid, would barely compensate our incessant labours, reimburse our expences and the losses incurred by neglect of our private affairs; yet even these rewards, confessedly moderate, are withheld from us, in a great proportion, by the unworthy part of our clients. Some regulation, therefore, is become absolutely requisite to establish terms more equal between the client and his council. To effect this we have come to the following resolution, for the invariable observance of which we mutually pledge our honour to each other: 'That after the 10th day of October next we will not give an opinion in any case stated to us but on payment of the whole fee, nor prosecute or defend any suit or motion unless the tax, and one half of the fee, be previously advanced, excepting those cases only when we choose to act gratis'; and we hope no person whatever may think of applying to us in any other way...."

This action was but a palliative. Six years later, when engaged in the revision of the laws of Virginia, Jefferson took up with Wythe this troublesome problem and its correlations. "Since I left you," he wrote on March 1, 1779, "I have reflected on the bill regulating the practising of attornies, and, of our omitting to continue the practitioners at the county and general courts separate. I think the bar of the general court a proper and excellent nursery for future judges; if it be so regulated that science may be encouraged, and may live there. But this can never be if an inundation of insects is permitted to come from the county courts, and consume the harvest. These people, traversing the counties, seeing the clients frequently at their own courts, or, perhaps, at their own houses, must of necessity pick up all the business. The convenience of frequently seeing their counsel, without going

"OLD COKE" 93

from home, cannot be withstood by the country people. Men of science, then, if there were to be any, would only be employed as auxiliary counsel in difficult cases. But can they live by that? Certainly not. The present members of that kind, therefore, must turn marauders in the county courts, and, in future, none will have leisure to acquire science. I should therefore be for excluding the county court attornies, or rather, for taking the general court lawyers from the incessant drudgery of the county courts and confining them to their studies, that any may qualify themselves as well to support their clients, as to become worthy successors to the bench...." [46]

Two of Jefferson's arguments while a practicing lawyer survive. These, fortunately for us, were printed in his "Reports of Cases Determined in the General Court of Virginia" already mentioned. "When I was at the bar of the General Court," he writes, in the introduction to the book, "there were in the possession of John Randolph, Attorney-General, three volumes of manuscript reports of cases determined in that Court." One volume had been taken down by Sir John Randolph, the father of the Attorney General. There were cases of English law as well as "those peculiar to our own country." These Jefferson abstracted. The English cases he considered as of no consequence, but "on our own peculiar laws, their [47] judgments, whether formed on correct principles of law or not, were of conclusive authority. As precedents they established authoritatively the construction of our own enactments and gave them the shape and meaning, under which our property has ever since been transmitted and is regulated and is held to this day." From 1740 to 1768 no reports were taken. In the latter year Jefferson "began to commit to writing some leading cases of the day, confining myself to those arising under our peculiar laws." He continued to do so until 1772, "when the Revolution dissolved our courts of justice."

The first of Jefferson's own cases included in these reports, Howell *vs.* Netherland, was argued in April 1770. It is perhaps not without significance that he pleaded the cause of the unfortunate; certain it is that the argument he advanced was far beyond the thought of the times. It was, likewise, the first expression of the ideas that had been growing in his mind, nurtured by the books he had recently acquired. As he summarizes the case it "was referred to the determination of the court, on the facts stated by the counsel for both parties, which were, that the plaintiff's grandmother was a mulatto, begotten of a white woman by a negro man, after the year 1705, and bound by the church wardens, under the law of that date, to serve to the age of thirty-one. That after the year 1723, but during her servitude, she was delivered of the plaintiff's mother, who, during her servitude, to wit, in 1742, was delivered of the plaintiff, and he again was sold by the person to whom his grandmother was bound, to the defendant, who now claims his service till he shall be thirty-one years of age." After a thorough summary of the statutes he boldly declares: "I suppose it will not be pretended that the mother being a servant, the child would be a servant also under the law of nature, without any particular provision of the act. Under the law of nature all men are born free, everyone comes into the world with a right to his own person, which includes the liberty of moving and using it at his own will. This is what is called personal liberty, and is given him by the author of nature, because necessary for his own sustenance. The reducing of the mother to servitude was a violation of the law of nature: surely then the same law cannot prescribe a continuance of the violation to her issue, and that too without end, for if it extends to any, it must be to every degree of descendants. Puff. b. 6c. 3. s. 4. 9 supports this doctrine." In conclusion he states, "so that the position at first laid down is now proven, that the act of 1705, makes servants of the first mulatto, that of 1723, extends it to her children, but that it remains for some future legislature, if any shall be found wicked enough, to extend it to the grandchildren and other issue more remote, to the *nati natorum et qui nascentur ab illis.*" The young lawyer's eloquence was in vain. "Wythe, for the defendant, was about to answer," he tells us, "but the Court interrupted him, and gave judgment in favor of his client." [48]

In the October session of the general court of 1771, Jefferson argued the case of Godwin *et al. vs.* Lunan—and was more successful. "The plaintiffs were churchwardens and vestrymen of the upper parish, in the county of Nansemond," he says, "and filed a libel in the General Court, as a court of ecclesiastical jurisdiction, against the defendant, charging that he was minister of the Gospel of Christ, regularly ordained, according to the rites of the church of England; that he was received to the care of said parish, that he was of evil fame and profligate manners; that he was much addicted to drunkenness, in so much, as to be often drunk at church, and unable to go through divine service, or to baptize or marry those who attended for that purpose; that he officiated in ridiculous apparel unbecoming a priest; that he was a common disturber of the peace, and often quarrelling and fighting; that he was a profane swearer." After preferring even more disgraceful charges, "the libellants prayed that the said Patrick Lunan might be corrected, punished and deprived, or otherwise, that right and justice might be administered. The defendant pleaded to the jurisdiction of the court, and in that plea it came to be argued." Jefferson argued brilliantly, calling on a wealth of historical precedents back to the year 854 and the days of Ethelwolf. "The Court," says Jefferson, "adjudged that they possessed ecclesiastical jurisdiction, and that as an ecclesiastical court they might proceed to censure or deprive the defendant, if there should be just cause." [49]

As an appendix to these reports, Jefferson printed a learned and lengthy discussion of "the pious disposition of the English judges to connive at the frauds of the clergy," entitled "Whether Christianity is a Part of the Common Law." He says of it, "I have added a disquisition of my own on the most remarkable instance of judicial legislation that has ever occurred in English jurisprudence or perhaps in any other. It is that of the adoption in mass of the whole code of another nation, and its incorporation into the legitimate system by usurpation of the judges alone, without a particle of legislative will having ever been called on, or exercised towards its introduction, or confirmation." [50] This discussion was first set down in Jefferson's legal commonplace book (Nos. 873 and 879). It comes there not long after his excerpts from Voltaire, whose writings may well have contributed to intensify his hostility to the priests. The latter follow abstracts from Eden's

"Principles of Penal Law" and from Helvétius' "De l'homme," both published in 1772, so that Jefferson's argument is from this period and not from about 1764, as has been supposed.

In the spring of 1769, when he was twenty-six years old, Jefferson was elected to the House of Burgesses to represent Albemarle. It was the first step in a career that was to wean him from the practice of the law. These were stirring times in the colony, and, as his political activities and interest grew, the time he could devote to his private practice dwindled. He was a rich man who had no need of income from the law. The urge to public service was even now strong upon him. By 1774 he had decided to dispose of his practice, and on August 11 of that year he turned it over to Edmund Randolph, one of the outstanding lawyers of the colony. In his account book he notes, under date of August 11, "the following is a list of balances assigned to Edmund Randolph, for which the clients must have credits in my accounts." [51] Then follows a list of 132 names, with the notation "By a rough estimate Mr. Randolph will have about 2/3 of the whole fees to receive." The amount involved was £519 3s 1¾d. The list and amounts due are repeated in the fee book.[52]

Jefferson's interest in the law was far from ceasing with the abandonment of his practice. Indeed, his contributions to it were not to be exceeded by any of his contemporaries. An urge to be active in the creation of the law drove him on, rather than the desire to devote himself to its execution and application. His greatest service to his chosen field was, without doubt, the part he was to play in the revision of the laws of Virginia, which will be discussed in a later chapter. He was a very young man at the time this was undertaken, only thirty-three years old, and it is a tribute to his knowledge, his abilities, and his personality that he was not only able to take the lead from men much older and more experienced, but was permitted to do so.

Of equal importance was to be Jefferson's painstaking collecting of the laws of Virginia from the earliest times—material which was ultimately turned over to Hening to be embodied in his "Statutes at Large." [53] In 1795 "an act was passed directing that all laws relating to lands, tenements and hereditaments within this commonwealth, at any time passed since the first settlement of Virginia," [54] should be published. George Wythe was made a member of the committee in charge of the matter, and, knowing of Jefferson's collection of laws, wrote him asking for the use of them. In his reply, after stating that the unprinted laws are scattered through many manuscript volumes, some of which are so decayed that the leaves fall to powder when touched, Jefferson sketches his efforts in behalf of Virginia law.

"Very early in the course of my researches into the laws of Virginia," he writes, "I observed that many of them were already lost, and many more on the point of being lost, as existing only in single copies in the hands of careful or curious individuals, on whose deaths they would probably be used for waste paper. I set myself therefore to work to collect all which were then existing, in order that when the day should come in which the public should advert to the magnitude of their loss in these precious monuments of our property and our history, a part of the regret might be spared by information that a portion had been saved from the wreck, which is worthy of their attention and preservation. In searching after these remains I spared neither time, trouble nor expense; and am of the opinion that scarcely any law escaped me, which was in being as late as the year 1770, in the middle or southern part of the state. In the northern part something might still be found. . . .

"My collection of fugitive sheets forms as we know, two volumes, and comprehends all the extant laws from 1734 to 1783; and the laws which can be gleaned up, from the revisals, to supply the chasm between 1710 and 1734, with those of 1783, to the close of the present century (by which term the work might be completed) would not be more than the matter of another volume." [55]

Another phase of Jefferson's service to American law is the "Manual of Parliamentary Practice" he was to prepare for the use of the United States Senate. Once again, as was so often the case with him, we find that he had laid the foundation for this in his youth. In another of his small, neatly written books, inscribed on the flyleaf "Parliamentary Note-Book," [56] he had made notes on the rules and regulations of parliamentary law. It was not until he was elected Vice-President and had, consequently, to preside over the Senate, that he was again to turn to this subject. He found that the legislative bodies of the new state managed their business in a way not only unparliamentary, as he says, but "the forms were so awkward and inconvenient that it was impossible some times to get at the true sense of the majority." [57] This was something utterly antipathetic to Jefferson's orderly spirit. He set about at once to remedy the situation. In January 1797, he wrote George Wythe, "it seems probable that I will be called on to preside in a legislative chamber. It is now so long since I have acted in the legislative line, that I am entirely rusty in the Parliamentary rules of procedure. I know they have been more studied and are better known by you than by any man in America, perhaps by any man living. I am in hopes that while enquiring into the subject you made notes on it. If any such remain in your hands, however informal, in books or in scraps of paper, and you will be so good as to trust me with them a little while, they shall be most faithfully returned." [58]

Jefferson continued to work on this problem until after his election to the presidency, in 1800. In February of that year he again wrote Wythe, "in the course of this business I find many perplexities... so little has the Parliamentary branch of the law been attended to, that I not only find no person here [*i.e.*, in Philadelphia], but not even a book to aid me. I had, at an early period of life, read a good deal on the subject and commonplaced what I read. This commonplace has been my pillar; but there are many questions of practice on which that is silent, some of them are so minute indeed, and belong too much to every-day practice, that they have never been thought worthy of being written down. Yet from desuetude they have slipped my memory. You will see by the enclosed paper what they are. I know with what pain you write: therefore I have left a margin in which you can write a simple negative or affirmative opposite every position or perhaps, with as little trouble, correct the text by striking out or interlining. This is what I have earnestly to solicit from you, and I would not have given you the trouble if I had had any other resource. But you are, in fact, the only spark of Parliamentary science now remaining to us. I am the more anxious because I have been forming a manual of Parliamentary law which I mean to deposit with the Senate as the standard by which I judge and am willing to be judged." Then he adds: "Though I should be opposed to its being printed, yet it may be done perhaps without my consent; and in that case I should be sorry indeed should it go out with errors that a Tyro should not have committed." [59]

Anything so fundamental and so useful was not destined to remain long in manuscript. The manual was printed within a very few years. It has been called "the highest authority in legislative proceedings known to the civilized world," [60] but Jefferson continued to think of it modestly. In 1809, when he was to be approached concerning a complete edition of his writings, he wrote, after discussing the "Notes on Virginia" and "The Summary View," "I do not mention the Parliamentary Manual, published for the use of the Senate of the United States, because it was a mere compilation, into which nothing entered but my own arrangement, and a few observations necessary to explain that and some of the cases." [61]

Although Jefferson never returned to the practice of the law, he did not regret his training in it. Writing from Paris to young Thomas Mann Randolph, who looked to a political career, he said, "I have proposed to you, to carry on the study of law with that of politics and history. Every political measure will, forever, have an intimate connection with the laws of the land, and he who knows nothing of them will always be perplexed, and often foiled by adversaries having the advantage of that knowledge over him." [62] It was an advantage that Jefferson's adversaries never possessed when he undertook to incorporate his political principles in the law of the land.

VI. A Taste for Literature

A MISFORTUNE OF the first order was to befall Jefferson on February 1, 1770, when the house at Shadwell was destroyed by fire. However devastating the loss may have been to Mrs. Jefferson, it was catastrophic to her son. He lost all that he valued most in the world, his books and his papers, both private and legal. On the twenty-first he wrote to Page:

"My late loss may perhaps have reached you by this time; I mean the loss of my mother's house by fire, and in it of every paper I had in the world, and almost every book. On a reasonable estimate I calculated the cost of the books burned to have been £200 sterling. Would to God it had been the money, *then* it had never cost me a sigh! To make the loss more sensible, it fell principally on my books of common law, of which I have but one left, at that time lent out. Of papers too of every kind I am utterly destitute. All of these, whether public or private, of business or of amusement, have perished in the flames. I had made some progress in preparing for the succeeding General Court, and having, as was my custom, thrown my thoughts into the form of notes, I troubled my head no more with them. These are gone, and like the baseless fabric of a vision, leave not a trace behind. The records also, and other papers which furnished me with states of the several cases, having shared the same fate, I have no foundation whereon to set out anew." [1]

Exactly how many books Jefferson lost in the fire we do not know, but if we may judge by the average value of books in his bills and inventories at this period, £200 would represent about four hundred volumes. His first thought, now, was to try to reconstitute his library, and he appears immediately to have made out a list of what he most needed. This he enclosed in a letter to his friend, Thomas Nelson, Jr., of York, whom he had known in his Williamsburg days, to be forwarded to his bookdealer. His second thought was for his law practice, and he considered it wise to whisper a word to a friend at court. Jefferson's letter on this subject seems not to have survived, but we have Nelson's reply, hitherto unpublished, dated York, March 6, 1770. "I just received your melancholy account of the loss you have sustained, and have only time to assure you that nothing can give me so much pleasure as to render you every service that is in my power. You may depend on your letter to your bookseller being sent by the first opportunity, it would be prudent to send a copy of the letter for fear the original should miscarry. If by 'the door that might be opened to relieve your distress,' you mean the courts indulging you with a continuance of your causes, my father says you may be certain of that, as the court has frequently done it where there have been good reasons for it."

Thomas Nelson himself, known as "Mr. Secretary," as he held the post of Secretary of the Colonial Council of Virginia, enclosed a note with that of his son: "I was extremely concerned to hear of your loss, the account of which had reached us some time ago. As I have a pretty good collection of books, it will give me pleasure to have it in my power to furnish you with any you may want." A hasty note from John Page, likewise enclosed, condoles with Jefferson on his misfortune and observes: "I am much pleased with the philosophy you manifest in your letter, which I this moment rec'd." Other friends rallied, as though there had been a death in the family. Even George Wythe was moved to write. He sent his young friend some grafts of nectarines and apricots, along with some grape vines, and remarked, "You bear your misfortune so becomingly that, as I am convinced you will surmount the difficulties it has plunged you into, so I foresee you will hereafter reap advantage from it several ways. *Durate et vosmet rebus servate secundus.*" [2]

Jefferson also set about ordering books through other channels. In a letter to Thomas Adams, a Virginian engaged in business in

London, and in the house of whose brother, Richard, Jefferson lodged, he wrote on February 20, 1771, "In consequence of your recommendation I wrote to Waller (a London bookdealer) last June for £45 sterl. worth of books inclosing him a bill of exchange to that amount. Having written to Benson Pearson for another parcel of nearly the same amount, I directed him to purchase them also of Waller. I acquainted both with the necessity of my situation brought on by the unlucky loss of my library, and pressed them most earnestly not to lose a day in sending them; yet I have heard not a tittle from either gentleman." [3]

Jefferson had very early begun the systematic accumulation of a library. Peter Jefferson's account book shows that in 1754 he had paid "By Books for my son, £1-10-6," [4] and on March 6, 1759, the accounts of his guardian, John Harvie, reveal that £5 3s 10d were spent "By Books per the Caesar for Mr. Thos. Jefferson." [5] Of course this is only the very beginning of the books worth £200 which composed his library in 1770, but no other early records seem to have been preserved. Even Jefferson's own pocket account books, which are an amazingly useful source of information, not only on what he paid for things, but on his activities, are of little help in this early period.

In these account books he noted not merely his daily expenses but whatever he wished particularly to remember, whether it were how large an area "4 good fellows, a ladd and 2 girls of about 16 each" could dig in a day, whether it were a sketch of a Chippendale ladderback chair, the fence at Rosewell, a Latin jingle, or the price of an egg. Just what year he started keeping them we do not know. The first one preserved begins in the summer of 1767, and the last ends with Jefferson's death in 1826. The earliest are small volumes which he apparently had bound and obviously carried with him constantly. Some are written in the blank pages of an almanac, whereas in the later ones he reverted to having sheets bound, and occasionally used blank books.[6]

On going to Williamsburg, Jefferson had found constant stimulation in the college library. Just how large it was at this time is not known, but it is said to have reached about three thousand volumes by the Revolution.[7] The libraries of private individuals both in the town and on nearby plantations were likewise accessible to him. We know that he was familiar with William Byrd's great collection for, in 1773, when he was busy planning a room to house his own books, he made a count of the number and size of the volumes at Westover, as well as their estimated cost. It may thus well have been Jefferson's ambition to equal, if not to outrival, this library, which was the finest one in the colony.

It was not necessary to send to England for everything. The bookstores in Williamsburg offered a ready opportunity and Jefferson availed himself of this to some extent, as we know by his purchases from the publisher of the *Virginia Gazette*. Curiously enough, as we have seen, his pocket account books show very few entries for books prior to his going to Philadelphia to the Second Continental Congress in 1775. Unless books were included in such items as "pd. J. Dixon ex^r of Royle, £25"—the publisher of the *Virginia Gazette* at this time—and unless the greater part of his library was being bought abroad, Jefferson apparently did not regularly enter his expenses for books in these accounts. On May 30, 1769, he notes that he "gave M. Maury to pay for books in England £9-17-3," along with £7 10*s* for a silver coffeepot, but all books ordered from European dealers were charged against his tobacco.

In any case, the acquisition of books became a passion that stayed with him all his life and led him to form no less than three great collections as disaster, in one form or another, overtook him at various intervals. His friends and associates did not remain unaware of this absorbing interest, and from his early days he was constantly being asked to help them form libraries, to suggest collections of books that would be suitable for their tastes, just to buy books for them, or lend them his books. Thus, in an unpublished letter, Robert Skipwith, who had married the half sister of the future Mrs. Jefferson, wrote on July 17, 1771, "This I have left at the Forest to remind you of your obliging promise and withal to guide you in your choice of books for me, as to the number and matter of them. I would have them suited to the capacity of a common reader, who understands but little of the classics and has not leisure for any intricate or tedious study. Let them be improving as well as amusing and among the rest let there be Hume's History of England, the new edition of Shakespeare, and the short Roman history you mentioned, and all Sterne's Works.... Let them amount to five and twenty pounds sterling, or, if you think proper, to thirty pounds. With the list please send me the particular directions for importing them, including the bookseller's place of residence." The address of Tho. Waller, Fleet Street, London, is noted in Jefferson's hand at the bottom of the letter.[8]

On August 3 Jefferson sent his reply, along with a list of suggested books.[9] This document, hitherto unpublished, is a remarkable one, revealing, as it does, a breadth and maturity of outlook unusual in so young a man. It is equally noteworthy as the earliest known expression of Jefferson's literary tastes at this still formative period of his life. The list doubtless contains many of the books he himself had ordered from Waller the preceding summer, although we know that by then his own library, despite the fire, was larger than the one proposed for Skipwith. At the end of his letter to the latter he says, "But whence the necessity of this collection? Come to the new Rowanty,[10] from which you may reach your hand to a library formed on a more extensive plan. Separated from each other but a few paces the possessions of each would be open to the other. A spring centrically situated might be the scene of every evening's joy. There we should talk over the lessons of the day, or lose them in music, chess, or the merriments of our family companions." [11]

In writing Skipwith about his proposed library Jefferson observes, "I sat down with a design of executing your request to form a catalogue of books to the amount of about 50 lib. sterling. But could by no means satisfy myself with any partial choice I could make. Thinking, therefore, it might be as agreeable to you I have framed such a general collection as I think you would wish and might in time find it convenient to procure. Out of this you will choose for yourself to the amount you mentioned for the present year and may hereafter as shall be convenient proceed in completing the whole." [12]

The desiderata are grouped under eight headings, starting with

"Fine Arts." Although this category, which embraces 73 items, begins with "Observations on Gardening, published by Payne," and "Webb's Essay on Painting," it includes poetry and general literature. Pope's "Homer's Iliad and Odyssey," early favorites with Jefferson, are first in order, followed by Milton's "Works," Shakespeare, Young, Dryden, Swift, Goldsmith, and Fielding, along with other standbys of English literature. To give young Skipwith a glimpse of authors other than English, Rousseau's "Héloïse," "Emile," then great novelties, and Marmontel's "Moral Tales," in translation, were included, as well as Smollett's edition of "Don Quixote" and "Gil Blas." With his amazing ability to keep abreast of current literary sensations in Europe, although he was in a colony several weeks' journey distant, Jefferson recommended Ossian's "Works," which had startled the world only a few years before and which he admired most extravagantly. Percy's "Reliques," published in 1765, his "Hankion-Chouan," a translation from the Portuguese of a Chinese tale, "Runic Poems," translated from the Icelandic, and "Chinese Pieces" were likewise on the list.

"If you are fond of speculation the books under the head of criticism will afford you much pleasure," Jefferson wrote of the second category on his list. These books included Lord Kames' "Elements of Criticism," Burke "On the Sublime and Beautiful," and Hogarth's "Analysis of Beauty." The third group is of particular interest as showing what Jefferson considered the fundamental books on the subject to which he was to dedicate his life. "Of Politics and Trade," he informed Skipwith, "I have given you a few only of the best books, as you would probably choose to be not unacquainted with those commercial principles which bring wealth into our country and the constitutional security we have for the enjoyment of that wealth." These books were, first, Montesquieu's "Spirit of Laws," followed by Locke "On Government," Marmontel's "Belisarius," Bolingbroke's "Political Works," Montesquieu's "Rise and Fall of the Roman Empire," Stuart's "Political Œconomy," Petty's "Political Arithmetic."

"Religion" forms the fourth group on the list, with 14 entries, embracing such varied works as Locke's "Conduct of the Mind in Search of Truth," Lord Kames' "Natural Religion," Cicero's "Offices," Sterne's "Sermons," and Lord Bolingbroke's "Philosophical Works." There are only three entries under "Law," the "few systematical books" Jefferson described as "necessary for a private gentleman." These are Lord Kames' "Principles of Equity," Blackstone's "Commentaries," and Cunningham's "Law Dictionary." The Bible heads the fifth class, labeled "Ancient History," which includes also Livy, Caesar, Plutarch, and Stanyan's "Graecian History," excerpts from which appear in Jefferson's commonplace book. Among the eight works listed under "Modern History" are Hume's "History of England" and Stith's "History of Virginia." The final category "Mathematics, Natural Philosophy, etc." contains an assortment of 17 books with which a gentleman should be acquainted in these subjects. They range from "Nature Displayed," and "Franklyn On Electricity," to works on husbandry and gardening, books of travel, a compendium of surgery, Voltaire's "Works" and two volumes of "Dialogues of the Dead." There were in all 140 volumes.

The earliest books we definitely know Jefferson to have owned, aside from the forty-odd he inherited from his father, are those whose purchase is listed in the daybook of the *Virginia Gazette*, already mentioned. As always, they reflect what was preoccupying him at the moment. In the early days of 1764 he seems to have been deep in the study of Italian. On February 4 he bought Barrit's Italian-English Dictionary, "Della Istoria D'Italia," in two volumes, Davila's "Guerre Civili Francia," [13] in two volumes, the "Opera di Machiavelli," likewise in two volumes. Apparently he put the books to good use, if we may judge from the remarks of Phillip Mazzei, the Italian doctor who came to Virginia in December 1773, in an attempt to introduce the cultivation of the grape and the olive in the colony. "Jefferson knew the Italian language very well," Mazzei says, "but he had never heard it spoken. Nevertheless, speaking with my men (Tuscan vignerons) he understood them and they understood him. I was impressed by their demonstrations of joy at the circumstance." [14] Other books which Jefferson bought on the same day as his Italian ones were "Scapulae Lexicon," and "Duchamel's Husbandry." On February 10 he acquired "Milton's Works, gilt," and on the twenty-second "Death of Abell." Hume's "History of England," in six volumes, and Robertson's "History of Scotland" were added to his library on March 2, and on the twenty-eighth Stith's "History of Virginia." The law books he bought at this period have already been discussed.

Except for the Italian books purchased at this time, none of the early bills show books in any other modern language except French. Indeed, the catalogue of his library he took with him to Europe, which states that he owned 2640 volumes in the spring of 1783, contains no works in Spanish or German, only in French, Italian, Greek, and Latin, aside from English. Nevertheless Jefferson had a certain acquaintance with Spanish, for in 1775 John Adams observed that "Duane says Jefferson is the greatest rubber off of dust that he has met with; that he has learned French, Italian, Spanish and wants to learn German." [15] In 1817, indeed, Jefferson himself wrote Delaplaine, "I read Greek, Latin, French, Italian, Spanish and English, of course, with something of its radics, the Anglo-Saxon." [16] Concerning the latter he spoke with too great modesty, for he had actually made a profound study of the language. In writing to Herbert Croft, a distinguished English scholar who was engaged in the preparation of an etymological dictionary in 1798, he tells how he was "led to set a due value on the study of the northern languages, and especially of our Anglo-Saxon, while I was a student of the law, by being obliged to recur to that source for an explanation of a multitude of law terms." He goes on to say that in a preface to certain "Reports" written by Fortescue Aland, he learned what books a beginner could use in acquiring the language. "I accordingly devoted some time to its study," he continues, "but my busy life has not permitted me to indulge in a pursuit to which I felt great attraction. While engaged in it, however, some ideas for facilitating the study by simplifying its grammar, by reducing the infinite diversities of its unfixed orthography to single and settled forms, indicating at the same time the pronunciation of the word by its correspondence with the characters and powers of the English alphabet. Some of these ideas I noted in the blank leaves of my

Elstob's Anglo-Saxon Grammar; but there I have left them, and must leave them, unpursued, although I still think them sound and useful." [17] The indefatigable Jefferson was incapable of leaving these ideas "unpursued," however. He turned his notes into literary form and to his letter appended as a "sequel" a fifty-page "Essay on the Anglo-Saxon Language" that is a classic.

That Jefferson also attempted German is evidenced by a card, preserved among his papers and in the handwriting that can be dated after 1767, on which he copied some verses popular at the time.[18] The German is far from being that of a master of his subject, or even of one well advanced. Capitalization of words and the *Umlaut* presented to Jefferson the pitfall usual to the student of the language. Beneath each German word he has written the English equivalent, in the time-honored manner of the schoolboy.

    Falle doch auf Doris augenlieder
    fall   oh! on Doris' eyelids

    Holder schlaaf leich wallend sanft hernieder
    gentle sleep light   soft down

    Drucke doch du Geber susser ruh
    shut   oh   thou giver soft repose

    Jetzt das paar der schonsten augen zu.
    now the pair of prettiest eyes   up.

    Dann so lass der schonen auf mein flehen
    then so let the fair   on my   prayer

    Doch im schlaaf auch dessen bildnis sehen
    too   in sleep   even   his   image to see

    Der nach ihr schon   tausend seuftzer schickt
    who for her already a thousand sighs   sends

    Seit   er sie zum letzten mahl erblickt
    after he has for the last time   seen...".[19]

A TASTE FOR LITERATURE

A second poem begins as follows:

>Ohne   lieb und ohne   wein
>without love and without wine
>
>Wass ist unser leben
>what is our life
>
>Alles was uns kann erfreun
>all   which us can   rejoice
>
>Mussen diese geben
>must   these give
>
>Wenn die grossen   sich   erfreun
>when the great themselves rejoice
>
>Wass ist ihre freude
>what is their joy?
>
>Hubsche madjens, guter wein
>pretty   maidens, good wine
>
>Eintzig diese beyde.
>only   these both...[20]

How much beyond this rudimentary study of the German language Jefferson went, we do not know, but apparently not far. On John Adams' inquiry, in 1814, whether he were familiar with the works of Goethe, whose fame, by that time, had swept the world, Jefferson answered an emphatic "Never." It is significant, too, that the work of the two German philosophers which had a place in his library, Puffendorf and Wolff, were in French translation, not in German. The "Droit de la nature et des gens," as each man's views on this subject were entitled, first appeared in Latin.

Another source for our knowledge of the books in Jefferson's early library, is the second commonplace book in which he copied extracts from his favorite poets, philosophers, and writers, whether English, Latin, or Greek. This little book was originally written on loose sheets and subsequently bound, as is indicated by the irregular numbering of the pages of the manuscript, as well as the variations in the handwriting, much of which can readily be dated. As the book is now bound, it opens with three selections from Herodotus, two of which deal with theories of immortality, a favorite subject of speculation with the very young. Jefferson had a thorough education in both Greek and Latin, and his familiarity with the great writers and thinkers in these languages is abundantly evidenced in the commonplace book. He did not read them as does the usual schoolboy, merely to effect some sort of translation of the words. He read them as living authors, whose language and whose wisdom were not dead. To him they were not the last relics of a bygone world but storehouses of "real science deposited and transmuted to us in these languages, to wit: in history, ethics, arithmetic, geometry, astronomy, natural history, etc.," and, he continued, "among the values of classical learning, I estimate the luxury of reading the Greek and Roman authors in all the beauties of their originals. And why should not this innocent and elegant luxury take its permanent stand ahead of all those addressed merely to the senses? I think myself more indebted to my father for this than for all the other luxuries his cares and affections have placed within my reach." [21]

This interest never flagged. Many years later, in his retirement, we find him addressing a letter to William Short, himself a very cultivated man, discussing the doctrines of Epicurus, Epictetus, Plato, and Socrates as though they were burning questions of the moment. "My business is to beguile the wearisomeness of declining life," he concludes, "as I endeavor to do, by the delights of classical reading and of mathematical truths, and by the consolation of a sound philosophy, equally indifferent to hope and fear." [22]

Among other Greek writers from whom Jefferson transcribed passages in his commonplace book are Anacreon, Quintus Smyrnaeus, Homer, and Euripides. The latter is represented with seventy selections, often of only a line or two. For the taste of the present, many of the quotations seem to have a somewhat threadbare homeliness: "His every friend flees from the path of a poor man," or "They are friends in name, not in reality, who are not friends in misfortune," or, again, "Change in all things is sweet." Yet we must not forget that for a youth of the 1760's, whose sophistication was not that of the 1940's, the words had a freshness and a meaning of which today they seem drained.

It is unfortunate that we have no extensive basis for comparison of the Greek characters Jefferson inscribed at varying periods of his life, as we have of his English. Positively to attribute the period at which he copied these Greek passages thus presents difficulties. However, he headed his section on Euripides with the author's name in English script, and that handwriting betrays an early date. Furthermore, the cynical tone of many of the extracts, and the frequent, derogatory remarks about womankind, tend to give color to the idea that some of them were inscribed after the unhappy ending of his love affair with Rebecca Burwell. "O Zeus," he cries, "why hast thou established women, a curse deceiving men, in the light of the sun?"

Homer appears in a dozen quotations, along with a number from Pope's translation. "I thank on my knees him who directed my early education," Jefferson was to write, "for having put into my possession this rich source of delight, and I would not exchange it for anything which I could then acquire, and have not acquired." [23] Nevertheless, the stirring scenes which we associate with the great poet are strangely missing in the passages Jefferson chose to copy; it cannot even be said that profound philosophical reflections abound. Largely they again reflect the youth's serious pseudo-melancholy in such phrases as "nothing more feeble than man doth earth nourish" or "there is nothing more pitiable than man, of all creatures that breathe and crawl upon the earth."

Of the Latin writers Jefferson singled out Cicero for particular attention, with 24 excerpts from his works. To judge by the handwriting, the majority seem to have been transcribed at an early period. Certain other extracts, notably those on page 66 of the manuscript, are obvious later additions. On April 9, 1764,

Jefferson bought "Thoughts on Cicero" from the publisher of the *Virginia Gazette*, and we have every reason to believe that he was concerning himself with Cicero's philosophy at this time. "Although Cicero," he says, "did not wield the dense logic of Demosthenes, yet he was able, learned, laborious, practised in the business of the world, and honest. He could not be the dupe of mere style, of which he was himself the first master in the world." [24] It was not the famous orations that appealed to Jefferson, indeed he declared that "the models for that oratory which is to produce the greatest effect by securing the attention of hearers and readers, are to be found in Livy, Tacitus, Sallust, and most assuredly not in Cicero." With a single exception all the selections which Jefferson commonplaced are from one of Cicero's philosophical works, the "Tusculan Disputations," as they are known in English. This work, which reports five dialogues or discussions between Cicero and his friends at his villa in Tusculum, after the death of his beloved daughter Tullia, is divided into as many books. The first "teaches us how to contemn the terrors of death, and to look upon it as a blessing rather than an evil; the second, to support pain and affliction with manly fortitude; the third, to appease all our complaints and uneasinesses under the accidents of life; the fourth, to moderate all our other passions; and the fifth explains the sufficiency of virtue to make men happy." [25]

We scarcely need the evidence of the handwriting of these transcriptions to tell us that this work had a particular appeal for the very young Jefferson, discussing, as it does, the human phenomena of death, grief, pain, and happiness—problems which eternally plague the adolescent. The philosophy of the Stoics, which Cicero admired and which this work reflects, fascinated Jefferson at this time, too. He was not to cling to it, however, but to advance in his thought until, many years later, he wrote his friend and protégé, William Short, "I, too, am an Epicurean. I consider the genuine (not the imputed) doctrines of Epicurus as containing everything rational in moral philosophy which Greece and Rome have left us. Epictetus, indeed, has given us what was good of the Stoics; all beyond, of their dogmas, being hypocrisy and grimace." [26]

The great Latin poets, Virgil and Ovid, were of course in Jefferson's early library, but he seems very thoroughly to have assimilated what they had to say to him before he started his commonplace book. There are only a few quotations from each, reflecting, for the most part, the young man's rather cynical point of view at this period. Horace fares somewhat better, with 12 selections, more poetical in character. A good part of these were, apparently, among the first passages Jefferson transcribed, as they are in the large, regular hand of his youth, at the period when he used the long "s" on all occasions.

Among the earliest English books Jefferson appears to have owned were the philosophical works of Lord Bolingbroke. He admired them extravagantly. No less than 58 pages of his commonplace book are devoted to this writer. The entries were transcribed at various periods, as is readily discernible by the handwriting, and show that Jefferson kept close to Bolingbroke for a long time. Some selections show the use of the long "s" throughout, indicating that they were probably copied in 1764; others appear to be in the writing of 1766-1767. None of them seem to be later than this, although Jefferson's admiration did not wane. With the exception of Montesquieu, whose works he did not acquire until December 1769, no writer had greater influence on the formation of Jefferson's ideas. The high regard in which, in his youth, he held Bolingbroke, now generally considered rhetorical and lacking in solidity, is best evidenced by how constantly and copiously he commonplaced the man. During his presidency he told John Bernard, an English actor who visited him, that his prose favorites were Swift and Bolingbroke,[27] and as late as 1821, from the fullness of his wisdom, he wrote his grandson, Francis Eppes: "You ask my opinion of Lord Bolingbroke and Thomas Paine. They were alike in making bitter enemies of the priests and pharisees of their day. Both were honest men; both advocates for human liberty.... He [Bolingbroke] was called indeed a tory, but his writings prove him a stronger advocate for liberty than any of his contemporaries....

These two persons differed remarkably in the style of their writing, each leaving a model of what is most perfect in both extremes of the simple and the sublime.... Lord Bolingbroke's ... is a style of the highest order. The lofty, rhythmical full-flowing eloquence of Cicero. Periods of just measure, their members proportioned, their close full and round. His conceptions, too, are bold and strong, his diction copious, polished and commanding as his subject. His writings are certainly the finest samples in the English language, of the eloquence proper for the Senate. His political tracts are safe reading for the most timid religionist, his philosophical, for those who are not afraid to trust their reason with discussions of right and wrong." [28]

Jefferson seems very early to have acquired Pope's works. Many passages from the "Essay on Man," as well as from the translation of Homer, found their way into the commonplace book, all but two in the hand of Jefferson's early youth. From its character it would appear to be one of the earliest examples we have of Jefferson's writing, probably preceding the period 1762-1763. The passages copied are of no particular literary significance. Although Jefferson later came to feel with Bentley that this was "a fine poem, Mr. Pope, but you must not call it Homer," at the time he transcribed the selections he seems to have been entranced by the rumble of the words and the vigor of the rhythm. Thomson's "Seasons" makes its appearance in the commonplace book at this same period, in the same handwriting. Two long and fine passages from "Spring" are much more poetical in character than those Jefferson usually selected, which tended to be moralistic in tone. From the daybook of the *Virginia Gazette* we know that Bathurst Skelton, who was in Williamsburg at the same time as Jefferson, bought this book on August 27, 1764, and he may very well have loaned it to his friend. On February 10, 1764, Jefferson acquired Milton's "Works" from the same source, and we have every reason to assume that those of the 29 passages from this writer which occur in the early handwriting were copied not long afterwards. Jefferson seems to have continued to read and reread Milton, as other selections are written in a later hand and reflect his changing views and preoccupations. On July 12, in the same year, Jefferson purchased Young's "Works," in four volumes. The famous "melancholy and moonlight" for which the "Night Thoughts" are distinguished were perfectly suited to the young man's temperament at this period, and he diligently transcribed many passages with emphasis rather on the side of melancholy. Young was another writer to whom Jefferson turned back at various times in his life, and some of the 21 selections were copied at later periods.

Dramatists whom Jefferson admired and with whom he was familiar were Dryden, Congreve, Otway, and Rowe. Twenty-three pages of the commonplace book are devoted to excerpts from these writers, some in Jefferson's very early hand, some in his mature script, and some which do not appear to be in his writing at all. It is perfectly possible that he and his young friends such as John Page, Dabney Carr, or Jack Walker exchanged extracts which they admired, and thus a piece not in Jefferson's writing came to be bound with the selections he had copied.

We do not know just when Shakespeare's "Works" came into Jefferson's possession, but excerpts from Julius Caesar, Henry IV, Coriolanus, and Troilus and Cressida appear in the commonplace book. Curiously enough, none of the famous passages so often quoted for sheer beauty of diction and elevation of thought, none of the so-called "beauties of Shakespeare," attracted Jefferson sufficiently to cause him to copy them. In Shakespeare, as in most other poets, it was what he called "the moral rules of life" that he delighted to cull. Indeed this moral overtone is conspicuous throughout. In the many letters Jefferson was to write for the guidance of young relatives or friends in their education, and all turned to him, he continued to stress the importance of reading that would nurture the moral sense. Xenophon's "Memorabilia," Plato's "Socratic Dialogues," Cicero's philosophical works, Antoninus, and Seneca were particularly recommended to his young nephew, Peter Carr.[29] Again he wrote: "The moral sense, or conscience, is as much a part of man as his leg or arm. It is given to all human beings in a stronger or weaker degree.... It may be strengthened by exercise, as may any particular limb of the body.... In this branch, therefore, read good books, because they will encourage, as well as direct your feelings. The writings of Sterne, particularly, form the best course of morality that ever was written." [30]

It must not be overlooked that Jefferson's views in this regard were the views of the majority of his contemporaries. They are not the animadversions of a prig, but the reflection of the taste of the eighteenth century, before the beneficent advent of romanticism.

Jefferson was certainly not one to underrate Shakespeare. At the very time he was transcribing excerpts from the great poet in his commonplace book, he was writing his friend, Bernard Moore, to "read the best of the poets, epic, didactic, dramatic, pastoral, lyric, etc. But among these Shakespeare must be singled out by one who wishes to learn the full powers of the English language. Of him we must advise as Horace did of the Grecian models, *vos exemplaria Graeca nocturna versate manu, diversate diurna,*" [31] Later he was to remark that Shakespeare and Pope gave him "the perfection of imagination and judgement, both displaying more knowledge of the human heart—the true province of poetry," than could be found elsewhere.[32]

Selections from such popular poets of the day as David Mallet, Edward Moore, and John Langhorne likewise appear in the commonplace book. Shenstone was another poet whose works he bought in 1765, but his value to Jefferson doubtless lay less in his poetry than in the famous description of "The Leasowes," which was to be so influential in the development of Monticello. Akenside, whose "Pleasure of the Imagination" had created a furor on its appearance, was likewise commonplaced. Jefferson owned this book before the fall of 1764, as we have seen. How much this work must have appealed to the young Jefferson we realize in reading in the preface that the purpose of the author was "not so much to give formal precepts, or enter into the way of direct argumentation, as, by exhibiting the most engaging prospects of nature, to enlarge and harmonize the imagination, and by that means insensibly to dispose the minds of men to a similar taste and habit of thinking in religion, morals, and civil life."

Jefferson seems to have had little taste for poetry after his

A TASTE FOR LITERATURE 117

first youth. "I was bred to the law," he once remarked. "That gave me a view of the dark side of humanity. Then I read poetry to qualify it with a gaze upon its bright side."[33] In these younger days he was fond of copying verses and is even suspected of having taken a hand in writing some. Among his papers there is preserved a poem entitled "Lovely Peggy."[34] It is written upon a diminutive sheet of paper in a handwriting that may be dated as between 1767 and 1770. It has hitherto generally been attributed to Jefferson.[35] Actually it was written by David Garrick and addressed to the actress, Peg Woffington. About 1749 it was set to music by James Oswald and again, in 1760, by S. Howard. It became a popular street ballad during the latter part of the eighteenth century.[36]

"Lovely Peggy" is by no means great poetry, not even good poetry. It tinkles along through nine stanzas in the following vein:

> Once more I'll tune the vocal shell
> To hills and dales my passion tell
> A flame which time can never quell
> That burns for lovely Peggy....
>
> And when in Thetis lap to rest
> He streaks with gold the ruddy West
> He's not so beauteous as undrest
> Appears my lovely Peggy....

Some fragmentary and cumbersome lines of a different character have come down to us and have likewise been attributed to Jefferson. The question of authorship again arises. They are so feeble in character and construction that it would seem as though they had come from the pen of an amateur, such as Jefferson was in versifying.

> 'Tis hope supports such noble flame,
> 'Tis hope inspires poetic lays,
> Our heroes fight in hopes of fame,

> And poets write in hopes of praise
> She sings sweet songs of future years,
> And dries the tears of present sorrow;
> Bids doubting mortal cease their fears,
> And tells them of a bright tomorrow.
> And where true love a visit pays,
> The minstrell is always there,
> To soothe young cupid with her lays
> And keep the lover from despair.
> Why fades the rose upon thy cheek;
> Why drop the lillies at the view?
> Thy cause of sorrow, Ellen, speak,
> Why altered thus thy sprightly hue?
> Each day alas! with breaking heart,
> I see thy beautous form decline;
> Yet fear my anguish to impart.
> Lest it should add a pang to thine.
> I will not be afraid wh
> have to [37]

In his "Thoughts on English Prosody," written some years after the period under discussion, Jefferson was to give, perhaps, the fullest expression to his views on poetry. "What proves the excellence of blank verse," he observes, "is that the taste lasts longer than for rhyme. The fondness for the jingle leaves us with that for the rattles and baubles of childhood, and if we continue to read rhymed verse at a later period of life it is such only when the poet has had force enough to bring great beauties of thought and diction into this form. When young any composition pleases which unites a little sense, some imagination, and some rhythm, in doses however small. But as we advance in life these things fall off one by one, and I suspect we are left at last with only Homer and Virgil, perhaps with Homer alone." [38] By the time he became President he was left only with this last pleasure. "The very feelings to which it is addressed are among those I have lost," he was to write of poetry. "In earlier life," he adds, "I was fond of it and easily pleased. But as age and care advanced the powers of fancy have declined. Every year seems to have plucked a feather from her wings till she can no longer waft one to those sublime heights to which it is necessary to accompany the poet, so much has my relish for poetry deserted me that at present I cannot read even Virgil with pleasure.[39]

During the early years there was one poet, above all others, who won Jefferson's heart, and that was Ossian. He was in good company in believing the poems were what they were represented to be—did not Herder and the young Goethe express similar opinions? The "Fragments of Ancient Poetry" had appeared in 1760, "Fingal" in 1761, "The Works of Ossian" in 1765, and Jefferson was swept off his feet. Just how early he acquired these books we do not know. There are extracts from "Fingal" in the commonplace book, but they are in Jefferson's mature hand. We do know, however, that Ossian was on the list of books he recommended to Robert Skipwith in 1771.

James Macpherson, the gifted Scotsman who perpetrated the greatest literary hoax in history, was appointed Secretary to General Johnstone and stationed at Pensacola, Florida, for two years, beginning in 1764. Whether Jefferson was aware he was in this country, or whether he was at that time familiar with the poems of Ossian, is questionable. In any case, it was not until February 1773 that he addressed a letter to Charles McPherson, whom he had met in Virginia, in which he wrote:

"I understand you are related to the gentleman of your name (Mr. James McPherson), to whom the world is so much indebted for the elegant collection, arrangement and translation of Ossian's poems. These pieces have been and will, I think, during my life, continue to be to me the sources of daily and exalted pleasures. The tender and the sublime emotions of the mind were never before so wrought up by the human hand. I am not ashamed to own that I think this rude bard of the North the greatest poet that ever existed. Merely for the pleasure of reading his works, I am become desirous of learning the language in which he sung, and of possessing his songs in their original form.... If they are printed, it will abridge my request and your trouble, to the sending me a printed copy;

but if there be more such, my petition is that you would be so good as to use your interest with Mr. McPherson to obtain leave to obtain a manuscript copy of them, and to procure it to be done.... I would further beg the favor of you to give me a catalogue of the books written in that language, and to send me such of them as may be necessary for learning it. These will, of course, include a grammar and dictionary.... You can, perhaps, tell me whether we may ever hope to see any more of those Celtic pieces published. Manuscript copies of any which are in print, it would at any time give me the greatest happiness to receive. The glow of one warm thought is to me worth more than money." [40]

It was doubtless a little difficult to explain that there were no originals, that the much-admired poems were entirely modern, and that Macpherson's authorities existed only in the imagination. All this, as is well known, was not revealed until years later. Meanwhile Jefferson continued to enjoy his Ossian and to discuss this phenomenal writer with those of kindred intellectual interests who spied him out on his mountain top. In 1782, before Mrs. Jefferson's death, the Marquis de Chastellux came to Monticello to pay the family a visit. "I recollect with pleasure," he writes in the account of his trip to America, "that as we were conversing over a bowl of punch, after Mrs. Jefferson had retired, our conversation turned on the poems of Ossian. It was a spark of electricity which passed rapidly from one to the other; we recollected the passages in those sublime poems which particularly struck us, and entertained my fellow-travellers, who fortunately knew English well, and were qualified to judge of their merits, though they had never read the poems. In our enthusiasm the book was sent for, and placed near the bowl, where, by their mutual aid, the night imperceptibly advanced upon us." [41] The words of the Marquis leave us in no doubt that truly Attic evenings were enjoyed at Monticello, as they had been at the Governor's Palace in Williamsburg in the brilliant days under Governor Fauquier.

The novel, as a literary form, was likewise the subject of Jefferson's scrutiny and study, and his opinion of it was destined to change with the passage of time. The works of the leading English novelists of the period were on his shelves, and in the list of books he recommended to Robert Skipwith the novel was liberally represented. Indeed, Jefferson went out of his way to explain the presence of so many.

"A view of the second column in this catalogue," he writes, "would I suppose extort a smile from the face of gravity. Peace to its wisdom! Let me not awaken it. A little attention, however, to the nature of the human mind evinces that the entertainments of fiction are useful as well as pleasant. That they are pleasant when well written every person feels who reads. But wherein is its utility asks the reverend sage, big with the notion that nothing can be useful but the learned lumber of Greek and Roman reading with which his head is stored? I answer, everything is useful which contributes to fix the principles and practice of virtue. When any original act of charity or of gratitude, for instance, is presented either to our sight or imagination, we are deeply impressed with its beauty and feel a strong desire in ourselves of doing charitable and grateful acts also. On the contrary, when we see or read of any atrocious deed, we are disgusted with its deformity, and conceive an abhorrence of vice. Now every emotion of this kind is an exercise of our virtuous dispositions, and dispositions of the mind, like limbs of the body acquire strength by exercise. But exercise produces habit, and in the instance of which we speak the exercise being of the moral feelings produces a habit of thinking and acting virtuously. We never reflect whether the story we read be truth or fiction. If the painting be lively, and a tolerable picture of nature, we are thrown into a reverie, from which if we awaken it is the fault of the writer. ... We are, therefore, wisely framed to be as warmly interested for a fictitious as for a real personage. The field of imagination is thus laid open to our use and lessons may be formed to illustrate and carry home to the heart every moral rule of life. Thus a lively and lasting sense of filial duty is more effectually impressed on the mind of a son or daughter by reading King Lear, than by all the dry volumes of ethics and divinity that were ever written. This is my idea of well written Romance, of Tragedy, Comedy and Epic poetry." [42]

A lifetime of observation and experience was to teach Jefferson that most readers of fiction did not seek in their reading what he hoped and believed they would. Rather bitterly, many years later he wrote Nathaniel Burwell, a friend of long standing, a propos of a plan for female education—which may, in part, explain his words—"A great obstacle to a good education is the inordinate passion prevalent for reading novels and the time lost in that reading which should be instructively employed. When this poison infects the mind, it destroys its tone and revolts it against wholesome reading. Reason and fact, plain and unadorned, are rejected. Nothing can engage attention unless dressed in all the figments of fancy, and nothing so bedecked comes amiss. The result is a bloated imagination, sickly judgment, and disgust towards all the real business of life. This mass of trash, however, is not without some distinction; some few modelling their narratives, although fictitious, on incidents of real life, have been able to make them interesting and useful vehicles of sound morality. Such, I think, are Marmontel's new moral tales, but not his old ones, which are really immoral. Such are the writings of Miss Edgeworth, and some of those of Madame Genlis. For a like reason, too, much poetry should not be indulged. Some is useful for forming style and taste. Pope, Dryden, Thompson, Shakspeare, and of the French, Molière, Racine, the Corneilles, may be read with pleasure and improvement." [43]

In 1773, three years after the destruction of his original library, Jefferson paused to take stock of the books he had collected since that time. First of all he noted the number from the library of "The Forest," which his wife was to receive as her share in the division of her father's estate. Six hundred and sixty-nine volumes, representing a value of £218 19s, came to the Jeffersons, a handsome library in itself for that time. On August 4 Jefferson made a résumé of his own books, 1254 in number. He does not list the titles but indicates the number in the various bookcases and on the shelves in the room, as well as the 31 "lent out" and 10 lying about. "This," he notes, "does not include vols. of Music; nor my books in Williamsburgh." Edmund Randolph in speaking of Jefferson's library the following year says: "He had been ambitious to collect a library, not merely amassing a number of books, but distinguishing authors of merit and assembling them in subordination to every art and science; and notwithstanding losses by fire, this library was at this time more happily calculated, than any other private one, to direct to objects of utility and taste, to present to genius the scaffolding, upon which its future eminence might be built, and to approve the restless appetite which is too apt to seize the mere gatherer of books." [44] By March 1783, Jefferson's library had increased to 2640 volumes, as an endorsement on the flyleaf of a catalogue of his books, which he took to Europe in 1784, testifies. Most of these must have been acquired by the outbreak of the Revolution, as trade, during the war, was virtually at a standstill and was not resumed until after the peace of 1783.

No discussion of Jefferson's literary tastes can be complete without mention of what many consider the greatest work of all time, the Bible. This, in turn, raises the question of his religion and of the many unjust charges that have been leveled against him. That the wise and liberal man who sponsored the "Statute of Virginia for Religious Freedom" should by some have been considered an infidel, is one of those amazing anomalies that occasionally occur. Perhaps the greatest harm Jefferson ever did himself was the observation in his "Notes on Virginia" that "it does me no injury for my neighbor to say there are twenty gods or no God." This was immediately taken up by his enemies, as well as by many right-thinking people with no critical faculty, as a confession of atheism, and to this day some of the stigma still clings to Jefferson's reputation. It is overlooked that he was elected a vestryman of Fredericksville parish in November 1767, and served there until St. Anne's parish was formed. Here he again served as vestryman from 1772-1785. Even in his old age, when religious services were held in the courthouse in Charlottesville, he would ride to town on horseback bringing his own seat, "some light machinery which folded up, was carried under his arm, and, when unfolded, served for a chair on the floor of the courthouse."[45] That he was a faithful disciple of the principles of Jesus Christ, that he felt "there never was a more pure and sublime system of morality delivered to man than is to be found in the four evangelists," was as nothing in view of his independence in applying the principles of historical criticism to the divine word.

Again quoting Edmund Randolph, we learn at first hand how Jefferson's contemporaries viewed this independence of spirit. "When Mr. Jefferson first attracted notice, Christianity was directly denied in Virginia only by a few. He was an adept however in the ensnaring subtleties of deism, and gave it, among the rising generation, a philosophical patronage; which repudiates as falsehoods things unsusceptible of strict demonstration. It is believed, that while such tenets as are in contempt of the gospel, inevitably terminate in espousing the fullest latitude in religious freedom, Mr. Jefferson's love of liberty, would itself have produced the same effects. But his opinions against restraints on conscience ingratiated him with the enemies of the establishment, who did not stop to enquire, how far those opinions might border on scepticism or infidelity. Parties in religion and politics rarely scan with nicety the peculiar private opinions of their adherents."[46]

Some writers have felt that it was the reading of Bolingbroke's philosophical essays—"the blunderbuss charged against religion and morality," as Johnson said—that first caused Jefferson to question the Bible and probe into his own religious beliefs. It seems more likely that what he acquired from Bolingbroke was the critical attitude—the attitude that questions before it believes. This was undoubtedly augmented by his contact with William Small, to whom, as we have seen, Jefferson often paid tribute. He was one of the first truly liberal and broad-minded men with whom young Jefferson had come in contact, and his influence was proportionate. Furthermore, it was inevitable that Jefferson should share in the attempt of the eighteenth century to put religion on a rational basis. He was too intelligent and too broadly educated not to have been early puzzled and disturbed by problems concerning religious dogma. His open mind, his willingness to discuss the pros and cons of a question, was undoubtedly one of the bonds that linked the young Jefferson to the worldly Fauquier and the wise Wythe. The latter likewise suffered under the charge of being an heretic. Among the few papers of Wythe that are preserved is a statement he delivered on his attitude on this subject. "As to religion: I have ever considered it our best and greatest Friend, those glorious views which it gives of our relation to God, and of our destination in Heaven, on the easy terms of a good life, unquestionably furnish the best of all motives to virtue; the strongest disuasives from vice; and the richest cordial under trouble.... The Christian religion (the sweetest and sublimest in the World) labours throughout to infix in our hearts this great truth, that God is love.... While others, therefore, have been beating their heads, or embittering their hearts with disputes about forms of baptism and modes of faith, it has always, thank God, struck me as my great duty, constantly to think of this—God is love; and he that walketh in love, walketh in God and God in Him." [47]

We have no actual statement from Jefferson's pen of his religious opinions, his hopes and doubts and fears, at this early period, except insofar as they are reflected in the excerpts he copied in his commonplace book. In a letter he was later to write to his young nephew, Peter Carr, however, he discourses upon the religious crisis which inevitably comes to young people of intelligence and independence of spirit. In his gentle and wise words we see how forthrightly he himself met the situation when a young man, for the letter can be nothing but a reflection of his own experience.

"Your reason is now mature enough," he writes, "to examine this object [religion]. In the first place, divest yourself of all bias in favor of novelty and singularity of opinion.... On the other hand, shake off all the fears and servile prejudices, under which weak minds are servilely crouched. Fix reason firmly in her seat, and call to her tribunal every fact, every opinion. Question with boldness even the existence of God; because if there be one, he must more approve of the homage of reason, than that of blindfolded fear. You will naturally examine first, the religion of your own country. Read the Bible, then, as you would read Livy or Tacitus. The facts which are within the ordinary course of nature, you will believe on the authority of the writer, as you do those of the same kind in Livy and Tacitus. The testimony of the writer weighs in their favor, in one scale, and their not being against the laws of nature, does not weigh against them. But those facts in the Bible which contradict the laws of nature, must be examined with more care, and under a variety of faces. Here you must recur to the pretensions of the writer to inspiration from God. Examine upon what evidence his pretensions are founded and whether that evidence is so strong, as that its falsehood would be more improbable than a change in the laws of Nature, in the case he relates. For example, in the book of Joshua, we are told, the sun stood still for several hours. Were we to read that fact in Livy or Tacitus, we should class it with their showers of blood, speaking of statues, beasts, etc. But it is said, that the writer of that book was inspired. Examine, therefore, candidly, what evidence there is of his having been inspired. The pretension is entitled to your inquiry, because millions believe it. On the other hand, you are astronomer enough to know how contrary it is to the law of nature that a body revolving on its axis, as the earth does, should have stopped, should not, by that sudden stoppage, have prostrated animals, trees, buildings, and should after a certain time have resumed its revolution, and that without a second general prostration. Is this arrest of the earth's motion, or the evidence which affirms it, most within the law of probabilities?

"You will next read the New Testament. It is the history of a personage called Jesus. Keep in your eye the opposite pretensions: 1, of those who say he was begotten by God, born of a virgin, suspended and reversed the laws of nature at will, and ascended bodily into heaven; and 2, of those who say he was a man of illegitimate birth, of a benevolent heart, enthusiastic mind, who set out without pretensions of divinity, ended in believing them, and was punished capitally for sedition, by being gibbeted according to the Roman law, which punished the first commission of that offence by whipping, and the second by exile, or death *in furea*.... These questions are examined in the books I have mentioned, under the head of

Religion, and several others. They will assist you in your inquiries; but keep your reason firmly on the watch in reading them all. Do not be frightened from this inquiry by any fear of its consequences. If it ends in a belief that there is no God, you will find incitements to virtue in the comfort and pleasantness you feel in its exercise, and the love of others which it will procure you. If you find reason to believe there is a God, a consciousness that you are acting under his eye, and that he approves you, will be a vast additional incitement; if that there be a future state, the hope of a happy existence in that increases the appetite to deserve it; if that Jesus was also a God, you will be comforted by a belief of his aid and love. In fine, I repeat, you must lay aside all prejudices on both sides, and neither believe nor reject anything, because any other persons, or descriptions of persons, have rejected or believed it. Your own reason is the only oracle given you by heaven, and you are answerable, not for the rightness, but uprightness of the decision...." [48]

These brave words express Jefferson's independence of spirit and indifference to cant as completely as anything he ever wrote. It may be charged, as it often was and has been, that he denied many of the articles of faith that distinguish the Christian religion as ordinarily taught and observed. Indeed, in the heat of the presidential elections of 1800, which were distinguished for their display of acrimony and vilification, his religious beliefs, or supposed lack of them, became a political issue. It was the major topic in the many pamphlets published at that time. The answer to these charges is best found in his own words. "I have a view of the subject," he wrote Dr. Benjamin Rush of Philadelphia at this period, "which ought to displease neither the rational Christian nor Deist, and would reconcile many to a character they have too hastily rejected. I do not know that it would reconcile the *genus irritabile vatum* who are all in arms against me. Their hostility is on too interesting ground to be softened." [49] What this genus could not forgive Jefferson was his passion to shake off, as he said, "all the fears and servile prejudices," and "fix reason firmly in her seat." What was even more unforgivable was that, essentially, he was a religious revolutionist, that he was "a preacher of an American religion, of certain ideas which were not only destroying feudalism and monarchism, but were destined also to destroy the power of all mere priesthoods and of the creeds that had been inherited." [50] Thus, in writing Horatio Spafford, he declared that "in every country and in every age, the priest has been hostile to liberty.... They have perverted the purest religion ever preached to man into mystery and jargon, unintelligible to all mankind." [51]

Religion was thus a problem that occupied Jefferson's thoughts throughout his life. We see this reflected not only in early entries in his commonplace book, but in his correspondence over a long period of years, culminating in a constant interchange of letters on the subject with John Adams and others during the last decade. In a letter to Dr. Rush, while President, he speaks of "the delightful conversations" on the subject of the Christian religion they had in the evenings of 1798-99, when he was in Philadelphia. With this letter he enclosed a "Syllabus of the Estimate of the Doctrine of Jesus, compared with those of others," which is remarkable for the lucidity of its analysis of the figure that was Jesus Christ and of the historical development of the faith He inaugurated. Jefferson states that his views "are the result of a life of inquiry and reflection, and very different from that anti-Christian system imputed to me by those who know nothing of my opinions. To the corruption of Christianity I am, indeed, opposed; but not to the genuine precepts of Jesus himself. I am a Christian, in the only sense He wished anyone to be; sincerely attached to His doctrines, in preference to all others; ascribing to Himself every human excellence; and believing that He never claimed any other." [52] On another occasion he expressed similar sentiments in writing to William Short. "The greatest of all the reformers of the depraved religion of His own country, was Jesus of Nazareth. Abstracting what is really His from the rubbish in which it is buried, easily distinguished by its lustre from the dross of His biographers, and as separable from that as the diamond from the dunghill, we have the outlines of a system of the most sublime morality which has ever fallen from the lips of man." [53]

A TASTE FOR LITERATURE 129

Although Jefferson, as he said, rarely permitted himself to speak about religion and "never but in a reasonable society," any more than he would write on it—"should as soon as think of writing for the reformation of Bedlam," [54] he observed—the result of his reflections on these topics was ultimately to be embodied in what has come to be known as the "Jefferson Bible." While he was President, "after getting through the evening task of reading the letters and papers of the day," he made certain extracts from the Bible which he called "the Philosophy of Jesus." It is a "paradigma of His doctrines, made by cutting the texts out of the book, and arranging them on the pages of a blank book, in a certain order of time or subject. A more beautiful or precious morsel of ethics I have never seen; it is a document in proof that I am *a real Christian*, that is to say, a disciple of the doctrines of Jesus, very different from the Platonists, who call *me* infidel and *themselves* Christians and preachers of the Gospel, while they draw all their characteristic dogmas from what its Author never said nor saw. They have compounded from the heathen mysteries a system beyond the comprehension of man, of which the great Reformer of the vicious ethics and deism of the Jews, were He to return to earth, would not recognize one feature." [55]

The work of arranging this "precious morsel of ethics" occupied Jefferson "two or three nights only," as he tells us. It was his ambition to add to the English text "Greek, Latin and French texts in columns side by side." This he finally accomplished some time between January 1816, when he wrote the letter just quoted, and his last years. A handsome volume, bound in red leather with gold tooling, survives. Inscribed on the flyleaf, in the trembling hand of Jefferson's late years, are the words, "The Life and Morals of Jesus of Nazareth, Extracted textually, from the Gospels in Greek, Latin, French & English." Family tradition has it that this was the volume he read last each night, carrying out his own recommendation to others: "I never go to bed without an hour, or a half hour's previous reading of something moral, whereon to ruminate in the intervals of sleep." [56]

VII. Young Blood

THE YEARS Jefferson spent in Williamsburg, after leaving college, were far from being all work and no play. Although he was at first an earnest and hard-working student, and, subsequently, a busy young lawyer with a large practice, he was anything but the ascetic his intellectual achievements might indicate. He played cards—his winnings and losses were reckoned in farthings rather than pounds—as well as backgammon, and seems to have been particularly fond of chess, as he ordered chessmen on various occasions. His accounts also show an occasional "won at shooting 1/6," or "pd at race at Charlottesville 5/9." In these early days he was an ardent fiddler; strings for his instrument were bought at frequent intervals while he was in Williamsburg. With his intimates among his former college friends and the girls who were the belles of the day, he was part of a gay young group that enjoyed the many pleasures and diversions the town afforded.

Their amusements would, by the youth of today, be considered unsophisticated beyond belief. There were balls in the season, walking and dancing and much music. Proficiency on the spinet or the harpsichord, the violin or guitar, was a *sine qua non* of good breeding. Singing also played a great role in a day when music was not to be had by turning a button, but was acquired by the way that is long, and laborious, and true. It was courting time and mating time, and always it was visiting time in Virginia—visiting from one plantation to another, usually for weeks at a time, with the young people thrown together in the simple pleasures of the country. Thus it was not surprising that many of

Jefferson's young friends should have pledged their vows during these years.

Marriage was not made as complicated as it is today. A girl expected to have a husband at sixteen or seventeen, and the young men married, as a rule, in the early twenties. The economic problem was relatively non-existent. There were many honored ways of circumventing the necessity of cash in the bank. A portion of the ancestral acres was frequently set aside for the young couple. Slaves were at hand to be bestowed upon them; the combination produced tobacco, which meant credit, as money of a certain number of pounds, sterling, was understood in the Virginia of that day. Often the actual marriage portion was not paid until the death of the father, when there was a general distribution. Thus when Jefferson's friend, John Walker, married the lovely and vivacious Betsey Moore, granddaughter of Governor Spotswood, a portion of the eleven thousand acres of Castle Hill was cut off for the young couple and named Belvoir. Subsequent marriages in the family brought about the creation of the various plantations of Turkey Hill, Peachylorum, and Kinloch, all from the Castle Hill property.

John Walker's marriage was the occasion of a famous interchange of letters illustrative not only of how these matters were arranged at the time, but of Dr. Walker's superlative frankness. "My son Mr. John Walker," the senior Walker writes to the young man's prospective father-in-law, Bernard Moore, "having informed me of his intention to pay his addresses to your daughter, Elizabeth, if he should be agreeable to yourself, lady and daughter, it may not be amiss to inform you what I feel myself able to afford for their support, in case of an union. My affairs are in an uncertain state; but I will promise to pay one thousand pounds, to be paid in 1766, and the further sum of two thousand pounds I promised to give him; but the uncertainty of my present affairs prevents my fixing on a time of payment—the above sums are all to be in money or lands and other effects, at the option of my said son, John Walker." [1]

Not to be outdone, Mr. Moore replied: "Your son, Mr. John Walker, applied to me for leave to make his addresses to my daughter Elizabeth. I gave him leave, and told him at the same time that my affairs were in such a state that it was not in my power to pay him all the money this year that I intended to give my daughter, provided he succeeded; but would give him five hundred pounds more as soon after as I could raise or get the money; which sums you may depend I will punctually pay to him." ²

The majority of these young people who formed Jefferson's circle came from plantations not far removed from Williamsburg. There was Jenny Taliaferro, whose family lived not three miles from town and of whom Jefferson wrote that he had been "particularly happy" in her company, and that he "was vastly pleased with her playing on the spinette and singing, but could not help calling to mind those sublime verses of the Cumberland poet, 'Oh! I was charmed to see, Orpheus' music all in thee.'" Then there was lovely Nancy Randolph—Nancy Wilton, as she was called, after her father's place on the James—to distinguish her from her many cousins. She became the bride of Jefferson's friend, Benjamin Harrison of Brandon. Pert Susannah Potter, the Sukey of Jefferson's letters and the daughter of Dr. Henry Potter, came from Middlesex County, on the south side of the Rappahannock, as did Alice Corbin, from whom Jefferson won a "pair of jemmy worked garters." Of course there was Rebecca Burwell, and her cousin Fanny Burwell of Isle of Wight County, who married John Page, Jefferson's closest friend, in 1765, and who ultimately became the mother of no less than 12 of John Page's 20 children. At this same time John Walker was beauing Betsey Moore. William Bland and Betsey Yates, two others of the group, were married the same year, "whether it was for money, beauty or principle," Jefferson observed, with the charity of a good friend, "it will be so nice a dispute that no one will venture to pronounce. Two days before the wedding I was not a little surprised, on going to the door at my house, to see him alight from his horse. He stepped up to me and desired the favour of me to come to Mr. Yates' at such a time. It was so unexpected, that for some time I could make no reply; at last I said 'Yes,' and turned about and walked into my room. I accordingly attended, and to crown the joke, when I got there, was dubbed a bridesman. There were many other curious circumstances too tedious to mention here." [3]

Once delivered from his own romantic entanglement, Jefferson seems to have regarded the love affairs of his friends with an air of tolerant amusement. He chides his friend, John Page, already a paterfamilias of some standing, with "being always in the moon." [4] We find him writing, in the spring of 1764, about their mutual friend, Warner Lewis, of Warner Hall on the Severn, who was at this time courting a distant cousin of Jefferson, Mary Chiswell, the daughter of Colonel John Chiswell of Hanover and Elizabeth Randolph of Turkey Island. "Poor fellow!" Jefferson writes, "never did I see one more sincerely captivated in my life. He walked to the Indian camp with her yesterday, by which means he had an opportunity of giving her two or three love squeezes by the hand; and like a true Arcadian swain, has been so enraptured ever since, that he is company for no one." [5] The walk to the Indian spring proved successful. Warner Lewis won his suit, and the young couple were married in 1766.

By the time Jefferson was concluding his law studies, most of his friends had married. He found himself in what seems to many the most attractive of situations, a rich young bachelor—and a very eligible one. We have no indication that he was pursued by the debutantes of the day or their designing mothers, although doubtless many an eager eye followed the tall, spare figure when it appeared in the streets of Williamsburg. There seems to have been no response. This was the time when Jefferson was writing in his commonplace book: ". . . wed her! No! were she all desire could wish, as fair as would the vainest of her sex be thought, with wealth beyond what woman's pride could waste, she should not cheat me of my freedom. Marry! when I am old & weary of the world I may grow desperate, and take a wife to mortify withal." He fancied himself a good deal of a misogynist at this period and took pleasure in crying: "I'd leave the world for him that hates a woman, woman the fountain of all human frailty!"

Jefferson's duties at this time took him to the various courthouses, Goochland, Orange, Culpepper, Fauquier, and New

Kent, his pleasure carried him across the York to the hospitable doors of Rosewell, Warner Hall, Fairfield, or White Hall. Here his college friends, newly enough married still to be full of fun, to enjoy games and music, and, perhaps, exhibit a recently arrived heir, bade him welcome. With them he would talk over old times, or become involved in long discussions, as he did with Page. "I reflect often with pleasure on the philosophical evenings I passed at Rosewell on my last visits there," [6] Jefferson writes his friend, and, referring to the fire that destroyed Shadwell, he adds: "If this conflagration, by which I am burned out of a home, had come before I had advanced so far in preparing another, I do not know but I might have cherished some treasonable thoughts of leaving these my native hills; indeed I should be much happier were I nearer to Rosewell and Severn hills [7]—however, the Gods, I fancy, were apprehensive that if we were placed together, we should pull down the moon, or play some such devilish prank with their works." [8]

The distance from plantation to plantation was not great, even for those days. From Williamsburg to York, where he took the ferry to Gloucester, was about ten miles. Rosewell and Fairfield were within a couple of miles of each other and about five miles from Gloucester. Frank Willis and Warner Lewis were about ten miles distant. On a good horse, such as Jefferson was sure always to have, the distance was covered in a very short time. Once back in Williamsburg there was plenty, aside from his practice, to claim his attention—the coffeehouse, concerts, and, above all, the playhouse, which he sometimes visited every other day.

If we want to follow Jefferson's peregrinations in a typical period of his bachelorhood, such as the spring of 1768, we find that he was with his family at Shadwell in early March. The thirtieth found him at Goochland Court House, and by April 3 he was in Williamsburg, where he went to his favorite coffeehouse and attended the play the following evening. On the seventh he set out again and visited the Lewises at Warner Hall until the ninth. He notes giving the servants 2s 6d on his departure. The tenth he spent with Francis Willis, at White Hall, on the Ware, but he left the same day, as his expenses for ferriage are entered under that date. This time he paid 7½s for seeing an elk in Williamsburg, and went to the play. Within a few days he was off again for Rosewell, which he left on the eighteenth; then followed an intensive session at the coffeehouse and playhouse, with a visit to the Ludwells at Greenspring on the twenty-fourth. On May 3, he was staying with Lewis Burwell at Fairfield; on the tenth, with the Pages. The following day found him at Hanover Court House whence he seems to have gone to Albemarle, for we find him making an agreement with a Mr. Moore "that he shall level 250 f. square on the top of the Mountain [*i.e.*, Monticello] at the N. E. end by Christmas." On the twentieth he was at Staunton, where his horse ran away and he "paid a negro for finding my horse, 5 shillings," on the twenty-fourth he went to New Kent Court House, and on the twenty-fifth back to Williamsburg. He bought a violin that day from Dr. Pasteur, and celebrated at the coffeehouse. All this involved riding about five hundred miles in a little less than two months. June was almost as busy. On the fifth Jefferson went to Rosewell and stayed three days with the Pages. The eleventh he again notes paying ferriage, and as he "gave Col° Lewis's George 2/6" on the fourteenth, we must conclude he had been staying at Warner Hall. On the twenty-first he again crossed the York, but as he does not note leaving a gratuity for the servants, it is not possible to tell which family he visited at this time. Two days later he "pd ferriage at Westpoint 3/," where the Pamunkey and Mattaponi unite to form the York, and proceeded to Amherst, the county that had been newly formed from Albemarle.

Dreams of travel had obsessed the young Jefferson. As early as January 1763, he had written Page of his desire to visit Europe. In the spring of 1766, in the month of May that is so lovely in Virginia, he left his native soil for the first time and undertook a trip to New York, stopping en route in Annapolis and Philadelphia. His adventures were numerous. Fortunately for us, he has left a gay account of them in a letter to John Page. "Surely," he says, "never did a small hero experience greater misadventures than I did on the first two or three days of my travelling. Twice did my horse run away with me and greatly endanger the breaking my neck on the first day. On the second I drove two hours through as copious a rain as I have ever seen, without meeting with a single house to which I could repair for shelter. On the third in going through Pamunkey, being unacquainted with the ford, I passed through water so deep as to run over the cushion as I sat on it, and to add to the danger, at that instant a wheel mounted a rock which I am confident was as high as the axle, and rendered it necessary for me to exercise all my skill in the doctrine of gravity, in order to prevent the center of gravity from being left unsupported, the consequences of which would, according to Bob Carter's opinion, have been the corruition of myself, chair and all into the water...."

Following the good Virginia custom of a leisurely trip and of stopping on the way at the houses of friends which lay in his path, Jefferson tells us that he "had the pleasure of passing two or three days on my way hither at the two Will Fitzhugh's and Col° Harrison's where were S.[ukey] Potter, P. Stith and Ben Harrison, since which time I have seen no face known to me before, except Capt Mitchell's who is here."

Jefferson was writing this letter on May 25 at Annapolis, the first town of any size, outside of Williamsburg, that he had ever seen. All was novel enough for him to give Page a detailed description, especially of what interested them most at the time. "I will now give you some account of what I have seen in this metropolis," he continues. "The Assembly happens to be sitting at this time. Their upper and lower house, as they call them, sit in different houses. I went into the lower, sitting in an old courthouse, which, judging from its form and appearance, was built in the year one. I was surprised on approaching it to hear as great a noise and hubbub as you will usually observe at a publick meeting of the planters in Virginia. The first object which struck me after my entrance was the figure of a little old man dressed but indifferently with a yellow queüe wig on, and mounted in the judge's chair. He, the gentleman who walked with me, informed me, was the speaker, a man of a very fair character, but who, bye the bye, has very little the air of a speaker. At one end of the justices' bench stood a man, whom in another place, I should from his dress and phiz have taken for Goodall, the lawyer in Williamsburg, reading a bill then before the house with a schoolboy tone and an abrupt pause at every half dozen words. This I found to be the clerk of the Assembly. The mob (for such was their appearance) sat covered on the justices' and lawyers' benches, and were divided into little clubs, amusing themselves in the common chit chat way. I was surprised to see them address the speaker without rising from their seats, and three, four and five at a time, without being checked. When a motion was made, the speaker instead of putting the question in the usual form, only asked the gentlemen whether they chose that such a thing should be done, and was answered by Yes sir, and no sir: and tho' the voices appeared frequently to be divided, they never would go to the trouble of dividing the house, but the clerk entered the resolutions, I supposed, as he thought proper. In short, everything seems to be carried without the house in general's knowing what was proposed."

Turning to the physical aspect of the capital of the rival colony, Jefferson writes, "The situation of this place is extremely beautiful, and very commodious for trade, having a most secure port capable of receiving the largest vessels, those of 400 hh'ds being able to brush against the side of the dock. The houses in general are better than those in Williamsburgh, but the gardens more indifferent. The two towns seem much of a size. They have no public buildings worth mentioning except a Governor's house, the hall of which after being nearly finished, they have suffered to go to ruin."

"I would give you an account of the rejoicing here on the repeal of the stamp act," he goes on, "but this you will probably see in print before my letter can reach you. I shall proceed tomorrow to Philadelphia where I shall make the stay necessary for inoculation, thence going on to New York. I shall return to Williamsburgh about the middle of July." [9]

Aside from indulging in the pleasure of travel, Jefferson had undertaken this trip with a view of being inoculated against smallpox. Dr. George Gilmer, a physician and friend in Williamsburg, had given him a letter to Dr. John Morgan of the University of Pennsylvania, just returned from extensive studies in Edinburgh where Dr. Gilmer had also been a student. "Give me leave," the letter reads, "to introduce the bearer, my particular friend Mr. Thomas Jefferson. I need say nothing to recommend him to your esteem, your penetrating genius will discover him to be a gentleman eminently worthy of your acquaintance." [10]

Little more is known of this trip, except that after the inoculation he proceeded to New York where he chanced to meet Elbridge Gerry, who was later to play a prominent rôle in the struggle for American independence. Writing many years later, in 1812, Jefferson recalls their early meeting: "I think our acquaintance commenced in 1764 [1766 is what he means], both then just of age. We happened to take lodgings in the same house in New York. Our next meeting was in the congress of 1775 and at various times afterwards in the exercise of that and other public functions." [11]

This trip to New York and Philadelphia was a revelation in more ways than one to the young Virginian who had just passed his twenty-third birthday. It was the first time he had visited the urban centers of the New World. The buildings there, in which Jefferson's interest is patent, did not yet include all those that graced them on the eve of the Revolution—indeed, in 1766 the most classical and ambitious houses were yet to be built. It was the moment when ornaments in "the French taste" of Louis XV, filtered through such English books as Chippendale's or Abraham Swan's "British Architect," were being first applied. These made the richness of detail in the great Brice house in Annapolis, which, with the Paca and Rideout houses, was then among the finest. The unfinished Governor's house, of which Jefferson speaks, was the one begun by Governor Paca in 1744, now the central building of St. John's College.

In Philadelphia, the State House, with its arcades and fine staircases and its handsome paneling of Doric cast, had already been built. So had Christ Church, its columned nave and storied tower fresh from London via James Gibbs's engraved folio. The new vogue of the Chippendale was spreading rapidly among the fashionable, superseding the heavier, earlier Georgian, which was to be seen in the stucco ceilings of Judge Peters's country house, Belmont. Samuel Powel had not yet occupied his splendid house downtown, but the privateer captain, Macpherson, was already installed with his pretty daughters at Mount Pleasant, where rocaille ornament enlivened the chimney pieces. If Jefferson rode out to Germantown, as he may very well have done, he saw, beside the hooded houses of the village street, the handsome mass of Cliveden, the Chew place, academically correct in detail, with its Doric doorway and columned hall. Governor Penn, however, was yet to build his country house, Lansdowne, which, with its portico of columns above columns in two stories, was to exceed all houses of the Colonies in magnificence and luxury.

The old Town House in New York was unpretentious enough when Jefferson visited it, and old Trinity Church was of "Gothic architecture improved by rules and proportions." In St. Paul's Chapel, however, still without its steeple, the Scotch builder, McBean, was erecting another church out of Gibbs. At the upper end of the island Frederick Van Cortlandt had his house, modest, yet handsomely finished internally, like the Phillipse Manor across the Harlem. Roger Morris had just built his mansion with its portico of four tall columns rising through the height of both stories, the only one of its kind in America before the Revolution. Unless in such a portico, or in the richness of Chippendale carving which adorned certain houses, there was little new to surprise the young Virginian, or to surpass the solid Georgian of such James River houses as Carter's Grove, erected in 1751 for Carter Burwell by the English master builder, David Minitree, or as Westover, which the luxurious William Byrd kept fashionable by more than one internal remodeling.

Jefferson's taste for travel seems to have been whetted by his journey to New York. In the summer of 1767 he made his first trip to the Natural Bridge, a phenomenon which exercised an incredible fascination upon him throughout his life. It is not surprising that the first page of his extant pocket account and memorandum books should be devoted to a diagram and description of this natural wonder. He subsequently amplified the notes made at this time and included them in his "Notes on Virginia." Jefferson speaks of the Natural Bridge as "the most sublime of nature's wonders. . . . It is impossible for the emotions arising from the sublime to be felt beyond what they are here; so beautiful an arch, so elevated, so light, and springing as it were up to heaven. The rapture of the spectator is really indescribable." [12] To the neighboring countrymen the bridge was only "a commodious passage over a valley which cannot be crossed elsewhere for a considerable distance"; to Jefferson it was a miracle and its possession a cherished dream. Seven years later, on July 4, 1774, his dream came true. He was granted a patent for 157 acres "including Natural Bridge on Cedar Creek." [13]

With his desire to see something of the world satisfied, to a degree, Jefferson settled back into the pleasant routine of life among his friends, partly in Williamsburg and the surrounding country, partly in Albemarle. At each place he had his particular friend and close associate. In the Tidewater it was John Page, whom he had first encountered at William and Mary; in Albemarle it was Jack Walker, with whom he had grown up and gone both to school and college. To John Page he confided his inmost thoughts and with him he engaged in philosophical speculations. Walker seems to have been more of a boon companion, the man with whom Jefferson hunted and jested and played. Early in life Walker started to concern himself with public affairs. He accompanied his father to Fort Stanwix in 1768, when a treaty with the Indians was under negotiation, he was a delegate to the various Virginia colonial conventions, and during the Revolution he acted as an aide to General Washington. The latter, in a letter to Patrick Henry, spoke highly of Walker's "ability, honour and prudence." He acted as a burgess in 1775, but subsequently took no further part in public life except for a brief six months in 1790, when he was appointed by the Governor of Virginia to fill the place of Senator William Grayson, deceased.

Although not many letters of this period of Jefferson's life are in existence, there is at least one to show his high spirits and the geniality of his nature, and this is a letter to Jack Walker, dated September 1769. In this missive, written in the "hog Latin" of

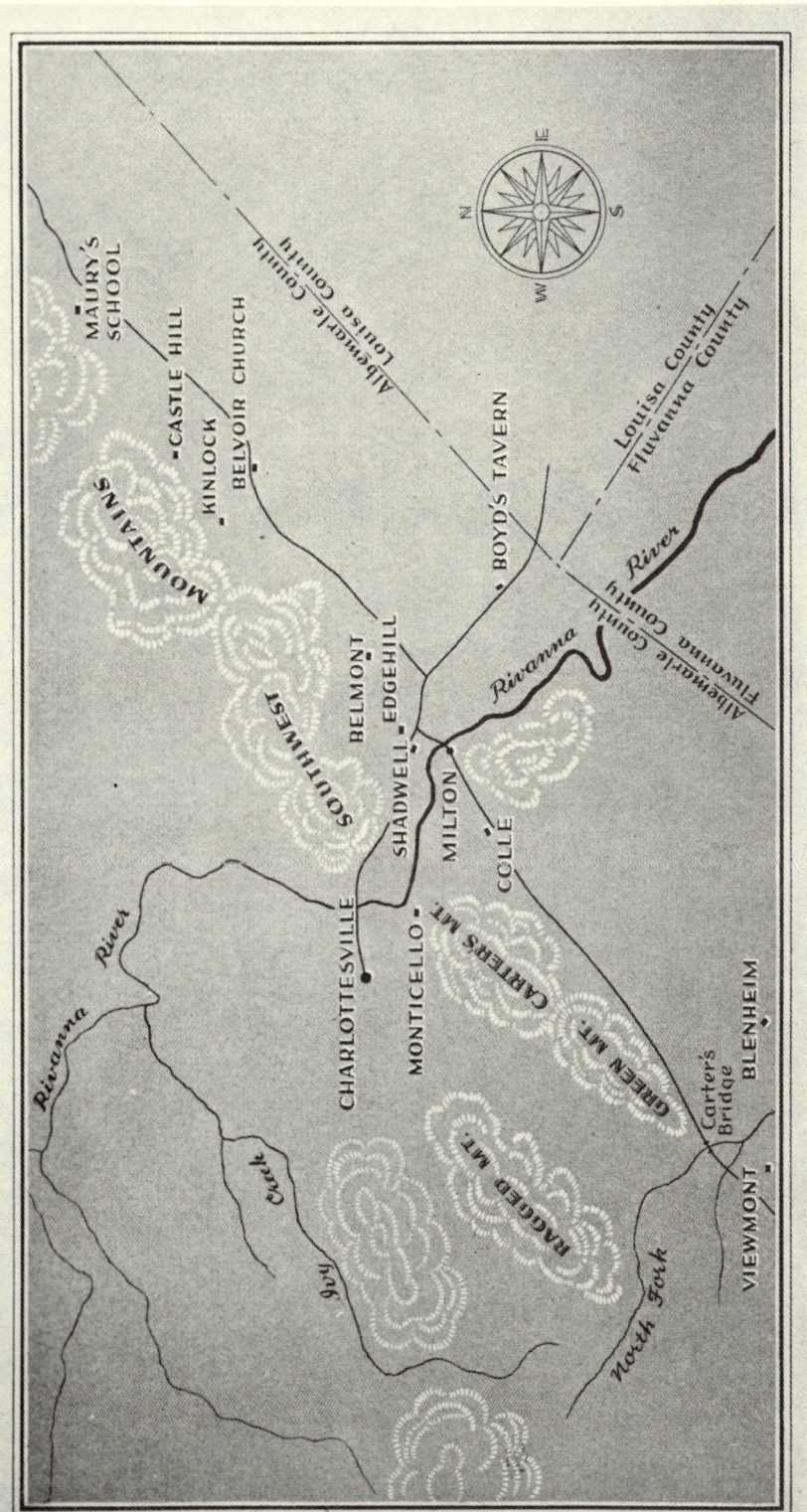

PLANTATIONS ALONG THE SOUTHWEST MOUNTAINS

their youth, Jefferson takes obvious pleasure in making puns in Latin on English words.[14]

"Galfridi-filius Ambulatori S.," the letter reads, "Ero apud society spring on Tuesday per quatuor. Fortasse et J. Lepus-aemula veniet. Apis ibi et tu quoque. Ferto sequelam tuam Septentrionalem. Ferto etiam ut ante tibi praecepi, tabulam scaccariam. Oculus feram viros. Si possemus gignare tabulam pro hac vice expressi factam, lignum apis putens. Sed de hoc postea confabulemur. Suntne tabulae terrae patris tui in Augusta salvae? Id est nonne sint lapsabiles pro defectu cultus vel quitrentorum? Non dubito quin salvae sint, tamen vide dum potes. Verbum sat sapienti. Magna clades mox erit iis qúi aliter sunt. Vale.
Sep. 3, 1769.
"P. S. Celeberrimus ille Ferguson, qui scripsit de astronomia, venturus est, ut fertur, ad coll. Gul. et Mar. successor dignus digninissimi Parvi?"[15]

The opening of the letter is cast in the form of a legal document, with a pun on the names of both men: "Jefferson to Walker, greetings." In translation the language is inevitably stilted rather than idiomatic, as otherwise the puns would not be apparent. Only one has resisted solution. The letter continues:

"I shall be at the spring society on Tuesday at four. Perhaps J. Lepus-aemula will be there. Be there, and you, too. Bring your northern following. Bring also, as I commanded you before, your chessboard. I will bring the men. If we are able to make a board for this special occasion, it would be well. But let us talk this over later. Are the tablelands of your father in Augusta safe? That is, have they lapsed or not for default of cultivation or quitrents? I do not doubt but that they are safe, nevertheless, see while you are able. A word to the wise is sufficient. Great loss will soon come to those who are otherwise. Farewell.
"P. S. That most celebrated Mr. Ferguson, who has written about astronomy, is going to come, it is said, to the College of William and Mary, a worthy successor to the most worthy Small."[16]

This letter is particularly significant in view of its relation to an event that had occurred the preceding year. It was an episode, not at all at variance with the conventions of the day, which seems to have been lightly passed over at the time by all concerned, but which was to take on ugly proportions many years later in the bitter political vilifications hurled at Jefferson during his presidency. It is, in many ways, the most human thing we know about him. That once, and only once, he displayed a modicum of the frailty that marks many in this transgressing world, that during these early years hot blood was coursing through his veins, inevitably renders him less austere and set apart from the ordinary run of mankind. Thus the man who was subsequently to resist the charms of one of the most dazzling women in Europe,[17] remaining true to the memory of the wife he had loved beyond all measure, as a young bachelor was not immune to the attractions of a saucy and comely young matron on a near-by plantation.

Among the disgruntled Federalists turned out of power in the great republican revolution following the elections of 1800, none was more frantic in his partisanship than Lighthorse Harry Lee, the brilliant but erratic Revolutionary officer then deeply sunk in unfortunate speculations which were soon to put him in a debtor's prison. In his eagerness to destroy Jefferson, whom he thought of as the author of all his misfortunes, he stooped to make use of an episode of Jefferson's youth, which rankled also in the mind of John Walker, now likewise disaffected from the President. Lee secured from Walker a statement of this old affair, as it remained in his embittered memory after a lapse of nearly forty years, and sought to make this the implement of his revenge. These were violent and electric times. Alexander Hamilton had been shot in a duel with Aaron Burr during the summer of 1804, and, although Lee and Walker realized the latter could not challenge the President, as feeling against dueling now ran so high, the two men set out to ruin him, if possible, and gain "satisfaction" for Walker after all these many years.

Walker's statement, dated March 28, 1805, and hitherto unpublished, was written during the height of the scandalous attacks upon Jefferson in the Massachusetts legislature. After mentioning the date of his marriage and speaking of the early friendship that existed not only between him and Jefferson, but between their fathers, Walker says:

"In '68 I was called to Fort Stanwix, being secretary, or a clerk to the Virginia commissioners at the treaty with the Indians there. ... I left my wife and infant daughter at home, relying on Mr. Jefferson as my neighbor and fast friend, having in my will, made before my departure, named him first among my executors. I returned in November, having been absent more than four months. During my absence Mr. Jefferson's conduct to Mrs. Walker was improper, so much so as to have laid the foundation of her constant objection to my leaving Mr. Jefferson my executor, telling me that she wondered why I could place such confidence in him.

"At Shadwell, his own house, in '69 or '70, on a visit common to us being neighbors [illegible] he renewed his caresses, placed in Mrs. Walker's gown sleeve cuff, a paper tending to convince her of the innocence of promiscuous love. This Mrs. Walker, on the first glance, tore to pieces. After this we went on a visit to Col. Coles, a mutual acquaintance and distant neighbor. Mr. Jefferson was there. On the ladys retiring to bed, he pretended to be sick, complained of a headache and left the gentleman, among whom I was. Instead of going to bed, as his sickness authorized belief, he stole into my room where my wife was undressing or in bed. He was repulsed with indignation and menaces of alarm, and stole off.

"In '71 Mr. Jefferson was married and yet continued his efforts to destroy my peace until the latter end of the year '79. One particular instance I remember. My old house had a passage upstairs with a room on each side and opposite doors. Mr. Jefferson and wife slept in one.—I and my wife in the other. At the end of the passage was a small room used by my wife as her private apartment. She visited it early and late. ... Mr. Jefferson, knowing her custom, was found in his shirt ready to seize her on her way from her chamber—indecent in manner. In '83 Mr. Jefferson went to France. His wife died previously. From '79 Mr. Jefferson desisted in his attempts on my peace.

"All this time I believed him to be my best friend and so felt and acted toward him.... Soon after his sailing for France was known, Mrs. Walker then referred to my will and being as before asked her objections, she related to me these base transactions, apologizing for her past silence from her fear of its consequence, which might have been fatal to me.

"I constantly wrote to him. You have seen our correspondence, and you go now to Mr. Jefferson. My [injury?] is before you. Let my redress be commensurate. It cannot be complete and therefore ought to be as [illegible] as possible." [18]

Some time later, Lee duly had an interview with Jefferson, and an account, in the form of a rough draft of what passed between them, written in Lee's almost illegible hand, is preserved among Jefferson's papers. It was written at Belvoir, the Walker plantation, on September 8, 1806. In it Lee says that Walker demands "a written paper from you giving only to his and his lady's entire exculpation, without the possibility (?) of any exculpation of yourself. This paper he desires should be acknowledged before any two of your friends known to the world, to prevent at any future day the possibility (?) of its being a forgery. This document he engaged to hold upon the express condition of using it, instead of the correspondence in his possession, whenever self-defence shall require it, and upon the condition that after your retirement from public life, he may publish it (?)...." The letter ends with a pious "hope that social intercourse may be restored between two friends from earliest years. I was truly satisfied in finding kindred feelings in his breast." [19]

These letters were the outgrowth of a scandal that had been increasing in virulence and importance for four years or more; Jefferson had befriended a certain English journalist, Thomas Callendar, whom he considered "a man of science fled from prosecution." [20] When Jefferson became President, Callendar asked to be appointed postmaster at Richmond. Jefferson, considering him, as he said, "totally unfit for it," declined to name him to this post. Callendar now turned upon his benefactor with unparalleled venom. He had become editor of *The Recorder* in

Richmond, and in this paper proceeded to publish a series of slanders against Jefferson, charging him, among other things, with having a family of children by a certain Black Sally, and with having been ordered by Jack Walker to leave Belvoir because he had written a love letter to Mrs. Walker.

This was the mere beginning of trouble. Papers all over the country took up the charges. With political feeling running as high as it did at the time, any rumor or piece of gossip was promptly seized upon for political capital, as, indeed, has been the case since politics and the world began. "I am really mortified at the base ingratitude of Callendar," Jefferson wrote. "It presents human nature in a hideous form. It gives me concern, because I perceive that relief, which was afforded him on mere motives of charity, may be viewed under the aspect of employing him as a writer." [21] And to Levi Lincoln, his Attorney General, he voiced his disgust in a note accompanying an enclosure: "I had no conception there were persons enough to support a paper whose stomachs could bear such aliment as the inclosed papers contain. They are far beyond even the Washington Federalist. To punish, however, is impracticable. Until the body of the people, from whom juries are taken, get their minds to rights; and even then I doubt its expediency." [22]

On January 18, 1805, the *New England Palladium*, under the innocuous heading "miscellany," brought a series of unlovely charges against Jefferson. In a discussion nominally of "monarchy and federalism," Jefferson was accused of having "quitted his station and hid his head in a cave" when the British invaded Virginia, of having written that there "was no matter whether there were twenty gods or one," of having dismantled the navy, had Callendar in his employ, and, finally, of having "assaulted the domestic happiness of Mr. Walker, and, after a failure in so honourable an attempt," of having "taken to his bosom a sable damsel." The publishers of the *Palladium*, Messrs. Minns and Young, were printers to the House of Representatives in Massachusetts. A motion was promptly made to dismiss them for having published scandalous stories concerning the President, and the charges against Jefferson were thus thoroughly aired in the legislature. The *Columbian Sentinel* for February 6, 1805, likewise published in Boston, contained the debate on this motion, and Mr. Hulbert, the member from Sheffield, took particular pleasure in mouthing over the libels.

The affair, of course, came to the attention of the President and other officers of the federal government. It had reached proportions that could not be ignored. In July 1805, Jefferson wrote to his Attorney General, Levi Lincoln, and to Robert Smith, Secretary of the Navy. He faced the issue squarely, in a letter notable for dignity and manliness. "The inclosed copy of a letter to Mr. Lincoln," he writes, "will so fully explain its own object, that I need say nothing in that way. I communicate it to particular friends because I wish to stand with them on the ground of truth, neither better nor worse than that makes me. You will perceive that I plead guilty to one of the charges, that when young and single I offered love to a handsome lady. I acknoledge its incorrectness. It is the only one founded in truth in all their allegations against me. . . . I will thank you for these papers when perused, and consider their contents as communicated with the same latitude, as well as restriction, as to Mr. Lincoln and that you will ascribe the trouble I give you in reading them to my counting you among those whose esteem I value too much to risk it by silence." [23]

Thus Jefferson denies not only the scurrilous charge of miscegenation, which has never found any respectable support, but any imputation of the slightest unfaithfulness after his marriage. With this straightforward avowal of his youthful indiscretion, he closes the page.

VIII. The House on a Mountain

BUILDING, A passion of country gentlemen in all countries and ages, was early in Jefferson's thoughts, as it was to remain until the day of his death. From the time of Lord Burlington, a knowledge of architecture had been one of the accomplishments of the English gentleman. Much the same was true of the Tidewater planters of the eighteenth century, who had long been building in friendly emulation. Their houses were, for the most part, of the vernacular, early Georgian type, not dissimilar to many provincial houses of about the same size and the same date in the English shires.

Soon after his majority Jefferson began to look forward to establishing himself more handsomely than had his father at Shadwell. From the very beginning he seems to have dreamed of something more advanced in style, more classically correct, and to have sought the necessary knowledge in books. William Short, who became his secretary and lifelong friend, was to write, many years later, that he had often heard Jefferson say he had acquired his first book on architecture while at college, from an old cabinetmaker who still lived near the college gate when Short was a student at William and Mary. From this accident, said Jefferson, had developed his fondness for building.[1]

The first stirrings of what was to become an all-absorbing interest occurred while Jefferson was still studying law in Williamsburg. In a letter to his crony, John Page, he proposes to build "a small house, which shall contain a room for myself and another for you, unless Belinda should think proper to favour us with her company, in which case I will enlarge the plan as much as she pleases."[2] No plan or design for this little house survives among Jefferson's papers, however, and we can by no means be certain he had a specific one for it.

When the idea of building finally became definitely crystallized, Jefferson chose as his site one very different from the characteristic location of the existing Virginia mansions. These were never far from the river banks, with formal gardens gently sloping toward the water. He followed the newer, romantic impulse of England, where garden temples and towers were crowning rugged eminences of the landscape. Indeed, he was in advance of his times. To build a country seat itself in such a location was unexampled even in England. Thus it was an act of the greatest originality that led the young enthusiast to build on the high mountain top dominating Shadwell, with its superb panorama of plain and hill and valley, bounded only by the distant outline of the Blue Mountains.

Among the influences which may well have stimulated Jefferson to take this romantic initiative were the works of William Shenstone, which he acquired in 1765.[3] More than as a poet, he is celebrated for the development of his estate, The Leasowes. It became one of the most famous of the smaller landscape gardens of England. The second volume of his works, in the edition of 1764 which Jefferson apparently bought, includes his "Unconnected Thoughts on Gardening" as well as Dodsley's "Description of The Leasowes," with a map and observations on the various scenes and prospects. The novel ideas here represented seem instantly to have superseded in Jefferson's mind those of an earlier generation embodied in "James on Gardening," which he had bought only two months before.[4] The latter was a translation, published in 1728, of the French treatise of Dargenville and Le Blond, who had codified the style of Le Nôtre, the great master of the French formal style, with its parterres and bosquets.

Although Shenstone urged "Let sweet concealment's magic art, your mazy bounds invest," and preferred the gentler effects, Jefferson may well at this time have identified himself with Polydore, the hermit. "Polydore, a new inhabitant in a sort of wild uninhabited country," we read, "was now ascended to the top of a mountain, and in the full enjoyment of a very extensive prospect.

Before him a broad and winding valley, variegated with all the charms of landskip. Fertile meadows, glittering streams, pendent rocks, and nodding ruins ... distant hills almost concealed by one undistinguished azure." [5] Thus, some years later, Jefferson was to write of his mountain top with even greater fervor to the lovely Maria Cosway: "And our own dear Monticello, where has nature spread so rich a mantle under the eye? Mountains, forests, rocks, rivers. With what majesty do we ride above the storms! How sublime to look down into the workhouse of nature, to see her clouds, hail, snow, thunder, all fabricated at our feet! and the glorious sun when rising as if out of a distant water, just gilding the tops of the mountains and giving life to all nature." [6]

The earliest mention made by Jefferson of his eyrie is in this memorandum: "Work to be done at Hermitage. Plant raspberries—gooseberries—currants—strawberries—asparagus—artichokes—fill up trees—sow grass—hen house—cherry tree—lucerne—road—waggoning wood and sand." Two changes were subsequently made, in darker ink. "Top cherry trees" was added at the end of the list. The word "Hermitage" was crossed off and replaced by the name "Monticello." Obviously, any work on the mountain top was just in its beginning, and the name which was to become so famous—the fruit of his recent study of Italian—was not long in being adopted. This entry is in the first of Jefferson's pocket account books, the one headed with the date of 1767. That work had indeed started, and the new name been adopted, is confirmed by an entry in Jefferson's manuscript garden book, the little volume in which he made notes on the planting and other gardening activities, under the date of August 1, "Inoculated common cherry buds into stocks of large kind at Monticello." [7]

By early 1768, if not the year before, Jefferson had determined to build on his mountain. It was to be not merely an hermitage or retreat, but, ultimately, a mansion house. A study of Jefferson's early accounts and memoranda, available only in the last few years, now permits a much more precise dating of the planning and construction of Monticello than has hitherto been possible.[8] Among the miscellaneous notes at the back of this first account book we find several pages of calculations for brick work. These were not only for two "outhouses, 18 f. sq. 10 f. to water table, 12 f. upper story," but for a "Principal building, wings 18 f. square to water table 10 f. 1st order 18 f." Thus the principal building was to have a central mass, for which no dimensions or calculations are given, with wings. These, in a fashion not uncommon in Virginia, were to be built first. The calculations themselves make clear that the dimensions of "18 f. square" were taken at the outside of the walls.

These notes do not conform exactly in the dimensions given to those of any of the surviving early plans drawn by Jefferson. We do find, however, two such plans, already drawn with competence, showing buildings of the general scheme indicated, one of wood, the other of brick. They have wings, one story high and of a single room, and are approximately the size proposed.[9] Both show a central building with a pediment. The type was one hitherto uncommon in Virginia. It seems to find its source in Robert Morris's "Select Architecture," published in 1757. This book is known to have been in Jefferson's library before he went abroad, and he must have acquired it very early. Indeed, there survives a tracing he made from Morris's Plate 3, showing a plan of this type and general scale.[10] It was a house of such character, no doubt, which Jefferson first had in mind to build.

Already in 1767 Jefferson was beginning to prepare building lumber. By December 24, when the sawyers stopped working, they had completed 650 feet of inch chestnut plank and 520 feet of 2¼ inch, as well as 2500 pales and 220 rails toward fences.[11] On May 7, 1768, he took the first step toward assembling other materials when he gave Thomas Munford £8 4s sterling "to lay out in the best crown glass and 150 yds window line," which had to be secured from England. It was enough window line for about 36 windows, sufficient for both outbuildings and house on the early plans with wings. On May 18 he "agreed with Mr. Moore that he shall level 250 f. square on the top of the mountain at N.E. end by Christmas, for which I am to give him 180 bushels of wheat and 24 bushels of corn." [12]

The two early designs just. mentioned are shown by accom-

VIEW FROM MONTICELLO TOWARDS THE BLUE RIDGE. (*Photograph by Holsinger Studio, Charlottesville*)

panying notes to have had cornices carried around above both stories. The second design, with arches below, was to have an "Upper order Tuscan ... 14 f." Both conform to a rule stated on one of them: "The pediments should be in height two-thirds of their span," a formula not given by Morris or others among the first architectural books owned by Jefferson. Accordingly we may assume that Jefferson had already acquired the great folio which was to become his mentor, Palladio's famous "Four Books of Architecture"—the bible of academism, the ancestor and exemplar of the eighteenth-century handbooks which alone had hitherto been followed in America.[13]

We can imagine with what satisfaction Jefferson read Palladio's noble chapter "Of the Situation which ought to be chosen for country houses." In this, after speaking of the convenience for a gentleman of a house in the city, "where he is obliged sometimes to reside, either as occupying some public post in the government, or for the management of his own private affairs," he continues: "so perhaps he may receive no less pleasure and advantage from a house in the country, where he passes the rest of his time in seeing and improving his own possessions, in augmenting his substance by industry and agriculture; where by exercising himself, either in walking or on horseback ... he preserves his body strong and healthy; and where, in a word, the mind ... will be singularly recruited and recreated: so that he may then quietly apply himself to the study of books, or the contemplation of nature ..." and commends "building in elevated and agreeable places." "None ought to build," says he, "in vallies enclosed by mountains: because houses hid in such places, besides their being deprived of distant projects ... are moreover in every respect injurious to health ... the resolution being taken therefore to build upon an eminence." [14]

The first supplies ordered, the dwelling begun, Jefferson had further time to consider his designs. These he elaborated in many studies. As the position and form of the first building, erected in the autumn of 1769, depended on them, it is obvious that they were prepared during the intervening year. In them is evident an intense study of Palladio, which was now to take Jefferson far beyond the simplicity of his first proposals. In the earliest plan we have for the general treatment of the mountain top, there recurs the figure of 250 feet for a "square circumscribing the house." [15] Here, however, this square constitutes the eastern half of a great rectangle, 250 by 500 feet, surrounded on all sides by a continuous terrace 18 feet in breadth. At the western corners of this square, and thus near the middle of the northern and southern sides of the rectangular terrace, are shown two outbuildings 20 feet square. Down their eastern sides were to run steps from the upper level to the lower. Further out, the terrace was surrounded by an outer line with semicircular ends—the boundary of the home lot—where it is stated with Jefferson's exaggerated exactness that "the whole circumference is 3715.88 feet or 1238.62 yards."

The mansion house is not drawn on the plot plan, but its position is marked there as with a margin of 91.25 feet, in all three directions, within the easterly end of the rectangle, and its length as 67.5 feet. The plan for the house, conforming to this dimension, was a most remarkable one for its place and time. It proposed a rectangular building with four corner rooms, having between them a loggia of three arches on the eastern front, a saloon adorned by niches on the western front, and a portico there of four columns. Many plans generally similar appear among Palladio's designs for country houses. The rectangular mass, the loggia, the niches, the portico are all commonly found in them, so that it is as difficult as it is needless to tell which served as the primary model. Like many of Palladio's villas, the house was to be all in a single story, with no interior staircase.[16] A calculation on the margin showed that this design would require 420,000 brick, far more than Jefferson had previously envisaged.

A second plan for the house, of exactly the same length, is evidently derivative from the first. It has many of the same Palladian features but returns, in general form, to Jefferson's own earlier schemes, being less extravagant of space and of brick. The saloon, with its niches and portico, remains the same as before, but the great loggia is reduced to a narrow, recessed porch or "lodge." In front of this, the portico of the other side is repeated. Instead of two rooms at each end in a single story, the house was now

THE HOUSE ON A MOUNTAIN 153

again to have wings of but one room, 20 feet square, in two stories, with a staircase rising beside the lodge. When he drew the plot plan, Jefferson was evidently still hesitating between these two schemes for the mansion house. It was the second one which carried the day. He wrote on the plot plan, in darker ink, "27.08469," which is just the depth, in feet, of the second plan from portico to central axis. This figure, added to the margin of 91.25, thus established this axis as "118.33469" inside the proposed eastern terrace. That is the point at which the house was later built, conforming to this plan—the nucleus of the house we know today.

The calculations for brickwork which Jefferson made in 1767-1768 already indicate that he planned to have his "first order," for the lower story, 18 feet in height. This height, above the pedestal, still prevails in the earliest surviving elevation.[17] It shows a Doric order with a total height, including the pedestal, of 22½ feet. The proportions of the order were calculated from James Gibbs's "Rules for Drawing the Several Parts of Architecture," which Jefferson evidently had meanwhile acquired, and to which, as well as to Palladio, he refers in notes subsequently added to his memorandum book of 1767.

Jefferson had hoped to have all the molded elements of his design in stone. As this was obviously quite beyond the abilities of any native stonecutter available, he had correspondents secure in England estimates for having the work executed there. There are two estimates, one by Thomas Petty, mason in Bristol, another by William Gates, mason in London, for the molded work of a house with "a Doric pedestal . . . the order entire of which should be 22½ feet." Even the price for a column is included.[18]

The drawing to which these figures correspond was left unfinished, nor did Jefferson add the upper story, which was implied by the staircase shown in the plan and for which he had left room on the sheet. Instead, as he notes, "after determining to have my Doric orders in Palladio's proportions,"[19] he recalculated and redrew it in an elevation more competent and more handsome than any yet made in the colonies. Over the central Doric portico he placed one of the Ionic order; over the wings, merely an attic.[20]

As he designed and went on with his figuring, Jefferson thought of many other needs or desires to fulfill, requiring advance orders. There were sheet lead for flashing, cartridge paper for walls, papier maché for ornaments of ceilings, "a Scotch carpet 17 f. 3 I. sq."[21] Those specifically to be ordered first were for "my dining room" in the wing which, as we shall see, was to be the first part of the main house undertaken. His ideas, however, soared far beyond these practical requirements. One page of an early notebook dealing with Monticello is headed "Statues, Paintings, etc." Here are listed "Venus of Medicis, Florence, Hercules Farnese, Rome: Apollo of Belvedere; Antinous, Florence," and others, the repertory of academic admirations in sculpture. Paintings, likewise, are among the desiderata: "St. Paul preaching at Athens," "St. Ignatius at prayer," "Jeptha Meeting his daughter," and "Diana Venatrix (See Spence's Polymetis)." Later, after the arrival of Mazzei and Bellini, the two Italians with whom he became closely associated, he added: "Bellini tells me that historical paintings on canvas 6 f. by 12 f. will cost £15 sterl. if copied by a good hand."[22] Thus the ambitions of the isolated young planter passed all colonial bounds.

Before beginning the house, Jefferson planned to construct the first of the outbuildings, or outchambers, as he was later to call them. This was to serve, for the moment, as self-contained bachelor quarters. Studies for this go back very early. One even proposes a building of wood: In the lower story are a chariot house and stalls for horses, in the upper, one fair-sized room, a cubicle and closet. The plot plan and other drawings of 1768-1769, however, show it as it was to be built, of brick, twenty feet square outside, with a kitchen below. He was also already canvassing the plans of necessary adjuncts in the way of domestic offices for the whole establishment. These were, at first, to be in two outer ranges, beyond the terraces on the north and south. Many studies exist for their disposition. The earliest are for ranges of a single story, a hundred feet in length, fronted by "Piazzas" and connected with the outchambers by "covered ways" with arches.[23] In

THE SOUTH OUTCHAMBER AT MONTICELLO, BUILT 1769-1770. (*Photograph by Holsinger Studio, Charlottesville*)

exactly these positions and these dimensions they are marked on the first general plan of the whole group we have already mentioned. In the one adjoining the kitchen, the laundry, dairy, dry well, smoke house, wine room, storeroom, meal room, hen house, and cook's room were to be placed. In the other, the chariot rooms, "little house," lumber room, stable, and fattening room. Space was cramped and Jefferson was driven to propose lengthening them. He even canvassed the addition of a second story. Here, above the stables, would have been placed retired quarters, away from the great house, for study, laboratory, lumber room, "solitudini volum," office, and bedroom. This scheme for placing and treating the outbuildings, again of a single story, was still the one envisaged in notes as late as August 2, 1771, long after the main house had been begun.

The work of actual construction on the first outchamber, the one built against the south brink of the summit, began in 1769. On July 16 George Dudley commenced making bricks, Will Beck blowing rocks and digging the deep well, where it still remains near the kitchen—both with increasing numbers of helpers. At first water had to be hauled up the mountain. In his garden book Jefferson notes that it required six hogsheads of water to make two thousand bricks. Toward fall the walls must have been begun; their finished measurements are noted in the old memorandum book of 1767. Recent excavations have disclosed a fireplace and oven in one corner of the basement, and even part of the flight of outside steps along the eastern side. In October 1769, Jefferson sent James Ogilvie £13 14s 6d sterling "to buy articles for the house in England." [24]

The fire which destroyed Shadwell on February 1, 1770, provided a new motive for hastening construction at Monticello. In March, Thomas Nelson wrote Jefferson from York, "The bearer carries 4 p. dovetail hinges for doors, 2 mortise locks, 20 pullies and 20 pr. of shutter hinges." [25] In July the plasterer was at work in the outchamber. By September Jefferson was sketching designs for slave quarters along the "roundabout" drive at the southern boundary of the home lot. The first to be built which survives, the present superintendent's house, was of stone. All the brick was evidently needed for the master's buildings. Finally, on November 26, 1770, his account book records the event so eagerly awaited, "Moved to Monticello."

The first extant letters dated from Monticello are of February 20, 1771. In one of them, to James Ogilvie, Jefferson, after mentioning the fire, writes: "I have lately removed to the mountain from whence this is dated.... I have here but one room which, like the cobbler's, serves me for parlour, for kitchen and hall. I may add, for bedchamber and study, too.... I have hope, however, of getting more elbow room this summer." [26] It was time he did, for the same letter speaks of his courtship, although its outcome was still uncertain. From early April until the end of July of this year he was constantly in the Tidewater, burgessing and on business, with frequent visits to "The Forest," the home of his future wife. Nevertheless he was much concerned over the progress of work in his absence. On June 1 he wrote from Williamsburg to Thomas Adams, the Virginia merchant who was doing business in London at this time: "I desired the favour of you to procure me an architect. I must repeat the request earnestly, and that you will send him as soon as you can." [27] Jefferson, needless to say, following the custom of the day, used the word "architect" for builder. The general drawings of the house were already complete. What he needed was someone to conduct their execution. None came. In August and September, despite numerous absences, he was himself pressing the work at Monticello.

A beginning on the mansion house, to which his hopes of more elbow room were turned, was made with the northwest wing. We have a measured plan of it, standing alone, with a "beaufet" where the future door to the parlor was to be. There is at least a possibility that Jefferson's hopes were not disappointed and that this wing was enclosed, if not completed, by winter. Randall, to be sure, relying on family tradition 75 years later, believes that nothing but the little outchamber was habitable when Jefferson brought home his bride in January, and this view has been accepted by later biographers. All the evidence does not point that way, however.

From the middle of January until the end of March 1772,

THE HOUSE ON A MOUNTAIN 157

Jefferson was steadily at home. Then, after an absence of the next three months in the Tidewater, he was back again until October 10. The long summer, particularly, he devoted to building. His interest extended to every phase of the task, practical as well as artistic. We find minute observations not matched again until the time studies of the "efficiency engineer," Gilbreth, in the twentieth century. Thus Jefferson notes: "July 23.... Julius Shand fills the two-wheeled barrow in 3 minutes and carried it 30 yds. in 1½ more—Now this is 4 loads of the common one-wheeled barrow, so that, suppose the 4 loads put in in the same time, viz. 3 minutes, 4 trips will take $4 \times 1\frac{1}{2}$ minutes $=$ 6 minutes which added to 3 minutes filling $=$ 9 minutes to fill and carry the same earth which was filled and carried in the large barrow in 4½ minutes." [28] He now calculated the brick needed for the "middle building": "N. E. walls and partitions of parlour 77½ f. in length, to raise the story, 82,000 bricks, S. W. walls to raise the story, 40,000, whole, to raise second story, 63,000." The total was 185,000 bricks. Sometime in the fall of 1772 he made an agreement with Dudley to make him, during the years 1773 and 1774, 100,000 workable bricks, of which 50,000 were to be made in 1773.[29]

For this new campaign of building, which had as its goal the completion of the main house, Jefferson revised his designs. There is a new plan for the mansion house and a general plan of the mountain top, with a note dated August 4, 1772.[30] Whereas only a year before he still intended to build the offices in a range outside the terrace,[31] he now had the idea of putting them under the terrace itself. The great rectangle was abandoned, the terrace being turned to join the house in two L-shaped wings, similar to many in Palladio's plates. It was fronted, like Palladio's, with arcades. At Monticello, these faced outwards, down the mountain. All the offices were at basement level, leaving the house with its unrivaled panorama unobstructed. The lawns to the east and west were given oval terminations, paralleling the circular ends of the "roundabout" further out. At the same time the house itself, of which the basement had already been constructed on the old plan, was enlarged by octagonal bows. There was a great one for the central parlor on the west, smaller ones at either end. The suggestion came again from Morris's book, the only one in his possession with such features, of which it made great use.

The house itself was now to consist of five major rooms on the main floor: the "Parlour," flanked on the north by the dining room and the "North Bow room," later called the tea room; on the south, correspondingly, by a large square "Dressing Room" and by a bedroom in the south bow. The stairs to the upper story remained north of the little open "Lodge," on the south of which was a small "antichamber" with a smaller, private staircase. Above, the great room over the parlor was to be the library, with a bedroom at either side. Of this library we have a plan showing the arrangement of bookcases. The house was on a very ingenious scheme, economical of space, with privacy for the master's suite, with air and outlook everywhere.

Jefferson was already making plans to subdivide the basement under the house and terraces into rooms for domestic uses, with a continuous corridor to the stairs.[32] Below the parlor was to be a large ware-room, below the dining room a beer cellar, below the dressing room a rum cellar. Under the terraces to the south, not yet built, were to be, in order, a meal room, a pantry, a summer dairy, and a room for servants. At the corner, the kitchen, with its great fireplace and oven; then, in the wing extending toward the west, a laundry with big kettles, a dry well, a smoke room, and, in place of the old kitchen then under the outchamber and still in use, a brewing room. Toward the north of the house were to be a storeroom, a saddle room, the "Hosterie" or roasting room; at the corner, a room for the grooms; then, in the wing, a "solitude," stalling for twenty horses, a chariot house for three carriages, and the corn room.

Progress in construction was steady but slow. By August 4, 1773, Jefferson's books were installed, for he made an enumeration of them, as we have seen, and gave their location. However, they cannot yet have been housed in the great room on the second floor, as it had not been completed. Bricks were being made in 1774, doubtless for the southern wing, to contain the dressing room and the bedroom. In June of that year he wrote to Cary and Co. in London for 14 pairs of sash windows.[33] There were, indeed, just 14 windows on the ground story of the "middle building" and of the south wing. In the fall, when the non-importation agreement threatened to exclude the sash, his account book reveals an order for much glass to James McDowell in the Tidewater.[34] Thus it is clear that Jefferson and his wife could only enjoy these parts of the house on the very eve of the Revolution.

In April 1775, Jefferson was checking over the dimensions of the Doric columns and cornices of the first story, which, obviously, were not yet executed. In July of that year, while attending the Continental Congress in Philadelphia, he made the most of the opportunity to buy hardware for the house. Like Washington, Jefferson was to continue building all through the Revolution. In 1776 and even in 1778, bricks were still being laid and made, and a hundred thousand more were yet to be burned. In February 1778, he contracted with William Rice for making three stone columns, doubtless for the east portico, which alone is of stone today. One column, it would seem, must already have been finished. By October 1779, Jefferson, as Governor, was living in the palace at Williamsburg. Throughout 1780, when his duties kept him in Richmond, there are no entries in his accounts for building at Monticello. In April 1781, however, he hired a British deserter, a joiner by trade, to work there. The finishing of the house was still in progress when, on June 4, the "British horse came to Monticello."

Jefferson had thus substantially completed his house in its first form at the close of the Revolution. It was likewise the very eve of his wife's death and his own subsequent departure for France. None of the terraces were yet built. The intended upper Ionic portico is believed never to have been erected. There are no payments for it and no references to removing it when the house was remodeled after 1793. Even without it, Monticello was of harmonious aspect, and attained a Palladian correctness not elsewhere found in the colonies.

The best description of the house at just this moment is that of the Marquis de Chastellux, who visited Jefferson in the spring of 1782. "The house," he writes, "of which Mr. Jefferson was the architect and often one of the workmen, is rather elegant, and in the Italian taste, though not without fault; it consists of one large square pavillion, the entrance to which is by two porticoes, ornamented with pillars. The ground floor consists chiefly of a very large, lofty saloon which is to be decorated entirely in the antique style; above it is a library of the same form; two small wings with only a ground floor and attic story, are joined to this pavillion, and communicate with the kitchen, offices, etc., which will form a kind of basement story, over which runs a terrace. My object in this short description is only to show the difference between this and the other houses of the country; for we may safely aver, that Mr. Jefferson is the first American who has consulted the fine arts to know how he should shelter himself from the weather." [35]

The complement to building, in the activity of a country gentleman, was, of course, gardening. "Gardens," Jefferson was to write, "[are] peculiarly worth the attention of an American, because it is the country of all others where the noblest gardens may be made without expense. We have only to cut out the superabundant plants." [36] Jefferson's planting, like his house, was not to be in the conventional Virginia manner, but in the newer style of landscape gardening fashionable in England. In 1766, to be sure, Richard Stockton of Morven, in Princeton, New Jersey, had written his wife from London: "I design to ride out to view Mr. Pope's garden and grotto, which, I am told, remain nearly as he left them, and ... I shall take with me a gentleman who draws well, to lay down the exact plan of the whole." [37] But, as Searle's engraved plan shows, Pope's garden with its formal *allées* was still far from foreshadowing such a plan as The Leasowes. Jefferson had undoubtedly formed his ideas with the acquisition of Shenstone in 1765. Thus he was the first of all Americans to propose the adoption of the landscape style.

In 1767, as we have seen, Jefferson had grafted the first fruit trees of an orchard to extend down the south side of the mountain. In September of the following year, by dint of scores of small purchases here and there, he had accumulated nearly 35 quarts of precious clover seed, besides grass seed, to try to turn

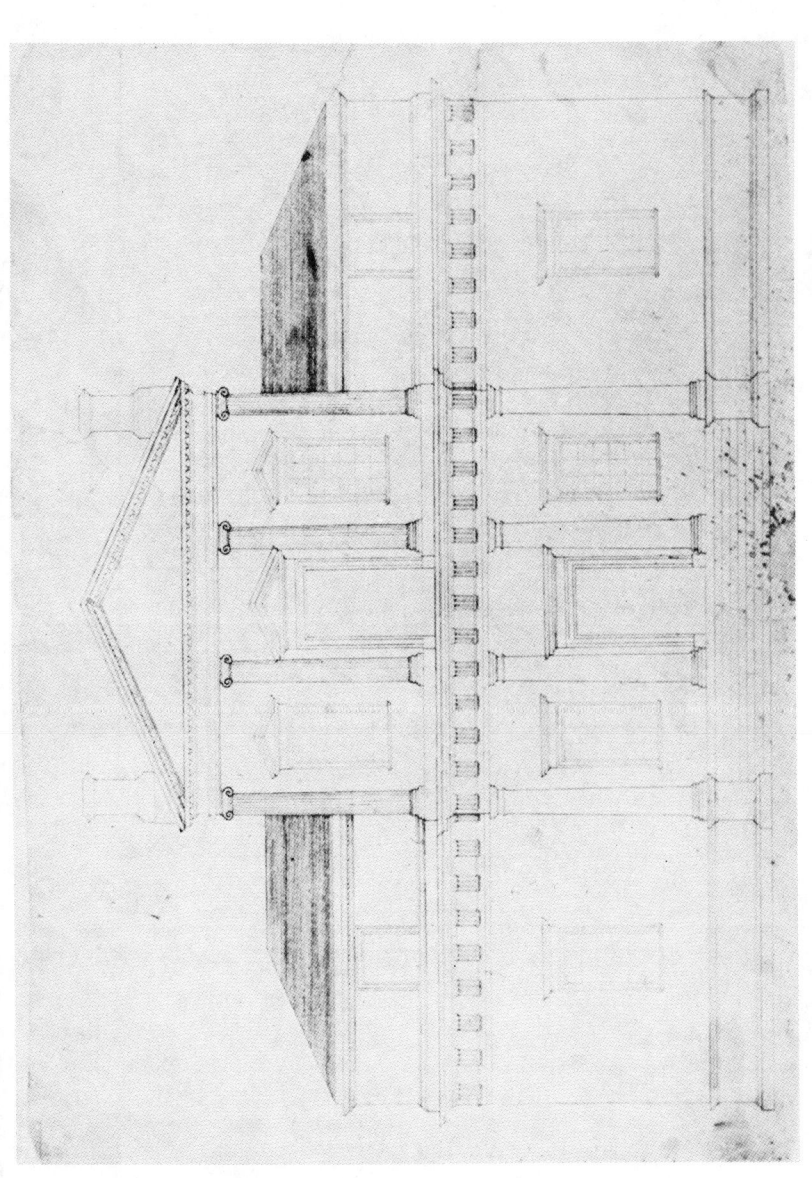

JEFFERSON'S DESIGN FOR MONTICELLO, DRAWN IN 1771-1772. (*Courtesy of the Massachusetts Historical Society*)

the ungrateful clay of Albemarle into an English lawn. In 1769 Richard Sorrels and helper were mauling eight thousand rails for "my park on the north side of the mountain ... in circumference 1850 yards," [38] or about forty acres.

Sometime before the summer of 1771, when he recommended it to Robert Skipwith, Jefferson had acquired a book which was to be of the greatest importance to him. This was Thomas Whately's "Observations on Modern Gardening," published in 1770 by T. Payne. Its influence upon him was to be far greater than that of Shenstone. Indeed, later it was to become his constant companion when, in March and April, 1786, he made his "Tour to some of the Gardens of England described by Whately." "I always walked over the gardens with his book in my hand," wrote Jefferson, "examined with attention the particular spots he described, found them so justly characterized by him as to be easily recognized, and saw with wonder, that his fine imagination had never been able to seduce him from the truth." [39]

How Jefferson pored over this treasure, how diligently he studied every word when it first came into his hands, we see reflected in certain proposals for the improvement of the grounds at Monticello, which fill the last four pages of his account book for 1771. They are in the romantic, sentimental style of the English landscape gardens, with their grottoes, cascades, temples, and inscriptions. The proposals have been discounted by Jefferson's biographers as the idle vaporings of a young man on the eve of his marriage. Actually they are of great importance in the history of landscape gardening in America, of which Jefferson was the pioneer.

"Gardening," writes Whately, "in the perfection to which it has been lately brought in England, is entitled to a place of considerable rank among the liberal arts. It is as superior to landskip painting, as a reality of a representation: it is an exertion of fancy; a subject for taste: and being released now from the restraints of regularity, and enlarged beyond the purposes of domestic convenience, the most beautiful, the most simple, the most noble scenes of nature are all within its province." [40] To the young man who "panted after the fine arts," as Edmund Randolph said, these words must have been music. "Nature, always simple," Whately continues, "employs but four materials in the composition of her scenes, *ground, wood, water* and *rocks*. The cultivation of nature has introduced a fifth species, the buildings requisite for the accommodation of men. . . . Every landskip is composed of these parts only: Every beauty in a landskip depends on the application of their several varieties." [41] After discussing these elements in their various aspects he proceeds to take up picturesque beauty, art, and "character" in a garden and the nature of a farm, whether pastoral, simple, or "ornamented," as compared to a park, a garden, or a "riding." The book is enhanced with descriptions of a romantic glow.

Jefferson's plans for his garden were very elaborate and no less tinged with the sweet melancholy then coming into fashion. His park on the north side of the mountain he planned to cover with grass. "Intersperse jessamine, honeysuckle, sweetbriar and even hardy flowers which may not require attention. Keep in it deer, rabbits, peacocks, guinea poultry, pigeons, etc. Let it be an asylum for hares, squirrels, pheasants, partridges and every other wild animal (except those of prey). Court them to it, by laying food for them in proper places. Procure a buck elk, to be, as it were, monarch of the wood; but keep him shy, that his appearance may not lose its effect by too much familiarity. A buffalo might be confined, also. Inscriptions in various places, on the bark of trees or metal plates suited to the character or expression of the particular spot. Benches or seats of rock or turf." [42]

The romantically minded young man was not satisfied merely with the development of his park. He visioned a near-by spring falling from an upper level to a lower in the form of a cascade. "Then conduct it along the foot of the terrace to the western side of the level, where it may fall into a cistern under a temple." The temple was to be of two stories, the lower arched, the second "to have a door on one side, a spacious window in each of the other sides. The room eight feet cube with a table and a couple of chairs. The roof may be Chinese, Grecian, or in the taste of the Lantern of Demosthenes at Athens." [43] Close to the spring was to be a sleeping figure reclining on a marble slab, with an appropriate inscription in Latin, and, under the temple, an Aeolian harp. Beech and aspen trees were to add their tremulous shade, and vistas were to be opened to the distant mill pond and river.

No plantation could, of necessity, be complete without its graveyard, and the young Jefferson, as practical as he was romantic at this period, turned his thoughts to that. "Choose out for a burying place," he writes, "some unfrequented vale in the park, where is 'no sound to break the stillness but a brook.' ... Let it be among ancient and venerable oaks; intersperse some gloomy evergreens. The area circular, about sixty feet in diameter, encircled with an untrimmed hedge of cedar, or of stone wall with a holly hedge on it in the form below. In the centre of it erect a small Gothic temple of antique appearance. Appropriate one half to the use of my own family; the other of strangers, servants, etc. Erect pedestals with urns, etc., and proper inscriptions. ... Let the exit ... look on a small and distant part of the Blue Mountains. In the middle of the temple an altar, the sides of turf, the top a plain stone. Very little light, perhaps none at all, save only the feeble ray of a half extinguished lamp."[44] He soon went so far as to write, and insert in these pages, epitaphs for his favorite sister, Jane, who had died in 1765, and for "an African slave."

Visionary as these plans may seem, with the romantic touches dear to the heart of a youth of this period, they were, to some extent, realized during the course of a long life. Cascades and temples may not have been brought into being, but a lavish flower garden embellished the fringe of the vast lawn, and the burying place was laid out under great oaks on the south side of the roundabout just as Jefferson had planned, without a temple, however. Whether he stocked peacocks we do not know, but hares, squirrels, pheasants, and guinea fowl abounded, and deer were to roam the park, as the Marquis de Chastellux tells us. "Mr. Jefferson amused himself by raising a score of these animals in his park," he recounts. "They are become very familiar, which happens to all the animals of America; for they are in general much easier to tame than those of Europe. He amuses himself by feeding them Indian corn, of which they are very fond, and which they eat out of his hand. I followed him one evening into a deep valley, where they are accustomed to assemble towards the close of the day, and saw them walk, run and bound; but the more I examined their faces, the less I was inclined to annex them to any species in Europe." [45]

In the buildings with which he proposed to ornament his garden, Gothic, Chinese, and Grecian, Jefferson again followed Whately. "In a garden, where objects are intended only to adorn," the latter writes, "every species of architecture may be admitted, from the Grecian down to the Chinese.... Few scenes can bear more than two or three; in some a single one has a greater effect than any number.... The Grecian architecture can lay aside its dignity in a rustic building; and the caprice of the Gothic is sometimes not incompatible with greatness; our choice therefore may be confined to one species, or range through the contrasts of many." [46] Seemingly written in the year 1771 is a page in Jefferson's notebook for Monticello headed, "Chinese Temples, Chamb. Chinese designs." [47] These, but briefly envisaged, were to be of two stories, standing at the angles of the terraces. Another page contains studies for two towers, doubtless for the higher neighboring Montalto, now known as Carter's Mountain. The front windows were to be so much lower than those in the back "as to direct the line of site to Monticello," the columns "planks only with the projections cut." [48]

Jefferson did not readily relinquish these ideas. Even during the Revolution he was revising his projects for decorative structures.[49] One of these was a battlemented mediaeval tower for Montalto.[50] It long anticipated any other appearance of mediaevalism in America. As he acquired other books showing English gardens, such as Kent's folio of designs by Inigo Jones and Lord Burlington, as well as Gibbs', and Perrault's "Vitruvius," he proposed to transform his outchambers by domes and porticoes. He likewise planned to place circular temples, instead of Chinese pavilions, at the corners of the terraces.[51] These proposals, however, were never executed.

In 1771, when his thoughts were entirely given over to courtship and to getting his house ready to receive his bride, Jefferson made no entries at all in his garden book. He was nonetheless eager to realize his plans. On September 7 he wrote to Alexander McCaul, in Glasgow, to "send me a gardener for 10 to 15 £ a year, indentured for 5 yrs." [52] It was a request which, like that for an architect, was not fulfilled, so far as we know. In 1772 the garden book was resumed. Most of the entries deal with kitchen gardening. There are occasional ones, however, which show that Jefferson's more ambitious plans were not forgotten: the cost of park paling, the size of a carriage turn for coach and six. In November of that year men were at work making the "roundabout walk," which encircled the home lot on top of the mountain. It was the first of several, further down, which were ultimately to follow. It was not until after the Revolution, and after his wife's death, that the carriage turn could be laid out and the flowering shrubs planted around the lawns near the house. The full fruits of Jefferson's planning and observations of gardens, however, were only to be gathered many years later—after 1800, indeed, when he was to lead in realizing, as he had led in proposing, the landscape garden in America.

IX. True Love

However unique and beautiful a situation on a mountaintop, however superb the panorama that spread below, Monticello was incomplete with only a solitary young man to enjoy its charms. Thoughts of marriage had early absorbed the young Jefferson, as we have seen, and now, in his solitude, he was once more preoccupied with it. Some time after the termination of his tenuous love affair with Rebecca Burwell, as we know from the handwriting, he wrote out certain reflections concerning the holy state of matrimony.[1] Whether they are his own views, or whether he copied them, is difficult to say. Certain it is, however, that he believed himself to be thoroughly in sympathy with them. This fragment, for it is nothing more, has hitherto been overlooked by Jefferson's biographers. It is, essentially, an adjuration addressed to an abstraction—half woman, half child, who is definitely the inferior and the handmaiden of the male. The burden of a happy marriage is placed mainly on the shoulders of the wife. Any young woman to whom he may have had the temerity to read or show this disquisition on the philosophy of marriage may well have quailed before the responsibilities that faced her. It is in such striking contrast to his devoted and indulgent conduct as a husband that it can only have been written by a young man who had not yet experienced true love.

"Sweetness of temper," Jefferson writes, "affection to a husband and attention to his interests, constitute the duties of a wife and form the basis of matrimonial felicity.

"The charms of beauty and the brilliancy of wit, though they may captivate in the mistress will not long delight in the wife:

they will shorten even their own transitory reign if, as I have often seen, they shine more for the attraction of everybody else than their husbands. Let the pleasing of that one person be a thought never absent from your conduct. If he loves you as you would wish he should, he will bleed at heart should he suppose it for a moment withdrawn; if he does not, his pride will supply the place of love, and his resentment that of suffering.

"Never consider as a trifle what may tend to please him. The great articles of duty he will set down as his own; but the lesser attentions he will mark as favours; trust me there is no feeling more delightful to one's self, than that of turning those little things to so precious a use.

"But wedlock, even in its happiest lot, is not exempted from the common fate of all sublunary blessings. The rapture of extravagant love will evaporate and waste; the conduct of the wife must substitute in its room, other regards, as delicate and more lasting. I say the conduct of the wife; for marriage, be a husband what he may, reverses the prerogative of sex; his will expect to be pleased, and ours must be sedulous to please.

"This privilege a good-natured man may waive: he will feel it, however, his due; & third persons will have penetration enough and may have malice enough to remark the want of it in his wife.

"The office of a wife includes the exertion of a friend. There are situations, where it will not be enough to love, to cherish, to obey: she must teach her husband to be at peace with himself, to be reconciled to the world, etc., etc.—

"There are afflictions less easy to be endured. Those which a husband inflicts, & the best wives feel most severely. The fortitude that can resist can only cure. Complaints debase her who suffers, and harden him who aggrieves. Let not a woman always look for their cause in the injustice of her lord: They may proceed from many trifling errors in her own conduct, which virtue cannot blame though wisdom may [illegible]. If she makes this discovery, let them be amended without a thought if possible, at any rate without an expression [illegible] in amending them.

"Above all, let a wife beware of communicating to others any want of duty or tenderness she may think she has perceived in her husband. This untwists, at once, those delicate cords which preserve the unity of the marriage engagements. Its sacredness is broken forever, if third parties are made witnesses of its failings.

"I am astonished at the folly of many women who are still reproaching their husbands for leaving them alone, preferring this or that company to theirs, for treating them with this or the other mark of disregard or indifference, when to speak the truth, they have themselves in a great m[easure] to blame, not that I would justify the men in any thing wrong on their part; but had you behaved to them with a more respectful observance, and a more equal tenderness, studying their humours, overlooking their mistakes, submitting to their opinions in matters indifferent, passing by little instances of unevenness, caprice, or passion, giving soft answers for hasty words, complaining as seldom as possible and making your daily care to relieve their anxieties...." [2]

It may have been the example of his dear friend Dabney Carr, who had married Martha Jefferson in 1765, that led Jefferson to feel a deficiency in his situation and realize there were heights of felicity still to be reached. Shortly after moving to Monticello he had written John Page, "He [Carr] speaks, thinks and dreams of nothing but his young son. This friend of ours, Page, in a very small house, with a table, a half dozen chairs and one or two servants is the happiest man in the universe. Every incident in life he so takes as to render it a costly pleasure." [3] In any case, Jefferson's dreams at this time were not confined entirely to his books, his house, or the ornamentation of his grounds. A more gentle passion had been aroused. It was no schoolboy infatuation, no hesitant, questioning love, as it had been in the case of Belinda, but a deep affection that flowered in a tenderness and devotion he was never to outgrow or to outlive. Of Jefferson's marriage it can truly be said that death did not part him from his beloved.

It was not one of the Albemarle belles that won Jefferson's heart, but the young widow of Bathurst Skelton, whom Jefferson had known at William and Mary. She was the daughter of John Wayles of Lancashire, who had come to the colony after completing his law studies in England and settled on the James River in Charles City County. His plantation was known as "The Forest." The house survived until burned by the Federal troops in the War between the States.

Wayles became a prominent attorney in Williamsburg and amassed a handsome fortune. He is described by Jefferson as being "a lawyer of much practice, to which he was introduced more by his great industry, punctuality and practical readiness, than to eminence in the science of his profession. He was a most agreeable companion, full of pleasantry and good humor, and welcomed in every society." [4]

Martha Wayles, his daughter, was the child of his second marriage, with Martha Eppes, of the Bermuda Hundred family. On November 20, 1766, at the age of seventeen, she was married to Bathurst Skelton, a young man of twenty-two. He was the fifth child of James Skelton and Jane Meriweather. Large grants of land in Henrico were made to the father in the 1720's. He also patented land on Elk Island which ultimately came to Mrs. Jefferson.[5] He served as sheriff of Hanover County for two terms and as justice of the peace. In 1751 he was engaged in remodeling the Capitol in Williamsburg, as we learn from the diary of John Blair.[6] Little is known of Bathurst Skelton except that he was a student at William and Mary from March 1, 1763, to December 16, 1764,[7] and was a friend of Jefferson, Page, Walker, and their circle. He was a younger brother of Reuben Skelton, whose widow, Elizabeth Lomax, became the third wife of John Wayles in July 1751.[8]

Some faint inkling of Bathurst Skelton's interests and personality may perhaps be gained from the books he left at his untimely death. These eventually found their way into the library at Monticello, as one with his bookplate, still extant, testifies. They formed not unworthy companions to the books already in place. There was "Ferguson's Astronomy, Boyer's French dictionary, abridged, Johnson's dictionary, abridged, 2 vols., The Preceptor, 2 vols., Ferguson's Lectures in Mechanics, etc., Milton's Paradise Lost of Newton, 2 vols., Potter's Mathematics, Maclauren's Algebra, Ward's Algebra, Ladies Geography, 2 vols., Terrence Delphini, Boyer's French Grammar, Rollin's Ancient History, 10 vols.,

Dryden's Virg, 3 vols., Cotton's Virg., Table of the Bees, 2 vols., Roderic Random, 2 vols., The World, 4 vols., Telemaque, Buckingham's Works, Spectator, 8 vols., Swift's Works, 8 vols., Pope's Works, 10 vols., Prayer Book, French." [9]

During the brief period of their marriage, Bathurst Skelton and his wife lived at Elk Hill, high on the bluffs of the James River overlooking Elk Island, near the confluence of the James and the Rivanna. As Elk Hill was ravaged by Cornwallis in 1781 and sacked by the Federal troops in 1865, we have little idea of the house which stood there at that time.[10] It was a favorite spot of the Jeffersons after their marriage. Here they often spent months at a time, and here Mrs. Jefferson fled with her children in the Revolution when the British approached Monticello before they had penetrated to Elk Hill. Elk Island forms a prosperous, green farm of some eleven thousand acres. In good years, when the river is benign, the land is very fertile. When heavy rains come, at least part of the island is invariably submerged. In the great flood of 1771 the losses were enormous. An account in the *Virginia Gazette* on May 30 of that year tells us that "at Elk Island John Wayles, Esq. is said to have suffered to the amount of 4000 pounds, nothing being saved but the people and 5 horses." A week later the *Gazette* reported that "Off Elk Island between 6 and 700 head of cattle, hogs, horses and sheep have been lost" and that in some places trees and carcasses were matted together in masses from 12 to 20 feet in height.

After scarcely two years of marriage, Bathurst Skelton died very suddenly on September 30, 1768.[11] In his desperate condition he made a will, which he was too weak to sign, but the witnesses noted that "at his request his name was signed by Jos. Harris."[12] He was only twenty-four years old. An infant son, John, survived until after Mrs. Skelton's marriage to Jefferson, four years later.[13]

We have, unfortunately, no picture and no description of the young woman who became Jefferson's wife, although her beauty and her charms have been celebrated by all his biographers. The children who survived were too young at the time of her early death to have remembered her. Jefferson seemed determined to

LETTER OF MARTHA WAYLES JEFFERSON. (*Courtesy of Miss Mary V. Perley*)

obliterate from profane eyes every trace of the woman he loved and to keep her enshrined only in his heart. Among the countless relics of the Jefferson family that are preserved, which include everything from shoe buckles to nightcaps and baby bonnets, there has not come to light one scrap of a garment she may have worn, not one ringlet of her hair, nor a trifle she may have used for adornment. Every letter from her pen seems to have met with destruction, except for two brief notes. One was found a few years ago folded in a receipt which Jefferson had made out to Mrs. Mary Lewis of Albemarle.

Mrs. Jefferson's letter, written in a delicate, angular script, is dated Richmond, August 8, 1780. The Revolutionary War was in full swing, and it was a period of very great hardship for the American forces. In May of that year the ladies of Philadelphia had formed an association for the purpose of collecting money and clothing for their relief.[14] The plan was, apparently, extended to other states, and the help of Mrs. Jefferson, as wife of the Governor of Virginia, was invoked. "Madame," the letter reads, "Mrs. Washington has done me the honor of communicating the inclosed proposition of our sisters of Pennsylvania and of informing me that the same grateful sentiments are displaying themselves in Maryland. Justified by the sanction of her letter in handing forward the scheme I undertake with·chearfulness the duty of furnishing to my countrywomen an opportunity of proving that they also participate of those virtuous feelings which gave birth to it. I cannot do more for its promotion than by inclosing to you some of the papers to be disposed of as you think proper. I am with the greatest respect, Your most humble servant, Martha Jefferson."[15]

One or two brief allusions by contemporaries to Martha Jefferson give us a fleeting glimpse of her; all refer to her spirit rather than to her physical appearance. Thus Philip Mazzei, an Italian doctor who had come to Virginia before the Revolution to experiment with wine making and who had bought Colle, a property adjoining Monticello, mentions Mrs. Jefferson in his memoirs. He had known her well during the early days of her married life. When he returned to Virginia about 1784, after an interval in

Europe, he writes: "Monticello was a sad place for me, because I often remembered the angelic deceased wife of Jefferson. She vivified that home." [16] There is also a letter dated The Forest, September 20, 1771, a few months before Jefferson's marriage, from Robert Skipwith, who seems to have married Mrs. Skelton's younger sister Tabitha.[17] He wrote of Martha to her fiancé: "My Sister Skelton, Jefferson I wish it were, with the greatest fund of good nature, has all that sprightliness and sensibility which promises to insure you the greatest happiness mortals are capable of enjoying. May business and play-musick and the merriments of your family companions lighten your hearts, soften your pillows and procure you health, long life and every human felicity." [18]

In her household accounts,[19] which have lain unobserved since a casual mention of their existence by Randall in 1858, Martha Jefferson has unwittingly given us a picture of the young woman who captured Jefferson's heart. They are written in the back of a leather-bound book in which Jefferson, in 1768, had recorded certain cases that came up in the general court, and which, as we have seen, were later published as "Report of Cases Determined in the General Court of Virginia from 1730-41 and from 1768-1772." Bravely, devotedly, trying to follow in the footsteps of her methodical husband, Martha Jefferson picked up his memorandum book, turned it upside down, and gaily set out to be a good housewife. In her singularly delicate hand, she dutifully inscribed: "1772, Feb. 10, opened a barrel of col. harrison's flower; 13, a mutton killed; 17, two pullets killed; 27, a cask of small beer brewed, 15 gallon cask." On the twenty-eighth she decided to take stock of the "house linen" of her new domain. There were "6 diaper tablecloths, 10 ditto damask, 12 diaper napkins marked T. J. 71, 12 ditto towels, T. J. 71, 6 pr. sheets, 15 pillow cases, T. J. 71." Presently she was supervising the making of 46 pounds of soft soap and a similar amount of hard soap. Then, like a good child, she emulated her husband in an "experiment of coffee. Two oz. of beans Troy weight made a pint, 12 oz. 1 lb. weighed made 6 pints. the Troy lb. is to the Avoidupoize lb. as 14:17."

A "list of our clothes" was compiled. For Mr. Jefferson "9 ruffled shirts and 18 plain ditto, 20 old cambrick stocks, 15 old rags of pocket handkerchiefs, 3 pr of English cordied breeches, 4 of Virginia ditto, 6 Virginia cordied dimity waistcoats, 13 pr. white silk stockings, 5 red waistcoats, 2 buff, 1 white flannel ditto, 1 green coat, 1 black princes ditto" were among the items. Mrs. Jefferson was possessed, in part, of "16 old shifts, 4 new ditto, 6 old fine aprons, 4 Virginia pettycoats, 9 pr. of silk stockings, 10 pr. of old cotton, 8 silk gowns, 6 washing ditto old and 2 new to make up, 2 suits of brussels lace, one suit of worked muslin." It was too much; more than her lively spirit could bear. Her pen hesitated at such prosaic facts. Instead, it drew two solemn little birds perched on a leafy twig. A goose was killed, a beef; on May 14 they began to eat cherries at Monticello; six hams, four shoulders, two middlings were consumed in three weeks and two days. Another bird fluttered into the book. With them, one feels, Martha Jefferson had found an escape.

It is small wonder Mrs. Jefferson found her accounts and the running of her establishment something of a burden. There were some two hundred slaves to be directed, fed, and clothed, and the plantations at Elk Hill and Bedford seem to have been managed from Monticello. There was a constant sending back and forth of bedding and clothing for the negroes, as well as provisions.[20] Of all this she tried to keep account—and it must be admitted that her abilities, or taste, in this direction lagged far behind those of the man she had married.

Whether Jefferson knew Martha Wayles before her first marriage or during it, we have no way of knowing. The first time he went to pay court, apparently, was in early October 1770, when, his pocket account book tells us, he gave a "Smith at Wayles's 1/3." [21] On December 10 he was back again, and once more on the twentieth, for the Christmas holidays. By this time he knew he was definitely in love. He may even already have proposed marriage, for on February 20, 1771, a letter to James Ogilvie comments on a friend who "is wishing to take to himself a wife, and nothing obstructs but the unfeeling temper of a parent." He adds "I too am in that way; and have still greater difficulties to encounter not from the forwardness of parents, nor perhaps want of feeling in the fair one, but from other causes as unpliable to my wishes as these." [22] In a letter written to Thomas Adams on the same day concerning some books, he concludes with a request quite in line with his intentions of establishing a family. "One farther favor," he writes, "and I am done; to search the Herald's office for the arms of my family. I have what I have been told are the family arms, but on what authority I know not. It is possible there may be none. If so, I would with your assistance become a purchaser, having Sterne's word for it that a coat of arms may be purchased as cheap as any other coat." [23]

During 1771 his visits to The Forest increased; he was there every ten days or fortnight, and by midsummer he may well have become engaged. In June we find him writing his correspondent, Thomas Adams, to make a change in one article ordered from England. "I wrote therein for a Clavichord," he says. "I have since seen a Forte-piano and am charmed with it. Send me this instrument then instead of the Clavichord: let the case be of fine mahogany, solid not veneered, the compass from Double G to F in alt, a plenty of spare strings; and the workmanship of the whole very handsome and worthy of the acceptance of a lady for whom I intend it." [24]

Martha Wayles was an accomplished musician, and family tradition has it that the love of this art is one of the things that drew her and Jefferson together. However that may be, we find in Jefferson's account with John Wayles, of whose estate he was the executor, that on July 13, 1772, he "pd Wm Allegre 2 years teaching Mrs. Jefferson on the spinet."

In August 1771, Jefferson was begging Robert Skipwith to "offer prayers for me too at that shrine to which tho' absent I pray continual devotions. In every scheme of happiness she is placed in the foreground of the picture, as the principal figure. Take that away and it is no picture for me." [25] Jefferson's friends in Williamsburg were, of course, not unaware of the situation. Among his unpublished papers is a letter from Mrs. Drummond, who seems to have been an older woman and a close friend. It is dated March 12 (no year) and addressed to "Jefferson, Esqre on

Monticello." After regretting that it is too late to send him "roots or graffs for fruits and flowers," she continues: "But hang this long preamble, about nothing. Let me recollect your description which bars all the romantic, poetical ones I ever read.... No pen but yours could surely so butiful discribe, especially those few lines in the Milton style.—Thou wonderful young man, so piously entertaining.... Indeed I shall think spirits of a higher order inhabits your airy mountains or rather mountain, which I may contemplate but never may aspire to [see]. I will first mention what needs no explanation in your letter, and say, persevere thou, good young man, persevere. She has good sense and good [missing] and I hope will not refuse (the blessing, shall I say)— why not, as I think it—of your hand. I've only now to tell you how happy I should think my Jeff if only you would throw away a few leisure hours in talking to me ... and believe me, that I most sincerely wish you the full completion of all your wishes, both as to the lady and everything else." [26]

Jefferson's fondest dreams were soon to come true. After an intensive courtship during the fall of 1771, such obstacles as existed were overcome. On December 14 he notes in his account book that he "pd. Will Beck for Dafoe's bringing curtains from Williamsburg," doubtless for his house at Monticello, and on the 16th he "pd. Richard Scott in part for a bed £3/16/3, the remainder £4, I am to pay to Robt. Baine." On the thirtieth he sent 40s for a license. The marriage bond is written in Jefferson's own hand and reads:

"Know all men by these presents that we Thomas Jefferson and Francis Eppes are held and firmly bound to our sovereign lord the King his heirs and successors in the sum of fifty pounds current money of Virginia, to the paiment of which well and truly to be made we bind ourselves jointly and severally, our joint and several heirs executors and administrators. In witness whereof we have hereto set our hands and seals this twenty-third day of December in the year of our lord one thousand seven hundred and seventy one. The condition of the above obligation is such that if there be no lawful cause to obstruct a marriage intended to be had and solomnized between the above bound Thomas Jefferson and Martha Skelton of the county of Charles City, widow,[27] for which a licence is desired, then this obligation is to be null and void; otherwise to remain in full force." [28]

The wedding was celebrated at The Forest on New Year's Day, 1772. On January 2 the *Virginia Gazette* announced "Thomas Jefferson, Esqre married to Mrs. Martha Skelton, relict of Mr. Bathurst Skelton." The bride was twenty-three and the groom was approaching his thirtieth birthday. The Reverend Mr. W. Coutts and the Reverend Mr. Davies performed the ceremony and received £5 each for their services.[29] The festivities seem to have been extensive and to have lasted some days, with fiddlers, whom Jefferson feed, and the usual attendant gaieties. It was not until the eighteenth, when Ben, Jamey, Martin, Tom, and Kikey and Betty Hemmins, the house servants at The Forest, had been duly rewarded,[30] that Jefferson and his bride set off in a phaeton for Monticello. They may well have stopped with the Randolph cousins at Tuckahoe, en route, for Jefferson notes giving a smith there 2*s* 6*d* on the twenty-second. For the rest of the month, indeed until February 8, the pocket account book is discreetly and completely silent.

We have no record of those first early days at Monticello except one written many years later by Martha Jefferson Randolph, Jefferson's eldest daughter, who repeated the story her father had often related. "They left The Forest," she writes, "after a fall of snow, light then, but increasing in depth as they advanced up the country. They were finally obliged to quit the carriage and proceed on horseback. Having stopped for a short time at Blenheim,[31] where an overseer only resided, they left it at sunset to pursue their way through a mountain track rather than a road, in which the snow lay from eighteen inches to two feet deep, having eight miles to go before reaching Monticello. They arrived late at night, the fires all out and the servants retired to their own houses for the night." [32] In Jefferson's garden book, under date of January 26, 1772, probably the day after their arrival at Monticello, he writes:

"The deepest snow we have ever seen. In Albemarle it was about three feet deep." [33]

The next weeks were busy ones, with work going forward on the house and planting in the garden, for spring comes early in Virginia. In April there was a journey to Williamsburg. Although Jefferson was a member of the House of Burgesses at this time, the journal of that body does not reveal that he attended this spring session. The Jeffersons stayed in Williamsburg for two months, with frequent visits to the theater, an occasional one to Dr. Brown and Dentist Baker. At the end of May they went to The Forest for a month, and were back at Monticello by the first of July. On September 27, 1772, their eldest child was born, a daughter named Martha, for her mother. No visitor has chronicled these peaceful, happy years of domesticity. Jefferson ever after looked back at them in wistful retrospect. They represented what he hoped life was abundantly to give him, but what, in reality, he was to be denied. Years later, on his retirement from the presidency, when he eagerly "shook off the shackles of power," he wrote: "The whole of my life has been a war with my natural tastes, feelings and wishes. Domestic life and literary pursuits were my first and my latest inclinations, circumstances and not my desires led me to the path I have trod."

We are fortunate in having just one glimpse of the life at Monticello while Mrs. Jefferson was still there to grace it. This was written by the Marquis de Chastellux, in the spring of the year she died. In speaking first of Jefferson he says, "Let me describe to you a man, not yet forty, tall and with a mild and pleasant countenance, but whose mind and understanding are ample substitutes for every exterior grace. An American, who without ever having quitted his own country, is at once a musician, skilled in drawing; a geometrician, an astronomer, a natural philosopher, legislator and statesman. A senator of America who sat for two years in the famous Congress which brought about the revolution . . . a governor of Virginia, who filled this difficult station during the invasions of Arnold, of Philips and of Cornwallis; a philosopher, in voluntary retirement from the world and public business, because he loves the world, inasmuch only as he can flatter himself with being useful to mankind.... A mild and amiable wife, charming children of whose education he himself takes charge, a house to embellish, great provisions to improve, and the arts and sciences to cultivate; these are what remain to Mr. Jefferson after having played a principal character in the theatre of the New World." [34]

How Chastellux's words struck Jefferson, always the most modest of men where his own person or abilities were concerned, we may gather from a letter he wrote the Marquis on his arrival in Paris in 1785. The manuscript, or the proof, of that part of Chastellux's book dealing with Virginia had been submitted to Jefferson for criticism. After remarking that he had "devoured it in a single meal," he continued, "from this general approbation, however, you must allow me to except about a dozen pages in the earlier part of the book which I read with a continued blush from beginning to end, as it presented me a lively picture of what I wish to be, but am not. No, my dear Sir, the thousand millionth part of what you there say, is more than I deserve. It might perhaps have passed in Europe at the time you wrote it, and the exaggeration might not have been detected. But consider that the animal is now brought there, and that everyone will take his dimensions for himself. The friendly complexion of your mind has betrayed you into a partiality of which the European spectator will be divested. Respect to yourself therefore will require indispensably that you expunge the whole of those pages except your own judicious observations interspersed among them on animal and physical subjects." [35]

Something more than a year after her marriage, in May 1773, Mrs. Jefferson lost her father. As his eldest daughter she had been very close to him and was unquestionably his favorite. John Wayles died a rich man and, as Jefferson says in his "Autobiography," "the portion which came on that event to Mrs. Jefferson, after the debts should be paid, which were very considerable, was about equal to my own patrimony, and consequently doubled the ease of our circumstances." [36] Mrs. Jefferson inherited 142 slaves and some forty thousand acres of land. This embraced nine farms, including Poplar Forest, in Bedford County, where

Jefferson later built a retreat, Elk Hill, and other farms known variously as Indian Camp, Angola, Guinea, Bridge-quarter, and Liggons.[37] Mr. Wayles likewise left a large number of debts. According to Colonel Thomas Jefferson Randolph, who managed his grandfather's business affairs in the latter years of his life, the share of debts that fell to Jefferson was £3749 12s. "He sold property immediately to pay for it," says Randolph. Referring to the depreciation in Virginia currency which began in 1773 and lasted until after the Revolution, he continues, "the payments for this property were made in paper money which he deposited in the Loan Office, and received it back again at a depreciation out to him, of one to forty. He sold again in 1785 and 1792 to discharge the debt with its accumulated interest. This swept nearly half of his estate." [38]

An advertisement for the sale of some of his property appeared in the *Virginia Gazette* on July 15, 1773, and again on September 16 of the same year. The first offered 2520 acres of land in Cumberland, 1420 in Goochland and Cumberland, on both sides of the James River, 1480 acres on Herring Creek in Charles City County. Only the lands on Herring Creek appear to have been sold at this time. The same property was advertised in September, along with 550 acres of land in Charles City County, "with a convenient Dwelling house and other Improvements. Two Hundred and twenty acres, in the same County, pleasantly situated on James River. The above Tracts of Land were of the Estate of the late John Wayles, deceased, devised to the Subscribers, and are now offered for Sale. Persons disposed to purchase may be informed of the Terms, on application to any one of the Subscribers; and the Times of Payment will be made easy, on Bond and Security to Thomas Jefferson, Francis Eppes, Henry Skipwith." [39]

In his will, dated April 1760, Wayles states "Whereas my daughter Martha is amply provided by a settlement made by myself and her mother, and the slaves contained in the settlement have been devised to me by her mother, Now I hereby give and confirm unto my said daughter Martha all and singular the slaves mentioned in the said settlement to her and her heirs forever, except Betty Hennings and Jenny the cook, which I desire may be part of twenty-five slaves devised as above to my dear wife, to continue with her during her natural life and after her death to my said daughter Martha.... It is my desire that if my daughter Martha thinks her portion not equal to her sisters that her portion may be thrown into hotch-potch with her three sisters above and the same equally divided among them."[40] In a codicil Jefferson was appointed one of the executors. The slaves which Martha Wayles was to inherit went, potentially, on her first marriage, to her husband, Bathurst Skelton. In the will made on his deathbed he states: "Whereas my wife Martha will be intitled to sundry slaves at the deth of her father by virtue of a marriage settlement made betwixt him and her mother, all which slaves I give to her and her heirs forever in case my son dies under age or unmarried, but if he attains to lawfull age or marries, then the said slaves to be equally betwixt them, my wife and son."[41] No attempt was made to probate this will until September 1771, when Mrs. Skelton's marriage to Jefferson seemed imminent. She, John Wayles, and Francis Eppes gave a £6000 bond at this time.

Three inventories, hitherto unpublished, of the estate of Skelton were filed by the executors, one for his property in Charles City County, one for Goochland, and one for Cumberland. The slaves in Charles City County, seven in number, were valued at £260. There was a dark bay horse named Dick, worth £12, a man's saddle, a phaeton with "a pair of Harness," valued at £20I, an old trunk and one of sealskin, a case of pocket instruments, an old silver spoon, a gold watch, his books, and other small objects. The total value of this property is given as £322.[42]

The appraisers for the Goochland assets met at Elk Island on October 7, 1771, to determine the value of the property. Twenty-six slaves, including one "Bobb (if alive, being run away)," were valued at £1130, and eight horses, varying from a "Ball faced sorrel mare" to an "Iron grey filley," were considered worth £76 10s.[43] Skelton's property in Albemarle was negligible, amounting to only £63 8s 4½d. It consisted chiefly of small household items such as "a silver crewet and stand, £3, 2 bottle stands 2/, mahogany waiters, 4/, silver ladle 6 oz. 5 dwt. 12 gm. @ 5/7 £2.9, 1 dozen table spoons, £9/16/6, 1 dozen teaspoons, £2/17/10, 2 pr. gadroon salts, 4 salt shovels," candlesticks, bread basket, knife basket, and various other small objects.[44] In the back of Jefferson's fee book, preceding the account of John Skelton, is the account of "the estate of Bathurst Skelton, dec'd" with Thomas Jefferson. Under date of January 18, 1772, the very day Jefferson and his bride left The Forest, is noted, "By sundry European goods on hand at the death of B. Skelton & taken by me."[45] There follows a list of articles identical with the inventory of Skelton's Albemarle property, an inventory of which was not made until November 16, 1773, when a final settlement of the rather involved Skelton and Wayles estates was undertaken.

Many years later, in 1810, Jefferson replied to an inquiry of Archibald Thweatt, a Skelton relative, concerning the Skelton estate, that he had not given it a thought for 35 years. "I never doubted," he added, "that on a fair settlement Mr. Skelton would be considerably indebted to Mr. Wayles. The thing spoke for itself. He had not a shilling of property but the island [*i.e.*, Elk Island]. He purchased every negro, horse and other animal for stocking it, had no resource for money or credit but in Mr. Wayles, and he did not live long enough for the place to repay the capital which stocked it."[46]

Martha Jefferson bore her husband six children in the ten years of their married life. Only two, Martha, the eldest, and Mary, survived infancy. It was a proud moment when Jefferson recorded, on May 28, 1777, "our son born 10 o'clock P.M.," and one equally sad on June 14 as he wrote "our son died 10-20 P.M." The last of the five daughters, Lucy Elizabeth, was born on May 8, 1782, and Mrs. Jefferson never rallied from this experience. Her health seems to have been impaired after the first few years of her marriage. As early as July 29, 1776, when Jefferson was in Philadelphia, he wrote Richard Henry Lee: "I receive by every post such accounts of the state of Mrs. Jefferson's health that it will be impossible for me to disappoint her expectation of seeing me at the time I have promised, which supposed my leaving this place on the eleventh of next month.... I pray you to come," he concludes. "I am under a sacred obligation to go home." [47] By October 1781, he was writing General Washington, in a letter of congratulation on his success at Yorktown, of the "state of perpetual decrepitude to which I am unfortunately reduced." The draft of this letter, much interlined, gives every evidence of the distraction of mind under which Jefferson was laboring.[48]

During the many months of his wife's illness Jefferson seldom left her side. All correspondence, all the ordinary activities of life were suspended—there are but six letters from his facile pen in the year 1782. Although he was a member of the General Assembly, he did not attend the spring session. James Monroe, likewise a member, and unaware of the domestic tragedy in progress, wrote sharply from Richmond: "It is publicly said here, that the people of your country informed you that they had frequently elected you in times of less difficulty and danger than the present to please you; but that now they had called you forth into public office to serve themselves. This is a language which has often been used in my presence; and you will readily conceive that, as it furnishes those who argue on the fundamental maxims of a Republican government with ample field for declaration, the conclusion has always been, that you should not decline the service of your country." [49]

Much as these words must have stung him, Jefferson replied in measured terms. "I ... am always mortified when anything is expected from me which I cannot fulfill, and more especially if it relate to the public service. Before I ventured to declare to my countrymen my determination to retire from public employment, I examined well my heart to know whether it were thoroughly cured of every principle of political ambition, whether no lurking particle remained which might make me uneasy, when reduced within the limits of mere private life. I became satisfied that every fibre of that passion was thoroughly eradicated. I examined also, in other views, my right to withdraw. I considered that I had been thirteen years engaged in public service—that, during that time, I had so totally abandoned all attention to my private affairs as to permit them to run into great disorder and ruin—that I had

TRUE LOVE 183

now a family advanced to years which require my attention and instruction—that to these was added the hopeful offspring of a deceased friend, whose memory must be forever dear to me, and who have no other reliance for being rendered useful to themselves or their country. . . ." Hidden at the end of the letter, after a lengthy discussion, and denial, of the right of the state to command the services of its citizens in an official capacity, is the real motive for Jefferson's conduct: "Mrs. Jefferson has added another daughter to our family. She has been ever since, and continues to be very dangerously ill." [50]

Jefferson's anxiety, the grief and desolation that filled his heart from the summer of 1781 onwards, when the steady flow of his pen ceases, were unconsciously to bear fruit of a most extraordinary character. Since boyhood he had, he writes, "always made it a practice whenever an opportunity occurred, of obtaining any information of our country [*i.e.*, Virginia], which might be of use to me in any station public or private, to commit it to writing. These memoranda were on loose papers, bundled up without order, and difficult of recurrence when I had occasion for a particular one." In 1781 he "had received a letter from M. de Marbois, of the French legation in Philadelphia, informing me he had been instructed by his government to obtain such statistical accounts of the different states of our Union, as might be useful for their information, and addressed to me a number of queries relative to the state of Virginia. . . . I thought this a good occasion to embody their substance, which I did in order of Mr. Marbois' queries, so as to answer his wish and to arrange them for my own use." [51]

It thus happened that during the last, sad year of his wife's life Jefferson's famous "Notes on Virginia" came to be written. In June 1781, he suffered a fall from a horse which incapacitated him for a time, and the work was begun then, with some additions and corrections made the following winter. What mental anguish he suffered during the composition of this work we may gather from a statement in the preface to the "Notes," dated February 27, 1787: "The subjects are all treated imperfectly, some scarcely touched on," Jefferson modestly observes. "To apologize for this by developing the circumstances of the time and place of their composition, would be to open wounds which have already bled enough."

"My dear wife died this day at 11-45 A.M." reads the entry in Jefferson's account book for September 6, 1782. No amount of care or solicitude, no medical science available in that day, had been able to save her life. Their eldest daughter later wrote of this time: "As a nurse, no female ever had more tenderness or anxiety. He nursed my poor mother in turn with Aunt Carr and her own sister, sitting up with her and administering her medicines and drink to the last. For four months that she lingered [*i.e.*, after the birth of her last child], he was never out of calling; when not at her bedside, he was writing in a small room which opened immediately at the head of her bed. A moment before the closing scene, he was led from the room almost in a state of insensibility by his sister, Mrs. Carr, who, with great difficulty, got him into the library, where he fainted, and remained so long insensible that they feared he never would revive. The scene that followed I did not witness; but the violence of his emotion, when almost by stealth I entered his room at night, to this day I dare not trust myself to describe. He kept to his room three weeks, and I was never a moment from his side. He walked almost incessantly night and day, only lying down occasionally, when nature was completely exhausted, on a pallet that had been brought in during his long fainting fit.... When at last he left his room, he rode out, and from that time he was incessantly on horseback, rambling about the mountain, the least frequented roads, and just as often through the woods. In those melancholy rambles, I was his constant companion, a solitary witness to many a violent burst of grief...."

Some time after his wife's death Jefferson seems to have addressed a letter to Mrs. Eppes of Eppington, if we may judge by the context. It was intended to give their aunt news of his three little daughters. Patsy, his eldest child, was ten at the time, Polly four, and the baby, Lucy Elizabeth, but four months old. A draft of this letter, a cry of agony, has been preserved but never published.

"The girls being unable to assure you themselves of their welfare," he writes, "the duty devolves on me and I will undertake it the more willingly as it will lay you under the necessity of sometimes letting us hear from you. They are in perfect health and as happy as if they had had no part in the immeasurable loss we have sustained. Patsy rides with me five or six miles a day and presses me for permission to accompany me on horseback to Elkhill, whenever I shall go there. When that may be, however, I cannot tell, finding myself absolutely unable to attend to anything like business. This miserable hand of existence is really too burthensome to be borne and were it not for the infidelity of deserting the sacred charge left me, I could not wish its continuance a moment. For what could it be wished? All my plans of comfort and happiness reversed by a single event and nothing arising in prospect before me but a gloom, unabridged with one cheerful expectation. The care and instruction of our children indeed affords some temporary abstractions from wretchedness, and nourishes a soothing reflection that if there be beyond the grave any [illegible] for the things of this world, there is one angel at least, who views these attentions with pleasure and wishes continuance of them, while she must pity the miseries to which they confine me.

"But I forgot that I began this correspondence on behalf of the children and am afflicting you at the distance of seventy or eighty miles with sorrows which you had a right to ... [illegible].

"I will endeavor to correct myself and keep what I feel to myself that I may not dispirit you from a communication with us. News from hence you will not expect. Mrs. Gilmer's getting better and better is the only event I can recollect which can be interesting to you. I say nothing of coming to Eppington. I promised you this should not be until I could support such a countenance as might not cast a damp on the cheerfulness of others. I shall begin to expect Jack in a week...." [52]

Late November found Jefferson at Ampthill, where he had taken his children and those of Dabney Carr to be inoculated against smallpox. From here he wrote his valued friend, the Marquis de Chastellux: "I received your friendly letters of ——

and June 30th, but the latter not till the 17th of October. It found me a little emerging from the stupor of mind which had rendered me as dead to the world as was she whose loss occasioned it. Your letter recalled to my memory that there were persons still living of much value to me. If you should ever have thought me remiss in not testifying to you sooner, how deeply I had been impressed with your worth in the little time I had the happiness of being with you, you will, I am sure, ascribe it to its true cause, the state of dreadful suspense in which I have been kept all summer, and the catastrophe which closed it." [53]

The inscription that marks the grave of Martha Jefferson probably tells more of her husband's love and devotion than other words could convey:

> To the memory of
> Martha Jefferson
> Daughter of John Wayles;
> Born October 19th, 1748, O. S.
> Intermarried with
> Thomas Jefferson
> January 1st, 1772
> Torn from him by death
> September 6, 1782:
> This monument of his love is inscribed

> If in the melancholy shades below,
> The flames of friends and lovers cease to glow,
> Yet mine shall sacred last; mine undecayed
> Burn on through death and animate my shade.[54]

X. Impulse to Revolution

IN 1769 JEFFERSON was elected to the House of Burgesses—"the most dignified body of men ever assembled to legislate," as he later observed.[1] It was at once a privilege and a duty that fell to the lot of the two men most outstanding in each county. He succeeded Edward Carter as one of the representatives of Albemarle, and served with Dr. Thomas Walker, his neighbor and former guardian. We are fortunate in having a picture of Jefferson at this period from the gifted pen of Edmund Randolph. He was Jefferson's second cousin and with him worked and lived through the stirring years of the formation of the new republic. No man more ably described his contemporaries, or was in a better position to do so. "As yet Thomas Jefferson had not attained a marked grade in politics," he writes. "Until about the age of twenty-five years he had pursued general science, with which he mingled the law as a profession with eager industry and unabated thirst. His manners could never be harsh, but they were reserved towards the world at large. To his intimate friends he shewed a peculiar sweetness of temper, and by them was admired and beloved."[2]

On April 3, Jefferson left Shadwell. After a leisurely journey to the Tidewater he settled down in Williamsburg, where he spent a month, with a hasty visit to Charles City County. He took his seat for the first time in the spring session of the Assembly, which opened on May 8. As the young legislator hurried from his lodgings toward the Capitol, he little suspected that the sunny spring day in the lovely month of May was to be a momentous one for him. An event, apparently routine for a man of his station, was transpiring which was to turn the whole trend of his thoughts, and was to be of the utmost importance not only for his own life but for the history of the world.

As an onlooker, to be sure, Jefferson had hitherto not failed to take an interest in politics—indeed he may be said to have grown up with them. The last ten years had been stormy ones in the Virginia Assembly, and Jefferson, although but a youth, had, as he tells us, "paid attention to what was passing in the legislature." [3] Not only had his father been a burgess, but the "Parson's cause" had rocked the colony while he was still a student with the Reverend James Maury, the very parson who brought the famous suit. There, in the violent discussions concerning the "two-penny act" of 1758, which was the cause of the trouble, he had received his initiation into politics. When the suit was finally decided, in 1763, and Patrick Henry leaped to fame as the advocate of the people, Jefferson was a student at Williamsburg. In his recollections of this period he tells of "listening at the door of the lobby, for as yet there was no gallery," to the debates in the Assembly which were "most bloody." [4] No one could have remained unaware of what was in progress there with Henry electrifying the burgesses, first by pleading before them as an advocate, subsequently as a tempestuous and eloquent member. "He appeared to me to speak as Homer wrote," Jefferson declared, and in these words he seems to have echoed the opinion of the majority of his contemporaries.

Patrick Henry played an important rôle in Jefferson's formative years. The reminiscences which he was later to contribute to Wirt's "Life of Patrick Henry" leave us in no doubt of this. This shiftless genius, at heart a vagabond, who went about in the garments of a plain countryman, whose sole education in the law had been the reading of a few fundamental books extending over a period of six weeks, and whose admission to the bar George Wythe refused to countenance, dominated the scene in Williamsburg from the moment of his first appearance. Jefferson had first encountered him at Colonel Dandridge's in Hanover, whose neighbor Henry was, at Christmas 1759. "During the festivity of the season I met him in society every day, and we became well acquainted, although I was much his junior, being then but in my seventeenth year and he a married man," [5] Jefferson writes of their meeting. "His manners had something of the coarseness of the society he had frequented; his passion was fiddling, dancing, and pleasantry. He excelled in the last and it attached everyone to him," Jefferson continues, giving a clue to the man's capacity to charm. "The occasion perhaps, as much as his idle disposition, prevented his engaging in any conversation which might give the measure either of his mind or information. Opportunity was not wanting, because Mr. John Campbell was there, who had married Mrs. Spotswood, the sister of Colonel Dandridge. He was a man of science and often introduced conversation on scientific subjects." [6]

In the spring of 1760, Henry, who had been unsuccessfully keeping a country store which, as Jefferson says, he broke up "or rather it had broken him up," decided to become a lawyer. He went to Williamsburg to obtain a license and called on young Mr. Jefferson, who had just entered upon his studies at the college. Thus began a friendship based on intense admiration on the part of the youthful student, strengthened, as he observes, "by the exact conformity of our political opinions." [7] Although it was a friendship destined later to be shattered as their politics diverged, Jefferson, in his old age, could still write of Henry that he was "the idol of the country beyond anyone that ever lived." [8] To this he added, with the clear vision and justice that distinguish his estimates of the abilities of his contemporaries: "He could not draw a bill on the most simple subject which would bear legal criticism, or even the ordinary criticism which looks to correctness of style and ideas, for indeed there was no accuracy of idea in his head. His imagination was copious, poetical, sublime, but vague also. He said the strongest things in the finest language, but without logic, without arrangement, desultorily." [9]

Henry's debut in the "Parson's cause" was followed, in 1764, by his sensational appearance in the House of Burgesses before the Committee of Privileges and Elections on behalf of Colonel Nathaniel Dandridge, who contested the election of James Littlepage, accused of bribery and corruption. A routine occasion—elections were contested at every meeting of the Assembly—was transformed into a dramatic event of the first order. Despite the reputation Henry had gained in the "Parson's cause," John Tyler, father of the President, could write of his appearance on this occasion: "He was ushered with great state and ceremony into the room of the committee, whose chairman was Colonel Bland. Mr. Henry was dresed in very coarse apparel; no one knew anything of him, and scarcely was he treated with decent respect by anyone except the chairman, who could not do so much violence to his feelings and principles, as to depart on any occasion, from the delicacy of a gentleman. But the general contempt was soon changed into general admiration; for Mr. Henry distinguished himself by a copious and brilliant display on the great subject of the rights of suffrage, superior to anything that had been heard before within those walls. Such a burst of eloquence, from a man so very plain and ordinary in his appearance, struck the committee with amazement; so that a deep and perfect silence took place during the speech, and not a sound but from his lips was to be heard in the room." [10]

The year 1765 was an important one both for Patrick Henry's career and for Virginia. Henry had removed from Hanover to "Round Top," a plantation in Louisa, and was elected a burgess to represent that county. He was immediately to distinguish himself in the famous Robinson case, which shook the colony to its very foundation.

John Robinson was one of the outstanding men of Virginia, wealthy, well connected, of distinguished presence, for many years speaker of the House of Burgesses and treasurer of the colony. He was the leader of the group that had long dominated the Assembly. Jefferson says of him, and of the circumstances in which he became involved, "he was an excellent man, liberal, friendly, rich. He had been drawn in to lend on his own account great sums of money to persons of this description [*i.e.*, gentlemen 'deeply involved in a state of indebtment'] and especially those who were of the Assembly. He used freely for this purpose the public money, confiding for its replacement in his own means and the securities he had taken on those loans. About this time, however, he became sensible that his deficit to the public

THE CAPITOL, WILLIAMSBURG. (*Photograph by F. S. Lincoln*)

IMPULSE TO REVOLUTION 191

was become so enormous as that a discovery must soon take place, for as yet the public had no suspicion of it. He devised therefore with his friends in the Assembly a plan for a public loan office to a certain amount, from which monies might be lent on public account and on good landed security to individuals. This was accordingly brought forward in the House of Burgesses, and had it succeeded, the debts due to Robinson on these loans would have been transferred to the public, and his deficit thus completely covered. This state of things, however, was not yet known." [11]

It was the sort of opportunity for which Henry had been waiting. In a manner which today would seem more than tinged with the theatrical, "he attacked the scheme on other general grounds in that style of bold, grand and overwhelming eloquence for which he became so justly celebrated afterwards." Jefferson, who was listening to the debate, tells us that Henry exclaimed: " 'What, Sir! is it proposed then to reclaim the spendthrift from his dissipation and extravagance, by filling his pockets with money.' The expressions are indelibly impressed on my memory. He laid open with so much energy the spirit of favoritism on which the proposition was founded, and the abuses to which it would lead, that it was crushed at its birth." [12] "Henry," Jefferson concludes, "carried with him all the members of the upper counties, and left a minority composed merely of the aristocracy of the country. From this time his popularity swelled apace, and Robinson dying four years after, his deficit was brought to light, and discovered the true object of the proposition." [13]

What Patrick Henry had really achieved was not merely a minor political victory, nor a great personal triumph. More significant than the defeat of the bill was the challenge he had issued to the ruling class in the colony, and the essential division of Virginia into two parties. Insofar as they were determined by the Assembly, the affairs of the colony had hitherto been directed by a handful of rich and powerful Tidewater planters—"the cyphers of the aristocracy," Jefferson called them. As the gifted and compelling spokesman of the common people, of whom he was one and to whom he first gave voice, Henry very truly "gave the first impulse to the ball of the Revolution." [14]

A further and determining impulse was given, a few months later, by Henry's fiery leadership of the opposition to the Stamp Act. This act, which involved placing a stamp on all newspapers, on most business papers, and on "every skin or piece of vellum or parchment or sheet or piece of paper, on which shall be embossed, written or printed, any declaration, plea, replication, rejoinder or demurrer, or other pleading, or any copy thereof in any court of law within the British Colonies and plantations in America," [15] had been passed by the British Parliament in January 1765, to take effect on November 1 following. The plan had been outlined by Grenville, the Chancellor of the Exchequer, in March of the preceding year, and the Virginia Assembly, along with the assemblies of most of the other colonies, had sent addresses to the King, the House of Lords, and the House of Commons, assuring their most gracious sovereign of their loyalty but, at the same time, protesting the right of Parliament to impose this tax. These addresses, however, were ignored. When the act became law and word of this finally reached Virginia, shortly before the spring meeting of the Assembly in 1765, feeling was running high. With his unfailing appreciation for the psychological moment, Henry seized upon the occasion to introduce his famous resolutions denying the right of Parliament to levy taxes on the colony, and declaring that it could only be taxed lawfully by its own Assembly.

The moment was dramatic in the extreme. Before the assembled burgesses, punctiliously dressed in the best London had to offer, stood the gaunt and homely representative from Louisa. "The court party failed not to remark," says Burk, "with some appearance of exultation, his supposed defect in ease and good breeding; and by titterings and whispers, attempted to embarrass and depress him. The plainness of his dress and the awkwardness of his figure furnished new food for ridicule, and the whole of their court graces were ostentatiously played off for the purpose of rendering the contrast between polish and rusticity more striking and decisive. But their triumph was short lived. Soon as the great faculties of his mind began to enlarge and expand their volumes before them, their feelings were instantly converted into apprehension and astonishment. Expectation now being at its height, Mr. Henry rose, and, having called the attention of the house to the alarming pretensions of the English government, and their late encroachments on the just rights and liberties of British America, as exemplified in the late passage of that obnoxious statute, the Stamp Act," [16] he offered his resolutions.

Standing spellbound at the door of the lobby stood a tall, young law student following the debate and drinking in the "torrents of sublime eloquence from Mr. Henry," [17] as Jefferson later described the scene to Wirt. When the orator reached the climax of his speech, after summarizing "those examples of successful resistance to oppression which rendered glorious the annals of Greece and Rome," he burst into a frenzied appeal "which seemed like the inspiration of prophecy," according to Burk. " 'Caesar,' he exclaimed, 'had his Brutus, Charles his Cromwell and (pausing) George the third (here a cry of treason, treason, was heard, supposed to issue from the chair, but with admirable presence of mind he proceeded), may profit by their examples. Sir, if this be treason,' continued he, 'make the most of it.' " [18]

Confusion and wild shouting greeted this dramatic appeal, and the resolutions were passed by a large majority. Opposed were Peyton Randolph, Robinson, Wythe, Bland, Pendleton, Nicholas, and "all the old members whose influence in the house had till then been unbroken," Jefferson tells us. "They opposed him on the ground that the same principles had been expressed in the petition etc. of the preceding year, to which an answer, not yet received, was daily expected, that they were therein expressed in more conciliatory terms and therefore more likely to have a good effect. The resolutions were carried chiefly by the vote of the upper and middle country." [19]

With these last words Jefferson signalizes at once the passing of the old order and the rise of the new—the emerging to dominance of the type Henry represented, the very people whose rights Jefferson himself was later to champion. How subtly and how inexorably the change which made possible the passage of the resolutions had come over Virginia, Jefferson well describes in a letter to Wirt:

"To state the difference between the classes of society and the lines of demarkation which separated them, would be difficult. The law, you know, admitted none except as to the twelve councillors. Yet in a country insulated from the European world, insulated from its sister colonies, with whom there was scarcely any intercourse, little visited by foreigners, and having little matter to act upon within itself, certain families had risen to splendor by wealth and the preservation of it from generation to generation under the law entails; some had produced a series of men of talents; families in general had remained stationary on the grounds of their forefathers, for there was no emigration to the westward in those days. The wild Irish, who had gotten possession of the Valley between the Blue Ridge and North Mountain, forming a barrier over which none ventured to leap, and would still less venture to settle among. In such a state of things, scarcely admitting any change of station, society would settle itself down into several strata, segregated by no marked lines, but shading off imperceptibly from top to bottom, nothing disturbing the order of their repose. There were then aristocrats, half breeds, pretenders, a solid independent yeomanry, looking askance at those above, yet not venturing to jostle them, and last and lowest, a seculum of human beings called overseers, the most abject, degraded, and unprincipled race, always cap in hand to the Dons who employed them, and furnishing materials for the exercise of their pride, insolence and spirit of domination." [20]

For better or for worse, the Assembly had passed the resolutions, and Virginia found herself on the road that was to lead to revolt and separation from the mother country. Henry's eloquence fired the other colonies, whose assemblies were quick to enact resolutions similar in character.[21] Determined resistance, led by Virginia and Massachusetts, reinforced by mob violence in the larger centers and by pressure from the London merchants whose American trade was facing ruin, ultimately brought about the repeal of the Stamp Act on March 17, 1766. At the same time the so-called Declaratory Act was passed, which affirmed the right of Parliament to "bind the colonies in all cases whatsoever." This act, as Burk observes, may "well have been only a salve to the wounded and mortified pride of authority," but, he adds, "it did not escape the sagacity of the people" that it "was suggested with a view to future encroachment." [22]

The widespread rejoicing and celebrating on the repeal of the Stamp Act was short-lived. The English government had no idea of relinquishing its right to tax the colonies. Despite the rebuff and the great loss of prestige occasioned by the repeal of the Stamp Act, Parliament still believed it could achieve its ends by finding a more palatable method of taxation. In 1767 Charles Townshend, who became Chancellor of the Exchequer in this period of rapidly changing ministries, introduced the famous acts that bear his name. His plan was a simple one. Seemingly, it took the colonists at their word when they had agreed that they were willing to pay external taxes, and not internal, such as they claimed the Stamp Act to be. Townshend's Act of Trade and Revenue imposed a duty on glass, lead, painters' colors, and tea. Out of the revenue thus raised were to be paid the salaries of governors and judges.

The struggle against taxation began again with renewed vigor. In January 1768, the Massachusetts Assembly addressed a petition to the home government protesting against the new law and, at the same time, sent a circular letter to the other colonies asking their views and inviting co-operation. On March 21 the Virginia Assembly met and protested even more vigorously than had Massachusetts. Appalled by the determined opposition of its two most important and powerful colonies, the British government decided upon drastic measures. In July the Massachusetts Assembly was ordered to rescind its circular letter and the other colonies were directed to treat it with contempt. Two regiments were sent from Halifax to Boston, and several warships made their appearance in the harbor. When the Massachusetts legislature refused to rescind, it was dissolved by the Governor. The greater number of the other colonial assemblies paid no attention to the order to disregard the letter, but sent warm and approving replies. It was by this time almost clear to the British government that the American colonies resented any dictation or restrictions, indeed that Massachusetts was already guilty of treason or misprision of treason.

Such was the turbulent background of that May day, in 1769, when the burgesses gathered in Williamsburg for their spring meeting. Young Mr. Jefferson was greeted warmly by his colleagues, many of whom were old friends. There was his cousin, Richard Randolph of Henrico, Benjamin Harrison, representing Charles City County, Lewis Burwell of Gloucester, with whom he had long been friendly, the second Lewis Burwell of James City County, Thomas Nelson, Jr., of York, Carter Braxton of King William, besides such distinguished figures as Richard Bland, "the most learned and logical man of those who took prominent lead in public affairs," Peyton Randolph, Robert Carter Nicholas, the eminent lawyer and treasurer of the colony, Edmund Pendleton, Richard Henry Lee, and Henry Lee. At this time there were 118 burgesses, representing 57 counties, with one burgess each for the College of William and Mary, Williamsburg, Jamestown, and Norfolk Borough.[23]

The day was an eventful one, not only for Jefferson, but for the new royal governor whose first session of the Assembly this was. The gifted and popular Francis Fauquier, who had done so much for the social and intellectual life of Williamsburg, had lain dead beneath the stone floor of Bruton Parish Church for more than a year. In his place the home government had dispatched to the turbulent colony Norborne Berkeley, Baron de Botetourt, a title that the holder had finally succeeded in having revived four years before, after a lapse of four hundred years.[24] He was a member of the Berkeley family which had sent men to Virginia since the early days of the colony. Walpole speaks of him as "a court favourite yet ruined in fortune," and certain it is that he was utterly impoverished and involved in financial scandal in England.[25] Virginia, however, received him with open arms, and he unquestionably made a good governor. He arrived in Williamsburg on October 21, 1768, just as the sun was setting. The 12 councilors and other distinguished gentlemen of Williamsburg met him and accompanied him to the Capitol where he read his commission as governor and took the oath. "Immediately on his arrival," says the *Virginia Gazette*, "the city was illuminated and all ranks vied with each other in testifying their gratitude and joy that a nobleman of such distinguished merit and abilities is appointed to preside over and live among them."

Lord Botetourt commanded the Assembly to convene on May 8. In the leisurely tradition of Virginia, "about ten o'clock in the morning," as the Journal of the Burgesses recounts, "such of said members of the House of Burgesses as appeared," had meanwhile assembled in the council chamber to take the oath before assuming their seats. George Wythe, Clerk of the House of Burgesses, "attending, according to his duty, with a book containing the list of the names of such members as had been returned," was present, with eight commissioners appointed by the Governor to administer the oaths, "which being done the members repaired to their seats in the House of Burgesses, after which a message was delivered by Nathaniel Walthoe, Esqr, Clerk of the General Assembly." The burgesses were thereby instructed to meet the Governor in the council chamber, to which they promptly betook themselves.

Meanwhile the Governor rode from the palace to the Capitol in "much greater state than any Governor of Virginia had ever before displayed. The chariot he rode in was a superbly finished one, presented him by William, Duke of Cumberland, uncle of George III, and was intended for his state carriage, the Virginia arms being substituted for the royal English." [26] He entered the council chamber dressed "in the ordinary costume of the day, but handsome and rich, the coat of a light, red colour, of gold thread tissues." [27] His manner pleased the burgesses; they considered that his "deportment was very dignified and his delivery solemn. It is said by those who had heard and seen George III speak and act on the throne of England, that his Lordship on the throne of Virginia was true to his prototype. He spoke very slow, with long pauses." [28]

"Gentlemen of the Council, Mr. Speaker, and Gentlemen of the House of Burgesses," he began. "The King having been graciously pleased to appoint me to the high office of his Lieutenant and Governor-General of this his ancient and loyal colony and dominion of Virginia, I lost no time in repairing to my government in order to enter as soon as possible upon the execution of the important trust committed to my charge: and give me leave to assure you that it is with the greatest satisfaction I have now, in obedience to his Majesty's command, the honour to meet you in General Assembly.

"You, Gentlemen, who know intimately the true interests of the colony, are the best judges of the measures necessary to be pursued for its advantage and prosperity; and the frequent experience his Majesty has had with your zeal and wisdom leave no room in the Royal breast to doubt that you will give me all such advice and assistance as may enable me to promote and render permanent the happiness of Virginia...." [29] Then, addressing himself to the burgesses, he said: "Mr. Speaker and Gentlemen of the House of Burgesses, I have nothing to ask but that you consider well, and follow exactly, without passion or prejudice, the real interests of those you have the honour to represent. They are most certainly consistent with the prosperity of Great Britain, and so they will forever be found when pursued with temper and moderation." The Governor thereupon announced that henceforth the governors of Virginia would "reside within their government," instead of living in London and conducting the affairs of the colony through a deputy.

Subsequently the Governor directed the burgesses to select a Speaker, "and the House being returned, Archibald Cary, Esqr, one of the members of the county of Chesterfield, addressing himself to the clerk (who, standing up, pointed to him and then sat down) putting the House in mind of the Governor's command to proceed to the choice of a Speaker, proposed the Gentleman whose eminent virtues and keen abilities qualified him for and recommended him to, that important trust." [30]

The name proposed was that of Peyton Randolph, the Speaker of the preceding session. Cary was seconded by Edmund Pendleton of Caroline County. "The House calling Mr. Randolph to the Chair, he was taken out of his place by two members, who led him from thence to the chair; and having ascended the uppermost step and standing there, Mr. Randolph returned his thanks to the House for the honour they had conferred upon him for advancing him a second time to an office of so much dignity, and declared his resolution to perform the duties of it with fidelity, diligence and impartiality, desiring at all times the assistance of the House and their benign interpretation of his conduct, and thereupon he sat down in the chair, and then the mace (which before lay under the table) was laid upon his table." [31]

Mr. Cary and Mr. Pendleton thereupon sent a message to the Governor informing him that a Speaker had been chosen and "to know his Pleasure, when they shall attend to present him." The Governor replied with proper ceremony and, as was usual when a meeting opened, it was "Resolved, *nemine contradicente,* that a most humble and dutiful address be presented to his Excellency the Governor, returning thanks for his very affectionate speech at the opening of this session." It was likewise "ordered, that a committee be appointed to draw up an address, to be presented to the Governor upon the said resolution, and a committee was appointed of Mr. Edmund Pendleton, Mr. Treasurer, Mr. Bland, Mr. Thompson Mason, Mr. R. H. Lee, Mr. Attorney-General and Mr. Jefferson." [32] The latter, who was already known for the quality of his pen, tells us, "Mr. Pendleton asked me to draw the resolutions, which I did. They were accepted by the house, and Pendleton, Nicholas, myself and some others, were appointed a committee to prepare an address. The committee desired me to do it, but when presented it was thought to pursue too strictly the diction of the resolutions, and that their subjects were not sufficiently amplified. Mr. Nicholas chiefly objected to it, and was desired by the committee to draw one more at large, which he did with amplification enough, and it was accepted. Being a young man as well as a young member, it made on me an impression proportioned to the sensibility of that time of life." [33]

The "young member" was likewise appointed on the Committee of Privileges and Elections, along with Edmund Pendleton, Richard Bland, Benjamin Harrison, Richard Henry Lee, George Washington, and others. They were to "meet and adjourn from day to day, and to examine, in the first place all returns of writs for electing burgesses to serve in this present assembly ... and to take into their consideration all such matters as shall or may come in question, touching returns, elections, privileges, and to report their proceedings." [34] It was furthermore "Ordered, that a Committee of Proposition and Grievances be appointed," and Mr. Jefferson found himself one of the 47 members of that group.

The meeting thus opened with an elaborate exchange of courtesies and with every appearance of success. The new Governor made a favorable impression—indeed, he was to become greatly beloved —and things seemed to be proceeding smoothly. Various routine matters were brought up to claim the attention of the burgesses; all seemed quiet, and ominous. Then "Mr. Speaker acquainted the House that according to the directions of the House last session of the General Assembly, he had written to the respective speakers of the Assemblies and Representatives on this continent, upon the subject of sundry acts of the British Parliament, and had received several letters in answer thereto, and he delivered the letters in at the clerk's table." It was "Ordered that the said letters do lie upon the table, to be perused by the members of the House." It was, furthermore, "ordered, that the letters which have passed between the Committee of Correspondence and the agent for this colony, for the last five years, and the papers they refer to, be laid before the House." [35]

With this the spirit of discontent and disquiet that had been flaring up in the colony at increasingly frequent intervals during the last years seized the members of the Assembly and ran through it like wildfire. Groups of the burgesses met first in this member's house, then in that. In hushed tones, but in fiery words, they pledged themselves to stand by Massachusetts. They likewise denounced Britain's right to impose taxes on any colony and to destroy their jury system, as Parliament's proposals threatened to do.

On May 16, "the order of the day being read, for the House to resolve itself into a Committee of the Whole House, to consider the present state of the colony... the House resolved itself in the said committee. Mr. Speaker left the chair. Mr. Blair took the chair of the committee. Mr. Speaker resumed the chair." It was as though they were waiting for the great moment yet, as loyal

British subjects, dreading it. Mr. Blair then "reported from the committee, that they had come to several resolutions; which he read in his place, and afterwards delivered in at the clerk's table where the same were read, and are as followeth, viz.:

'Resolved, that it is the opinion of this committee that the sole right of imposing taxes on the inhabitants of this his Majesty's colony and dominion of Virginia is now, and ever hath been, legally and constitutionally vested in the House of Burgesses, lawfully convened, according to the ancient and established practice, with the consent of the Council and of his Majesty the King of Britain, or his Governor for the time being.

'Resolved, that it is the opinion of this committee, that it is the undoubted privilege of the inhabitants of this colony to petition their sovereign for redress of grievances, and that it is lawful and expedient to procure the concurrence of his Majesty's other colonies in dutiful addresses, praying the Royal interposition in favour of the violated rights of America.

'Resolved, That it is the opinion of this committee, that all trials for treason, misprision of treason, or for any felony or crime whatsoever committed and done in his Majesty's said colony and dominion, by any person or persons residing therein, ought of right to be had and conducted in and before his Majesty's courts held within said colony, according to the fixed and known course of proceeding; and that seizing any person or persons residing in this colony suspected of any crime whatsoever committed therein, and sending such person or persons beyond the sea to be tried, is highly derogatory of the rights of British subjects, as thereby the inestimable privilege of being tried by a jury from the vicinage, as well as the liberty of summoning and producing witnesses in such trial, will be taken away from the party accused.

'Resolved, that it is the opinion of the committee that an humble, dutiful and loyal address be presented to his Majesty, to assure him of our inviolable attachment to his sacred person and government, and to beseech his Royal interposition, as the father of all his people, however remote from the seat of his Empire, to give to the minds of his loyal subjects in this colony and to avert from them those dangers and miseries which will ensue from the seizing and carrying beyond sea any persons residing in America, suspected of any crime whatsoever, to be tried in any other manner than by the ancient and long established course of proceeding.'"

It was also ordered that "the Speaker of this House, do transmit, without delay, to the Speaker of the several Houses of Assembly on this continent a copy of the resolutions now agreed to by this House, requesting their concurrence therein." [36] "The said resolutions being severally read a second time," the Journal continues, it was "Resolved, *nemine contradicente*, that this House doth agree with the committee in said resolutions."

The following day the House again convened as a Committee of the Whole and Mr. Blair read "the humble address" of the House of Burgesses to the King, which had been written by the committee appointed the day before. This committee consisted of Mr. Blair, Richard Henry Lee, Patrick Henry, Thompson Mason of Stafford County, Benjamin Harrison, and Mr. Treasurer, Robert Carter Nicholas. They assured his Majesty that "far from countenancing traitors, treasons or misprision of treasons" the members of the House of Burgesses "are ready at any time to sacrifice our lives and fortunes in defense of your Majesty's sacred person and government." They state that "with most heartfelt grief" they "find that their loyalty hath been traduced, and that those measures, which a first regard for the British constitution (dearer to them than life) made necessary duties, have been misrepresented as rebellious attacks upon your Majesty's government." They go on to say that they cannot "without horror, think of the new, unusual, and permit us, with all humility to add, unconstitutional and illegal mode, recommended to your Majesty, of seizing and carrying beyond the sea, the inhabitants of America, suspected of any crime; and of trying such persons in any other manner than by the ancient and long established course of proceeding."

With a humility thought suitable to the occasion, the address concludes: "Truly alarmed at the fatal tendency of these pernicious counsels, and with hearts filled with anguish, by such dangerous invasions of our dearest privileges, we presume to prostrate ourselves at the foot of your royal throne, beseeching your

Majesty, as our King and Father, to avert from your faithful and loyal subjects of America, those miseries which must necessarily be the consequence of such measures...." ³⁷

The news of the action taken by the burgesses spread rapidly and it was doubtless small surprise to them when, at noon on May 17, Nathaniel Walthoe, the clerk, appeared before them and announced that the Governor commanded their immediate presence in the council chamber. The Governor was waiting for them, "dressed in a suit of plain scarlet. The speaker advanced toward him, the members following. At the usual distance from the person of the representative of Majesty the speaker stopped. A solemn pause of a minute or two ensued, when the Governor with an assumed stern countenance and with considerable power, addressed the speaker and members of the house: 'Mr. Speaker and Gentlemen of the House of Burgesses, I have heard of your resolves, and augur ill of their effect. You have made it my duty to dissolve you; and you are dissolved accordingly.'" ³⁸

The Governor might dissolve the burgesses, but he could not dampen or dismay their spirit. Counsel was hurriedly taken, and the *Virginia Gazette* reports, the representatives of the people, "judging it necessary that some measures should be taken, in their distressed situation, for preserving the true and essential interests of the colony, resolved upon a meeting for that very salutary purpose; and therefore immediately, with the greatest order and decorum, repaired to the house of Mr. Anthony Hay ³⁹ in this city, where being assembled," it was proposed that a moderator should be appointed.⁴⁰ Peyton Randolph, the late Speaker, was elected to this office.

"The true state of the colony being then opened and fully explained," the *Gazette* continues, "and it being proposed that a regular association should be formed, a committee was appointed to prepare the necessary and most proper regulations for that purpose, and they were ordered to make their report to the general meeting the next day at ten o'clock." This was duly accomplished. The report was "read, seriously considered, and approved, and was signed by a great number of the principal gentlemen of the colony then present." Like little boys who had been naughty, but who wished to assure their sovereign that all was well meant and no hard feelings should be entertained, they proceeded to drink toasts to the King, the Queen and royal family, his Excellency, Lord Botetourt, the prosperity of Virginia, a speedy and lasting union between Great Britain and her colony, and a dozen more. Everyone felt quite merry and pleased with the proceedings. That Virginia had committed the first act of true rebellion against the King and his government was not emphasized.

On May 25 the *Virginia Gazette* printed "A Copy of the Association." After the usual preamble and most earnestly recommending "this our association to the serious attention of all gentlemen, merchants, traders and other inhabitants of this colony, in hopes that they will very reasonably and cordially accede thereto," the association, in eight articles of agreement, endorsed and adopted a strict non-importation policy. The agreement was drafted by George Mason and presented by George Washington. The signers, some 89 in number, bound themselves "not at any time hereafter, directly or indirectly, [to] import or cause to be imported any manner of goods, merchandise or manufactures which are, or shall hereafter be, taxed by Act of Parliament for the purpose of raising revenue in America ... nor purchase any such after the first day of September next, of any person whatsoever, but that they will always consider such taxation, in every respect, as an absolute prohibition, and in all future orders, direct their correspondents to ship them no goods whatever, taxed as aforesaid, except as is above excepted."

The list of contraband goods was enormous. It contained practically everything used in almost all phases of life; commodities such as meat, butter, cheese, sugar, oil, fruit, along with all wines and spirits, paper, all clothing materials, leather and skins of all kinds. It was most effectively and ruinously designed to stop all trade with the mother country. The members of the Association agreed to inform their correspondents in England not to send them anything on the long list until Parliament had repealed the acts to which they objected, and if such goods were sent, they were to be refused. No slaves were to be imported after the first of the following November, and no lambs were to be killed, so that there might be more wool to be woven into cloth for garments.

The Association flourished, and many of the other colonies passed similar resolutions. On July 27 the *Virginia Gazette* stated: "It is with the highest pleasure we can inform our readers the Association meets with the greatest encouragement in every county that we have yet heard from." John Page wrote from Rosewell on May 27, 1769, to his correspondent in London: "... I like the association because I think it will repeal the disagreeable acts of Parliament, open the eyes of the people with you, and must certainly clear us of our debts. All North America will join in this scheme. How must your manufacturers curse the Minister who has driven the colonies to this; I am astonished at Ld. Hillsborough. His method of quelling riots in London & supporting the civil power in America, as he terms it, will render him eternally ridiculous & odious to the English & Americans. I am amazed at the influence he seems to have over both houses of Parliament.... Is it not shocking to think that he not only executed that dangerous & impolitic scheme of sending troops to Boston, but was able to get the approbation of Lds. & Commons? Is not every honest Englishman alarmed at their resolves and addresses?" [41]

Even the ladies, accustomed, at that time, to remaining in the background, became ardent supporters, and the *Virginia Gazette* remarked that "we cannot refrain from publishing the names of the widow ladies who have acceded to the association." Martha Jacquelin of Jamestown, in sending an order to the firm of John Norton and Sons in London, wrote, in August 1769: "You will see by my invoice that I am an associator.... Our poor country never stood in more need of an effort to save her than now; not more from the taxes and want of trayd than from our own extravagances.... I expect to be dress't in Virginia cloth very soon, and as I am a little incommoded with corns, in mockasins likewise. I have given up the article of tea, but some are not quite so tractable; however if we can convince the good folks on your side of the water of their error, we may hope to see happier times." [42]

Within a few months "Virginia cloth," if not moccasins, was worn everywhere. Sacrifice and loyalty to the ideals of the colony had become popular. On December 14, 1769, the *Virginia Gazette* reported: "Last night there was a ball and elegant entertainment at the Capitol, given by the Gentlemen of the Hon. House of Burgesses to his Excellency the Governor, his Majesty's Council, and the Gentlemen and Ladies of this city, who were chiefly dressed in Virginia cloth, and made a genteel appearance. The Capitol was illuminated on this occasion."

Jefferson's account book, which sometimes tells so much, gives no account or clue to these stirring days. Although he was on several committees, he appears to have found time to visit John Page or Francis Willis, for on May 13 he notes paying ferriage at York and the same on his return two days later. On the eighteenth, however, there is an entry "pd expenses of association 10/." He seems to have remained in Williamsburg until the middle of June, when various small debts were settled. A trip to Staunton followed, as on the twentieth he "paid women at Staunton for singing," and by July 1 he was back at Charlottesville, deep in the problem of buying clover seed. On Friday, the fourteenth, George Dudley began making bricks for him at "Moncello," where he was taking the first steps toward building his future house.

On November 7, 1769, the Governor again summoned the Assembly to meet. He had good news for the burgesses and was all smiles and affability when he appeared before them in the council chamber. After speaking at some length of the "Boundary betwixt this colony and the Cherokees," he observed, "I think myself peculiarly fortunate to be able to inform you that in a letter dated May the 13th, I have been assured by the Earl of Hillsborough that his Majesty's present administration have at no time entertained a design to propose to Parliament to lay any further taxes upon America for the purpose of raising a revenue, and that it is their intention to propose in the next session of Parliament, to take off the duties upon glass, paper and colours, upon consideration of such duties having been laid contrary to the true principles of commerce." He then continued, "It is my firm opinion that the plan I have stated to you will certainly take place, and that it will never be departed from, and so determined am I forever to abide by it that I will be content to be declared infamous, if I do not to the last hour of my life, at all times, in all places, and upon all occasions, exert every power with which I either am or ever shall be legally invested, in order to obtain and maintain for the continent of America that satisfaction which I have been authorized to promise this day." [43]

This was good news for the burgesses. After duly presenting a "most dutiful and humble address" to his Excellency, the Assembly set busily to work on the many internal problems that had been neglected a full year. Forty-one acts and six resolves were passed.

Concerning his own part in this session, Jefferson has little to say. In his "Autobiography" he states that, "I made one effort in that body for the permission of the emancipation of slaves, which was rejected." [44] He doubtless refers to his work on the Committee of Proposition and Grievances, of which he was a member, which was instructed "to prepare and bring in a bill to amend the act entitled an act to amend the act for the better government of servants and slaves." [45] Instead of liberalizing the act, in accordance with Jefferson's views, it was made even more stringent, for the committee was empowered "to receive a clause or clauses for amending so much of said act as impowers the county court to order and direct dismembering of slaves, who are notoriously guilty of going abroad in the night or running away, and laying out, and who cannot be reclaimed by the common methods of punishment." [46] In 1814 he wrote Edward Coles an account of the incident: "In the first or second session of the legislature after I became a member, I drew to this subject the attention of Col. Bland, one of the oldest, ablest, and most respected members, and he undertook to move for certain moderate extensions of the protection of the laws to these people. I seconded his motion, and, as a younger member, was spared in the debate; but he was denounced as an enemy of his country, and was treated with the grossest indecorum." [47]

The burgesses remained in session until the approach of the Christmas holidays. On December 21 they were summoned to the council chamber where the Governor thanked them "for the material service you have rendered to his Majesty and this his ancient dominion ... in the course of your wise and temperate deliberations," and directed that both houses adjourn themselves until the twenty-first of the following May. After receiving his "burgesses wages" of £37 10*s*, Jefferson, on the twenty-second, set off for York where he spent several days visiting Warner Lewis and seeing old friends. It was not until the first of the year that the young burgess returned to his home in Albemarle.

XI. The Four Freedoms

UNTIL HE entered the House of Burgesses, it had been Jefferson's ambition to be a lawyer, to follow, most probably, in the distinguished footsteps of the man whom he admired above all others, George Wythe. He had pursued his studies with a thoroughness most unusual but entirely consonant with the determination with which he habitually threw himself upon any task. Since his induction to the bar, he had built up a promising practice, and he had otherwise occupied himself with the development of his farms and with plans for building himself a house. Almost overnight his interests shifted. In that brief spring meeting of the Virginia Assembly, it was brought home to him that the future held problems greater and infinitely more vital than any he would ever encounter as a barrister. The law already lay behind him, although he was not to be fully aware of this for some time. Neither could he know that in forsaking it he was taking the first steps along the road that was to lead to immortality. Henceforth his mind was to become fixed solely on the philosophy of government and on the solution of the many vexing and practical problems entailed in the relation of the colonies to the mother country.

It is our great good fortune that we possess a document which establishes, beyond question of a doubt, this fundamental shift in Jefferson's interests. It is a bill for books that he ordered in the summer of 1769, shortly after the closing of the legislature.[1] Instead of being an assortment of volumes of literature and books on law, as had been the only other known book bill of his early days—that of the *Virginia Gazette* of 1764-1765—every one of the 14 items on this bill deals with theories of government. There is not a single volume of any other character. The books were bought of T. Cadell, a London bookseller. In late September 1769, they were, as the invoice states, "shipped by Grace of God in good order and condition upon the good Sloop Industry, now riding at anchor in the river Thames, and by God's Grace bound for Virginia." An advertisement in the *Virginia Gazette* for December 14 of the same year, by Sarah Pitt, informs us that she has a variety of goods for sale "just imported on the Industry, Captain Lowes, from London." Thus we know that Jefferson received his books before the year was out.

The volumes ordered by the young legislator are informative in the extreme. The list of those shipped is headed by a "very elegant" copy in "gilt marble" of the "Petits Jus Parliamentum." Gordon's "History of Parliaments," in two volumes, follows. Then "Modus tenendi Parliamentum," "very scarce, could not be got otherwise bound," along with "Determinations of the House of Commons." Now come the books that are the real kernel of the order and which were to be so influential in the development and formation of Jefferson's thought. There is Locke "On Government," Burlamaqui's "Le Droit Naturel," Ellis's "Tracts on Liberty," Warner's "History of Ireland,"—"History of Civil Wars," Petty's "Survey of Ireland," the "Oeuvres de Montesquieu," Ferguson's "Civil Society," and Stewart's "Political Oeconomy."

As might be expected, the reading and study of these books is immediately reflected in Jefferson's commonplace book, that confidant of his inmost thoughts. The first 693 entries in this book, as we have already seen, dealt exclusively with abstracts from books on the law. Subjects such as treason, felony, murder, burglary, misprision, conspiracy, inheritance, history of property and privileges, history of entails, rules of descent, had occupied his attention. With the next entry Jefferson was just turning his attention to the history of the early populations of Europe, when his shipment of books from London arrived. He glanced through Ferdinand Warner's "History of Ireland," and noted: "The laws of the Tanistry among the antient Irish, like Alexander's will, gave the inheritance to the strongest." Then his eye fell upon

Montesquieu's "Esprit des Lois." He picked it up and began devouring its words. They seemed like a revelation to him, expressing, as they did, so many of the thoughts and ideas he had more than half sensed and been mulling over these many months. He laid aside the page on which he had been writing, turned to a new one, and inscribed "Le droit des gens est naturellement fondé sur ce principe que les diverses nations doivent se faire dans la paix le plus de bien, et dans la guerre le moins de mal qu'il est possible, sans nuire à leur véritables intérêts." It was the first of 27 excerpts from the French philosopher which Jefferson transcribed—more than he was to devote to the work of any other writer.

The question of Jefferson's debt to Montesquieu is one that has been much debated. As the date he secured the book has hitherto not been known, as there is no reference to him in Jefferson's letters prior to 1790, and as all subsequent allusions are bitterly antagonistic, recent opinion has tended to minimize Montesquieu's influence. No matter in what regard Jefferson may have held him later in life—and he was to alter his opinion of various writers and thinkers in the course of time—there can be no doubt that he was profoundly affected by Montesquieu at this early period. The freshness and originality of the Frenchman's views—despite a certain leaning on Locke—his theory of liberty, his warm impulse for reform and for the betterment of the human lot, were qualities inevitably stimulating to the young Virginia idealist. The eagerness with which he transcribed passages from Montesquieu, and the extent to which he did so, lead to the conclusion that this may well have been Jefferson's first contact with the work. French authors tended to make rare appearances in colonial libraries. Whether Wythe, Small, or Fauquier had a copy of the "Esprit des Lois," which had appeared in 1748, we have no way of knowing. The inventory of Lord Botetourt's library shows that he owned the work, but there is no indication that Jefferson was on such terms of intimacy with Botetourt as he had been with Fauquier—indeed, that they ever met, except as Governor and burgess. There was no copy in Dabney Carr's rather extensive library, or in William Byrd's magnificent one.

The catalogue of the Library Company of Philadelphia for 1770 shows that they had an English translation published in London in 1750, and it is within the realm of possibility that Jefferson visited this library on his trip north in 1766. Even so, it would, of course, not mean that he became acquainted with this particular book.

Although apparently novel to Jefferson, Montesquieu's ideas were, to be sure, more or less in the air at this time and were destined to become even more so within the following years. By the fall of 1772 an advertisement appeared in the *Massachusetts Gazette* advocating an American edition of his works with the recommendation that they "ought to be in every man's hands." [2] A series of letters which Robert Carter Nicholas addressed to Purdie and Dixon, publishers of the *Virginia Gazette*, in 1773, concerning paper money and the devaluation of Virginia currency, shows that he was thoroughly familiar with Montesquieu, as well as Puffendorf, from whom he claims the former derived his ideas.[3] So great became Montesquieu's vogue, so influential his theories, that the leaders in the revolutionary movement did not hesitate to bandy his name about in their innumerable pamphlets and letters to the papers, quite confident that it would be understood by their public. Thus Alexander Hamilton observed "I hold, with Montesquieu, that a government must be fitted to a nation much as a coat to the individual." [4] And James Madison, in discussing the separation of the departments of power, remarked in *The Federalist:* "The oracle who is always consulted and cited in this subject is the celebrated Montesquieu. If he be not the author of this invaluable precept in the science of politics, he has the merit at least of displaying and recommending it most effectually to the attention of mankind." [5]

Jefferson's later distaste for Montesquieu may be ascribed in part to his ever-increasing distrust and hatred of England, whose government and civilization the Frenchman admired most extraordinarily. "The British constitution was to Montesquieu what Homer has been to the didactic writers of epic poetry," Madison wrote,[6] and Jefferson came to be of this opinion. Furthermore, the passing years witnessed Jefferson's own growth in wisdom and enabled him to pass judgment on certain of Montesquieu's principles which experience had taught him were fallacious. This was particularly true of Montesquieu's theory that a republican form of government is suited only to small territories—an idea Jefferson eventually found very galling. Another reason for his veering from the French philosopher was that when he went to France, in 1785, he became a familiar in the circle dominated by Helvétius, who, although an intimate friend of Montesquieu, was antipathetic to his ideas, more particularly to his Anglomania. Thus it came about that from an enthusiastic endorsement and admiration of Montesquieu in 1769, Jefferson was writing to his son-in-law, Thomas Mann Randolph, in May 1790, "in the science of government, Montesquieu's 'Spirit of Laws' is generally recommended. It contains, indeed, a great number of political truths; but also an equal number of heresies: so that the reader must be constantly on his guard." [7] By September 1810, he had reached the conclusion that "I am glad to hear of everything which reduces that author [Montesquieu] to his just level, as his predilection for monarchy, and the English monarchy in particular, has done mischief everywhere, and here also, to a certain degree." [8] When, in 1809, the French philosopher, Destutt de Tracy, sent Jefferson his "Commentaire sur l'esprit des lois de Montesquieu," he wrote the author, "I cannot express to you the satisfaction which I received from its perusal. I had, with the world, deemed Montesquieu's work of much merit; but saw in it, with every thinking man, so much of paradox, of false principle and misapplied fact, as to render its value equivocal on the whole.... A radical correction of them, therefore, was a great desideratum. This want is now supplied, and with a depth of thought, precision of idea, of language and of logic, which will force conviction into every mind." [9]

That Jefferson's estimate of a work might alter in the course of time, that experience and rumination might lead him to change his opinion, instead of remaining slavishly true to an early impression, is well exemplified in his remarks on Hume's "History of England." He had first acquired the book on March 7, 1764, from the bookshop of the *Virginia Gazette,* and subsequently reordered it after the fire at Shadwell. "I remember well," he was to write William Duane, in 1810, "the enthusiasm with which I devoured it when young, and the length of time, the research and reflection which were necessary to eradicate the poison it had instilled in to my mind." Jefferson might, indeed, have written these very words about Montesquieu, at this time! "It is this book," he continues, "which has undermined the free principles of the English government, has persuaded readers of all classes that these were usurpations on the legitimate and salutary rights of the crown, and has spread universal toryism over the land." [10] This book, he says on another occasion, has "done more towards the suppression of the liberties of man than all the millions of men in arms of Bonaparte.... I fear nothing for our liberty from the assaults of force; but I have seen and felt much, and fear more from English books, English prejudices, English manners." [11]

Among the other books that reached Jefferson in December 1769 were Locke's essays on government. Curiously enough, there is just one extract from them included in the commonplace book: "because a king, *elected by the people,* is one of the branches to whom the people have deputed the power of making laws; and they have never bound themselves to submit to any laws but such as have received the approbation of the Commons, the Lords, and a king so elected, and his being merely a delegated power cannot be deputed to others by the whole delegates, much less by two branches of them only, to wit, the Lords and Commons." [12]

It would seem that Jefferson was already familiar with the English philosopher, otherwise his words would doubtless have been as copiously transcribed as were those of Montesquieu. The "Two Treatises on Government" had been published eighty years before, and Locke's "Works" were to be found on the shelves of every Virginia library of any pretensions. His ideas and principles were already part of the warp and woof of colonial thought. "Locke's little book is perfect as far as it goes," [13] Jefferson was to write, and this opinion was very generally shared not only by his coadjutors in the struggle against England and the shaping of the new nation, but by the majority of the thinking men of the period. It was music to their ears to read in Locke: "to understand political power right, and derive it from its original, we must consider what state all men are naturally in, and that is, a state of perfect freedom, to order their actions and dispose of their possessions and persons, as they think fit, within the bounds of the law of nature; without asking leave, or depending on the will of any other man." [14] The sorely tried colonists, smarting under the injustices they felt the British government had inflicted upon them and plotting alleviation of their woes, found solace as well as confirmation of their stand in the words of the English philosopher: "Revolutions happen not upon every little mismanagement in public affairs. Great mistakes in the ruling part, many wrong and inconvenient laws, and all the slips of human frailty, will be born by the people without mutiny or murmur. But if a long train of abuses, prevarications and artifices, all tending the same way, make the design visible to the people, and they cannot but feel what they lie under, and see whither they are going; it is not to be wondered, that they should then rouse themselves, and endeavor to put the rule in such hands which may secure to them the ends for which government was at first erected." [15]

As we know from the list of books recommended to Robert Skipwith in 1771, Jefferson was also familiar at this period with Algernon Sidney's "Discourses concerning Government," another work upholding the propriety of resistance to oppression by the King and defending the authority of legislative bodies, as well as with Montesquieu's "Rise and Fall of the Roman Empire," a work which has been called the "first important essay in the philosophy of history." A recent book with which Jefferson was likewise acquainted at the time was Marmontel's "Belisaire," a romance published in 1764. What obviously interested him in this was the famous chapter on religious toleration which called down upon the author the censure, not only of the Sorbonne, but of the Archbishop of Paris.

Although we have no record of when Jefferson acquired the works of the great German historian and philosopher, Puffendorf, it is obvious that he was thoroughly familiar with them before April 1770, when he appeared for the plaintiff in the case of Howell *vs.* Netherland and argued that "under the law of nature all men are born free." This, as we have seen, was Jefferson's first public pronunciamento of this theory. Puffendorf occupied the chair of "the law of nature and nations" at the University of Heidelberg, the first professorship of the sort in the world. His bold and independent ideas were of great influence upon subsequent writers, both in Europe and America.

The study of these and similar books in his library, the hours and days and weeks of reflection on them, was to bear fruit in many ways. It was to lead, for one thing, to the stellar rôle Jefferson was to play in the gigantic struggle that culminated in the Declaration of Independence. It was to lead, likewise, to something quite as important and revolutionary within his own Virginia, the revisal of the ancient laws of the new state. How urgent he considered this need, what emphasis he laid upon the principles expounded by these philosophers, and his eagerness to realize them in a practical way were subsequently to be manifested in his leaving Congress. It is clear that his whole program of social reform was conceived about 1770, and that he waited only for a favorable opportunity to put it in effect.

Jefferson was sitting in Congress in Philadelphia during the fateful summer of 1776, as a delegate from Virginia, when he was notified that "our delegation had been renewed for the ensuing year, commencing August 11." He was stunned, for he had indicated that he wished to withdraw. A feeling, perhaps, that he had accomplished his work in Congress—as, indeed, who could doubt! —along with a passionate devotion to a frail and lovely wife, a full ten days' journey distant, drew him back to Virginia. He wrote Edmund Pendleton in July, "I am sorry the situation of my domestic affairs renders it indispensably necessary that I should solicit the substitution of some other person here, in my room. The delicacy of the House will not require me to enter minutely in to the private causes which render this necessary. I trust they will be satisfied. I would not have urged it again, were it not unavoidable. I shall with cheerfulness continue in duty here until the expiration of one year, by which time I hope it will be convenient for my successor to attend." [16]

This same summer Jefferson was elected a member of the new Virginia state legislature to represent Albemarle. "I knew," he writes of this event, "that our legislation, under the regal government, had many very vicious points which urgently required reformation, and I thought I could be of more use in forwarding that." [17] He therefore resigned his seat in congress and set out on September 2 for Albemarle, where he arrived on the ninth. Early October found him back in Williamsburg, ready to take an active part in the session, which opened on the seventh of the month.

When Jefferson states that the laws of Virginia had hitherto had "many vicious points," he is putting the case gently. They were still enveloped in a sort of religious fog which countenanced the most barbarous cruelty—as was indeed true of the laws of the other colonies at that time. Man's inhumanity to man was never more perfectly exemplified than in some of the statutes as they then stood. In the "Notes on Virginia" Jefferson pictures the state of affairs before he introduced his far-reaching reforms. "The first settlers of this country," he says, "were emigrants from England, of the English Church, just at a point of time when it was flushed with complete victory over the religions of all other persuasions. Possessed, as they became, of the powers of making, administering, and executing the laws, they showed equal intolerance in this country with their Presbyterian brethren, who had emigrated to the northern government. The poor Quakers were flying from persecution in England. They cast their eyes on these new countries as asylums of civil and religious freedom; but they found them free only for the reigning set. Several acts of the Virginia assembly of 1659, 1662, and 1693, had made it penal in parents to refuse to have their children baptized; had prohibited the unlawful assembling of Quakers; had made it penal for any master of a vessel to bring a Quaker into the State; had ordered those already here, and such as should come thereafter, to be imprisoned till they should abjure the country; provided a milder punishment for their first and second return, but death for their third; had inhibited all persons from suffering their meetings in or near their houses, entertaining them individually, or disposing of books which supported their tenets." [18]

"At the common law," Jefferson continues, "*heresy* was a capital offense, punishable by burning. Its definition was left to the ecclesiastical judges, before whom the conviction was, till the statute of the 1 El. c. 1 circumscribed it.... By our own act of assembly of 1705, c. 30, if a person brought up in the Christian religion denies the being of a God, of the Trinity, or asserts there are more gods than one, or denies the Christian religion to be true, or the Scriptures to be of divine authority, he is punishable on the first offence by incapacity to hold any office or employment ecclesiastical, civil, or military; on the second by disability to sue, to take any gift or legacy, to be guardian, executor, or administrator, and by three years' imprisonment without bail. A father's right to the custody of his own children being founded in law on his right of guardianship, this being taken away, they may of course be severed from him, and put by the authority of a court into more orthodox hands. This is a summary view of that religious slavery under which a people have been willing to remain, who have lavished their lives and their fortunes for the establishment of their civil freedom." [19]

To a man of Jefferson's advanced ideas such a state of affairs was unendurable. It is small wonder that he felt driven to throw off the shackles of intolerance along with the bondage to England. He forthwith set himself the task of humanizing and liberalizing these archaic conceptions of right and wrong which had become woven into the law. On taking his seat in the House of Delegates he wasted no time in starting the machinery that was to effect the reforms he had so long contemplated. The House was scarcely organized before, with almost breathless haste, he set to work. On October 11 he "moved for leave to bring a bill for the establishment of courts of justice, the organization of which was of importance. I drew the bill; it was approved by the committee, reported and passed after due course." [20] The following day he introduced a bill so revolutionary in character that it was to shatter the very foundations of Virginia society, and win Jefferson more enemies than any other act of his long career. To this day there are many people who have hardly forgiven him what they consider treason to his own class. This bitterly contested bill, "declaring tenants in tail to hold their lands in fee simple," thus permitting lands to be divided among the several children of a landowner, was directed at the abolition of one of the most cherished laws of the Old Dominion. "In earlier times," Jefferson writes in explanation of his championship of this cause, "when lands were to be obtained for little or nothing, some provident individuals procured large grants, and, desirous of founding great families for themselves, settled them on their descendants in fee tail. The transmission of this property from generation to generation, in the same name, raised up a distinct set of families, who, being privileged by law in the perpetuation of their wealth, were thus formed into a Patrician order, distinguished by the splendor and luxury of their establishments. From this order, too, the king habitually selected his counsellors of State; the hope of which distinction devoted the whole corps to the interests and will of the crown. To annul this privilege, and instead of an aristocracy of wealth, of more harm and danger, than benefit, to society, to make an opening for the aristocracy of virtue and talent, which nature has wisely provided for the direction of the interests of society, and scattered with equal hand through all its conditions, was deemed essential to a well-ordered republic." [21]

"To effect it," he goes on, "no violence was necessary, no deprivation of natural right, but rather an enlargement of it by a repeal of the law." [22] This repeal was violently opposed by Edmund Pendleton, a distinguished and able adversary, "one of the most virtuous and benevolent of men, the kindest friend, the most amiable and pleasant of companions, which ensured a favorable reception to whatever came from him." [23] Despite this and despite the fact that he worried his adversary so that "you never knew when you were clear of him, but were harassed by his perseverance, until the patience was worn down of all who had less than himself" [24]—despite all this, the bill became law before the month was out.

But the fiery young reformer had only just started. The reading and thinking he had done in the years since he first sat in the

House of Burgesses had led him far afield from the traditional point of view of the majority of his contemporaries and put him in the vanguard of a new order. "When I left Congress in '76," he tells us, "it was the persuasion that our whole code must be reviewed, adapted to our republican form of government; and, now that we had no negatives of councils, governors, and kings to restrain us from doing right, it should be corrected, in all its parts, with a single eye to reason, and the good of those for whose government it was framed." [25] Jefferson thus presented a bill for the revision of the existing code of law and it was passed on October 26, three days after the final reading of his bill for the abolition of entails. George Wythe, Edmund Pendleton, George Mason, Thomas L. Lee, along with Jefferson, constituted the committee appointed to execute this prodigious undertaking.

On January 13, 1777, the committee met in Fredericksburg, as had been agreed. They discussed whether to "abolish the whole existing system of laws, and prepare a new and complete Institute, or preserve the general system and only modify it to the present state of things. Mr. Pendleton, contrary to his usual disposition in favor of ancient things, was for the former proposition, in which he was joined by Mr. Lee." [26] Wythe, Mason, and Jefferson inclined toward the latter. The work was divided between Wythe, Pendleton, and Jefferson. Mason excused himself on the ground of being no lawyer and Lee resigned. "The common law and statutes to the 4. James I (when our separate legislature was established) were assigned to me; the British statutes from that period to the present day, to Mr. Wythe; and the Virginia laws to Mr. Pendleton. As the law of Descents, and the criminal law fell of course within my portion, I wished the committee to settle the leading principles of these as a guide for me in framing them; and, with respect to the first, I proposed to abolish the law of primogeniture." [27]

Once again Jefferson was in advance of his contemporaries, once more he had designs upon a time-honored institution. Pendleton opposed him but, as Jefferson says, "seeing at once that he could not prevail, he proposed we should adopt the Hebrew principle, and give a double portion to the elder son." Jefferson's further comments on this are one of the rather rare occasions in which he descends from the Olympian heights he was likely to inhabit and gives way to his sense of humor. "I observed, that if the eldest son could eat twice as much, or do double work, it might be a natural evidence of his right to a double portion; but being on a par in his powers and wants, with his brothers and sisters, he should be on a par also in the partition of the patrimony; and such was the decision of the other members." [28]

The guiding principles of this great task being determined, the three men returned to their homes and set to work. "In the execution of my part," Jefferson writes, "I thought it material not to vary the diction of the ancient statutes by modernizing it, nor to give rise to new questions by new expressions." However, he thought it admissible "in all new draughts, to reform the style of the later British statutes, and that of our own acts of assembly, which from their verbosity, their endless tautologies, their inventions of case within case, and parenthesis within parenthesis ... are really rendered more perplexed and incomprehensible not only to common readers, but to the lawyers themselves." [29]

In February 1779, Wythe, Pendleton, and Jefferson met again, in Williamsburg, to examine "critically our several parts, sentence by sentence, scrutinizing and amending, until we had agreed on the whole." [30] When they came to Pendleton's part they found that he had "not exactly seized the intentions of the committee, which were to reform the language of the Virginia laws, and reduce the matter to a simple style and form. He had copied the acts verbatim." [31] Jefferson and Wythe then undertook the task of making Pendleton's part "what we thought it ought to be ... and reexecuted it entirely so as to assimilate its plan and execution to the other parts."

On June 18, Wythe and Jefferson, with Pendleton detained in Caroline County, but concurring, reported to the General Assembly. "We had, in this work," says Jefferson, "brought so much of the common law as it was thought necessary to alter, all the British Statutes from the Magna Charta to the present day, and all the laws of Virginia, from the establishment of our legislature ... to the present time, which we thought should be retained, within the compass of one hundred and twenty-six bills, making a printed folio of ninety pages only." [32]

The response to these labors was not to be immediate. "Some bills were taken out occasionally, from time to time, and passed, but the main body of the work was not entered on by the legislature until after the general peace, in 1785, when by the unwearied exertion of Mr. Madison, in opposition to the endless quibbles, chicaneries, perversions, vexations and delays of lawyers and demi-lawyers, most of the bills were passed by the legislature, with little alteration." [33]

During this memorable period that he sat in the Virginia legislature Jefferson, who had been placed on most of the important committees of the House, was to father other bills destined to shock the complacency of the conservatives. One was for moving the ancient seat of government from Williamsburg to Richmond, at the falls of the James, at this time no more than a village with a population of about six hundred persons. Jefferson felt that, owing to the western migration, the center of population had shifted and Williamsburg was no longer a suitable place for the Capital. Furthermore its situation was so exposed "that it might be taken at any time in war, and at this time particularly, an enemy might in the night run up either of the rivers, between which it lies, land a force above, and take possession of the place, without the possibility of saving either persons or things." [34]

On the same day, October 14, Jefferson was to introduce a bill for the naturalization of foreigners. Citizenship might be conferred after a residence of two years within the state and assurances, before the court, of "fidelity to the commonwealth." When we consider that even today a person without three or four generations of Virginia-born ancestors is considered "a foreigner," we realize how revolutionary was Jefferson's proposal of 1776.

Another undertaking of greatest importance was to be the bill for the reformation of the educational system of the state. Jefferson was asked to undertake this. He "prepared three bills for the Revisal, proposing three distinct grades of education reaching all classes. 1st, Elementary schools, for all children generally, rich and poor. 2d. Colleges, for a middle degree of instruction, calculated for the common purposes of life. . . . And, 3d, an ultimate grade for teaching the sciences generally, in their highest degree." [35] Not one of these was adopted. When it was discovered that "the expenses of these schools should be borne by the inhabitants of the county, everyone in proportion to his general tax rate," it was realized that the wealthy would be educating the poor, and nothing more unpalatable could have been imagined.

The question of slavery, which had long haunted Jefferson and over which, for years, the House of Burgesses had, from time to time, shown distress and concern, was one of the great problems the revisors had to face. The bill on this subject, Jefferson writes, "was a mere digest of the existing laws concerning them." [36] No one was as yet prepared to follow him in his ideas for the emancipation of the Negro and subsequent deportation "peaceably, and in such slow degree, as that the evil will wear off insensibly." With the words of a prophet, the far-seeing Jefferson added, "nothing is more certainly written in the book of fate, than that these people are to be free; nor is it less certain that the two races, equally free, cannot live in the same government." [37]

Many years later, utterly disillusioned by the failure to recognize the existence of the problem, much less remedy it, Jefferson expressed himself more fully. "The love of justice and the love of country plead equally the cause of these people, and it is a moral reproach to us that they should have pleaded it so long in vain, and should have produced not a single effort, nay I fear not much serious willingness to relieve them and ourselves from our present condition of moral and political reprobation. From those of the former generation who were in the fulness of age when I came into public life . . . I soon saw nothing was to be hoped. Nursed and educated in the daily habit of seeing the degraded condition, both bodily and mental, of these unfortunate beings, not reflecting that that degradation was very much the work of themselves and their fathers, few minds have yet doubted but that they were as legitimate subjects of property as their horses and cattle. The quiet and monotonous course of colonial life has been disturbed by no alarm, and little reflection on the value of liberty. And when alarm was taken at an enterprize on their own, it was not easy to carry them the whole length of the principles which they invoked for themselves.... From an early stage of our revolution ... till I returned to reside at home in 1809, I had little opportunity of knowing the progress of public sentiment here on this subject ... yet the hour of emancipation is advancing, in the march of time. It will come; and whether brought on by the generous energy of our own minds; or by the bloody pressure of St. Domingo ... is a leaf of our history not yet turned over.... My opinion has ever been that until more can be done for them, we should endeavor, with those whom fortune has thrown on our hands, to feed and clothe them well, protect them from ill usage, require such reasonable labor only as is performed voluntarily by freemen, and be led by no repugnancies to abdicate them and our duties to them. The laws do not permit us to turn them loose, if that were for their good; and to commute them for other property is to commit them to those whose usage of them we cannot control." [38]

Revision of the laws concerning crimes and punishments lay in Jefferson's particular sphere as a revisor. In this undertaking, he is free to say in his "Autobiography" that he leaned on the Italian jurist, Beccaria. His famous treatise, "Dei Delitti e delle Pene," had been published in 1764, translated into French in 1766, and into English in 1768, under the title "On Crimes and Punishments." It would seem as though Jefferson must have acquired the book at about the time he did Montesquieu, for no less than 26 extracts from Beccaria, in Italian, follow directly those from Montesquieu in Jefferson's commonplace book, and in the handwriting of the same period. Beccaria was enormously influential in Europe—the reformation of the penal code of most European countries is due to his work. Jefferson had, of course, absorbed Beccaria's ideas, along with those of many other writers, by the time he started to prepare his "Bill for proportioning crimes and punishments in cases heretofore capital." By November 1778, he had completed his work, elaborately annotated with extracts from the Anglo-Saxon laws, and sent the draft to George Wythe for comment and criticism. "In its style," Jefferson wrote, "I have aimed at accuracy, brevity and simplicity, preserving, however, the very words of the established law, wherever their meaning had been sanctioned by judicial decisions, or rendered technical by usage.... I have thought it better to drop, in silence, the laws we mean to discontinue and let them be swept away by the general negative words of this.... I have strictly observed the scale of punishments settled by the committee, without being entirely satisfied with it. The *Lex talonis*, although a restitution of the common law, to the simplicity of which we have generally found it so advantageous to return, will be revolting to the humanized feelings of modern times. An eye for an eye, and a hand for a hand, will exhibit spectacles in execution whose moral effect would be questionable; and even the *membrum pro membro* of Bracton, or the punishment of the offending member, although long authorized by our law, for the same offence in a slave has, you know, been not long since repealed in conformity with public sentiment." [39]

The "unrightfulness and inefficiency of the punishment of crimes by death," had satisfied the revisors, and this penalty was abolished for all crimes except murder and treason. "Hard labor on roads, canals, and other public works" was to be the punishment for other felonies, although in some cases retaliation in kind was to be resorted to, something in which Jefferson did not concur. He was equally opposed to making prisoners "a public spectacle, with shaved heads and mean clothing," and sought for years to introduce the more humane practice of labor in solitary confinement. Indeed, the plan for a prison which he sent to Virginia from France in 1785 embodied this very revolutionary idea. The country, however, was not yet ready for such mitigation of the barbarous and inhuman treatment of the criminal. Once more Jefferson was to be in advance of the times. The bill was not to be introduced into the House until 1785, when it failed by one vote, and it was not until 1796, eighteen years after Jefferson had drafted it, that, in a modified form, "avoiding the adoption of any part of the diction of mine," it was to become law.

The bill which lay closest to Jefferson's heart, indeed which he regarded as one of the greatest achievements of his life, so much so that he wished it inscribed upon his tombstone, was the one that came to be known as the "Statute of Virginia for Religious Freedom." When he returned to the House of Delegates he had been placed on the standing committee for religion. The committee was, of course, predominantly Anglican, but Jefferson, although belonging to that church, led a small yet determined minority in a struggle to rectify some of the abuses. In the "Notes on Virginia," he says, "the Anglicans retained full possession of the country about a century. Other opinions began to creep in, and the great care of the government to support their own church, having begotten an equal degree of indolence in its clergy, two thirds of the people had become dissenters at the commencement of the present revolution." [40] The unfortunate and illegal situation of these dissenting bodies demanded redress. This first meeting of the new legislature was "crowded with petitions to abolish this spiritual tyranny."

The ensuing struggle proved the most severe in which Jefferson had ever engaged, according to his own words. Edmund Pendleton and Robert Carter Nicholas, zealous churchmen, led the opposition. After some weeks, with the aid of a few of the more enlightened members of the House, the minority was able to obtain "feeble majorities" on certain points. They managed to secure the repeal of "the laws which rendered criminal the maintenance of any religious opinions, the forbearance of repairing to church, or the exercise of any mode of worship; and further, to exempt dissenters from contributing to the support of the established church, and to suspend, only until the next session levies on the members of the church for the salaries of their own incumbents." [41]

This, of course, Jefferson could regard only as a palliative, not as a solution. He could be satisfied with nothing short of true toleration, which to him meant absolute freedom of conscience, unhampered by religious bias or considerations of state. "The error seems not to be sufficiently eradicated," he writes in the "Notes on Virginia," "that the operations of the mind, as well as the acts of the body, are subject to the coercion of laws. But our rulers can have no authority over such natural rights, only as we have submitted to them. The rights of conscience we have never submitted; we could not submit. We are answerable only to our

God. The legitimate powers of government extend to such acts only as are injurious to others, but it does me no injury for my neighbor to say there are twenty gods, or no god. . . . Reason and free inquiry are the only effectual agents against error. Give a loose to them, they will support the true religion by bringing every false one to their tribunal, to the test of their investigation. They are the natural enemies of error, and of error only." [42]

With such toleration in his heart, "well aware that the opinions and belief of men depend not on their own will, but follow involuntarily the evidence proposed to their minds; that Almighty God hath created the mind free, and manifested His supreme will that free it shall remain by making it altogether insusceptible of restraint," [43] Jefferson was to set to work on his "Bill for Establishing Religious Freedom." He says of it, in his "Autobiography," that it was drawn "in all the latitude of reason and right," but although, or perhaps because, it meant "to comprehend, within the mantle of its protection, the Jew, the Gentile, the Christian and Mohammedan, the Hindoo, and Infidel of every denomination," [44] it was to meet with such violent opposition in the Assembly that it was not written in the statute books until ten years later, when Jefferson had long since gone across the seas as Minister to France.

"I considered four of these bills," Jefferson observes in evaluating this work, "passed or reported, as forming a system by which every fibre would be eradicated of ancient or future aristocracy; and a foundation laid for a government truly republican. The repeal of the laws of entail would prevent the accumulation and perpetuation of wealth, in select families. . . . The abolition of primogeniture, and equal partition of inheritances, removed the feudal and unnatural distinctions which made one member of every family rich, and all the rest poor. . . . The restoration of the rights of conscience relieved the people from taxation for the support of a religion not theirs; for the establishment was truly of the religion of the rich, the dissenting sects being entirely composed of the less wealthy people; and these, by a bill for a general education, would be qualified to understand their rights, to maintain them, and to exercise with intelligence their parts in any government; and all this would be effected without free violation of a single natural right of any one individual citizen." [45]

Great as we know his services to have been, Jefferson was not to take credit for effecting these reforms single-handed. In paying tribute to his fellow workers, in his "Autobiography," he modestly observes of his own part that "in giving this account of the laws of which I was myself the mover and draughtsman, I, by no means, mean to claim to myself the merit of obtaining their passage. I had many occasional and strenuous coadjutors in debate, and one, most steadfast, able and zealous; who was himself a host. This was George Mason, a man of the first order of wisdom among those who acted in the theatre of the revolution, of expansive mind, profound judgment, cogent in argument, learned in the lore of our former constitution, and earnest for the republican change on democratic principles.... Mr. Wythe, while speaker in the two sessions of 1777, between his return to Congress and his appointment to the Chancery, was an able and constant associate in whatever was before a committee of the whole. His pure integrity, judgment and reasoning powers, gave him great weight." [46]

To this task, so stupendous that it was to have repercussions throughout the United States of America, Jefferson was to bring a boldness of conception, a maturity of thought, and an elevation of spirit that set him apart from all his fellow legislators, not excluding even George Wythe. It was as though he had already said to himself, as he was to write many years later, "I have sworn upon the altar of God eternal hostility against every form of tyranny over the mind of man." [47] With this in his heart he set to work to bestow upon man, as has been remarked, the four great freedoms—the like of which had never been known. By destroying the last remnants of feudalism, the laws of entail and primogeniture, he gave man the freedom of the land; by advocating the abolition of slavery, the freedom of the body; by fostering universal education, freedom of the mind; and by the statute for religious freedom he conferred upon man the supreme boon, freedom of the soul.

XII. The Rights of British America

FROM 1770-1773 THERE was a lull in the series of crises that had shaken the colony of Virginia in the past dozen years and that was destined to be resumed. Jefferson dutifully fulfilled his functions as a burgess in this period, except, as we have seen, during his protracted honeymoon. He served, as usual, on various committees, and his facile pen was frequently called on to draw up an address or a bill. He says of these years in his "Autobiography," "nothing of particular excitement occurring for a considerable time, our countrymen seemed to fall into a state of insensibility to our situation."[1] Another association had been formed, to be sure, in June 1770, by certain burgesses and many of the leading Williamsburg merchants. They agreed not to import various foodstuffs, spirits, oil, paint, and many manufactured articles after the first of the next September. Committees of five men were elected in each county to see that the provisions of the association were carried out. Nevertheless it languished, and by the following June we find Jefferson writing his correspondent in London, to whom he had sent an order the preceding summer, "as it was somewhat doubtful when you left the country how far my little invoice delivered you might be complied with till we should know the fate of the association, I desired you to withhold purchasing the things till you should hear farther from me. The day appointed for the meeting of the associates is not yet arrived; however from the universal sense of those who are likely to attend, it seems reduced to a certainty that the restrictions will be taken off everything but the dutied articles."[2]

Lord Botetourt had died suddenly on October 15, 1770, and William Nelson of Yorktown acted as Governor of the colony until the arrival of Lord Dunmore on September 25, 1771. The latter was received with the usual honors and apparent jubilation, but, from the first, he was a thoroughly unpopular figure. Even before his arrival Richard Bland had written Thomas Adams, in London, "We know nothing as yet of our new Governor's coming amongst us. We entertain a very disadvantageous opinion of him from the accounts brought us from New York." He then relates at great length that a Mr. Wood, a member of the Assembly from Frederick County, who had recently been north, told how Lord Dunmore, "with a set of drunken companions sallied from the Palace" and attacked Chief Justice Horsemanden's coach and horses. The coach was destroyed and the poor animals lost their tails. The Chief Justice applied for redress and a reward of £200 was offered for the discovery of the culprit. "We have not heard whether the Governor demanded the reward," Bland concludes.[3]

Edmund Randolph says of Dunmore that "he generally preferred the crooked path, possessed not the genius to conceive, nor temper to seek the plain and direct way.... A governor, who could withstand a popular current must possess more than ordinary qualifications. But of those which shed a beam of false lustre, and certainly those of an exalted kind, Dunmore was wholly destitute. In stature he was low; and though muscular and healthful he bore on his head hoary symptoms of probably greater age, than he had reached. To external accomplishments he pretended not; and his manners and sentiments did not surpass substantial barbarism; barbarism, which was not palliated by a particle of native genius, nor regulated by one ingredient of religion. His propensities were coarse and depraved. But," Randolph adds with engaging candor, "it must be confessed that probably no British Viceregent, not Botetourt himself, had he been on earth, could have gained ten revolters from their country's cause."[4]

Neither in his letters nor in his reminiscences has Jefferson indicated that he was on the same terms with Botetourt or Dunmore that he was with Fauquier, or that he came in contact with them in anything more than the most superficial way. There is, however, one extant document which shows not only that Jefferson's abilities as an architect were recognized by the early seventeen-seventies, but that Dunmore consulted him on the subject. This is a drawing endorsed in Jefferson's hand "Plan for an addition to the College of William and Mary, drawn at the request of Ld. Dunmore." The old college had been U-shaped, its two rear wings toward the west, containing the chapel and hall, being connected by an arcade. Jefferson's plan doubled this U to form a closed interior court, reached by four vestibules at the cardinal points, and extended the arcade around the court. He thus created a scheme like that of the Italian palaces, as he may have seen them in Palladio.[5] It was a brilliant and monumental solution of the problem, wholly novel in the colonies.

The Assembly was scheduled to meet in May 1773. In January of that year the treasurer of the colony, Robert Carter Nicholas, had received several spurious notes for redemption. It developed that wholesale forgeries of a very deceptive character had been committed and the soundness of Virginia currency was threatened. Dunmore summoned the Assembly to meet on March 4 in order that "they might fall upon such measures as they thought best for reestablishing its credit."[6] The burgesses attended to the matter with great dispatch, then turned to something they had much more at heart—further action for the defense of colonial liberty. Two recent incidents had once more prodded them into action: the burning of the schooner "Gaspee" in Narragansett Bay in June 1772, and the establishment of a special court of inquiry in Rhode Island empowered to send colonists to England for trial.

This was something the independent burgesses of Virginia could not tolerate. What happened in New England might happen to them. They immediately took affairs in hand. "Not thinking our old and leading members up to the point of forwardness and zeal which the times required," Jefferson writes, "Mr. Henry, Richard Henry Lee, Francis L. Lee, Mr. Carr and myself agreed to meet in the evening, in a private room of the Raleigh, to consult on the state of things." They met to good purpose. "We were all sensible," he continues, "that the most urgent of all measures was that of coming to an understanding with all the other colonies, to consider the British claims as a common cause to all, and to produce a unity of action." [7] A committee of correspondence to communicate with the other colonies was proposed, and the assembled men drew up a set of resolves which were to be offered to the burgesses on the following day. The feeling in Williamsburg was tense on the morning of March 12 when the representatives of the people took their seats. Students of William and Mary had learned what was going on and crowded the Capitol. St. George Tucker, who was present, has left a description of some of the actors in the scene. Patrick Henry, upon whom all eyes centered, "wore a peach blossom colored coat, and a dark wig, which tied behind, and I believe a bag to it, as was the fashion of the day. When pointed out to me as the orator of the Assembly I looked at him with no great prepossession. On the opposite side of the house sat the graceful Pendleton and the harmonious Richard Henry Lee, whose aquiline nose and Roman profile struck me much more forcibly than that of Mr. Henry, his rival in eloquence." [8]

It was neither of these gentlemen, however, who was to occupy the center of the stage, but a new and unknown member from the county of Louisa, which had already contributed one brilliant member to the House of Burgesses. After patiently transacting such routine business as voting an addition to the house of the public jailer and the appointing of new ferries, the house resolved itself into a Committee of the Whole House to consider the state of the colony. Jefferson had been urged to move the resolutions but had declined in favor of Dabney Carr, "my friend and brother-in-law, then a new member, to whom I wished an opportunity should be given of making known to the House his great worth and talents." [9] This he did "with great ability, reconciling all to it, not only by the reasonings, but by the temper and moderation with which it was developed." [10] Carr is described as having "a person at once dignified and engaging, and the manner and action of an accomplished gentleman.... His education was a finished one.... His voice was finely toned, his feelings acute, his style free, and rich and various; his devotion to the cause of liberty, verging on enthusiasm; and his spirit firm and undaunted, beyond the possibility of being shaken." [11] This engag-

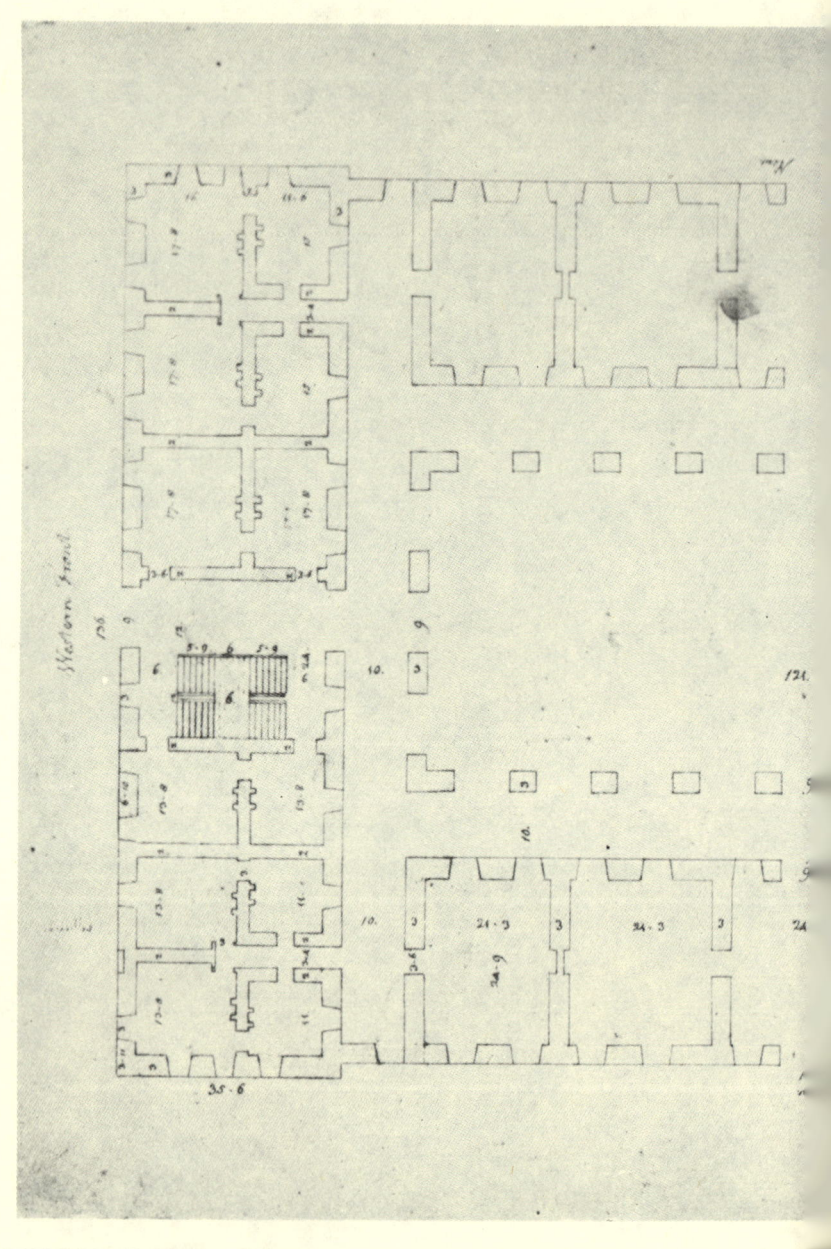

JEFFERSON'S PLAN FOR THE ENLARGEMENT OF WILLIAM AND MA[RY]

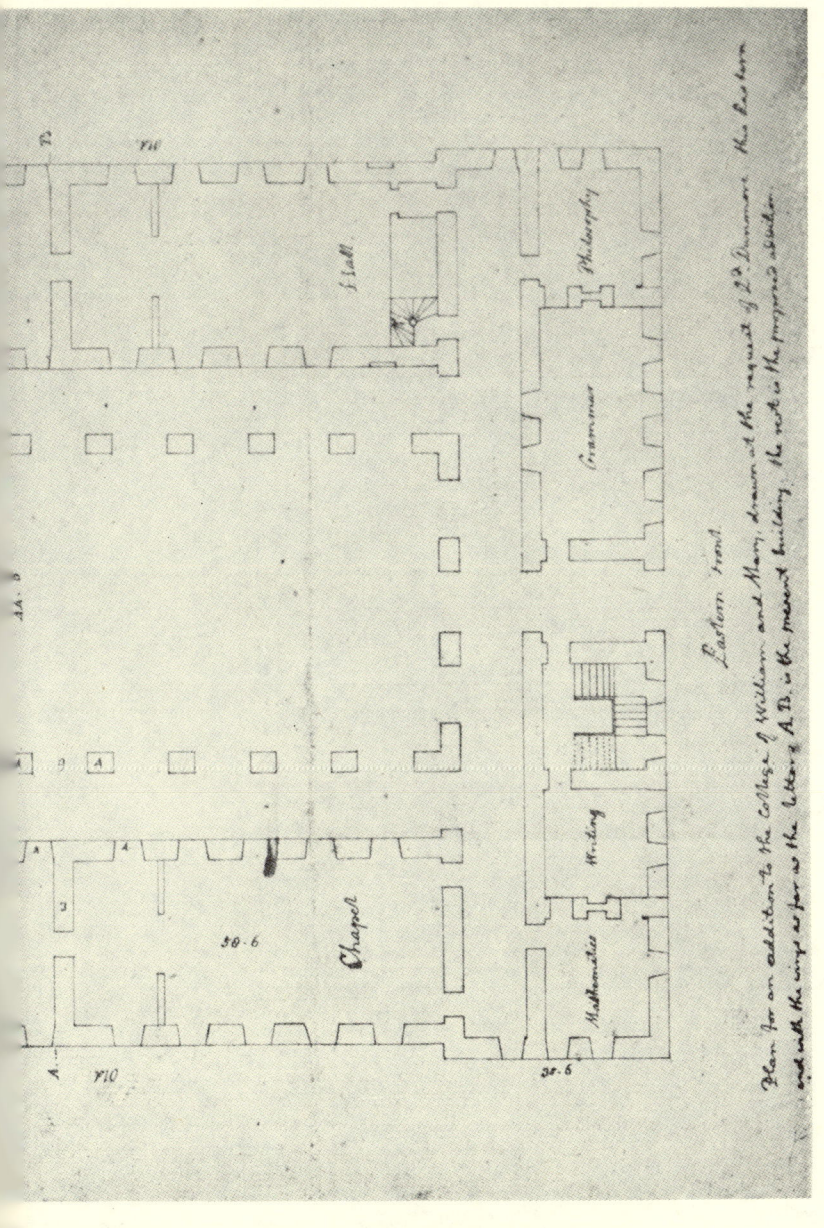

OLLEGE. (*Courtesy of the Henry E. Huntington Library*)

ing young man, upon whom every eye was fixed, rose to his feet and offered the resolutions that will always be connected with his name.

"Whereas," he began, "the minds of his Majesty's faithful subjects in this colony have been much disturbed, by various rumours and reports of proceedings tending to deprive them of their ancient, legal, and constitutional rights,
"And whereas, the affairs of this colony are frequently connected with those of Great Britain, as well as of the neighboring colonies, which renders a communication of sentiments necessary; in order, therefore, to remove the uneasiness, and to quiet the minds of the people, as well as for the other good purposes above mentioned,
"Be it resolved, that a standing committee of correspondence and inquiry be appointed, to consist of eleven persons, to wit, the Honourable Peyton Randolph, Esquire, Robert Carter Nicholas, Richard Bland, Richard H. Lee, Benjamin Harrison, Edmund Pendleton, Patrick Henry, Dudley Digges, Dabney Carr, Archibald Cary, and Thomas Jefferson, Esquire, any six of whom to be a committee, whose business it shall be to obtain the most early and authentic intelligence of all such acts and resolutions of the British Parliament, or proceedings of administration, as may relate to or affect the British Colonies in America, and to keep up and maintain a correspondence and communication with our sister colonies, respecting these important considerations; and the result of such proceedings, from time to time, to lay before this house." [12]

The committee was further instructed to inform themselves on what authority the special court of inquiry in Rhode Island was formed "with powers to transport persons accused of offences committed in America, to places beyond the seas, to be tried." Finally, the Speaker of the House was directed to send copies of the resolutions to "the Speakers of the different Assemblies of the British colonies on the continent ... and request them to appoint some person or persons of their respective bodies, to communicate from time to time, with the said committee." [13] Nine members of the committee met on the next day and duly composed a circular letter which was sent as directed, along with a copy of the resolutions. A select corresponding committee, to which Peyton Randolph, Nicholas, and Digges were named, was given power to call meetings of the whole committee whenever an occasion arose which demanded prompt action. It was likewise to carry out the instructions of the resolves in regard to the other colonies and to secure the acts of Parliament.

The Governor did not immediately dissolve the Assembly, as might have been expected. He took occasion to send the burgesses an ungracious message on another matter; then, after a session of only 11 days, in which he claimed they had attended to all necessary business, he prorogued them until June 17. He made no comment at all upon the unprecedented and revolutionary steps they had taken, but dismissed them with a sanctimonious observation. "I recommend to you," he adjured them, "to use your endeavours, in the several counties, to abolish that spirit of gaming which I am afraid but too generally prevails among the people, and to substitute in its place a love of agriculture and attention to their private affairs, by which you will render a most essential service to them and to your county." [14]

The burgesses returned home and did not meet again for over a year. Dunmore repeatedly prorogued the Assembly until May 5, 1774, when a session could no longer be postponed. The meeting that then took place was to exceed in importance and in high feeling even the thrilling sessions attending the repeal of the Stamp Act, eight years before. On the day set the burgesses gathered in Williamsburg, but, as their number was less than fifty, they adjourned until the following day. In his address, the Governor made no reference to any unusual circumstances, merely observing that they had been called together to transact the regular business of the colony which he hoped would be promptly dispatched, and that he trusted their deliberations might be influenced by "prudence and moderation." They proceeded with the business in hand. The recently imposed tea tax was of course in everyone's thoughts and mind, but it was hoped to postpone action on it for the time being. Suddenly, in the midst of their deliberations, came the news of the Boston Port Bill. The port was to be closed to all commerce on June 1, only a few days later, in reprisal for the famous "tea party" of the preceding December, when 340 chests of tea had been dumped into the harbor during a popular uprising against paying a three-penny tax at the port of entry.

The Virginians, with whom love of liberty was spiced with the spirit of rebellion, were aflame at this news. The younger and more radical of the burgesses, led by Jefferson, Patrick Henry, Richard Henry Lee, and a few others, seized the leadership, "agreeing," as Jefferson says, "that we must boldly take an unequivocal stand in the line with Massachusetts. . . . We were under conviction of the necessity of arousing our people from the lethargy into which they had fallen, as to passing events." [15] Jefferson makes no reference to the very real sacrifice the Virginians were making in considering the cause of Massachusetts their own. In their zeal, and in their conviction that they were the protagonists of a just cause, one that was of supreme importance for the future of the colonies, he and his associates seem willingly to have acquiesced in the idea that their actions not only might mean the destruction of Virginia's trade, but might very well bring down on them punishment similar to that which had been visited on other unruly colonies.

The burgesses now took a most unusual step. They decided on a day of fast and prayer. Edmund Randolph credits Jefferson and Charles Lee with originating the idea, "to electrify the people from the pulpit." "No example of such a solemnity had existed since the day of our distresses in the war of '55," Jefferson writes.[16] On Tuesday, May 24, Robert Carter Nicholas, the chairman of the committee on religion and one of the most conservative of the burgesses, "whose grave and religious character was more in unison with the tone of our resolution," presented the resolve, which was immediately adopted, and printed in the *Virginia Gazette* on the twenty-sixth. "This house, being deeply impressed with apprehension of the great dangers to be derived to British America from the hostile invasion of the city of Boston," the resolution reads, "in our sister colony of Massachusetts Bay, whose commerce and harbours are, on the first day of June next to be stopped by an armed force, deem it highly necessary that the said first day of June be set apart, by members of this house, as a day of fasting, humiliation and prayer, devoutly to implore the divine interposition for averting the heavy calamity which threatens destruction of our civil rights, and the evils of civil war: to give us one heart and one mind firmly to oppose, by all just and proper means, every injury to American Rights, and that the minds of his Majesty and his Parliament, be inspired from above with wisdom, moderation and justice, to remove from the loyal people of America all cause of danger from a continued pursuit of measures pregnant to their ruin." [17]

The burgesses were instructed to meet at ten o'clock in the morning of June 1 and "to proceed with the Speaker and the Mace, to the church in this city, for the purpose aforesaid," where services were to be held. "The style, in which the fast was recommended was too bold to be neglected by the governor, as an effusion, which would evaporate on paper," Randolph tells us. When Dunmore saw the news in the *Gazette*, he at once called the burgesses to the council chamber and addressed them. "I have in my hand a paper," he observed, "published by order of your House, conceived in such terms as reflect highly upon his Majesty and the Parliament of Great Britain, which makes it necessary for me to dissolve you, and you are dissolved accordingly." [18]

Undaunted, the burgesses retired once more to the Raleigh Tavern. In the Apollo room, where a decade before Jefferson and the impish Rebecca had danced so gaily, another association was formed, much more severe in its absolute restriction on exportation and importation. At the same time the committee of correspondence was instructed to "propose to the corresponding committees of the other colonies, to appoint deputies to meet in Congress at such place, annually, as should be convenient, to direct, from time to time, the measures required by the general interest; and," Jefferson adds, "we declared that an attack on any one colony, should be considered as an attack on the whole." [19] The meeting of this congress, to be known as the Continental Congress, was set for September 5, 1774, in Philadelphia. Not content with this, "we further recommended to the several counties to elect deputies to meet at Williamsburg, the 1st of August ensuing, to consider the state of the colony, and particularly to appoint delegates to a general congress." [20]

Midsummer found the freeholders of every county "assembled in their collective body, at the Court House of said county" and as Jefferson observed, "re-electing every man of the former assembly as a proof of their approbation of what they had done." [21] On July 26 the electors of Albemarle met and appointed "Thomas Jefferson and John Walker our Deputies to act for this County at said convention, and we instruct them to conform themselves to these our Resolutions and Opinion." [22] The Albemarle resolutions minced no words. So fearless and advanced a stand was adopted that it was plain to everyone who was responsible. They resolved, first of all, that "the inhabitants of the several States of British America are subject to the laws which they adopted at their first settlement, and to such others as have been since made by their respective Legislatures ... that no other Legislature whatever can rightly exercise authority over them; and that these privileges they hold as the common rights of mankind." They proceeded to speak of "these their natural and legal rights" which have "in frequent instances been invaded by the Parliament of Great Britain" and mentioned especially the "act lately passed to take away the trade of the inhabitants of the town of Boston, in the province of Massachusetts Bay" as an assumption of unlawful power "dangerous to the rights of the British Empire in general" and one which they consider a common cause. They pledged themselves ready to join with their fellow subjects "in executing all those rightful powers which God has given us, for the re-establishment and guaranteeing such their constitutional rights, when, where, and by whom invaded." [23]

Thereupon they stated that "the most eligible means of effecting these purposes, will be to put an immediate stop to all imports from Great Britain." All exports to England were likewise to be stopped on October 1, 1775, and all commercial intercourse was immediately to be discontinued with "every part of the British Empire which shall not in like manner break off commerce with Great Britain." They furthermore agreed immediately to cease importing "all commodities from every port in the world which are subject by British Parliament to payment of duties in America."[24]

With these stringent instructions in hand, Jefferson and Walker prepared to set off for the convention. Jefferson, however, was destined not to reach Williamsburg. He seems to have left Monticello late on the twenty-ninth or on the thirtieth, for on the former date he notes sending Jupiter, a servant, to Holliday of Williamsburg to buy paint, and sums up various little debts which are to be settled. From then until the middle of August his account book is completely silent. As he and Walker rode through the woods that covered the first part of their way, Jefferson was taken violently ill with an attack of dysentery. He had only strength enough to ride home, where he spent several weeks in bed and, subsequently, recuperating. Although he may not have been there in the flesh, he was very much present in the amazing document he dispatched as his spiritual ambassador.

Peyton Randolph was elected to preside over the convention, which essentially took over the activities, if not the legal functions, of the ancient House of Burgesses. The terms of the association were made much more strict—it was agreed not to import any more British goods or slaves after November 1 of the current year and, what must have been very difficult, not to export any tobacco after August 10, 1775—and the penalties for violation were severe indeed. Carrying out its further function, the convention elected delegates to the congress which the other colonies had concurred in holding in Philadelphia the first Monday of the next month. They were Peyton Randolph, Richard Henry Lee, George Washington, Patrick Henry, Richard Bland, Benjamin Harrison, and Edmund Pendleton. "Some of the tickets on the ballot," says Edmund Randolph, "assigned reasons for the choice expressed in them. These were, that Randolph should preside in congress; that Lee and Henry should display the different kinds of eloquence, for which they were renowned, that Washington should command the army, if an army should be raised; that Bland should open the treasures of ancient colonial learning; that Harrison should utter plain truths, and that Pendleton should be the

THE RIGHTS OF BRITISH AMERICA 239

penman for business. Perhaps characters were never better discriminated." [25]

During the weeks preceding the Williamsburg convention Jefferson had not been idle; indeed he was engaged on a work of so astonishing a nature and so revolutionary a character as to startle the civilized world. In the few letters remaining from this period we find little clue as to what was going on in his mind. Neither do we in the account books, which often reflect many hidden thoughts and ideas. For all they tell us, he was leading the life of a country gentleman, deep in the problems of his farms. Work on the house at Monticello was being pushed forward as rapidly as possible. A second baby was expected in April, which proved to be another little daughter, instead of the much-desired son. Life had not been all smiles, however. On February 21, about two o'clock in the afternoon, the family and servants were startled to feel the "shock of an earthquake at Monticello. It shook the houses so sensibly that everybody ran out of doors." [26] The following day, at almost the same hour, another earthquake caused the mountain to tremble, and it was some time before the hands could be quieted and induced to go back to work. Meanwhile Jefferson's sister, Elizabeth, a year and a half younger than he and somewhat deficient in intellect, had wandered away from home—whether terrified by the earthquake, or for some other reason, we do not know. Her body was found on the twenty-fourth and the funeral, amazingly enough, was not held until March 7, when Jefferson notes selling Mr. Clay, the preacher, his two old bookcases for £5 "of which credit him forty shillings for performing the funeral service this day on burying my sister Elizabeth & 40/ more for preaching Mr. Carr's funeral sermon, which last sum charge to D. Carr's estate. ye other 20/ is a gratuity." [27] The day before the funeral there had been a flood, the Rivanna had risen to "the highest ever known except the great flood of May, 1771." It is small wonder that the little family on the mountaintop felt it had come upon dire days.

By the middle of April 1774, Jefferson had been in the Tidewater—he notes paying small sums to the smith at Tuckahoe, the coffeehouse, the barber, borrowing a little money from Mr. Mazzei, who had not long since arrived, and buying a trifle from Craig, the jeweler. He makes no mention of having been present at the opening of the Assembly on May 5, or of any of the stirring events in which he took part. On May 26 he merely observes: "the assembly dissolved this day. pd. towards a ball for Lady Dunmore 20/." The first two weeks of June seem to have been spent in traveling about. He paid ferriage at Westover, at York, at Gloucester, at Colonel Bland's, went to Eppington, and, finally, the last of the month, reached home.

Although it was not until July 26 that Jefferson was chosen one of the delegates to the Williamsburg convention, he knew that his election was inevitable, and there can be no question that he spent the time from the dissolution of the Assembly to the end of the month in preparing what he calls "a draught of instructions to be given to the delegates whom we should send to the congress in Philadelphia." "They were drawn in haste," he modestly observes, "with a number of blanks, with some uncertainties and inaccuracies of historical facts, which I neglected at the moment, knowing they could readily be corrected at the meeting." [28] Jefferson made two copies of the instructions or resolutions. One was sent to Patrick Henry, whose golden voice was sure to be raised in behalf of the colonies. Henry either lost this or, as Jefferson says, was too lazy to read it and cast it aside. The second was dispatched to Peyton Randolph, who seemed certain to be in the chair; it was laid on the table and considered by the members. "I distinctly recollect the applause bestowed on most of them [the resolutions]" Edmund Randolph writes, "when they were read to a large company at the house of Peyton Randolph, to whom they were addressed.... The young ascended with Mr. Jefferson to the source of these rights; the old required time for consideration, before they could tread this lofty ground.... When the time of writing is remembered, a range of inquiry then not very frequent, and marching far beyond the politicks of the day, will surely be allowed them." [29] The conservatives prevailed. "Tamer sentiments were preferred and, I believe, wisely preferred," the author remarks, "the leap I proposed being too long, as yet for the mass of our citizens." [30] As Edmund Randolph truly observed, Jefferson was wont "to run before the times in which he lived."

This pronouncement, known as "A Summary View of the Rights of British America," although not ordered published by the convention, was promptly printed in Williamsburg by subscription by "several of the author's admirers," and very shortly afterward in London. It did not bear Jefferson's name, although everyone knew who had written it, but was said to be "By a Native and Member of the House of Burgesses." On the title page was an inscription from Cicero: "It is the insuperable duty of the supreme magistrate to consider himself as acting for the whole community, and obliged to support its dignity, and assign to the people, with justice, their various rights, as he would be faithful to the great trust reposed in him." In speaking of the views expressed in this paper, Jefferson says: "I took the ground that from the beginning, I had thought the only one orthodox or tenable, which was, that the relation between Great Britain and these colonies was exactly the same as that of England and Scotland, after the accession of James, and until the union, and the same as her present relation with Hanover, having the same executive chief, but no other necessary political connection; and that our emigration from England to this country gave her no more rights over us, than the emigration of the Danes and Saxons gave to the present authorities of the mother country, over England. In this doctrine, however, I had never been able to get anyone to agree with me but Mr. Wythe. He concurred in it from the first dawn of the question." [81]

This amazing document, which was destined to ring around the world, is written with a boldness and fearlessness that had never before been heard in the colonies. In 1766, to be sure, Richard Bland, a veteran politician and pamphleteer, who, most curiously, represented the conservative and, on occasion, the more radical points of view, had published his "Inquiry into the Rights of the British Colonies" in connection with the difficulties concerning the Stamp Act. In this he revealed familiarity with certain philosophical works, such as Locke and Vattel, which were likewise to contribute to the formation of Jefferson's views, but

Bland's work, although doubtless influential on the younger man, is very different in character. Jefferson, who had no cause for jealousy and who regarded Bland as "the most learned and logical man ... profound in constitutional law," says of this work, "he wrote the first pamphlet on the nature of the connection with Great Britain which had any pretension of accuracy of view on that subject, but it was a singular one. He would set out on sound principles, pursue them logically till he found them leading to the precipice which he had to leap, start back alarmed, then resume his ground, go over it in another direction, be led again by the correctness of his reasoning to the same place, and again back about, and try other processes to reconcile right and wrong, but finally left his reader and himself bewildered between the steady index of the compass in their hand, and the phantasm to which it seemed to point. Still, there was more sound matter in his pamphlet than in the celebrated 'Farmer's letters,' which were really but an *ignis fatuus,* misleading us from true principles." [32]

The "Summary View," inevitably, also invites comparison with another famous pamphlet, James Wilson's "Considerations of the Nature and Extent of the Legislative Authority of the British Parliament." Wilson, who was born a Scotsman and came to America in 1765, claims to have written his treatise in 1770, but it did not appear in print until August 14, 1774, eight days after we know George Washington to have paid "3s 9d" for Jefferson's "Bill of Rights," [33] as the "Summary View" was first called. Wilson's work is less direct, and more cumbersomely expressed than Jefferson's but the emphasis in both is much the same—that Parliament was vested with no constitutional authority to legislate for the colonies, and that the "connection and harmony between Great Britain and us, which it is her interest and ours mutually to cultivate, and on which her prosperity as well as ours so materially depends, will be better preserved by the operation of the legal prerogatives of the Crown, than by the exerting of an unlimited authority of Parliament." [34] "How would the Commons of Great Britain startle at the proposal to deprive them of their share in the Legislature!" he cries. He also rehearses the familiar ideas of the day that "all men are by nature equal and free. No one has a right to any authority over another without his consent. All lawful government is founded on consent of those who are subject to it.,... This rule is founded on the law of Nature. It must control every political axiom; it must regulate the Legislature itself. The people have a right to insist that this rule be served." [35] Appearing, as it did, in Philadelphia on the eve of the first Continental Congress, and being on everyone's tongue, it had, of course, great influence on that occasion.

Even today, allowing for the changes in taste and feeling which nearly two centuries have brought about, one is struck by the brave and undaunted tone that dominates the "Summary View." Essentially, it contains every idea that was to be immortalized two years later in a much more famous manifesto, the "Declaration of Independence." It is perfectly clear that any attempt at reform, any effort to mend the difficulties between the colonies and the mother country, was alien to Jefferson's mind. At heart he knew that this was impossible; that the only solution lay in rebellion. It was no wanton fancy that filled his mind, but a philosophical conclusion, born of profound study and reflection. A mere glance at the books which had preoccupied him in the years since the thinker had emerged from the student, reveals how early he had been captivated by the theory of the natural rights of man and the consequent idea of the freedom of the people.

We have seen how, immediately on his entrance to the House of Burgesses, his thoughts had turned from problems associated with the law to those involved in government, and he proceeded to inform himself more thoroughly on this subject. A survey of the books on politics and government which he owned prior to the Revolution, based on book bills and his library catalogue, reveals that the writers on whom he leaned, or in whose works he found substantiation of his own theories, were Locke and Montesquieu, whose works he acquired in December 1769, along with Puffendorf, Burlamaqui's "La droit naturel," Bolingbroke, and Algernon Sidney. Although we do not have bills for the acquisition of the last two, we know from the commonplace book that Jefferson was early familiar with Bolingbroke, likewise that in

1771 he recommended Sidney's "Discourses concerning Government" to his friend Skipwith. There was, of course, a more remote background supplied by the study of Aristotle, Plato, Cicero, and other ancient philosophers, just as more fugitive books of the period fell under his avid eye. Among these were Ellis's "Tracts on Liberty," Warner's "History of Ireland," and "History of Civil Wars." There was also the "Survey of Ireland" and "Political Arithmetic" of Petty, the English political economist regarded as one of the first to expound the science of comparative statistics, the "Essay on the History of Civil Society," by Adam Ferguson, Scotch philosopher and disciple of Montesquieu, celebrated in his day, and Stewart's "Political Oeconomy," to which George Wythe had probably introduced Jefferson. In May 1768, Wythe had written to his London correspondent, John Norton and Sons, "Please send me by the first opportunity Sir James Stewart's Political Oeconomy, a Book much celebrated by its reviewers." [36] By December 1769, it was in Jefferson's hands.

It was not until after he reached Paris in 1784, and then not immediately, that Jefferson acquired the works of other writers who figure prominently in this field. In the list of books he added to his library at this time, we find under the heading "Natural Law of Nations," Vattel's "Droit des gens," in the edition of 1758 and 1775 for which he paid 15 livres, Grotius' "De jure belli ac pacis," Burlamaqui's "Principes du Droit Politique," "Droit de la Nature et des gens de Wolff, Lat. Fr. par Lurac, 27 livres," "Questions de droit naturel de Vattel." He also bought "Droit de la Nature et des gens de Puffendorf, 27 livres," although, as we have seen, he was already familiar with this writer.

Except for Montesquieu, from whom, as has been shown, Jefferson excerpted many passages, and a brief reference to Locke, no one of these writers makes his appearance in Jefferson's political commonplace book. We can only assume that in them he found the reflection or confirmation of his own thoughts and opinions and did not feel the necessity of making elaborate notes. Although they are not bound in at that point in the political commonplace book, every evidence of the character of the handwriting indicates that the passages from Montesquieu and Beccaria (items No. 775-

831 inclusive) were transcribed right after Jefferson had laid aside the purely legal section (Nos. 1-693).[37] As he acquired Montesquieu in December 1769, we are justified in inferring that these notes were inscribed in 1770. The section between these excerpts (Nos. 696-744, inclusive) are in a later handwriting than the preceding, and as some of the books under consideration bear dates of publication from 1771-1774, it is fair to conclude that these were the very ones which were absorbing Jefferson in the period immediately preceding the "Summary View."

The subjects with which Jefferson was particularly concerned at this time were two, an investigation of the history and the forms of government of the early peoples of Europe, in an endeavor to ascertain how far they rested on popular sovereignty, and a study of the history and rise of feudalism. The latter was ultimately to bear fruit in the revisal of the laws of Virginia, when Jefferson was the prime mover in abolishing the laws of entail and primogeniture. William Robertson's "History of the Reign of the Emperor Charles V, with a view of the Progress of Society from the Subversion of the Roman Empire to the beginning of the Sixteenth Century," which had appeared in London in 1769 and in Philadelphia in 1770, and Francis S. Sullivan's "Historical Treatise on the Feudal Laws and the Constitution and Laws of England" (London, 1772) were the two books which were most helpful to him, and from them he copied many pages.

The majority of the excerpts in this part of the commonplace book, however, have to do with the question of kingly prerogatives and the rights of the citizen, or colonies. To this end he made, first of all, an elaborate study of Simon Pelloutier's "Histoire des Celtes" and "Histoire des Galates" (Paris, 1771), in which the author goes into great detail concerning the early history and customs of the Celts, Germans, and Gauls, as well as the Galatians, a people of Asia Minor. Subsequently, Jefferson analyzed Abraham Stanyan's "Grecian History," a book he had recommended to Skipwith in 1771. In this he was gratified to read in the very first chapter that "the first kings of Greece were elected by the free consent of the people," but he was even more pleased with Stanyan's account of the relation of the parent city to the colonies, and he took pains to note concerning Corinth and Corcyra, "these colonies were at first subject to Corinth their metropolis, and were governed much after the same manner; but as they increased in power, they renounced their obedience." Jefferson studied these words to good purpose. He found what he was seeking—a corroboration of his favorite theory of the natural rights of man as well as historical precedents for the right of colonies to break away from the mother country and achieve self-government.

Jefferson next turned his attention to a study of federative unions of Europe for further confirmation of these theories and their logical outgrowth. He scrutinized the works of Sir William Temple and made elaborate notes on the Union of Utrecht, likewise Stanyan's "Account of Switzerland written in the year 1714," and prefaced his résumé with the tendentious observation, "There are certain articles in the Constitution of the Helvetic body also worthy of attention in constituting an American congress." A lengthy study of the Anglo-Saxons followed, based on William Camden's "Britannia," Langhorne's "Elenchus Antiquitatum Albionensium," Paul Henri Mallet's "Introduction à l'histoire de Danemark," and William Guthrie's "History of England." In Robert Molesworth's "An Account of Denmark as it was in the year 1690" Jefferson found real comfort in reading and transcribing: "The estates of the realm being convened to that intent were to elect for their prince such a person as to them appeared personable, valiant, just, merciful, affable, a maintainer of the laws, a lover of the people, prudent and adorned with all the other virtues fit for government and requisite for the great trust imposed on him.... But if after such a choice they found themselves mistaken, and that they had advanced a cruel, vicious, tyrannical, covetous, or wasteful person, they frequently deposed him, often times banished, sometimes destroyed him." The government of Sweden and of Poland was likewise the subject of study, based on such authorities as René Aubert de Vertot, "Histoire des Révolutions en Suède," and Thomas Salmon's "Modern History" in three volumes. In all these cases particular stress was laid on the legislative bodies, their powers and methods of elec-

THE RIGHTS OF BRITISH AMERICA 247

tion. It is impossible to escape the idea that all this time the fate and the future of the united colonies were never out of Jefferson's thoughts.

Armed with an array of historical precedents, his mind alive with new ideas, Jefferson now devoted himself to casting them into shape for what he sensed was the coming conflict. They flowered in "The Summary View of the Rights of British America." In this document, with which he made his debut on the stage of world affairs, Jefferson poured out not only his grievances but his heart, a heart still young enough to hope, to trust, and to believe.

The "Summary View" is an indictment of the Kings of Great Britain, of Parliament, and of the colonial policy that had been pursued by the English government since the settlement of the colonies. In an endeavor to expound "our rights as well as the invasion of them," Jefferson gives an historical summary "from the origin and first settlement of these countries." He reminds his Majesty that "our ancestors, before their emigration to America, were the free inhabitants of the British dominions in Europe, and possessed a right, which nature has given to all men, of departing from the country in which chance, not choice has placed them." Thereupon he describes the Saxon migration to England and observes that there was never "any claim of superiority or dependence asserted over them by that mother country from which they had migrated ... and it is thought that no circumstance has occurred to distinguish, materially, the British from the Saxon emigration. America was conquered, and her settlements made and firmly established, at the expense of individuals and not of the British public. Their own blood was spilt in acquiring lands for their settlement, their own fortunes expended in making that settlement effective. For themselves they fought, for themselves they conquered, and for themselves alone they have right to hold."

The next object of unjust encroachment was upon the "exercise of a free trade with all parts of the world" which the American colonists possessed "as a natural right and which no law of their own had taken away or abridged." Jefferson discusses this at great length and with much feeling. He cites the numerous infringements and concludes that "the true ground on which we declare these acts void, is, that the British Parliament has no right to exercise authority over us."

Jefferson then summarizes the various "arbitrary acts" which marked the reigns of the monarchs preceding George III, "during which the violation of our rights was less alarming, because repeated at more distant intervals, than that rapid and bold succession of injuries, which is likely to distinguish the present from all other periods of American history. Scarcely have our minds been able to emerge from the astonishment into which one stroke of Parliamentary thunder has involved us, before another more heavy and more alarming is fallen on us. Single acts of tyranny," he charges, "may be ascribed to the accidental opinion of the day; but a series of oppressions, begun at a distinguished period, and pursued unalterably through every change of ministers, too plainly prove a deliberate, systematical plan of reducing us to slavery." The author thereupon rehearses the various grievances of the colonies against Parliament, laying particular stress on the act suspending the legislature of New York. "One free and independent legislature," he observes, "hereby takes upon itself to suspend the powers of another, free and independent as itself. Thus exhibiting a phenomenon unknown in nature, the creator, and creature of its own power. Not only the principles of common sense, but the common feelings of human nature must be surrendered up, before his Majesty's subjects here, can be persuaded to believe, that they hold their political existence at the will of a British Parliament. Shall these governments be dissolved, their property annihilated, and their people reduced to a state of nature, at the imperious breath of a body of men whom they never saw, in whom they never confided, and over whom they have no powers of punishment or removal, let their crimes against the American public be ever so great? Can any reason be assigned, why one hundred and sixty thousand electors in the island of Great Britain, should give law to four millions in the States of America?" Concluding his indictment of Parliament, Jefferson remarks, "that these are the acts of power, assumed by a body of

THE RIGHTS OF BRITISH AMERICA 249

men foreign to our constitutions, and unacknowledged by our laws; against which we do, on behalf of the inhabitants of British America, enter this our solemn and determined protest."

Turning to other problems, Jefferson reviews the policy of the government in trying to restrict the powers of the colonial legislatures, and lays particular emphasis on their frequent dissolution. "Your Majesty, or your Governors, have carried this power beyond every limit known or provided for by the laws. After dissolving one House of Representatives, they have refused to call another, so that for a great length of time, the legislature provided by the laws, has been out of existence. From the nature of things, every society must, at all times, possess within itself the sovereign powers of legislation.... While those bodies are in existence to whom the people have delegated the powers of legislation, they alone possess, and may exercise, those powers. But when they are dissolved, by the lopping off of one or more of their branches, the power reverts to the people, who may use it to unlimited extent, either assembling together in person, sending deputies, or in any other way they may think proper. We forbear to trace the consequences further," Jefferson ominously concludes, "the dangers are conspicuous with which this practice is complete."

The "Nature of our land holdings," now comes under Jefferson's observation, and, after an historical review, he asserts that the time has come "for us to lay this matter before his Majesty, and to declare, that he has no right to grant lands of himself. From the nature and purpose of civil institutions, all the lands within the limits, which any particular party has circumscribed around itself, are assumed by that society and subject to their allotment; this may be done by themselves assembled collectively, or by their legislature, to whom they may have delegated sovereign authority; and, if they are allotted in neither of these ways, each individual of the society may appropriate to himself such lands as he finds vacant, and occupancy will give him title." [38]

Jefferson was thirty-one years old at the time he wrote the "Summary View." The document fairly jubilates with the intrepid spirit of youth. Gone is the fearful and craven tone of humility that had heretofore marked addresses to the throne. Gone the tone of suppliance. No one but a very young man, fired with a passion for sifting the right from the wrong and confident of a God-given ability to do so, would have ventured to say of his address that it was "penned in the language of truth, and divested of those expressions of servility, which would persuade his Majesty that we are asking favors and not rights," or to have informed his Majesty that he was "no more than the chief officer of the people, appointed by the laws, and circumscribed with definite powers, to assist in the working of the great machine of government, erected for their use, and, consequently, subject to their superintendence." [39] Above all, no one but a very idealistic and totally unabashed young man could have had the temerity to conclude his address with the triumphant cry: "These are our grievances, which we have thus laid before your Majesty, with that freedom of language and sentiment which becomes a free people claiming their rights as derived from the laws of nature, and not as the gift of their Chief Magistrate. Let those flatter who fear; it is not an American trait." [40]

XIII. The Gentleman From Virginia

THE FIRST Continental Congress convened in Philadelphia on September 5, 1774. "At ten the delegates all met at the City Tavern," John Adams tells us, "and walked to the Carpenter's Hall, where they took a view of the room and of the chamber where is an excellent library; there is also a long entry where gentlemen may walk, and a convenient chamber opposite to the library. The general cry was that this was a good room." [1] Jefferson was not among the delegates. It may be that the illness which kept him from attending the Williamsburg convention in August, when they were chosen, was one reason he was not named. Perhaps, again, as Edmund Randolph observes, "he had not yet attained a marked grade in politics." "His presence at the convention would probably have multiplied the suffrages in his favor," Randolph continues, "but the seven who were nominated to that new assembly, had the advantage of being better known, of possessing more exclusive connections, and of being older servants of the public." [2] Meanwhile Jefferson, after recovering, remained in Albemarle and spent busy months overseeing improvements on his farms and, particularly, pushing forward the building of his house. There is no indication in his account books that he went from home until December 11 when he notes "arrived at Elk Hill." The only reference to politics, in this same source, is under date of December 8, "a list of the captains of Albemarle to whom association papers are to be sent." Thirteen men are named, eight in the parish of St. Anne and five in that of Fredericksville.

Although Jefferson was not present at this first Congress, his spirit animated the delegates. There can be no doubt that the bold sentiments expressed in the "Summary View," which they had applauded but had not dared adopt, did much to shape opinion and strengthen their determination. "These gentlemen from Virginia appear to be the most spirited and consistent of any," John Adams wrote in his diary. "Harrison said he would come on foot rather than not come. Bland said he would have gone, upon this occasion, if it had been to Jericho." [3] The instructions which had been voted by the Williamsburg convention to guide the conduct of the delegates, although more conciliatory in tone than those proposed by Jefferson, were sufficiently ominous from the British point of view. The delegates might express their "faith and true allegiance to his Majesty, King George the Third, our lawful and rightful sovereign," and "sincerely approve of a constitutional connection with Great Britain," but in the next breath they declared that "the power assumed by the British Parliament to bind America by their statutes *in all cases* whatsoever, is unconstitutional, and the source of these unhappy differences." [4]

After rehearsing the grievances of the colonists and the many infringements of their rights, the instructions politely threaten "to obtain redress of these grievances, without which the people of America can neither be safe, free, nor happy, they are willing to undergo the great inconvenience that will be derived to them, from stopping all imports whatever, from Great Britain, after the first day of November next, and also to cease exporting any commodity whatsoever, to the same place, after the tenth day of August, 1775." The delegates are thereupon instructed to "cordially cooperate with our sister colonies in General Congress, in such other just and proper methods as they, or the majority, shall deem necessary for the accomplishment of these valuable ends." [5]

The Virginia delegates took the lead in Congress. Peyton Randolph was unanimously chosen president. He "seems designed by nature for the business," Silas Deane wrote his wife. Patrick Henry promptly found his way into the spotlight with one of the arresting speeches for which he was known. "The completest speaker I ever heard," Deane called him. "I can give you no idea of the music of his voice or the high wrought yet natural elegance of his style and manner." [6] The credentials of the members had scarcely been read when Henry leaped to his feet. "Government is dissolved," he proclaimed. "Fleets and armies and the present state of things show that government is dissolved. Where are your landmarks, your boundaries of Colonies? We are in a state of Nature, Sir.... The distinction between Virginians, Pennsylvanians, New Yorkers and New Englanders are no more. I am not a Virginian, but an American." [7] Richard Henry Lee, whom John Adams describes as "a masterly man," took no less prominent a part. He "is for making the repeal of every revenue law," Adams writes, "the Boston Port Bill, the bill for altering the Massachusetts constitution, and the Quebec Bill, and the removal of all the troops, the end of the Congress, and an abstinence from all dutied articles, that means,—rum, molasses, sugar, tea, wine, fruits, etc. He is absolutely certain that the same ship which carries home the resolution would bring back the redress.... He said the opposition had been so feeble and incompetent hitherto, that it was time to make vigorous exertions." [8]

Most of the other delegates seem to have been as certain as Lee that the difficulties between the colonies and the mother country were capable of being negotiated out of existence. George Washington, "nearly as tall a man as Col. Fitch, and almost as hard a countenance, yet with a very young look and an easy, soldierlike air," [9] who attended the Congress and who was not much given to speechmaking, observed in a letter to Captain MacKenzie, "I am well satisfied that no such thing as independence is desired by any thinking man in all North America; on the contrary, that it is the ardent wish of the warmest advocates for liberty that peace and tranquillity on constitutional grounds will be restored and the horrors of civil war prevented." [10]

The first Continental Congress remained in session until October 26. Although Thomas McKean, delegate from Pennsylvania, claimed there were no "formal speeches such as are made in the British Parliament ... we had no time for speeches; little for deliberation; action was the order of the day," [11] John Adams viewed the proceedings differently. "The deliberations of the Congress are spun out to an immeasurable length. There is so much wit, sense, learning, acuteness, subtlety, eloquence, etc.

among fifty gentlemen, each of whom has been habituated to lead and guide in his own province, that an immensity of time is spent unnecessarily." [12] A declaration of rights was finally agreed upon, and a strict association, very much on the order of the last Virginia association, was imposed on all the colonies. They bound themselves not to import any British goods after the first of December 1774, and to export nothing after September 10, 1775. Articles arriving in the colonies in the two months following December 1774 were to be returned or handed to local committees, who would determine the disposal. It was agreed to "encourage frugality, oeconomy and industry, and promote agriculture, arts, and the manufactures of this country, especially that of wool." [13]

For the enforcement of these recommendations it was resolved "that a committee be chosen for every county, city and town ... whose business it shall be attentively to observe the conduct of all persons touching this association; and when it shall be made to appear ... that any person within the limits of their appointment has violated this association, that ... [they] cause the truth of the case to be published in the Gazette; to the end, that all such foes of the rights of *British-America* may be publicly known, and universally contemned as the enemies of American liberty." Any colony failing to subscribe to the association, or violating it, was to be considered "unworthy of the rights of freemen, and as inimical to the liberties of their country." [14]

No one was more zealous in the enforcement of the association than were the Virginians. Committees of Safety, as they were called, composed of the leading citizens, were speedily formed in the various counties. Such conservatives as Robert Carter Nicholas headed the one of James City County, Richard Bland of Prince George, Edmund Pendleton of Caroline, Peyton Randolph and George Wythe of Williamsburg, confident that they were serving the cause of peace and the restoration of friendly relations with England, scarcely aware that they were fostering a revolution. What had been efficacious once, as in the case of the Stamp Act, could be efficacious twice. Although, strictly speaking, these committees had no legal status, to all intents and purposes they took

JEFFERSON. By Mather Brown, 1786

over the functions of government. "The powers of the committees not being defined," says Girardin, "were almost unlimited. They examined the books of merchants in order to ascertain whether they imported prohibited articles, or, in consequence of the scarcity of the times, sold at a higher price than usual. . . . They kept a vigilant eye upon the conduct of every inhabitant without distinction, and such as were suspected they sent for into their presence and interrogated them upon every subject which they deemed connected with the public welfare. Such as were found to be disaffected . . . were disarmed, advertised, held up to the odium of the people and underwent a species of political and social excommunication. . . . Their regulations were strictly observed and carried into rigorous execution; and from their decisions there was no appeal." [15]

How strict was the boycott and how severe the possible penalties for violation we see from a letter of Jefferson written in December 1774, when he found himself in a predicament he had not anticipated. The preceding May, when the association in force at that time had placed an embargo on tea only, Jefferson had ordered in London "fourteen pairs of sash windows, to be sent me ready made and glazed, with a small parcel of spare glass to mend with." They were destined for Monticello, which he was desperately eager to get to some state of completion. Meanwhile the Continental Congress had recommended its general association with consequent prohibition of the importation of glass. Jefferson hastened to make his position clear to Archibald Cary and Benjamin Harrison, members of local committees where the goods might be landed. "As I mean to be a conscientious observer of the measures generally thought requisite for the preservation of our independent rights," he says, "so I think myself bound to account to my country for any act of mine which might wear an appearance of contravening them." After explaining the situation, he concludes: "As they come under the prohibitions of the Continental association (which, without the spirit of prophecy, could not have been foretold when I ordered them) so I mean they shall be subjected to its condemnation. To your committee, therefore, if landed within this county, I submit the disposal of them, which shall be obeyed as soon as made known." [16] The committee, however, seems to have decided to release the shipment to Jefferson, for on August 11, 1775, he notes in his account book "pd James Buchanan freight of my window frames from Norfolk, 18/." [17]

Apparently Jefferson did not feel the association was sufficiently strict or far-reaching. Among his papers was found a sheet headed "Defects of the Association." After listing six aspects with which he finds fault, particularly that "we are to conform to such resolutions only of the Congress as our deputies assent to: which totally destroys that union of conduct in the several colonies which was the very purpose of calling a Congress," he comes to the damning conclusion that "we have left undone those things which we ought to have done, and have done those things which we ought not to have done." [18]

Jefferson headed the Committee of Safety for Albemarle. There could be no question that by now he was its most prominent citizen. His pocket account book for 1775 opens with the names of the "committee chosen for Albemarle" and the number of votes each received. His own name, with 211 votes, stands first on the list. John Walker comes next with 200. There were 15 men in all, the others most prominent being George Gilmer and Thomas Walker. Shortly after, Jefferson and Walker were again elected to represent the county at the second Virginia Convention held in Richmond on March 20. Jefferson reached the Tidewater by the eighteenth of the month and seems to have taken his family to stay at The Forest while he was in Richmond, for he notes paying ferriage on that day. Richmond, which was shortly to become the seat of government of the colony, was at the time hardly more than a hamlet which would "afford scarce one comfort of life. With the exception of two or three families this little town is made up of Scotch factors who inhabit small tenements here and there from the river to the hill." [19]

The only place of meeting of suitable size was St. John's Church. There the delegates gathered for a momentous meeting, exciting and moving beyond what they had expected. As in previous conventions and sessions of the House of Burgesses, the delegates were divided between the conservative element that hoped for reconciliation with Britain and believed the present boycott would lead to favorable results, just as had the one in 1765, and the more progressive men led, as before, by Jefferson, Patrick Henry, and Richard Henry Lee. The first act of this convention was "entirely and cordially to approve of the proceedings and resolutions of the continental congress; to consider the whole continent as under the highest obligation to them for the wisdom of their counsels and their unremitted endeavours to maintain and preserve inviolate the just rights and liberties of his majesty's dutiful and loyal subjects in America. In correspondence with this resolution a second was passed for the warmest thanks to the delegates from Virginia for their cheerful undertaking and faithful discharge of the very important trust reposed in them." [20]

These preliminaries over, a petition and address to the King from the Assembly of Jamaica on behalf of the colonies was read. Thereupon a resolution was introduced thanking "the very respectable Assembly for its efforts" and assuring it "that it is the most ardent wish of the Colony (and they were persuaded of the whole continent of North America) to see a speedy return of those halcyon days, when we lived a free and happy people." These conciliatory words, this temporizing attitude, coming close after the actions of the Continental Congress, were too much for the radical members. Patrick Henry jumped to his feet and introduced a resolution "that a well regulated militia, composed of gentlemen and yeomen, is the natural strength and only security of a free government . . . that the establishment of such a militia is, at this time, peculiarly necessary by the state of our laws, for the protection and defence of the country. . . . Be it resolved, therefore," he thundered, "that this colony be immediately put into a state of defence, and that———be a committee to prepare a plan for embodying arming and disciplining such a number of men, as may be sufficient for that purpose." [21] Richard Henry Lee seconded the motion.

Pandemonium broke loose in the Convention. Few were prepared for so radical a step. The delegates were used to protesting, to boycotting, and to sending addresses across the sea, but actual revolution had an ominous sound. Richard Bland, Benjamin Harrison, and Edmund Pendleton, who had so actively advocated resistance at the Continental Congress, opposed the resolutions, along with Robert Carter Nicholas, urging "that the friends of American liberty in parliament were still with us... that the Sovereign himself had relented and showed that he looked upon our sufferings with an eye of pity.... Were we ready for war?" they argued. "Where were our stores—where were our arms—where our soldiers—where our generals—where our money, the sinews of war?" [22] Richard Henry Lee, John Page, George Mason, and other leaders of the radical element supported Henry. "Jefferson was not silent. He argued closely, profoundly and warmly on the same side. The post in the Revolutionary debate belonging to him, was that at which the theories of republicanism were deposited. Washington was prominent, though silent. His looks bespoke a mind absorbed in meditation on his country's fate." [23]

The moment was again one for which Henry, with his unfailing sense of the dramatic, had been waiting. "He rose at this time with a majesty unusual to him in an exordium, and with that self-possession by which he was so invariably distinguished," launched into a speech which has come down to us as one of the most famous and impassioned in American annals. "We have done everything that could be done," he cried, "to avert the storm which is now coming on. We have petitioned—we have remonstrated—we have supplicated—we have prostrated ourselves before the throne.... Our petitions have been slighted; our remonstrances have produced additional violence and insult; our supplications have been disregarded; and we have been spurned with contempt from the foot of the throne.... *There is no longer any room for hope.* If we wish to be free—if we mean to preserve inviolate those inestimable privileges for which we have so long been contending... we must fight! I repeat, sir, we must fight! An appeal to arms and to the God of Hosts is all that is left to us!" Not content with this stirring challenge, Henry went on to inflame his hearers still further. "Gentlemen may cry peace, peace—but there is no peace. The war has actually begun!... Our brethren are already in the field! Why stand we here idle?... Is life so dear, or peace so sweet, as to be purchased at the price of chains and slavery? Forbid it, Almighty God! I know not what course others may take; but as for me ... give me liberty, or give me death!" [24]

As he finished, there was no sound in the old church. Then Richard Henry Lee rose "and supported Mr. Henry with his usual spirit and elegance." The other delegates sat silent, "their souls were on fire for action." [25] "It was a proud day for a Virginian," Edmund Randolph declares, "feeling and acting with his country. Demosthenes invigorated the timid, and Cicero charmed the backward. The multitude, many of whom had travelled to the convention from a distance, could not suppress their emotion. Henry was his pure self.... It blazed so as to warm the coldest heart. In the sacred place of meeting, the church, the imagination had no difficulty to conceive, when he launched forth in solemn tones, various causes of scruple against oppressors, that the British King was lying prostrate from the thunder of heaven. Henry was thought in his attitudes to resemble St. Paul, while preaching at Athens, and to speak as man was never known to speak before." [26]

Warm debate followed, in which "artificial oratory fell in streams from the mouth of Lee" and "the generous and noble minded Thomas Nelson ... convulsed the moderate by an ardent exclamation, in which he called God to witness, that if any British troops should be landed within the county, of which he was lieutenant, he would wait for no orders, and obey none, which should forbid him to summon his militia and repel the invaders at the water edge.... His example told those, who were happy in ease and wealth, that to shrink was to be dishonoured." [27] The resolutions were adopted. No amount of rhetoric, or eloquence, however, could sway the conservative element beyond a certain point, and the vote was very close, 65 to 60, another example of "the inequality of pace with which we moved, and the prudence required to keep front and rear together," as Jefferson remarked.

A committee was then appointed to prepare a plan for arming and training the militia. Richard Henry Lee, Robert Carter Nicholas, Patrick Henry, Benjamin Harrison, George Washington, Edmund Pendleton, and Thomas Jefferson were the more prominent of the 12 men named. After making various further recommendations for the encouragement of manufactures and the relief of Boston, the convention, apprehending that "Peyton Randolph, who with his former colleagues had been elected to the succeeding congress holden in Philadelphia in May 1775, might be detained by sickness or his duties as the speaker of the house of burgesses, Thomas Jefferson was named, as his eventual successor. The convention then considered the delegation of its members as at an end, and recommended to the people to choose delegates to represent them for one year." [28] Jefferson now returned to Elk Hill, an easy journey from Richmond. On April 7 we find him noting, "in three months and one week (excluding time we have been absent) we have used at Elk Hill 2 doz. bottles of Madeira, 3 bottles of red wine, & 10 pint flasks of Syracuse, which is at the rate of 10 bottles a month." [29]

Meanwhile, Williamsburg had been, and continued to be, the scene of events preordained to speed the advent of revolution. On March 28, while the Richmond convention was still in session, Lord Dunmore had issued a proclamation, haughty and condescending in character, by no means calculated to soothe the disturbed state of the colony. "Whereas," he observed, "certain persons, styling themselves delegates of several of his majesty's colonies in America have presumed without His Majesty's authority or consent to assemble together at Philadelphia, in the months of September and October last, and have thought fit, among other unwarrantable proceedings, to resolve that it will be necessary that another congress should be held at the same place on the 10th of May next ... I am commanded by the King, and I do accordingly issue this my proclamation, to require all magistrates and other officers to use their utmost endeavours to prevent any such appointment of deputies and to exhort all persons whatever within this government to desist from such an unjustifiable proceeding...." [30] Three weeks later, "eager to acquit himself with some noise toward his royal master," as Randolph observes, Dunmore secretly had 15 barrels of gunpowder removed from the magazine at Williamsburg, and transferred to the *Fowey*, a man-of-war lying in the York River, 12 miles distant. Indignation over this was intense, the repercussions enormous. A broadside an-

THE GENTLEMAN FROM VIRGINIA   261

nouncing the Battle of Lexington, published in Williamsburg on April 29, fanned the flames. "The intelligence of the bloodshed at Lexington..." says Edmund Randolph, "had in Virginia changed the figure of Great Britain from an unrelenting parent into that of a merciless enemy."[31] In protest, volunteer troops gathered in Fredericksburg, and "Gentlemen volunteers" of Albemarle armed themselves and prepared to proceed to Williamsburg to force the return of the powder. On May 3, Patrick Henry led a detachment of men from Hanover County in a march on Williamsburg. Only 16 miles from the city he was met, early on the morning of the fourth, by Carter Braxton, representative of the Receiver General, Richard Corbin, and handed £330 in payment of the confiscated gunpowder. It was hoped thus to mollify the outraged colonists who could not agree that the powder was the property of his Majesty. The same day Dunmore issued another proclamation, more temperate in character, designed to justify his removal of the powder. The time for proclamations to be of any value had come to an end, however. In desperation, although still blustering, the Governor decided, on May 12, to call a meeting of the Assembly for June 1.

It was a recalcitrant and determined body of men who gathered in Williamsburg that day. Burk, in his "History of Virginia," dramatically describes them as appearing in hunting shirts, and armed with shotguns, ready for any emergency, but historical proof of this has generally been considered lacking. Edmund Randolph's remarks in regard to George Wythe may well be taken as referring to it, however: "on alarm of hostility from the last British Governor, he sallied forth in his hunting shirt and musket, at an age when his patriotism would have sustained no shock had he remained at home."[32] Again George Gilmer, writing to Jefferson, observes, "The confusion in our country daily increases ... Emmanuel Jones has ordered a hunting shirt; keeps three guns high charged beside him. Every rank and denomination of people is full of martial notions."[33] From Jefferson's account book we learn that he reached Williamsburg on the first. Conscious that he might be away for some time, he made a "memm of my tobo this year," how much he expected to receive and "how to be disposed of" in his absence. He was present as the session opened and was put on the Committee of Privileges and Elections as well as on that of Propositions and Grievances. He was also one of those selected to draft a reply to the Governor's address.[34] The latter had attempted to be more conciliatory. "I have called you together," it began, "to give you an opportunity of taking the alarming state of the colony into your consideration, and providing remedies against the evils which are increasing therein." In dulcet tones he informed the Assembly that their "well-founded grievances, properly represented, will meet with that attention and regard which are so justly due them," and proceeded to tell them news that would have been sweet to a less disillusioned audience. "No specific sum is demanded of you for these purposes [*i.e.,* taxation]," he said, "that (as I think obviously appears), your justice and liberality may be left full scope and that your gift, if you should be induced to offer any, may be in the most completest manner, free." [35] He further adjured the burgesses to "reflect upon the benefits this country hath received from the support given to it by the parent state" and trusted that it will be visible in the zeal with which they will attempt to restore harmony.

These so-called Conciliatory Proposals of Lord North, news of which had already reached the colony in May, met with a cold reception from the burgesses. The House took them under consideration, meanwhile approving the proceedings of the Continental Congress as well as the Richmond Convention. They then appointed a committee to inspect the public magazine from which the powder had been removed by the Governor on the twentieth of April. Three men who subsequently entered the arsenal were wounded by a musket trap Dunmore had had placed there, and the community was enraged. "A voluminous farrago of bitterness against the Governor" resulted. Armed men began gathering, and rumors flew about the town. The same detachment of marines who had originally carried off the powder were said to be advancing on the city. The Governor's palace had already been fortified for the past month. Excitement ran high. In the dark of the night of June 8 the Governor and his family retired to the *Fowey,* and with this act British rule in Virginia came to an end.

On June 12 the committee, appointed only two days earlier to draft the reply to Lord North's proposals, reported. The paper they presented had been written by Jefferson. In his "Autobiography," he says that Edmund Randolph "was anxious that the answer of our Assembly, likely to be first, should harmonize with what he knew to be the sentiments and wishes of the body he had recently left. He feared that Mr. Nicholas, whose mind was not yet up to the mark of the times, would undertake the answer, and therefore pressed me to prepare it. I did so, and, with his aid, carried it through the House, with long and doubtful scruples from Mr. Nicholas and James Mercer, and a dash of cold water here and there, enfeebling it somewhat, but finally with unanimity, or a vote approaching it." [36] Even though it may not entirely have conformed to Jefferson's ideas, the answer of the House of Burgesses was considered a "manly repulse of the snare." [37]

After the usual respectful preliminaries, "wishing nothing so sincerely as the perpetual continuance of that brotherly love which we bear our fellow subjects of Great Britain, and continuing to hope and believe that they do not approve the measures which so long have oppressed their brethren in America," it states that "we entered into consideration of that Resolution, we examined it minutely: we viewed it in every point of light in which we were able to place it; and, with pain and disappointment we must ultimately declare it only changes the form of oppression, without lightening its burthen. We cannot, my Lord, close with the terms of that Resolution, for these reasons:

"Because the British Parliament has no right to intermeddle with the support of the civil government of the Colonies. For us, not for them, has government been established here. . . .

"Because, to render perpetual our exemption from an unjust taxation we must saddle ourselves with a perpetual tax, adequate to the expectations and subject to the disposal of parliament alone. Whereas we have a right to give our money, as the parliament do theirs, without coercion, from time to time, as public exigencies may require. . . .

"Because on our undertaking to grant money as is proposed, the Commons only resolve to forbear levying pecuniary taxes on us;

still leaving unrepealed their several acts passed for the purpose of restraining trade, and altering the form of government of the Eastern colonies. . . .

"Because at the very time of requiring from us grants of money, they are making disposition to invade us with large armaments by sea and land, which is a style of asking gifts not reconcileable to our freedom. . . .

"Because, on our agreeing to contribute our proportion towards the common defence, they do not propose to lay open to us a free trade with all the world: whereas to us it appears just that those who bear equally the burthens of government, should equally participate of its benefits. . . .

"Because, the proposition now made to us involves the interest of all the other colonies. We are now represented in General Congress, by members approved by this House, where our former union, it is hoped, will be so strongly cemented that no partial application can produce the slightest departure from the common cause. We consider ourselves as bound in honour as well as interest to share the general fate with our sister colonies, and should hold ourselves base deserters of that union to which we have acceded, were we to argue on any measures distinct and apart from them."

The address concluded with a paragraph displaying Jefferson's art of expression at its best, the forthrightness, the succinctness, the utter simplicity that marks his great public utterances. "These, my Lord, are our sentiments on this important subject; which we offer, only, as an individual part of the whole empire. Final determination we leave to the general congress, now sitting, before whom we shall lay the papers your Lordship has communicated to us. To their wisdom we communicate this important advance. If it can be wrought into any good we are assured they will do it. To them, also, we refer the discovery of that proper method of representing our well-founded grievances, which your Lordship assures us, will meet with the attentions and regard so justly due them. For ourselves, we have exhausted every mode of application which our invention could suggest as proper and promising. We have decently remonstrated with Parliament, they have added new injuries to the old: we have wearied our King with supplications, he has not deigned to answer us; we have appealed to the native honour and justice of the British nation, their efforts in our favour have hitherto been ineffectual. What then remains to be done? That we commit our injuries to the even-handed justice of that Being who doth no wrong; earnestly beseeching him to illuminate the councils, and prosper the endeavours of those to whom America hath confided her hopes; that, through their wise direction, we may again see, reunited, the blessing of liberty and property, and the most permanent harmony with Great Britain." [38]

His work in the House of Burgesses completed, Jefferson set out for Philadelphia. Before leaving he had "rc'd of the Treasurer for use of myself & other delegates of congress £315." He started on June 11 and by evening reached Ruffin's Ferry, 12 miles distant. He drove a phaeton, as we learn from his account book, and was accompanied by a servant, Richard, who seems to have ridden postillion and for whom he bought a postillion whip in Fredericksburg. The following day he lodged at King William Court House and on the thirteenth arrived in Fredericksburg. Here he bought of Alexander Spotswood a horse that was to become his favorite, "The General," and consulted a "horse doctor." A guide was added to the little party as it set off on the fifteenth. Passing through Port Tobacco, Maryland, where they spent the night of the sixteenth, they reached Annapolis the next day. Jefferson paused only long enough to buy some books and to view the "apartments in the State house." He was on his way again the next day and finally, with the aid of another guide from Wilmington, reached Philadelphia on the twentieth. He took lodgings with Benjamin Randolph, the cabinetmaker, to whom he paid for "a fortnight's lodging for self and servant £3-15." His horses proved to be more expensive—Jacob Hiltzheimer charged him £3 10s a week for their care.

Judging by certain entries in his account book, Jefferson seems to have been asked to join a group of men who dined regularly at the City Tavern, or Smith's Tavern, as it was also called. This hostelry, on Second Street near Walnut, was newly completed and the most fashionable place in Philadelphia. It was advertised as a "genteel tavern, elegantly lighted." George Read, one of the delegates from Delaware, writing in May 1775, thus describes the scene to his wife, before Jefferson's arrival: "We sit in Congress generally till half-past three o'clock, and once till five o'clock, then dine at the City Tavern where a few of us have established a table for each day in the week, save Saturday, when there is a general dinner. Our daily table is formed by the following persons, at present, to wit: Messrs. Randolph, Lee, Washington, Harrison of Virginia, Alsop of New York, Chase of Maryland, and Rodney and Read. A dinner is ordered for the number, eight, and whatever is deficient of that number is to be paid for at two shillings and sixpence a head, and each that attends pays only the expense of the day." [39]

Jefferson was cordially received by the members of Congress. Except for John Jay of New York and Edward Rutledge of South Carolina, he was the youngest man present. He had behind him the prestige of the "Summary View" and he had in his pocket Virginia's answer to Lord North's proposals, "a very handsome public paper which he had written for the House of Burgesses." [40] Thus he brought with him, as John Adams says, "a reputation for literature, science, and a happy talent of composition. Writings of his were handed about, remarkable for the peculiar felicity of expression. Though a silent member of Congress, he was so prompt, frank, explicit and decisive upon committees and in conversation—not even Samuel Adams was more so, that he soon seized upon my heart." [41] This ability was immediately recognized and on the twenty-sixth Jefferson, the youthful progressive, and John Dickinson, the conservative, were added to the committee, appointed three days before to "draw up a Declaration to be published by General Washington upon his arrival at the camp before Boston." After some bickering, the "modest and virtuous, the amiable, generous and brave George Washington, Esqr.," had just been appointed commander-in-chief of the American army. Something was needed not only to signalize this great event, which marked the first actual step toward war, but to justify it. Jefferson set about preparing a draft, but, says he, "it was too strong for Mr.

Dickinson. He still retained the hope of reconciliation with the mother country, and was unwilling it should be lessened by offensive statements. He was so honest a man, and so able a one, that he was greatly indulged even by those who could not feel his scruples. We therefore requested him to take the paper, and put it into a form he could approve. He did so, preparing an entire new statement, and preserving of the former only the last four paragraphs and half the preceding one." [42]

The report was presented to Congress on July 6 and accepted the same day.[43] It was a happy compromise—Dickinson mollifying the conservatives, in the main body of the paper, Jefferson's last paragraphs giving hope to the more radical element. Despite Jefferson's statement, and despite his endorsement on the manuscript draft,[44] attempts have been made to claim the credit for the whole document for Dickinson. There is such a sharp break in character and in tone, however, in the latter part, that there can be no question of the authorship. Once more Jefferson applied his great talents strikingly to drive home his point. "We are reduced to the alternative of choosing an unconditional submission to the tyranny of irritable ministers," he writes, "or resistance by force. The latter is our choice. We have counted the cost of this contest, and find nothing so dreadful as voluntary slavery. Honour, justice and humanity forbid us tamely to surrender that freedom which we received from our gallant ancestors, and which our innocent posterity have a right to receive from us. . . . Our cause is just. Our union is perfect—our internal resources are great, and, if necessary, foreign assistance is undoubtedly obtainable. . . . We fight not for glory or for conquest. We exhibit to mankind the remarkable spectacle of a people attacked by unprovoked enemies, without any imputation, or even suspicion of offence. They boast of their privileges and civilization, and yet proffer no milder condition than servitude or death. . . . In our native land, in defence of the freedom that is our birthright, and which we ever enjoyed until the late violation of it; for the protection of our property, acquired solely by the honest industry of our fore-fathers and ourselves, against violence actually offered, we have taken up arms. We shall lay them down when hostilities shall cease on the part of the aggressors, and all danger of their being renewed shall be removed, and not before." This "spirited manifesto," as John Adams called it, ended with a prayer expressing "confidence in the mercies of the supreme and impartial Judge and Ruler of the Universe" and imploring "His divine goodness to conduct us happily through this great conflict ... and thereby to relieve the empire from the calamities of civil war." [45] These words, written by Jefferson and spoken by Washington, echoed throughout the colonies. They were read at public gatherings of every sort, to the soldiers, to the citizens, to worshipers in church. They did much to crystallize opinion and reassure the faint at heart.

There was still a good deal of pacifist feeling not only in Congress, but in the colonies as a whole. A break with the mother country was not lightly to be undertaken. One faction continued to place all its hopes in a petition to the King. Such an one was agreed to on July 5, engrossed and signed on the eighth. It was Dickinson's particular project, and he prepared it almost singlehanded. In a "secret and confidential" postscript to a letter addressed to James Warren, John Adams voiced his opinion of the document, as well as of the attitude of the congress. It "is not yet so much alarmed as it ought to be," he writes. "There are still hopes, that ministry and Parliament, will immediately recede as soon as they hear of the battle of Lexington, the spirit of New York and Philadelphia, the permanency of the union of the colonies etc.: I think they are much deceived, and that we shall have nothing but deceit and hostility, fire, famine, pestilence and sword from administration and Parliament. Yet the colonies, like all bodies of man, must and will have their way and their humour and even their whims." [46]

Meanwhile the Virginia delegates prepared a report of the proceedings in Congress for the convention in session at Williamsburg. The paper, dated July 11, 1775, is in Jefferson's handwriting and is signed by him as well as by Patrick Henry, Richard Henry Lee, Edmund Pendleton, and Benjamin Harrison. Its receipt was acknowledged,[47] but it appears not to have been published hitherto.

Sir [the communication reads], the continued sitting of Congress prevents us from attending the Colony Convention; but, directed by a sense of duty, we transmit to the convention such determinates of Congress as they have directed to be made public. The papers speak for themselves and require no comment from us. A petition to the King is already sent away. Earnestly entreating the royal interposition to prevent the further progress of civil contention by redressing American grievances, but we are prevented from transmitting a copy of it, because a public communication, before it has been presented, may be improper. The Convention, we hope, will pardon us for venturing our sentiments on the following subjects, which we submit to their superior wisdom. The continuance and the extent of this conflict we consider as among the secrets of providence; but we also reflect on the propriety of being prepared for the worst events, and, so far as human foresight can provide, to be guarded against probable evils at least. Military skill we are certainly not so well provided with as military violence opposed to us may render necessary. Will not this deficiency be supplied by sending at the public expense a few gentlemen of genius and spirit to the military school before Boston to learn the necessary art, which in these days of rapine can only be relied upon for public safety.

The present crisis is so full of uncertainty and danger that opinions here are various. Some think a continued sitting of Congress necessary, whilst others are of opinion that an adjournment to the Fall will answer as well. We conclude that our powers go not to the latter, but that a Fall Congress will be indispensable, with adjourning powers given to your delegates that they may be prepared to meet contingencies. The Convention will therefore see the propriety of proceeding to a new choice of delegates and being explicit about the time to which they chose to limit the continuance of their delegation. It is expected that at the next Congress the delegates from the respective colonies come provided with an exact account of the number of people of all ages and sexes, including slaves. The Convention will provide for this.

It is with singular pleasure that we congratulate you on the success with which providence has been pleased to favor our righteous cause by giving success to the operations in defence of American liberty.[48]

Before Congress adjourned, Jefferson's pen was once more called into use. On July 22 a committee of four was chosen for the important task of reporting "on the Resolution of the House of Commons, February 20, 1775, commonly called Lord North's Motion." Benjamin Franklin headed the committee, having received the most votes, Jefferson was second, then John Adams and Richard Henry Lee. "The answer of the Virginia assembly on that subject having been approved," Jefferson writes, "I was requested by the committee to prepare this report, which will account for the similarity of feature in the two instruments." [49] Much the same course of reasoning was followed; indeed, many of the words and phrases are almost identical. The dazzling quality of the first composition has not quite been recaptured, yet it closes with a stirring appeal. "When the world reflects how inadequate to justice are these vaunted terms; when it attends to the rapid and bold succession of injuries which, during a course of eleven years have been aimed at the colonies; when it reviews the pacific and respectful expostulations, which, during the whole time, were the sole arms we opposed to them; when it observes that our complaints were either not heard at all, or were answered with new and accumulated injuries.... When it considers the great armaments with which they have invaded us, and the circumstances of cruelty with which these have commenced and prosecuted hostilities; when these things, we say, are laid together and attentively considered, can the world be deceived into an opinion that we are unreasonable. Or can it hesitate to believe with us that nothing but our own exertions may defeat the ministerial sentence of death or abject submission." [50]

The reply was adopted on July 31. The following day Congress adjourned and Jefferson started for Virginia, in company with Benjamin Harrison. On August 3 they lodged in Annapolis, on the sixth at Port Royal. The next morning, after breakfasting at Bowling Green, the two gentlemen parted company. Jefferson continued on to Williamsburg. On the eleventh he was reappointed by the convention then in session to the next Congress, which was to meet in Philadelphia on September 5. His associates there were to be Peyton Randolph, Richard Henry Lee, Benjamin Harrison,

Thomas Nelson, Jr., and George Wythe. Richard Bland, who was also appointed, declined because of failing health, and Francis Lightfoot Lee was chosen in his place. George Washington and Patrick Henry likewise declined. From Williamsburg Jefferson appears to have gone to Elk Hill, as he made payment to a man near by on the nineteenth. Laden with the music and books he had bought in Philadelphia, and with four butter prints which seem to have been Mrs. Jefferson's heart's desire, he was home again at Monticello before the twenty-fifth of the month.

It was while in Williamsburg this time that he had revoked the legacy of £100 standing in his will for the benefit of his kinsman, John Randolph, in return for which Jefferson was to have received Randolph's violin, and gave instead an order on the treasurer for £13 in payment for it. This was not occasioned by any change of heart on Jefferson's part, but by Randolph's imminent removal to England. This "most elegant gentleman," this "polite scholar" and "profound lawyer," as Jefferson described him, was entirely unsympathetic with the revolutionary movement and felt he should leave Virginia. In Randolph's going, Jefferson, who always believed in leaving no stone unturned, saw an opportunity to effect a little propaganda on behalf of the colonies. No sooner had he reached Monticello than, on the twenty-fifth, he sat down to write his cousin, asking him to use his good offices in clarifying the position of the colonies to the British. Jefferson's letter is a clear and able summing up of the attitude and situation of British America in the summer of 1775, and of particular value for that reason.

"I am sorry the situation of our country should render it not eligible for you to remain longer in it," he writes, "I hope the returning wisdom of Great Britain will, ere long, put an end to this unnatural contest.... My first wish is a restoration of our just rights; my second, a return to the happy period when, consistently with duty, I may withdraw myself totally from the public stage. ... Looking with fondness towards a reconciliation with Great Britain, I cannot help hoping that you may be able to contribute towards expediting this good work. I think it must be evident to yourself, that the ministry have been deceived by their officers on this side of the water, who (for what purpose I cannot tell) have constantly represented the American opposition as that of a small faction, in which the body of the people took little part. This, you can inform them, of your own knowledge, is not true. They have taken it in their heads, too, that we are cowards, and shall surrender at discretion to an armed force. The past and future operations of the war must conform or undeceive them on that head. I wish they were thoroughly and minutely acquainted with every circumstance relative to America, as it exists in truth. I am persuaded this would go far towards disposing them to reconciliation. Even those in Parliament know nothing of our real determination.... I wish no false sense of honour, no ignorance of our real intentions, no vain hope that partial concessions of right will be accepted, may induce the ministry to trifle with accommodation, till it be out of their power ever to accommodate. If, indeed, Great Britain, disjointed from her colonies, be a match for the most potent nation of Europe, with the colonies thrown into their scale, they may go on securely. But if they are not assured of this, it would be certainly unwise, by trying the event of another campaign, to risk our accepting a foreign aid, which, perhaps, may not be attainable, but on condition of everlasting avulsion from Great Britain. This would be thought a hard condition, to those who still wish for reunion with their parent country. I am sincerely one of those, too, who would rather be in dependence on Great Britain, properly limited, than on any other nation on earth, or than on no nation. But I am one of those, too, who, rather than submit to the rights of legislating for us, assumed by the British Parliament, and which late experience has shown they will so cruelly exercise, would lend my hand to sink the whole Island in the ocean.

"If undeceiving the minister, as to matters of fact, may change his disposition, it will, perhaps, be in your power, by assisting to do this, to render service to the whole empire, at the most critical time, certainly, that it has ever seen. Whether Britain shall continue the head of the greatest empire on earth, or shall return to her original station in the political scale of Europe, depends, perhaps, on the resolutions of the succeeding winter...."

THE GENTLEMAN FROM VIRGINIA   273

"I shall be glad to hear from you as often as you may be disposed to think of things here. You may be at liberty, I expect, to communicate some things consistently with your honour, and the duties you will owe a protecting country, such a communication among individuals, may be mutually beneficial to the contending parties. On this or any future occasion, if I affirm to you any facts, your knowledge of me will enable you to decide on their credibility; if I hazard opinions on the disposition of men, or other speculative points, you can only know they are my opinions." [51]

Jefferson was late in arriving in Philadelphia for the Congress which was due to meet on September 5, but which actually did not convene until the thirteenth. His second little daughter, named for his mother, Jane Randolph, who had been born on April 3, 1774, died in the course of September, and it was not until the twenty-fifth that he was able to leave home. Once more he took lodgings with Benjamin Randolph and assumed his seat in the State House. "The Congress," writes Silas Deane, "tho' not numerous, are yet a very unwieldy body in their very nature. As no motion or resolution can be started or proposed, but what must be subject to much canvassing before it will pass with the unanimous approbation of Thirteen Colonies, whose situation and circumstances are various." [52] At this time the Congress was struggling with the stupendous task of raising, organizing, and maintaining an army. Hours were spent in argument before it was decided that on Monday a soldier would receive one pound of beef, one pound of bread, one pound of turnips or potatoes, that on Tuesday his fare would be the same except for the addition of pudding. A half pint of rum per man every day was decreed "with discretionary allowance on extra duty and in time of engagement." [53] Congress was likewise engaged in wooing Canada, hoping "to bring the Canadians into our Union." Jefferson did his duty in attending, but he marked time. The few letters of his from this period that are preserved are full of the latest news from England, from Canada, and from Boston. "Ninety brass cannon were embarked from the tower and may be hourly expected in N. York or Boston.... Two thousand troops were to sail from Ireland about the 25th of Sept.... In the Spring, 10,000 more men are to come over. They are to take possession of New York and Albany..." [54] are items of news he sends his brother-in-law, Francis Eppes, from the metropolis. He is particularly concerned with the ravages of the ruthless Dunmore in Virginia. "The plan is to lay waste all the plantations on our river sides," Jefferson writes on October 10. On November 21, he adds "I have written Patty [Mrs. Jefferson] a proposition to keep yourselves at a distance from the alarms of Ld. Dunmore... and shall hope to meet you as proposed." [55]

At the end of October Congress and the colonies received a piece of news which was to change the course of their deliberations as well as their sentiments. The old hope and habit of redress by petition was to give way to a definite sentiment toward independence—not, to be sure, until it had been dealt a death blow from across the sea. On the adjournment of Congress the preceding August, "The Declaration by the Representatives of the United Colonies of North America... Their Humble Petition to his Majesty"—the reply of the Congress to Lord North's proposals—had been entrusted to Richard Penn, who was going to England. He duly presented the document to Lord Dartmouth and was subsequently informed that no answer to it could be expected. When Parliament opened in October, the King faced the issue and declared that "the rebellious war now levied is become more general, and is manifestly carried on for the purpose of establishing a second empire." His Majesty could have performed no greater service to the cause of American independence.

On October 22, before the news of the King's pronouncement had reached the colonies, Jefferson noted in his account book "this evening the amiable Peyton Randolph, Esq., our Speaker, died about 9 o'clock of an apoplexy at the house of Mr. Richard Hill, 6 miles from this city, whither he had gone to dine." [56] The following month, on the twenty-ninth, he sat down to communicate to John Randolph "the melancholy intelligence" of the loss of his brother. Having accomplished this in two brief sentences, he turned his attention to giving Randolph the latest news concerning the progress of the war, particularly Dunmore's activities, which have "raised our countrymen to a perfect phrensy." Thereupon Jefferson embarks on a violent attack upon the King. Hitherto, as in the "Summary View"—and as in the various addresses by the burgesses to the crown—his arguments and his bitterness had been directed chiefly at the British Parliament, which he consistently described as having "no right to exercise authority over us." It was the many "unwarrantable encroachments and usurpations, attempted to be made by the legislature of one part of the empire, upon the rights which God, and the laws, have given equally and independently to all," [57] which particularly excited his wrath. The King, to be sure, came in for a share of reprobation, but he tended to be a somewhat shadowy figure, obscured by the "Parliamentary thunder" and still cloaked in the last shreds of divine right. In this letter to Randolph, not intended for publication, of course, but valuable as propaganda, Parliament is ignored. A direct and savage attack is launched against his Majesty, and the blame for the situation is placed squarely on his shoulders. There is no doubt that this letter, which preceded by six weeks or so Thomas Paine's indictment of the King in his famous pamphlet, "Common Sense," marks a turn in Jefferson's thought, a realization, as never before expressed, that the willful and obstinate George III, controlling Parliament and his ministers by corrupt patronage, was more responsible for the impasse than they. "It is an immense misfortune, to the whole empire," Jefferson wrote, "to have a King of such a disposition at such a time. We are told, and everything proves it true, that he is the bitterest enemy we have. His minister is able, and that satisfies me that ignorance or wickedness, somewhere, controls him. In an earlier part of this contest, our petitions told him, that from our King there was but one appeal. The admonition was despised, and that appeal forced on us. To undo his empire, he has but one truth more to learn; that, after colonies have drawn the sword, there is but one step more they can take. That step is now pressed upon us, by the measures adopted, as if they were afraid we would not take it. Believe me, dear Sir, there is not in the British empire a man who more cordially loves a union with Great Britain, than I do. But by the God that made me, I will cease to exist before I yield to a connection on such terms as the British Parliament propose; and in this, I think I speak the sentiments of America. We want neither inducement nor power, to declare and assert a separation. It is will, alone, which is wanting, and that is growing apace under the fostering hand of our King." [58]

From this letter there was but one step to the Declaration of Independence.

XIV. The Road to Glory

CONGRESS EXPECTED to adjourn in the winter of 1775-1776. Except for a brief recess, they had been sitting since May and were thoroughly tired of it, as well as of one another. On December 13 it was resolved "that when Congress shall adjourn, it will be necessary for a committee to sit during the adjournment, for the purpose of superintending the treasury, carrying on necessary correspondence, and such other services as shall be directed by Congress." A committee of five, headed by Jefferson, was appointed "to consider and prepare instructions for the committee above mentioned."[1] Such was the pressure of business, however, that adjournment was out of the question, except from Saturday, the twenty-third, to Tuesday, the twenty-fifth. Jefferson secured leave, however, and on the twenty-eighth set out for Monticello, where he arrived on the ninth or tenth of January. He was not to leave home again for four months.

There has been much conjecture as to what kept him away from his post at this important period. Concern over his family undoubtedly induced him to return when he did. On November 7, six weeks after leaving Monticello, he had written Francis Eppes, whose wife was Mrs. Jefferson's sister and with whom she appears to have been staying at this time, that he had "never received the script of a pen from any mortal in Virginia since I left it, nor been able by any inquiries I could make to hear of my family. I had hoped that when Mrs. Byrd came I could have heard something of them: but she could tell me nothing. The suspense under which I am is too terrible to be endured."[2]

When he finally reached home, he found his family safe, although his wife's frail health left much to be desired. His mother, however, was in her last illness. Although by no written word, by no family tradition do we have any indication that Jefferson had the same deep affection for his mother that he had for his wife and children—indeed, with a single exception, she is always referred to in his private accounts as well as in those of the estate in the old-fashioned way as "Mrs. Jefferson"—he undoubtedly considered it his duty to be near her in those last weeks. On March 31 he notes in his account book "My mother died about 8 o'clock this morning—in the 57th year of her age." [3]

There is no other reference to domestic events in any of the sources where we usually look for them. The account book has otherwise but few and routine notations for this period. The garden book, in which he kept a record of his planting and of the development of Monticello, is completely devoid of entries. The farm book merely lists the "number of souls in my family in Albemarle as given this year," in accordance with the request of the Continental Congress that "the delegates from the respective colonies come provided with an exact account of the number of people of all ages and sexes, including slaves." Jefferson's "family" at this time comprised 117, of whom 34 were free men and women, and 83 slaves.

The reason Jefferson did not return to Congress immediately on his mother's death is indicated in a letter he wrote Thomas Nelson shortly after reaching Philadelphia in May 1776. "I arrived here last Tuesday," he says, "after being detained hence six weeks longer than I intended, by a malady of which Gilmer can inform you." [4] George Gilmer, the son of the Williamsburg doctor of the same name, was his physician, who lived in the neighboring town of Charlottesville. We have, unfortunately, no record of what this illness was, indeed it has passed unobserved by Jefferson's biographers, but that it must have been serious is evidenced by his failure to return to Philadelphia. By a curious coincidence he was again stricken as he was about to set out on a mission of the first importance, just as he had been in August 1774, when he and Jack Walker started for the Williamsburg convention.

The months Jefferson spent at Monticello were not entirely

lost ones, however. Despite sorrows and illness he had been active not only in behalf of his native colony—which was still his "country" to him—but on behalf of the poor of Boston, as well. On September 26 he had been appointed by the Committee of Safety for the Colony of Virginia, lieutenant and commander-in-chief of the militia of Albemarle.[5] Not only had the militia to be organized, but their pay and maintenance arranged, firearms and powder purchased, and countless details attended to. Thus on May 1, a week before he set out for Philadelphia, we find in his accounts a summary of the "state of the money received for purchasing powder for the county and for the poor of Boston." He had enlisted the help of his neighbors and notes that he received "from John Henderson, Boston money, £0-10-0, Powder do £1-10-0. Bennet Henderson, Powder do, £3-16-0, Nicholas Lewis, Boston money, £29-2-2½, Powder do° £49-4-9½," making a total of £84 3s. "Besides the above," he adds, "J. Walker desires me to pay and charge to him £23-1-6, but qu. how much powder money and how much Boston?"

Meanwhile a profound change had been taking place, not only in the sentiments of most members of the Congress, but in public opinion as well. Although as late as the preceding winter the delegates of four important colonies, New York, Pennsylvania, Maryland, and New Jersey, had been instructed to vote against independence, by January 1776 a new spirit was in evidence.

The succession of engagements with the British, culminating in the burning of Norfolk by Dunmore in that very month, had done much to inflame popular opinion. Of even greater importance, however, was the publication, on January 10, of Thomas Paine's famous paper "Common Sense." It marked the climax of a steady outpouring of political pamphlets which the last few years had witnessed. The citizenry had been bombarded with endless assertions of the natural and inalienable rights to which man had been born, with countless discussions of the rights of the colonies, and of their relation to the British Parliament. All this was finally bearing fruit. Paine, an Englishman who had emigrated to America in 1774, came out openly for independence. He had the gift of dramatic expression, the power to inflame the imagination of the common man. He proposed to present "nothing more than simple facts, plain arguments and common sense." His words fell on fertile and well-prepared soil. "Society in every state is a blessing," he wrote, "but government even in its best state is but a necessary evil, in its worst state an intolerable one ... the palaces of kings are built on the ruins of the bowers of paradise." After dissecting the English constitution as well as the King, he proceeded, "Volumes have been written on the subject of the struggle between England and America ... but all have been ineffectual. The period of debate is closed. Arms as the last resource decide the contest; the appeal was the choice of the King and the Continent has accepted the challenge.... The sun never shined on a cause of greater worth ... now is the seed time of Continental union, faith and honour." [6]

Even more fervent was the appeal which trumpeted the opening of "The American Crisis," another of Paine's pamphlets. "These are the times that try men's souls: The summer soldier and the sunshine patriot will, in this crisis, shrink from the service of his country; but he that stands it *now* deserves the love and thanks of man and woman. Tyranny, like hell, is not easily conquered, yet we have this consolation with us, that the harder the conflict, the more glorious the triumph." [7]

Who could resist such words, such arguments? One edition of "Common Sense" succeeded another with the greatest rapidity as the demand for it grew by leaps and bounds. Washington's comment on it and its influence in shaping opinion in Virginia, are well known. Edmund Randolph almost forgets to be ponderous in his enthusiasm. Paine, says he, "poured forth a style hitherto unknown on this side of the Atlantic, for the case, with which it insinuated itself into the hearts of the people, who were unlearned, or of the learned, who were not callous to the feelings of man. From his pen issued the pamphlet of 'Common Sense,' pregnant with the most captivating figures of speech.... It was published under the reputed sanction of Dr. Franklin and was a text book from which many of the most respectable officers in our army warmed the coldest among their civil friends. Under all these advantages, the public sentiment which a few weeks before had shuddered at the tremendous obstacles, with which independence was environed, overleaped every barrier. The election of delegates for the convention, the stated meeting of which was to be in May, 1776, now depended in very many if not the majority of the counties, upon their candidates pledging themselves or being understood to be resolved, to sever, as far as their voices could extend, the colonies from Great Britain. But in truth this pamphlet put the torch to combustibles which had been deposited by the different gusts of fury, excited by the successive acts of the ministry and those who were their agents." [8]

Thus by the early spring of 1776 popular sentiment had definitely veered to separation. In the words of Richard Henry Lee, the conviction had become widespread that as well "might a person expect to wash an Ethiopian white, as to remove the taint of despotism from the British court." [9] Washington, whose words, of course, bore great weight, was writing Joseph Reed in February, "with respect to myself, I have never entertained the idea of an accommodation since I heard of the measures which were adopted in consequence of the Bunker's Hill fight.... If every man was of my mind, the ministers of G. B. should know in a few words upon what issue the cause should be put. I would not be deceived by artful declarations or specious pretences; nor would I be amused by unmeaning propositions, but in open, undisguised, and manly terms, proclaim our wrongs, and our resolutions to be redressed." [10] At about the same moment John Adams, somewhat in advance of the colony he represented, was declaring that "reconciliation if practicable and peace if attainable, you very well know will be agreeable to my inclinations, but I see no prospect, no probability, no possibility." [11] It was to take time, however, to transform these sentiments into action. As Adams philosophically remarked, "I do not at all wonder, that so much reluctance has been shown to the measure of Independency. All great changes are irksome to the human mind, especially those which are attended with great dangers and uncertain effects. No man living can foresee the consequences of such a measure, and therefore I think it ought not to have been undertaken untill the design of providence by a series of great events had so plainly marked out the necessity of it that he who runs might read." [12]

In his "Notes on Virginia," Jefferson says that in April 1776, "independence and the establishment of a new form of government, were not even yet the objects of her people at large" and that "one extract from the pamphlet called 'Common Sense' had appeared in all Virginia papers in February and copies of the pamphlet itself had got in a few hands. But the idea had not been opened to the mass of the people in April, much less can it be said that they had made up their minds in its favour." [13] Contemporary statements do not bear out this observation. Indeed, the desire for independence seems to have been widespread. The advertisement for the second edition of Paine's "Common Sense," which appeared on January 26, 1776, in the *Pennsylvania Evening Post*, announced that "several hundred copies are already bespoke, one thousand for Virginia." And in the very month of April, John Adams was writing James Warren, a propos of a letter from John Penn, one of the delegates to the Continental Congress from North Carolina who had returned home to attend the convention of his colony, "he heard nothing praised in the course of his journey, but Common Sense and Independence. That was the cry throughout Virginia.... 'In short, Sir,' says this letter, 'the vehemence of the Southern Colonies is such as will require the coolness of the Northern Colonies, to restrain them from running to excess.'" [14] Almost identical words were used by a young man writing from Petersburg on April 12: "In my way through Virginia I found the inhabitants warm for independence. I spent last evening with Mr. —— from South Carolina. He tells me the people there leave no expectation of ever being reconciled with Great Britain again, but only as a foreign power. Several letters he has received from North Carolina show these are for independence, too. I hear nothing but Common Sense and Independence." [15] In April, likewise, John Page addressed a letter to Richard Henry Lee from Williamsburg saying "almost every man here, except the Treasurer (Robert Carter Nicholas) is ready to declare Independency," [16] and William Aylett, a good citizen of King William, told the sympathetic Lee that "the people of this county almost unanimously cry aloud for Independence." [17]

Similar sentiments prevailed in most of the other colonies by this time. "I can't describe the sighing after independence," James Warren wrote Adams this same April from Watertown, Massachusetts. "It is universal. Nothing remains of that prudence, moderation or timidity with which we have so long been plagued and embarrassed. All are united in this question." [18]

The first definite steps were taken by the southern colonies. In March, the Provincial Congress of South Carolina framed a constitution for "regulating the internal policy of this colony." [19] No sooner had word of this reached Adams than he wrote Warren in great excitement, "the news from South Carolina has aroused and animated all the continent. It has spread a visible joy, and if North Carolina and Virginia should follow the example, it will spread through all the rest of the colonies like electric fire." [20] North Carolina and Virginia were not long in acting. On April 12, North Carolina resolved that "the delegates for this Colony in the Continental Congress be empowered to concur with the delegates of the other Colonies in declaring independency, and forming foreign alliances, reserving for this Colony the sole and exclusive right of forming a constitution and laws for this colony." [21]

Virginia did not lag far behind. Its convention was scheduled to meet on May 6. Everyone knew what to expect. Richard Henry Lee wrote Patrick Henry shortly before the meeting, "Ages yet unborn, and millions existing at present, must rue or bless that Assembly on which their happiness or misery will so eminently depend. Virginia has hitherto taken the lead in great affairs, and many now look to her with anxious expectation, hoping that the spirit, wisdom, and energy of her councils, will rouse America from the fatal lethargy." [22] On May 15, the Virginia Convention, the most forward-looking legislative body in the colonies, took this solemn step. It instructed its delegates in general congress to "propose to that respectable body to declare the United Colonies free and independent States, absolved from all allegiance to, or dependence on, the Crown or Parliament of *Great Britain;* and that they give the assent of this Colony to such declaration, and to whatever measures may be thought proper and necessary by the Congress for forming foreign alliances, and a Confederation of the Colonies, at such time and in the manner as to them shall seem best: *Provided,* that the power of forming government for, and the regulations of the internal concerns of each Colony, be left to the respective Colonial Legislatures." [23] There was only one dissenting vote, that of Robert Carter Nicholas, who "offered himself as a victim of conscience, being dubious of the competency of America in so arduous a contest." [24] Otherwise the passage of the resolution caused the most widespread rejoicing. It was read to the men under arms in the presence of General Andrew Lewis, the Committee of Safety, the members of the Convention and most of the population of Williamsburg. As on all great occasions, the city was brightly illuminated and a repast was given the soldiers in Waller's Grove. "The exultation here was extreme," Richard Henry Lee wrote Adams. "The British flag on the Capitol was immediately struck, and the Continental hoisted in its room. The troops were drawn out, and we had a discharge of artillery and small arms." [25]

This resolution was, of course, the culmination not only of weeks and months of effort, but of years. For the last seven Jefferson had played a prominent rôle in the movement. How much he had to do with the climax, with the actual framing of the resolution, is an enigma, and will probably remain so unless further papers come to light. In his "Autobiography" Jefferson merely observes, "On the 15th of May, 1776, the Convention of Virginia instructed their delegates in Congress to propose to that body to declare the Colonies independent of Great Britain, and appointed a committee to prepare a declaration of rights and a plan of government." [26] Although, with Charles Lewis, he had been elected a delegate from Albemarle to the Virginia Convention, he felt bound to return to the general congress in Philadelphia. His friend George Gilmer, who had been with him during his illness in April, sat in Jefferson's place in the Convention. What instructions Gilmer may have carried, whether oral or written, we do not know. The two men must often have discussed the coming assembly and the burning question of "independency," and there is little doubt that Gilmer was the standard-bearer of Jefferson's views. This is lent further color by Edmund Randolph's remarks in his "Essay on the Revolutionary History of Virginia," where he discusses this convention. "Mr. Jefferson, who was in Congress," he writes, "urged a youthful friend in the Convention, to oppose a *permanent* constitution, until the people should elect deputies for the special purpose. He denied the power of the body elected (as he conceived them to be agents for the management of the war) to exceed some temporary regimen. The member alluded to, communicated the ideas of Mr. Jefferson to some of the leaders in the house, Edmund Pendleton, Patrick Henry, and George Mason. These gentlemen saw no difference between the conceded power to declare independence, and its necessary consequence, the fencing of society by the institution of government. Nor were they sure that to be backward in this act of sovereignty might not imply a distrust, whether the rule had been wrested from the king. The attempt to postpone the formation of a constitution, until a commission of greater latitude, and one more specific should be given by the people, was a task too hardy for an inexperienced young man." [27] Since Gilmer, and no one else can be meant by the "youthful friend," appeared as Jefferson's advocate in the question of the constitution, there is every reason to suppose he did so in regard to other matters.

Meanwhile, on May 7, Jefferson started on his way to Philadelphia, where he arrived on the fourteenth. The journey was one of 280 miles, and his expenses were £14, as we learn from his account with the treasury of Virginia.[28] He varied the trip by taking the road he so often had ridden as a young lawyer, through Orange, Culpepper, and Fauquier Court Houses. At Knowlands he crossed the "Potowmack," then proceeded to Fredericktown, Maryland, Tarrytown, and McAlister's town in Pennsylvania, and finally York, Lancaster, and Philadelphia. Here he took lodgings at the house of a Mr. Graaf, a young German bricklayer. It was a new house, three stories in height, five windows wide and four deep, on the corner of Seventh and Market Streets. Jefferson rented the second floor, which contained a parlor and a bedroom, ready furnished. "In that parlour I wrote habitually," he stated later when questioned about the Declaration, "and in it wrote this paper, particularly."

Congress was meeting in the State House, and Jefferson took his seat on the day of his arrival. With William Livingston and John Adams he was immediately put on a committee to consider Indian and Canadian affairs, in response to letters from Washington and General Schuyler. The atmosphere in Congress was tense. The long hours of debate were grueling, the sense of responsibility overwhelming. Small wonder that John Adams lamented he was destined to "drudgery of the most wasting, exhausting, consuming kind, that I ever went through in my whole life. Objects of the most stupendous magnitude, and measures in which the lives and liberties of millions yet unborn are intimately interested, are now before us. We are in the very midst of a revolution, the most complete, unexpected, and remarkable, of any in the history of nations." [29]

A climax came on May 15. Five days before, Richard Henry Lee and John Adams had introduced a certain resolution. Consideration had been postponed to permit the addition of a preamble suitable to the occasion. This accomplished, and the reasons for Congress's action being made perfectly clear to his "Britannic Majesty, in conjunction with the lords and commons of Great Britain," the resolution was passed and ordered published. It was one of the milestones of the Revolution. "This day," Adams was moved to write, "the Congress has passed the most important Resolution that ever was taken in America." [30] He was quite right. The Congress had resolved that "it be recommended to the respective Assemblies and Conventions of the United Colonies where no government sufficient to the exegencies of their affairs hath been hitherto established, do adopt such government as shall in the opinion of the representatives of the people, best conduce to the happiness and safety of their constituents in particular and America in general." [31]

The day after the passage of this momentous resolution Jefferson sat down to write his old friend, Thomas Nelson, who was a delegate from York at the convention in Williamsburg. Although he remarked, "I have nothing new to inform you of," he did "inclose a vote of yesterday on the subject of government as the ensuing campaign is likely to require a greater exertion than our unorganized powers may at present effect." News of the action of the Virginia Convention, which took place on the same day as that of Congress, not yet having reached him, he devotes most of his letter to concerting plans for directing the course he hopes Virginia will follow. How close the affairs of Virginia lay to his heart, how desperately eager he was for the future of his own country, is revealed in every line. In the formation of a "plan of government" he saw an opportunity for the realization of the hopes and dreams he long had cherished, a chance to create a state in the image of his own thought. He makes no secret of the fact that he feels he could do more good in Williamsburg than in Philadelphia, and suggests to Nelson "should the Convention propose to establish now a form of government perhaps it might be agreeable to recall for a short time their delegates. It is a work of the most interesting nature and such as every individual would wish to have his voice in. In truth, it is the whole object of the present controversy; for should a bad government be instituted for us in future it had been as well to have accepted at first the bad one offered to us from beyond the water without the risk and expense of contest. But this I mention to you in confidence, as in our situation, a hint to any other is too delicate, however anxiously interesting the subject is to our feelings." He then adds a postscript to mark his point, "In the other Colonies who have instituted government they recalled their delegates, leaving only one other to give information to Congress of matters which might relate to their country particularly, and giving them a vote during the interval of absence." [32]

This word to a friend at court had no result. The Virginia Convention either considered itself perfectly capable of forming the "plan of government" without the aid of its delegates to Congress, or felt they were more needed where they were. In any case, they were not recalled. To be sure, Richard Henry Lee, as staunch a Virginian as Jefferson, felt that he could absent himself from Congress and gratify his desire of being in Williamsburg "at the formation of our new government." He did not, however, leave Philadelphia until June 13, nearly a week after he had done his part in introducing the famous resolutions that will always be connected with his name.

Thus the work on the Virginia constitution proceeded despite Jefferson's desire to be there and his efforts to effect his return. In accordance with the resolution a committee of twenty-eight men, including such distinguished compatriots and co-workers as Henry Lee, Robert Carter Nicholas, Archibald Cary, Patrick Henry, Edmund Randolph, Richard Bland, Thomas Ludwell Lee, John Page, and George Mason,[33] was appointed to prepare a declaration of rights, which was adopted on June 12, and a plan of government, voted on June 29. Jefferson's interest in and concern over the measures they were taking never flagged, however, and he was not satisfied until he was able to leave the general congress, in September, to throw himself into the struggle to make the laws and the government of Virginia enlightened beyond anything that had yet been known in the western world.

On May 27, the Continental Congress received the resolution of the Virginia Convention. Realizing that the die had been cast, likewise that no word had come recalling the Virginia delegates, Jefferson set to work in haste and with great determination to prepare a constitution for his native state. Neither at this time nor later did he concur in the idea that the Virginia Convention had the power to adopt a constitution. He contended that it was a body chosen when "independence and the establishment of a new form of government, were not even yet the objects of the people at large," [34] who had elected the delegates. Therefore he cast his proposed constitution in the form of "A Bill for newmodelling the form of Government and for establishing the Fundamental principles thereof in future." [35] Thus, as has been remarked, it contains certain elements which do not properly belong in a constitution. Within a month the draft was completed and sent posthaste by George Wythe to Edmund Pendleton, President of the Convention. Although in his old age Jefferson wrote that he had sent it "on the mere possibility it might suggest something worth incorporation into that [constitution] before the Convention," [36] there is no doubt that his memory here was slightly dimmed and that in the fire of youth he believed he had not only done much more than that, but trusted that it would, substantially, be adopted.

Two copies of Jefferson's proposed constitution were preserved among his papers, one a rough draft, the other a fair copy endorsed in his handwriting.[37] After declaring that George Guelf, King of Great Britain and Ireland and Elector of Hanover, had perverted the Kingly office into a "destestable and insupportable tyranny," Jefferson enters upon a lengthy recital of grievances against the King, concluding that the "said George Guelf be, and he hereby is deposed from the Kingly office within this government and absolutely divested of all its rights, powers, and prerogatives ... and that the said office shall henceforth cease and never more either in name or substance be re-established within this colony."

He then launches upon his "plan of government." After stating that the "Legislative, Executive and Judiciary Offices shall be kept forever separate," Jefferson fully describes the functions of each of these branches. The legislative, for instance, was to consist of a House of Representatives "elected by all male persons of full age and sane mind having a freehold estate in one fourth of an acre of land in any town or in 25 acres of land in the country, and all persons resident in the colony who shall have paid scot and lot to government the last two years." There was also to be a Senate appointed by the House of Representatives. In a fourth, and final, section he is back on a topic never far from his mind, "Rights, Private and Public." Many of the other features of the document were subsequently embodied in the revisal of the laws of Virginia.

A letter from Wythe, who had left the Continental Congress to attend the Virginia Convention, to which he was likewise a delegate, tells the fate of Jefferson's proposed constitution. The last sentence of the letter, omitted by Ford in his discussion, and by Jefferson's later biographers, is of particular significance. It indicates not only that Jefferson had already decided to leave the general congress at the expiration of his present term (the delegates were elected for a year at a time) but that he and Wythe were engaged in planning the far-reaching reforms Jefferson was to introduce into the legislature of Virginia in October 1776. "When I came here," he writes, "the plan of government had been committed to the whole House. To those who had the chief hand in forming it, the one you put in my hands will be shown. Two or three parts of this were with little alteration inserted in that; but such was the impatience of sitting long enough to discuss several important points in which they differ, and so many other matters were necessarily to be dispatched before the adjournment, that I was persuaded the revision of a subject the members seemed tired of, would at that time have been unsuccessfully proposed. The system agreed to, in my opinion, requires reformation. In October I hope you will effect it." [38]

Jefferson's efforts, however, were not entirely in vain. Although his constitution was not adopted as a whole, his preamble was affixed to the one already voted. In writing Judge Woodward, the year before his death, he describes how this came about. "The fact is unquestionable," he says, "that the Bill of Rights and the Constitution of Virginia, were drawn originally by George Mason, one of our really great men, and of the first order of greatness. The history to the preamble to the latter is this: I was then in Philadelphia with Congress; and knowing that the Convention of Virginia was engaged in forming a plan of government, I turned my mind to the same subject." He then describes how it was sent by Wythe and how the Convention, after endless altercation and debate, "could not, from mere lassitude, have been induced to open the instrument again; but that, being pleased with the Preamble to mine, they adopted it in the House, by way of amendment to the Report of the Committee; and thus my Preamble became tacked to the work of George Mason." [39]

Meanwhile events in the General Congress were leading gradually but inevitably toward the goal of independence. On May 20 John Adams had written James Warren, "Every post and every day rolls in upon us Independence like a torrent. The delegates from Georgia made their appearance this day in Congress with unlimited powers and these gentlemen themselves are very firm. South Carolina has erected her government and given her delegates ample powers, and they are firm enough. North Carolina has given theirs full powers, after repealing an instruction given last August against Confederation and Independence. This day's post has brought a multitude of letters from Virginia, all of which breathe the same spirit. They agree they shall institute a government—all are agreed in this they say. Here are four colonies to the southward who are perfectly agreed now with the four to the northward. Five in the middle are not yet quite so ripe; but they are very near it." [40] Despite the reluctance of these middle colonies, Maryland, Delaware, Pennsylvania, New Jersey, and New York, the sentiments of the more radical and advanced colonies prevailed.

On June 7, Richard Henry Lee, in accordance with the instructions of the Virginia Convention, introduced his celebrated resolutions: "Resolved that these United Colonies are, and of right ought to be, free and independent States, that they are absolved from all allegiance to the British Crown, and that all political connection between them and the State of Great Britain is and ought to be, totally dissolved." Secondly, "that it is expedient forthwith to take the most effectual measures for forming foreign alliances." And, finally, "that a plan of confederation be prepared and transmitted to the respective Colonies for their consideration and approbation." [41] The resolutions were seconded by John Adams.

Action of this sort had been expected for the last ten days or more, ever since news had reached Congress of the steps the Virginia Convention had taken, yet the assemblage was thrown into an uproar. "The Congress sat until 7 o'clock this evening, in consequence of a motion of R. H. Lee's rendering ourselves free and independent State," Edward Rutledge wrote John Jay the following day. As one of the leaders of the opposition, he continued in a tone of some disaffection, "the sensible part of the House opposed the motion—they had no objection to forming a scheme of a treaty which they would send to France by proper persons and uniting this continent by a confederacy; they saw no wisdom in a Declaration of Independence, nor any other purpose to be enforced by it, but placed ourselves in the power of those with whom we mean to treat, giving our enemy notice of our intentions before we had taken any steps to execute them." [42]

The upshot of the argument was a move to postpone the consideration of the "resolutions respecting independency" to the next day, and the members were "enjoined to attend punctually at ten o'clock, in order to take the same into consideration." [43] On Saturday, June 8, the Congress resolved itself into a Committee of the Whole, with Benjamin Harrison in the chair, and for two days gave their entire attention to debates on this engrossing and still highly controversial subject. "I wish you had been here," Rutledge wrote, "the whole argument was sustained on one side by R. Livingston, Wilson, Dickinson and myself, and by the power of all New England, Virginia and Georgia at the other." [44] Meanwhile Jefferson sat quietly taking notes "whilst these things were going on," and it is from his pen that we have the fullest and clearest account of these debates.[45] The middle colonies, with whom Rutledge had joined forces, argued that "tho' they were friends of the measures themselves, and saw the impossibility that we should ever again be united with Great Britain, yet they were against adopting them at this time." They were for "deferring to take any capital step till the voice of the people drove" them into it. They went further, and announced "that if such a declaration should now be agreed to, these delegates must retire and possibly their colonies might secede from the Union." In this event "such a secession would weaken us more than could be compensated by any foreign alliance." The question of alliances was next debated. Fears were expressed that there was little occasion to expect one with France and Spain who would have "reason to be jealous of that rising power, which would one day certainly strip them of all their American possessions; that it was more likely they should form a connection with the British court." It would be better, the opposition argued, to wait for information from the agent who had been sent to Paris to learn the disposition of the French court, and "by waiting the event of the present campaign, which we all hoped would be successful, we should have reason to expect an alliance on better terms."

John Adams, Richard Henry Lee, and George Wythe championed the cause of the radicals. "No gentleman had argued against the policy or the right of separation from Great Britain," they contended, "nor had supposed it possible we should ever renew our connection.... The question was not whether, by a declaration of independence, we should make ourselves what we are not; but whether we should declare a fact which already exists. ... As to the people or parliament of England, we had always been independent of them, their restraints on our trade deriving efficacy from our acquiescence only.... As to the King, we had been bound to him by allegiance ... but this bond is now dissolved by his assent to the late act of parliament, by which he declares us out of his protection."

The "backwardness" of Maryland and Pennsylvania was thoroughly discussed, and it was concluded that "it would be vain to wait either weeks or months for perfect unanimity, since it was impossible that all men should ever become of one sentiment on any question." It was further argued that "the conduct of some colonies from the beginning of this contest, had given reason to suspect it was their settled policy to keep in the rear of the Confederacy, that their particular prospect might be better, even in the worst event."

As for foreign alliances, "a Declaration of Independence alone could render it consistent with European delicacy for European powers to treat with us, or even to receive an Ambassador from us.... Though France and Spain may be jealous of our rising power, they must think it will be much more formidable with the addition of Great Britain; and will therefore see it their interest to prevent a coalition.... It would be idle to lose time in settling the terms of an alliance, till we had first determined we would enter into an alliance." And finally "that the only misfortune is that we did not enter into alliance with France, six months sooner, as besides opening their ports for the vent of our last year's produce, they might have marched an army into Germany and prevented the petty princes there from selling their unhappy subjects to subdue us." [46]

The time spent in these debates was fruitful. "It appearing," as Jefferson says, "that the colonies of New York, New Jersey,

Pennsylvania and Maryland and South Carolina were not yet matured for falling from the parent stem, but that they were fast advancing to that state, it was thought most prudent to wait a while for them, and to postpone the final decision until July 1." [47] Accordingly, on June 10, it was resolved that "the consideration of the first resolution [*i.e.*, of those offered by Richard Henry Lee] be postponed to Monday, the first day of July next; and in the meanwhile, that no time be lost, in case the Congress agree thereto, that a committee be appointed to prepare a declaration to the effect of the said first resolution." [48] The following day a committee of five was named "for preparing the declaration." Those chosen were "Mr. Jefferson, Mr. J. Adams, Mr. Franklin, Mr. Sherman, and Mr. R. R. Livingston." [49]

By Friday, June 28, the committee had concluded its work. Congress met as usual these days, at nine o'clock in the morning. It listened first to a report of the committee of claims. Then "Francis Hopkinson, one of the delegates from New Jersey attended and produced the credentials of their appointment." This was followed by the appointment of Monsieur le Chevalier de Kirmovan "to plan and lay out the fortifications agreed by Congress at Billingsport on the Delaware." Mr. Hopkinson was subsequently added to the committee for preparing a plan of confederation. Finally the moment for which everyone had been waiting, arrived. "The committee appointed to prepare a declaration etc.," the minutes read, "brought in a draught, which was read, ordered to lie on the table." [50] There was no discussion. At least a dozen other matters of ordinary business came up, then Congress adjourned to "nine o'clock Monday next." Such was the reception of this famous document on this day, as far as we may gather from the official record. The few surviving letters written by members of Congress on the twenty-eighth do not mention the Declaration. All stress the coming Monday. "The first day of July will be remarkable," John Penn writes, "then the question relative to Independence will be agitated and there is no doubt but a total separation from Great Britain will take place." [51]

To Jefferson, with his "happy talent of composition," had fallen the task of drafting the Declaration. He speaks of it very simply in his "Autobiography," merely stating that. "the committee for drawing the Declaration of Independence desired me to do it. It was accordingly done, and being approved by them, I reported it to the house on Friday the 28th of June when it was read and ordered to lie on the table." [52] Those who were present at the time of the report, at the debates which followed, and at the final adoption of the declaration, were not moved to record their impressions of the speakers, to recount their works, or to describe the scene. The only exception is Jefferson. He, however, reduced the notes he took at the time to so concise a form before he gave them to the world,[53] that all trace of personalities, of any discussions or disagreements, of local color of any sort, is wanting. What he left is more in the nature of a legal document. His remarks concerning these notes are contained in a letter to Samuel Adams Wells, written in 1819. "As yourself, as well as others," he observes, "appear embarrassed by inconsistent accounts of that memorable occasion [the Declaration], and as those who have endeavored to restore the truth have themselves committed some errors, I will give you some extracts from a written abstract on that subject. For the truth of which I pledge myself to heaven and earth; having, while the question of independence was under consideration before Congress, taken written notes, in my seat, of what was passing, and reduced them to form on the final conclusion. I have now before me that paper, from which the following are extracts." He then proceeds to quote certain passages based on the notes and later published in the "Autobiography," beginning with the events of June 7, 1776, and ending with the striking out of the declaration those passages "which conveyed censures on the people of England." [54]

Except for this, such descriptions as there are of these events were written many years later, when memories were likely to be dulled and events thrown out of focus by the passage of time. Thus John Adams says in his "Autobiography," written 29 years afterwards, "the committee had several meetings, in which were proposed the articles of which the declaration was to consist, and minutes made of them. The committee appointed Mr. Jefferson and me to draw them up in form, and clothe them in proper dress. The subcommittee met, and considered the minutes, making such observations on them as then occurred, when Mr. Jefferson desired me to take them to my lodgings, and make the draught. This I declined, and gave several reasons for declining. 1. That he was a Virginian, and I a Massachusettensian. 2. That he was a southern man, and I a northern one. 3. That I had been so obnoxious for my early and constant zeal in promoting the measure, that any draught of mine would undergo a more severe scrutiny and criticism in Congress, than anyone of his composition. 4. And lastly, and that would be reason enough if there were no other, I had a great opinion of the elegance of his pen, and none at all of my own. I therefore insisted that no hesitation should be made on his part. He accordingly took the minutes, and in a day or two produced to me his draught. Whether I made or suggested any correction I remember not. The report was made to the committee of five, by them examined, but whether altered or corrected in anything, I cannot recollect." [55]

Seventeen years after writing this, and when he was in his eighty-eighth year, Adams enlarged on these statements and dramatized them in a letter to Timothy Pickering, dated August 22, 1822. His statements called forth a sharp correction from Jefferson in a letter to Madison the following year, in which he states that he should not "venture to oppose my memory to his, were it not supported by written notes, taken by myself at the moment and on the spot." After rehearsing Adams's statements he says, "Now these details are quite incorrect. The committee of five met; no such thing as a subcommittee was proposed, but they unanimously pressed on myself alone to undertake the draught. I consented; I drew it; but before I reported it to the committee, I communicated it separately to Doctor Franklin and Mr. Adams, requesting their corrections, because they were the two members of whose judgments and amendments I wished most to have the benefit before presenting it to the committee: and you have seen the original paper now in my hands, with the corrections of Doctor Franklin and Mr. Adams interlined in their own handwritings.[56] Their alterations were two or three only, and merely verbal. I then wrote a fair copy, reported it to the committee, and from them unaltered, to Congress. This personal communication and consultation with Mr. Adams, he has misremembered into the actings of a subcommittee." [57]

The session of Congress which met on Monday, July 1, opened auspiciously. It was a day of "fine sunshine" which grew "very warm." At 4 came a thundergust with rain, cleared up by six ... "past 10 fine moon." [58] Every member realized the importance of the day. John Adams was up early writing Archibald Bullock, "This morning is assigned for the greatest debate of all. A declaration that these colonies are free and independent states has been reported by a committee appointed some weeks ago for that purpose, and this day or tomorrow is to determine its fate. May Heaven prosper the new-born republic, and make it more glorious than any former republics have been!" [59] News that another colony had come into the fold was brought in just as the members were about to enter on the great debate. The Maryland Convention had, on the preceding Friday, passed a resolution rescinding previous instructions to its delegates and directing them to "concur with the other united colonies, or a majority of them, in declaring the United Colonies free and independent States." [60] Congress then resolved itself into a Committee of the Whole, with Benjamin Harrison, as usual, in the chair, and continued its deliberations on the original motion made by Richard Henry Lee. The entire day was spent in the "greatest and most solemn debate." John Dickinson, not in the least shaken in his convictions by all that had happened, rose to defend the conservative point of view for the last time. "In a speech of great length, and with all his eloquence, he combined together all that had before been written in pamphlets and newspapers, and all that had from time to time been said in Congress by himself and others," John Adams observes.[61] "No member rose to answer him," he continues, "and after waiting some time ... I determined to speak." This he did, likewise at great length, ending with a recapitulation of the arguments for the benefit of the new delegates who had just arrived from New Jersey. That evening Adams was led to write of this exhausting session, that it was but "an idle mispence of time, for nothing was said but what had been repeated and hackneyed in that room before, a hundred times, for six months past." [62]

At the conclusion of the debate, in which others no doubt joined, a vote was taken. The four New England colonies, New Jersey, Maryland, Virginia, North Carolina, and Georgia voted in the affirmative, South Carolina and Pennsylvania in the negative. Delaware's vote was divided, and New York, although sympathetic, refrained from voting. Their instructions, issued nearly a year before, when reconciliation with Great Britain was still hoped for, forbade the delegates to take any steps which would hinder it. Hereupon the committee rose and "the resolution agreed to by the committee of the whole being read, the determination thereof was, at the request of a colony, postponed, till tomorrow." [63] The colony desiring this was South Carolina. Edward Rutledge believed that by this maneuver he would be able to induce the other delegates, who did not approve of the resolution, to vote for it, thus securing unanimity. "It was now evening," Jefferson writes in describing the scene, "the members exhausted by a debate of nine hours, during which all the powers of the soul had been distended with the magnitude of the object—without refreshment, without a pause—and the delegates of South Carolina desired that the final decision might be put off to the next morning that they might still weigh in their own minds their ultimate vote." [64]

The delay proved to be to good purpose. When the Congress resumed its consideration of the resolutions the following morning and a vote was taken, that of South Carolina was in favor of them. Meanwhile, Caesar Rodney, a third delegate from Delaware, arrived in Congress and added his vote to that of McKean in favor of the resolution. Pennsylvania, too, was experiencing a change of heart. When Congress assembled on July 2, John Dickinson and Robert Morris failed to attend. James Wilson, realizing that a new order had taken over, changed his vote and thus brought his colony into line. "Thus," says Jefferson, "the whole 12 colonies who were authorized to vote at all, gave their voices for it; and within a few days, the convention of N. York approved of it and thus supplied the void occasioned by the withdrawing of her delegates from the vote." [65] Only three men cast their ballots against the resolution on this final vote, Thomas Willing and Charles Humphreys of Pennsylvania, and George Read of Delaware, thereby bearing out Adams's prophecy of July 1 that "one or two gentlemen may possibly be found, who will vote point-blank against the known and declared sense of their constituents." [66]

On this second of July Jefferson's Declaration of Independence, which had been referred to the Committee of the Whole the preceding day, at last came up for discussion. Independence had, of course, actually been established by the passage of Lee's resolution. Adams was well aware of this when he wrote his wife, on July 3, "Yesterday, the greatest question was decided, which ever was debated in America, and a greater, perhaps, never was nor will be decided among men.... The second day of July, 1776, will be the most memorable epoch in the history of America. I am apt to believe that it will be celebrated by succeeding generations as the great anniversary festival. It ought to be commemorated, as the day of deliverance, by solemn acts of devotion to God Almighty. It ought to be solemnized with pomp and parade, with shows, games, sports, guns, bells, bonfires, and illuminations, from one end of this continent to the other, from this time forward, forevermore." [67] It was not Lee's second of July, however, but Jefferson's fourth that was destined to be celebrated in this manner.

The Declaration was essentially an affirmation or justification of the resolution introduced by Lee; indeed, the committee had been specifically instructed to "prepare a declaration to the effect of the said first resolution." When it was taken up on this sunny Tuesday morning, another "great and solemn debate" ensued, which lasted, so Jefferson tells us, "the greater part of the 2nd, 3rd, and 4th days of July." Page by page, sentence by sentence, word by word, the draft was dissected, discussed, and criticized. "The pusillanimous idea that we had friends in England worth keeping terms with," Jefferson writes, "still haunted the minds of many. For this reason those passages which conveyed censures on the people of England were struck out, lest they should give them offence. The clause, too, reprobating the enslaving of the inhabitants of Africa, was struck out in complaisance to South Carolina and Georgia, who had never attempted to restrain the importation of slaves and who, on the contrary still wished to continue it. Our northern brethren also, I believe, felt a little tender under those censures; for tho' their people have very few slaves themselves yet they had been pretty considerable carriers to others." [68]

To the author, the flower of whose thought and the passion of whose soul had been poured out in the Declaration, this discussion was scarcely palatable. He speaks of "writhing a little under the acrimonious criticism," and complains that "although the offensive expressions were immediately yielded, these gentlemen continued their depredations on other parts of the instrument." [69] Franklin, who was sitting by Jefferson during the debate and who perceived that he was "not insensible to these mutilations," turned to him with a philosophical observation born of the wisdom and experience of many years. "I have made it a rule," he observed, "whenever in my power, to avoid becoming the draughtsman of papers to be reviewed by a public body. I took my lesson from an incident I will relate to you." [70] He then recounted the famous story of the man who proposed to advertise his trade with a sign reading "John Thompson, Hatter, Makes and sells hats for ready money," with a figure of a hat subjoined. By a series of fortunate "mutilations" this was gradually reduced until it read merely to "John Thompson," with the figure of a hat.

Jefferson did not speak in behalf of his "instrument." He left that to John Adams, who "supported the Declaration with zeal and ability, fighting fearlessly for every word of it. As for myself," Jefferson adds, "I thought it a duty to be, on that occasion, a passive auditor of the opinions of others, more impartial judges than I could be, of its merits and demerits." [71] And again he pays tribute to Adams in stating that "he was the pillar of its support on the floor of Congress, its ablest advocate and defender against the multifarious assaults it encountered. For many excellent persons opposed it on doubts whether we were provided sufficiently with the means of supporting it, whether the minds of our constituents were yet prepared to receive it, etc., who, after it was decided, united zealously in the measures it called for." [72]

On the evening of July 4, Jefferson tells us, the debates finally came to an end. The "Journals of Congress" continue the story: "Mr. Harrison reported that the committee have agreed to a declaration which they desired him to report. The declaration being read was agreed to as follows 'A Declaration by the Representatives of the United States of America in General Congress Assembled.'" [73] The speaker paused, overcome himself by the solemnity of the occasion, then he continued: "When in the course of human events it becomes necessary for one people to dissolve the political bands which have connected them with another, and to assume among the powers of the earth the separate and equal station to which the laws of nature and nature's God entitle them, a decent respect of the opinions of mankind requires that they should declare the causes which impel them to the separation." Again there was a pause, then "we hold these truths to be self-evident, that all men are created equal; that they are endowed by their Creator with inherent and inalienable rights, that among these are life, liberty, and the pursuit of happiness; that to secure these rights, governments are instituted among men deriving their just powers from the consent of the governed; that whenever any form of government becomes destructive of these ends, it is the right of the people to alter or to abolish it, and to institute new government, laying its foundation on such principles, and organizing its powers in such form, as to them shall seem most likely to effect their happiness. Prudence indeed, will dictate that governments long established should not be changed for light and transient causes: and accordingly all experience hath shown that mankind are more disposed to suffer while evils are sufferable, than to right themselves by abolishing the forms to which they are accustomed. But when a long train of abuses and usurpations begun at a distinguished period and pursuing invariably the same object, evinces a design to reduce them under absolute despotism, it is their right, it is their duty, to throw off such government, and to provide new guards for their future security. Such has been the patient sufferance of these colonies, and such is now the necessity which constrains them to expunge their former systems of government." [74]

As the sonorous, organ-like tones of these opening words echoed through the great hall of the State House, where the delegates sat in utter silence, they seemed to be pealing a hymn to victory, a glorious chorus of divine tones. Then it was as though the crash of trombones took up its theme as each charge against the King was heralded with terrible and pitiless finality: "He has refused his assent to laws the most wholesome and necessary for the public good; he has forbidden his governors to pass laws of immediate and pressing importance; he has called together legislative bodies at places unusual and uncomfortable; he has dissolved representative houses repeatedly and continually; he has endeavored to prevent the population of these states; he has suffered the administration of justice to cease; he has made judges dependant on his will alone; he has abdicated government here; he has plundered our seas, ravaged our coasts, burnt our towns and destroyed the lives of our people; he has waged cruel war against human nature itself, violating its most sacred rights of life and liberty." [75]

Proudly and triumphantly this brave manifesto swelled toward a shattering conclusion, a paean to a new and united people. "The road to happiness and to glory is open to us," the words sang, and, then, in a final, victorious cry, "We, therefore, the representatives of the United States in General Congress assembled, in the name and by the authority of the good people of these states, reject and renounce all allegiance and subjection to the kings of Great Britain and all others who may hereafter claim by through, or under them; we utterly dissolve all political connection which may heretofore have subsisted between us and the people or parliament of Great Britain, and finally we do assert and declare these colonies to be free and independent, and that, as free and independent states, they have full power to levy war, conclude peace, contract alliances, establish commerce and do all other acts and things which independent states may of right do. And for the support of this declaration we mutually pledge to each other our lives, our fortunes and our sacred honour." [76]

The reading of the Declaration over, it was ordered engrossed

SIGNING THE DECLARATION OF INDEPENDENCE. Detail from the painting by John Trumbull. (*Courtesy of Yale University Art Gallery*)

and signed."[77] It was further "resolved, that copies of the declaration be sent to the several assemblies, conventions, and committees or councils of safety; and to the several commanding officers of the continental troops; that it be proclaimed in each of the United States and at the head of the army." [78] On July 8 it was "published and proclaimed from the awful stage in the State-House yard" in Philadelphia. Large crowds of people gathered and "three cheers rended the welkin," according to John Adams. "The battallions paraded on the Common and gave us the *feu de joie*, notwithstanding the scarcity of powder. The bells rang all day and all night. Even the chimers chimed away.... The arms are taken down from every public place." [79]

The glad news spread beyond the city as fast as it could be carried by post and express. The various members of Congress paused to write family and friends of the great event, and we have numerous expressions of the universal rejoicing. "The Declaration came on Saturday," James Warren wrote Adams, "and diffused a general joy. Every one of us feels more important than ever; we now congratulate each other as Freemen. It ... seems to animate and inspire every one to support and defend the Independency he feels." [80] John Hancock, President of Congress, wrote Washington on the fifth, enclosing a copy of the Declaration and requesting him to "have it proclaimed at the Head of the Army in the Way you shall think most proper." According to Washington's "Order Book" he directed that "the several brigades are to be drawn up this evening on their respective Parades, at six o'clock, when the Declaration of Congress, showing the grounds and reasons for this measure, is to be read with an audible voice. The General hopes this important event will serve as a free incentive to every officer, and soldier, to act with fidelity and courage, as knowing that now the peace and safety of his country depends (under God) solely on the success of our arms." [81]

In the days immediately following the adoption of the Declaration, Jefferson sent copies of it to certain of his friends and supporters. "Whenever, in the course of the composition, a copy became overcharged and difficult to read with amendments," he writes, "I copied it fair, and when that also was crowded with other amendments, another fair copy was made, etc. These rough draughts I sent to distant friends, who were anxious to know what was passing. But how many, and to whom, I do not recollect." [82] The known recipients were Richard Henry Lee, George Wythe, Edmund Pendleton, Philip Mazzei, and, it is believed, John Page. Lee's salty comments, along with Pendleton's and Page's acknowledgments, have been preserved. "I thank you much," Lee writes, "for your favour and its enclosures by this post, and I wish sincerely as well for the honour of Congress, as for that of the States, that the manuscript had not been as mangled as it is. It is wonderful and passing pitiful, that the rage of change should be so unhappily applied. However, the *Thing* is in its nature so good, that no cookery can spoil the dish for the palates of freemen." [83] With all the old enthusiasm that had so endeared him to Jefferson, Page sends his comments to his old friend. "I am highly pleased with your Declaration. God preserve the United States—We know the race is not to the swift nor the battle to the strong—Do you not think an angel rides in the whirlwind and directs this storm?" [84]

Almost from the moment of its publication, attempts have been made to find a prototype for the Declaration. Countless pages have been written in an endeavor to find the source of Jefferson's ideas. Richard Henry Lee, subsequently, perhaps not without some feeling that it was his countryman's Declaration that was being celebrated rather than his own Resolutions, was one of the first to disparage it, claiming as Jefferson said, that it was "copied from Locke's treatise on government." [85] This charge has been taken up at regular intervals in the passing years and endless, patient paragraphs have been devoted to pointing out similarity of thought and phrases. Various political pamphleteers of the day have been disinterred and their words placed beside the immortal ones of Jefferson, scarcely to his disadvantage.

It would be foolish to deny that Locke influenced Jefferson. Indeed, he was not the only one. Hobbes, Milton, Sidney, Vattel, and Montesquieu, as well, were familiar not only to him but to every political writer and thinker of the time, whether it were

Richard Bland, John Dickinson, Thomas Paine, James Wilson, or John Adams. Their works were likewise quite as well known to the majority of educated men who did not take up the pen. These writers formed the background, as well as the backbone, of the thought of the period, which was, for every thinking man, concerned primarily with politics. Jefferson's Declaration was no slavish copy of anyone's words or ideas. It was, as we have seen, the outgrowth of years of thoughtful and persistent reading—until a complete amalgamation had here been reached. It was a spontaneous outpouring of his own spirit, a burst at once of passionate feeling and lucid expression, brought into being by the mortal peril of his country. It was, indeed, as Jefferson remarked, "the genuine effusion of the soul of our country at that time." [86]

No one has answered his critics more ably than did the man who wrote the Declaration. In a letter to Madison, on the occasion of Timothy Pickering's Fourth of July oration which caused a furore in 1823, he wrote, "Pickering's observations, and Mr. Adams' in addition, 'that it contained no new ideas, that it is a commonplace compilation, its sentiments hackneyed in Congress for two years before, and its essence contained in Otis' pamphlet' may all be true. Of that I am not the judge.... Otis' pamphlet I never saw, and whether I had gathered any ideas from reading or reflection I do not know. I know only that I turned to neither book nor pamphlet while writing it. I did not consider it as any part of my charge to invent new ideas altogether, and to offer no sentiment which had ever been expressed before." [87] Even more illuminating was the letter he wrote Henry Lee, the year before he died, in answer to some questions Lee had put to him. "When forced, therefore," he wrote, "to resort to arms for redress, an appeal to the tribunal of the world was deemed proper for our justification. This was the object of the Declaration of Independence. Not to find out new principles, or new arguments, never before thought of, not merely to say things which had never been said before; but to place before mankind the common sense of the subject, in terms so plain and firm as to command their assent, and to justify ourselves in the independent stand we are compelled to take. Neither aiming at originality of principle or sentiment, nor yet copied from any particular and previous writing, it was intended to be an expression of the American mind, and to give to that expression the proper tone and spirit called for by the occasion. All its authority rests then on the harmonizing sentiments of the day, whether expressed in conversation, in letters, printed essays, or in the elementary books of public right, as Aristotle, Cicero, Locke, Sidney, etc." [88]

Jefferson was never one to overestimate his own abilities. Indeed, he was one of the most sincerely modest of men. How modest is nowhere better expressed than in the words he wrote Skelton Jones in 1809, when he had reached the pinnacle of his fame and had enjoyed all the rewards that come to a man who has achieved very great distinction. "I have been connected, as many fellow laborers were," he observed, "with the great events which happened to mark the epoch of our lives. But these belong to no one in particular. All of us did our parts, and no one can claim the transactions to himself." [89] As the author of the Declaration of Independence, which crowned the cause for which he had been battling since he entered the House of Burgesses in 1769, Jefferson would have been less than human, however, had he not experienced a little justifiable pride and satisfaction in his achievement. Well might he say with John Adams, who had stood shoulder to shoulder with him in the long struggle: "You will think me transported with enthusiasm, but I am not. I am well aware of the toil, and blood and treasure, that it will cost us to maintain this declaration, and support and defend these States. Yet through all the gloom I can see the rays of ravishing light and glory. I can see that the end is worth more than all the means, and that posterity will triumph in that day's transaction, even although we should rue it, which I trust in God we shall not." [90]

NOTES

CHAPTER I

1 *Cf. Journals of the House of Burgesses of Virginia*, vol. for 1619-59. His name is believed to have been John. He was one of a committee of eight appointed to read the second book of the "Greate Charter or commission of privilege and laws sent by George Yeardley out of England."
2 Patent Book No. 6 (1666-79), p. 131. Land Office, State Capitol, Richmond, Virginia.
3 *Cf.* Henrico County Records, Book 1, pp. 116, 209, 214, 217, 227, 356, 480, 481, 482; Book 2, pp. 135, 143, 152, 153, 154, 157, 158, 159, 160, 161, 178, 204, 209, 223, 243, 251, 267, 301, 302, 307, 316, 319, 341, 348, 361, 388, 420, 439; Book 3, p. 249; Book 5, pp. 51, 142, 523, 605, *et al.*, Virginia State Library.
4 *Ibid.*, Book 1, p. 209.
5 *Ibid.*, Book 3, p. 169. Virginia State Library. Published in the *Virginia Magazine of History and Biography* (cited henceforth as *Virginia Magazine*), vol. 1, pp. 208-12.
6 Henrico County Records, vol. 1688-97, p. 350. Virginia State Library.
7 *Cf.* P. A. Bruce, *Economic History of Virginia in the Seventeenth Century*, vol. 2, pp. 164 *ff.*, 250 *ff.*
8 *Tyler's Quarterly*, vol. 7, p. 119.
9 *Virginia Magazine*, vol. 2, p. 5.
10 *Executive Journals of the Colonial Council of Virginia*, vol. 3, pp. 470, 500.
11 William Meade, *Old Churches, Ministers and Families of Virginia*, vol. 1, pp. 125, 137, 440.
12 *The Secret Diary of William Byrd of Westover*, vol. 1, p. 410.
13 *Ibid.*, p. 414.
14 *Virginia Magazine*, vol. 23, pp. 173 *ff.*
15 *The Writings of Thomas Jefferson*, edited by A. E. Lipscomb and A. E. Bergh (cited henceforth as Lipscomb), vol. 1, p. 1.

16 Henrico County Records, Book 3, p. 249 (ordered recorded). Henrico County Deed Book (1697-1704), p. 158.
17 Henrico County Records, Book 10, p. 378.
18 *Journals of the House of Burgesses*, vol. 1712-26, p. 293.
19 *Ibid.*, Book 3, p. 182. Quoted in *Virginia Magazine*, vol. 2, pp. 296 ff.
20 *Tyler's Quarterly*, vol. 7, p. 122. The entry in the family Bible states that Thomas Jefferson died "Feb. 18, 1735, it being Thursday night, in the 53rd year of his age." This is an obvious error. There is only one year at that period in which February 18 falls on a Thursday, and that is 1731. It was in April of that year that his will was proved. *Cf.* Henrico County Records, vol. for 1725-37, p. 293.
21 *Ibid.*, p. 121. Isham Randolph, Thomas Jefferson's maternal grandfather, seems to have had command of a ship at various times. On March 14, 1710, William Byrd observes in his diary that the death of Ned Bolling by smallpox "makes way for Isham Randolph to command Colonel Hill's ship [Col. Edward Hill of Shirley], for which he shall have my recommendation." *Cf. The Secret Diary of William Byrd of Westover*, p. 152.
22 Henrico County Records, vol. for 1725-37, p. 293.
23 Field subsequently moved to Lunenburg County and settled near Clarksville, an area later embraced in Mecklenburg County. Here he patented a good deal of land and developed a large plantation called "Occaneechee." *Tyler's Quarterly*, vol. 7, p. 119.
24 Albemarle County Will Book No. 2, p. 41.
25 *Ibid.*, p. 59.
26 *Ibid.*, pp. 230-33.
27 *Ibid.*, p. 256.
28 Goochland County Deed Book No. 3, p. 58.
29 Henry E. Huntington Library, San Marino, California.
30 William W. Hening, *Statutes at Large* (cited henceforth as Hening), vol. 2, p. 244.
31 Isham Randolph inherited, on his father's death in 1711, a share in 3256 acres above the falls of the James. Five of his brothers likewise inherited parts of this property. (Henrico County Records, vol. for 1710-14, Pt. I, pp. 215-18.) From 1730-36 he patented 8800 acres adjoining this. See Goochland Records and *Executive Journals of the Colonial Council of Virginia*.
32 *Executive Journals of the Council*, vol. 4, p. 429. *Cf.* also, J. R. Anderson, "Tuckahoe and the Tuckahoe Randolphs," *Annual Report of the Monticello Association*, 1936, p. 33.
33 William Darlington, *Memorials of John Bartram and Humphry Marshall*, p. 88.

NOTES 309

34 Robert Isham Randolph, *The Randolphs of Virginia*, p. 107.
35 *Journals of Council*, published in *Virginia Magazine*, vol. 15, p. 120. At this same meeting of the Council the petition of Peter Jefferson and others for the far larger amount of 40,000 acres in Goochland was rejected "as being judged too great a grant to what is already granted petitioners."
36 Aside from the land inherited from his father on Fine and Manakin Creeks, the number of acres of which are not specified in the will, we find the following entries regarding Peter Jefferson's acquisition of land:

1730	322 acres, south side of James, adjoining P. Ford	Goochland Records, Book 13, p. 495
1734	400 acres on Sailor's Creek, Amelia County	Goochland Records, Book 15, p. 222
1734	3 surveys (acreage not given) on north side of North (*i.e.* Rivanna) River beginning at Secretary's Ford on north side of the First Ledge of Mountains and running down the river and back to Secretary's Line in Goochland	*Executive Journals of Council*, vol. 4, p. 330.
1734	1200 acres on south side of North River beginning at Secretary's Ford above the Mountains & so down ... to the Sandy Falls below the Mountains in Goochland	*Ibid.*, p. 340
1735	1000 acres (Monticello) south side of Rivanna	Goochland Records, Book 16, p. 60. Jefferson's Farm Book
1736	200 acres, north side of Rivanna (bought for bowl of punch) (Shadwell)	Goochland Records, Book 2, p. 222
1737	50,000 acres (with 5 others) between Blue Ridge and Third Ridge Mountains, near headwaters of Sherrando	*Executive Journals of Council*, vol. 4, pp. 403-404
1738	2000 acres on Davis Creek	*Ibid.*, p. 435
1740	150 acres (Portobello, adjoining Monticello)	Goochland Records, Book 19, p. 796. Farm Book

1741	1500 acres (with 2 others) in Brunswick County	*Journals of Council*, published in *Virginia Magazine*, vol. 15, p. 120
1741	200 acres, north side of Rivanna, bought of Wm. Randolph } (Shadwell)	Goochland County Deed Book No. 3, pt. 2, p. 535
1746	322 acres on south side of James bought of J. Smith	Goochland Records, Book 25, p. 120; Book 5, p. 133
1746	400 acres on south side of Fluvanna, surveyed for B. Harris Feb. 19. Transferred to P. J.	Albemarle Surveyor's Book, No. 1, p. 41
1746	Plot 400 acres on both sides Bold Branch of Ballenger's Creek	Book of Plots in back of Albemarle Surveyor's Book No. 1, p. 16
1747	225 acres south side of Fluvanna surveyed for D. Watkins, Feb. 1746. Watkins insolvent. P. J. acquired it 1747	*Ibid.*, p. 41
1748	10,000 acres (with 3 others) on New River	American Antiquarian Society, New Series, vol. 41, p. 87. Quoted from L. P. Summers' *History of Southwest Virginia*, p. 51
1751	1790 acres (with 5 others) on Tomahawk and Rock Castle Creeks of Blackwater	Albemarle Surveyor's Book No. 1, p. 177
1751	528 acres (with Th. Turpin) in Cumberland	Cumberland County Records, Book 31, p. 4
1751	Lots Nos. 57, 107, 108, 151 in Beverley Town	Farm Book
1751	11,770 acres (with 5 others) on branches of Blackwater of the Fluvanna (P. J. got 2000)	Albemarle Surveyor's Book, No. 1, p. 181
1755	300 acres (Tufton)	Farm Book
1755	650 acres (Pantops)	*Ibid.*
1756	400 acres (Pouncey's)	*Ibid.*

1756	225 acres in Albemarle, on the south side and adjoining the Fluvanna River.	Henrico Records, Land Book No. 32, p. 714
1756	364 acres on both sides Tye River including forks on mouth of Cox's & Elk Creeks	Book of Plots in back of Albemarle Surveyor's Book, No. 1, p. 6
1757	Houses in Charlottesville opposite Court House rented to R. Murray, ordinary keeper	John Harvie's account book, Huntington Library
undated	2050 acres south side of Fluvanna, opposite Totier Creek, 500 acres purchased from the Ladds, the other being new land (left to Th. Jefferson by will)	*Ibid.*
undated	Farm in Pittsylvania called "The Pockett." Sold to J. Smith in 1750	*Virginia Magazine*, vol. 23, p. 377
undated	560 acres, plot 4, part of large survey on Tuckahoe Creek (probably 1752-53)	Albemarle Surveyor's Book, No. 1, p. 231
undated	825 square yards of lot 335 in Richmond purchased by P. Jefferson from W. Byrd	Farm Book

37 From the land roll in Thomas Jefferson's farm book we learn that the other properties were Shadwell, acquired 1736-37, Portobello, 1740, Tufton, 1755, Pantops, patented by J. Smith and others in 1734, purchased subsequently by Peter Jefferson, and Pouncey's.
38 *Cf.* John Harvie's account book, Huntington Library.
39 Goochland County Deed Book No. 2, p. 222. An abstract is published in *William and Mary Quarterly*, Series 1, vol. 5, p. 112.
40 Lipscomb, vol. 13, p. 160.
41 Alexander Brown, *The Cabells and Their Kin*, p. 53.
42 Edgar Wood, *History of Albemarle County in Virginia*, p. 11.
43 Albemarle County Order Book, 1744-48, pp. 1-2, 7-8.
44 *Virginia Magazine*, vol. 23, p. 75. Tyler's Quarterly, vol. 6, p. 264.
45 *Journals of the House of Burgesses of Virginia*, vol. 1752-1758, pp. 214, 235.
46 Quoted from vestry records in *Virginia Magazine*, vol. 4, p. 324.
47 Henry S. Randall, *Life of Thomas Jefferson* (cited henceforth as Randall), vol. 1, pp. 2-3.

48 There is a note of Jefferson dated 1801 in the Coolidge Collection, Massachusetts Historical Society, concerning the repair of the "East end of Dwelling House and building the West end."
49 Peter Jefferson's account book, Huntington Library.
50 The stone monument placed by the Thomas Jefferson Memorial Foundation, some years ago, to mark the reputed site of Jefferson's birthplace, stands some way toward the north, below the top of the ridge. In the excavations of 1941 at this point, no antique remains of any building were found.
51 Hening, vol. 5, pp. 33-38.
52 *Dinwiddie Papers*, vol. 1, p. 8.
53 *Cf.* Sketch of Fry, *William and Mary Quarterly*, Series I, vol. 14, p. 75.
54 Edgar Wood. *History of Albemarle County*, pp. 8-9.
55 Sarah N. Randolph, *The Domestic Life of Thomas Jefferson*, p. 24.
56 Edward G. Mead, *Historic Homes of the South-West Mountains*, p. 75.
57 Albemarle Will Book No. 3, pp. 280-81.

CHAPTER II

1 Goochland County Deed Book No. 5, pp. 73 *ff*.
2 Goochland County Deed Book No. 1, p. 219.
3 Thomas Anburey, *Travels through the Interior Parts of America* (1791), vol. 2, pp. 318-19.
4 Peter Jefferson's account book. Huntington Library.
5 *Ibid.*, p. 12.
6 *The Fairfax Line*, Thomas Lewis's Journal of 1746, pp. 79 *ff*.
7 *Virginia Gazette*, January 5, 1738.
8 *Journals of the House of Burgesses*, 1742, 1747, 1748, 1749.
9 Peter Jefferson's account book, Huntington Library. A pistole was the equivalent of about $3.90.
10 *William and Mary Quarterly*, Series I, vol. 7, p. 179.
11 William Jones (editor), *The Douglas Register*, 1750-97, p. 5.
12 Louisa County Records, Will Book No. 5, pp. 196-97.
13 Peter Jefferson's account book, 1728-55, Huntington Library.
14 Lipscomb, vol. 1, p. 3.
15 Letter to Thomas Jefferson Randolph, November 24, 1808. Lipscomb, vol. 12, p. 196.
16 Albemarle County Will Book No. 2, p. 32.
17 *Ibid.*, p. 41.
18 Peter Jefferson's account book, p. 14, Huntington Library.

NOTES 313

19 Westmoreland County, Virginia, Records, Inventories and Accounts, Book 4, p. 77.
20 Hening, vol. 5, pp. 211, 262-63; vol. 7, p. 141.
21 Lipscomb, vol. 1, p. 3.
22 E. L. Goodwin, *The Colonial Church*, p. 292. The King's Bounty, amounting to £20, was given every clergyman licensed by the Bishop of London for service in the colonies. It was intended to assist him with his traveling expenses.
23 Journal of the Meetings of the President and Masters of William and Mary College. Reprinted in *William and Mary Quarterly*, Series 1, vol. 1, p. 220.
24 W. Meade, *Old Churches, Ministers and Families of Virginia*, vol. 2, p. 41.
25 E. Wood, *History of Albemarle in Virginia*, pp. 127, 268.
26 E. C. Mead, *Historic Homes of the South-West Mountains*, p. 232.
27 Accounts of John Harvie, Huntington Library.
28 J. Fontaine and A. Maury, *Memoirs of a Huguenot Family*, p. 379.
29 *Ibid.*, p. 342.
30 *Virginia Magazine*, vol. 5, p. 175.
31 *William and Mary Quarterly*, Series 1, vol. 16, p. 24; vol. 20, p. 172.
32 Albemarle County Will Book No. 2, p. 256.
33 Fontaine and Maury, *Memoirs of a Huguenot Family*, p. 342.
34 *Cf.* Lipscomb, vol. 2, p. 41.
35 Lipscomb, vol. 13, p. 149. Letter to James Maury, April 25, 1812.

CHAPTER III

1 *Writings of Thomas Jefferson*, edited by P. L. Ford (cited henceforth as Ford), vol. 9, p. 475.
2 Ford, vol. 1, p. 340.
3 Lyon G. Tyler, *Williamsburg, the Colonial Capitol*, pp. 134-38.
4 The statutes of the College were first printed in London in 1727, and in Williamsburg in 1736, in both Latin and English. They were reprinted, without change, in 1758. They were printed a third time, with many changes, in 1792. *Cf. William and Mary Quarterly*, Series 1, vol. 16, pp. 241-56.
5 Statutes, *William and Mary Quarterly*, Series 1, vol. 16, p. 248.
6 *Ibid.*, p. 254.
7 *Ibid.*, p. 227.
8 *William and Mary Quarterly*, Series 1, vol. 3, p. 129.
9 Herbert Adams, "The College of William and Mary," *Circular of Information* No. 1, Bureau of Education, p. 20.

10 *William and Mary Quarterly*, Series 1, vol. 2, pp. 55 ff.
11 Statutes, *William and Mary Quarterly*, Series 1, vol. 16, p. 247.
12 *Ibid.*, vol. 4, p. 44.
13 Ford, vol. 1, p. 353.
14 Weather data from Andrew Burnaby, *Travels through the Middle Settlements of North America in the Years 1759 and 1760*, 2d edition, p. 163.
15 *William and Mary Quarterly*, Series 2, vol. 1, p. 27.
16 H. B. Adams, *The College of William and Mary*, p. 29.
17 *Virginia Historical Register*, vol. 3, pp. 147-50.
18 S. N. Randolph, *Domestic Life of Thomas Jefferson*, p. 26.
19 William Wirt, *Sketches of the Life and Character of Patrick Henry*, p. 89.
20 *Idem.*
21 Jefferson's garden book. Coolidge Collection, Massachusetts Historical Society.
22 *Virginia Magazine*, vol. 2, pp. 221-28.
23 Lipscomb, vol. 14, pp. 400-401.
24 *Virginia Magazine*, vol. 24, pp. 327 ff.
25 Jefferson states that Small returned to Europe in 1762, but his memory must have failed him. The accounts of the college with Dr. Small (published in *William and Mary Quarterly*, Series 1, vol. 16, pp. 164 ff.) indicate that he was on its salary list until September 15, 1764.
26 Lipscomb, vol. 1, pp. 3-4.
27 L. G. Tyler in *Tyler's Quarterly*, vol. 2, p. 287.
28 *Virginia Magazine*, vol. 16, pp. 209 ff.
29 John Burk, *History of Virginia*, vol. 3, p. 333.
30 Lipscomb, vol. 14, pp. 231-32.
31 Burk, *History of Virginia*, vol. 3, p. 334.
32 Hugh Jones, *The Present State of Virginia*, p. 32.
33 William Meade, *Old Churches, Ministers and Families of Virginia*, vol. 1, p. 194.
34 Lipscomb, vol. 2, p. 212.
35 A. Burnaby, *Travels through North America*, 1759-60, pp. 6-7.
36 Randall, vol. 1, p. 132.
37 *William and Mary Quarterly*, vol. 12, p. 219.
38 *Ibid.*, vol. 23, p. 222.
39 *Ibid.*, vol. 11, p. 94.
40 *Ibid.*, vol. 3, pp. 251-53.
41 Randall, vol. 1, p. 131.

42 Jefferson's account book for 1768, deposited in the Library of Congress by General Jefferson Randolph Kean. "Dr. Pasteur" is probably William Pasteur, son of the surgeon who came to Williamsburg from Geneva in 1700 and was, to some small extent, a patron of the arts. He was a partner of Dr. John Galt and married Elizabeth, daughter of William Stith, President of the College of William and Mary.
43 Jefferson's account book for 1775. Huntington Library.
44 Randall, vol. 1, p. 131.
45 Jefferson papers, Library of Congress, vol. 1, no. 165.
46 Louis Morton, *Robert Carter of Nomini Hall*, p. 219.
47 Lipscomb, vol. 4, p. 41.
48 S. N. Randolph, *The Domestic Life of Thomas Jefferson*, p. 348.
49 *Virginia Gazette*, September 10, 1736.
50 *Ibid.*, April 4, 1738.
51 Jones, *The Present State of Virginia*, p. 45.
52 *Virginia Gazette*, February 27, 1752.
53 *The Diaries of George Washington*, edited by J. C. Fitzpatrick, vol. 1, p. 34.
54 *Virginia Gazette*, March 5, 1752.
55 *William and Mary Quarterly*, Series 1, vol. 8, pp. 133-53.
56 Nicholas Cresswell, *The Journal of Nicholas Cresswell*, pp. 52-53.
57 Lipscomb, vol. 12, pp. 197-98.

CHAPTER IV

1 Lipscomb, vol. 4, p. 4.
2 *Ibid.*, pp. 1-6.
3 *Ibid.*, vol. 1, pp. 1-3.
4 An ornament cut from paper for the inside of a watch case.
5 R. A. Brock, *Virginia and Virginians*, pp. 58-59.
6 W. Meade, *Old Churches, Ministers and Families of Virginia*, vol. 1, pp. 198 ff.
7 Lipscomb, vol. 1, pp. 6-8.
8 They are printed by kind permission of Yale University.
9 *Ibid*, pp. 122-23.
10 *Ibid.*, p. 12.
11 The word "Belinda" is written in Greek in the original of this letter.
12 Jefferson means Belinda. He uses the masculine pronoun to mislead anyone into whose hands the letter might fall. Jefferson sent the letter to Miss Sukey Potter, who said she delivered it to Mr. T. Nelson, the younger, who, in turn, handed it to John Page.

13 Lipscomb, vol. 1, pp. 13-14.
14 Ford, vol. 1, pp. 357-58.

CHAPTER V

1 Lipscomb, vol. 1, pp. 169-70.
2 Burnaby, A. *Travels through North America, 1759-60* (reprint of 1904), p. 53.
3 Lipscomb, vol. 1, p. 170.
4 *Virginia Historical Register,* vol. 5, p. 166.
5 Frances N. Mason, *John Norton and Sons, Merchants of London and Virginia,* p. 166.
6 *Ibid.,* p. 51.
7 Lipscomb, vol. 1, p. 167.
8 *Ibid.,* vol. 1, p. 165.
9 *William and Mary Quarterly,* Series 2, vol. 2, p. 40.
10 *Ibid.,* p. 157.
11 *William and Mary Quarterly,* Series 2, vol. 2, pp. 40 *ff.*
12 Lyon G. Tyler, *Life and Times of the Tylers,* vol. 1, p. 249 *ff.*
13 That is, Lord Coke's *Institutes of the Laws of England.*
14 Lipscomb, vol. 4, pp. 3-4.
15 *Ibid.,* vol. 14, pp. 119-20.
16 Ford, vol. 9, p. 480.
17 *Ibid,* note.
18 Jefferson habitually spelled the name of Lord Kames, the Scotch lawyer and philosopher, *Kaims.*
19 This letter will be found in full in Ford, vol. 9, pp. 480-85, note.
20 Letter to Thomas Cooper, Lipscomb, vol. 14, p. 85.
21 The dates for the acquisition of these books were determined from a manuscript belonging to Professor James Southall Wilson of the University of Virginia, who has most kindly permitted the author to consult it and quote from it. This is a *Virginia Gazette* Day Book, January 7, 1764-January 27, 1766.
22 Randall, vol. 1, p. 50.
23 *Virginia Magazine,* vol. 43, p. 123.
24 Letter to Thomas Cooper, Lipscomb, vol. 14, p. 85.
25 Jefferson papers, Library of Congress, vol. 432, no. 42,072. This scrap of paper was reverently preserved by Jefferson's secretary and grandson-in-law, Nicholas P. Trist.
26 The manuscripts of the two commonplace books are preserved among the Jefferson papers at the Library of Congress. Mercer's "Abridgement" is in the Alderman Library, University of Virginia.

NOTES

27 The manuscript is preserved in the Jefferson papers in the Library of Congress, ac1944.
28 Fiske Kimball, *Thomas Jefferson, Architect*, p. 109.
29 Johann Wolfgang von Goethe, *Dichtung und Wahrheit*, Part II, Book 8.
30 All attempts to locate the manuscript of the letter written to his guardian John Harvie, January 14, 1760, have proven futile.
31 The excerpts referred to are on the lower half of p. 32 and on p. 59 of Jefferson's manuscript, which is preserved in the Jefferson papers in the Library of Congress.
32 This document is preserved in the Library of Congress, Jefferson papers, vol. 232, no. 42,060.
33 Huntington Library, B. R. 13. I am much indebted to Professor Gilbert Chinard of Princeton University, who kindly loaned me his photostat of this manuscript, of which I had only part. He likewise very kindly put at my disposal his photostat of the legal commonplace book when the original from which I had been working ceased to be available on account of the war.
34 Hening, vol. 7, p. 397.
35 *Ibid.*, p. 399.
36 *Cf.* Jefferson's pocket account book for 1771, Coolidge Collection, Massachusetts Historical Society.
37 Jefferson's fee book, Huntington Library, also pocket account book for 1768, Library of Congress.
38 Jefferson's register of cases, Huntington Library, HM326.
39 Jefferson's fee book, Huntington Library.
40 Fee book, Huntington Library, also account book for 1774, Coolidge Collection, Massachusetts Historical Society.
41 Thomas Jefferson, *Reports of Cases Determined in the General Court of Virginia for 1730-1740 and from 1768-1772*.
42 Fee book, Huntington Library.
43 Jefferson's register of cases, Huntington Library.
44 Jefferson's fee book, Huntington Library.
45 Hening, vol. 7, p. 400.
46 Lipscomb, vol. 4, pp. 44-45.
47 That is, the judges of the General Court, who, Jefferson considered, were appointed largely on account of their social position and wealth.
48 Thomas Jefferson, *Reports of Cases Determined in the General Court of Virginia* (1829), pp. 90-96.
49 *Ibid.*, pp. 96-108.
50 *Cf.* letter to Thomas Cooper, Lipscomb, vol. 14, p. 185.
51 Jefferson's account book for 1774, Coolidge Collection, Massachusetts Historical Society.

52 Jefferson's fee book, Huntington Library.
53 Hening, vol. 1, p. iv.
54 *Ibid.*, p. vii.
55 Lipscomb, vol. 9, pp. 319 *ff*.
56 This notebook is preserved in the Coolidge Collection, Massachusetts Historical Society.
57 Lipscomb, vol. 2, p. 335.
58 *Ibid.*, vol. 9, p. 370.
59 *Ibid.*, vol. 2, p. 336.
60 *Ibid.*, vol. 12, p. xxviii.
61 *Ibid.*, p. 308.
62 *Ibid.*, vol. 6, p. 167.

CHAPTER VI

1 Ford, vol. 1, p. 370.
2 The letters from the two Nelsons, Page, and Wythe on the loss of Jefferson's library are unpublished. They are from the Coolidge Collection in the Massachusetts Historical Society.
3 Ford, vol. 1, pp. 387-88.
4 Peter Jefferson's account book, Huntington Library, p. 12.
5 John Harvie's account book, Huntington Library.
6 The Jefferson pocket account books are preserved in the following institutions: the Library of Congress, Manuscript Division, 1767-70, loaned by General Jefferson Randolph Kean, 1773, 1779-82. Coolidge Collection, Massachusetts Historical Society, 1771-72, 1774, 1776-78, 1783-90, 1804-26. Henry E. Huntington Library, San Marino, California, 1775. New York Public Library, 1791-1803.
7 James Thacker, "Military Journal during the American Revolutionary War from 1775-83," quoted in *William and Mary Quarterly*, Series 2, vol. 8, p. 247.
8 Coolidge Collection, Massachusetts Historical Society, vol. 1705-83, p. 31.
9 This list is preserved at the Massachusetts Historical Society, Coolidge Collection, undated papers.
10 Jefferson associates Monticello with Rowandiz (Rowanty), "The Accadian Olympus which was believed to be the pivot on which the heaven rested." Sayce, *Ancient Monuments*, pp. 173-78.
11 Lipscomb, vol. 4, p. 240.
12 *Ibid.*, pp. 237 *ff*.
13 In the fifth letter of the *Study of History* Bolingbroke highly recommends Davila as a writer in many ways equal to Livy.

14 "Memoirs of the Life and Voyages of Dr. Philip Mazzei," *William and Mary Quarterly*, Series 2, vol. 9, p. 164.
15 John Adams, *Works*, vol. 2, p. 430.
16 Lipscomb, vol. 19, p. 246.
17 *Ibid.*, vol. 18, p. 363.
18 Jefferson papers, Alderman Library, University of Virginia.
19 The Alderman Library of the University of Virginia has kindly made available the complete text of this poem and the following one.
20 I am much indebted to Carlton Sprague Smith, Chief of the Music Division of the New York Public Library, for identifying the first poem. It was written by Johann Wilhelm Gleim and entitled "An den Schlaf." Subsequently it was set to music by Friedrich G. Fleischer, appearing in his "Oden und Lieder, II" in 1757. Two other editions followed, in 1762 and 1775.
21 Lipscomb, vol. 15, pp. 208-209.
22 *Ibid.*, p. 221.
23 Lipscomb, vol. 10, p. 147.
24 *Ibid.*, vol. 14, p. 148.
25 Middleton, quoted in introduction to C. D. Yonge's translation of Cicero's *Tusculan Disputations*.
26 Lipscomb, vol. 15, p. 219.
27 John Bernard, *Retrospections of America, 1797-1811*, p. 238.
28 Lipscomb, vol. 15, pp. 305-306.
29 *Ibid.*, vol. 5, p. 85.
30 *Ibid.*, vol. 6, p. 257.
31 Ford, vol. 9, p. 484.
32 Bernard, *Retrospections of America*, p. 238.
33 *Idem.*
34 Dreer Collection, Historical Society of Pennsylvania.
35 *Cf.* Lipscomb, vol. 6, p. 414; *The Bookman*, vol. 31, pp. 648-49.
36 For the identification of this poem I am indebted to W. H. U. Harding, Esq., of Chicago, through the intermediation of *The New York Times Book Review*. The poem is to be found in Garrick's *Works* (1785), vol. 2, p. 366.
37 Jefferson papers, Library of Congress, vol. 1. Quoted by Gilbert Chinard in *The Literary Bible of Thomas Jefferson*, p. 27.
38 Lipscomb, vol. 18, pp. 447-48.
39 Ford, vol. 8, p. 65.
40 Lipscomb, vol. 4, pp. 21-23.
41 Marquis de Chastellux, *Travels in North America*, vol. 2, pp. 45-46.
42 Lipscomb, vol. 4, pp. 237-39.
43 *Ibid.*, vol. 15, p. 166.

44 Edmund Randolph, "Essay on the Revolutionary History of Virginia" (cited henceforth as Edmund Randolph's Essay), *Virginia Magazine,* vol. 43, p. 122.
45 William Meade, *Old Churches, Ministers and Families of Virginia,* vol. 2, pp. 50 and 52.
46 Edmund Randolph's Essay, *Virginia Magazine,* vol. 43, p. 123.
47 Quoted in *Virginia Magazine,* vol. 6, p. 102.
48 Lipscomb, vol. 6, pp. 258-61.
49 Ford, vol. 7, p. 460.
50 S. M. Crothers, *The Unitarianism of Thomas Jefferson,* pp. 7-8.
51 Lipscomb, vol. 14, p. 119.
52 *Ibid.,* vol. 10, pp. 379-80.
53 *Ibid.,* vol. 15, p. 220.
54 *Cf.* letter to Charles Clay, Lipscomb, vol. 14, p. 232.
55 *Cf.* letter to Charles Thompson, *ibid.,* pp. 385-86.
56 Lipscomb, vol. 15, p. 187.

CHAPTER VII

1 *Genealogy of the Page Family in Virginia,* p. 203.
2 *Idem.*
3 Lipscomb, vol. 4, pp. 16-17.
4 *Ibid.,* p. 19.
5 *Ibid.,* p. 16.
6 Lipscomb, vol. 4, p. 20.
7 In Gloucester County.
8 Lipscomb, vol. 4, pp. 19-20.
9 New York Public Library, Manuscript Division. Published in the *Bulletin of the New York Public Library,* No. 2, pp. 176-77.
10 Gratz Collection, Historical Society of Pennsylvania.
11 Lipscomb, vol. 13, pp. 161-62.
12 Lipscomb, vol. 2, pp. 31-32.
13 Patent Book, No. 42, p. 657. Cited in "Kegley's Virginia Frontier," p. 431.
14 In translating the word Walker as *ambulatori,* Jefferson puns, for instance, on his friend's name. Similarly *saccaria* means exchequer; *saccariam tabulam* is exchequer board, hence chess or checker board J. Lepus-aemula has escaped identification.
15 Published by kind permission of Yale University.
16 For assistance in the translation of this puzzling epistle I am greatly indebted to Professor Julius Goebel of Columbia University and to Professor Thomas Fitz-Hugh of the University of Virginia.
17. *Cf.* Marie Kimball, "Jefferson's Farewell to Romance," *Virginia Quarterly Review,* vol. 4, no. 3, pp. 402-19.

NOTES

18 Jefferson papers, Library of Congress, vol. 155. It has not been possible to locate the "correspondence" to which Walker refers, in any of the public repositories of Jefferson's papers.
19 Jefferson papers, Library of Congress, vol. 161, no. 28,252.
20 Letter to Governor James Monroe, Lipscomb, vol. 10, pp. 330-33.
21 *Idem.*
22 Jefferson papers, Library of Congress, vol. 121, March 24, 1802.
23 *Thomas Jefferson Correspondence, Printed from Originals in the Collection of William K. Bixby*, p. 114. The enclosed letter to Mr. Lincoln has not come to light, so far as the author has been able to ascertain. The Walker-Jefferson affair was rehearsed in a letter of Henry Lee, dated August 24, 1833, to Richard Brown of Windsor, Virginia. This letter was seen by B. J. Hendrick and referred to in his book, *The Lees of Virginia*, p. 400. Repeated search of the Jefferson papers in the Library of Congress, where this item is catalogued under accession 919, and is again listed in vol. 155 of the Jefferson papers, has failed to bring it to light. It was likewise not to be found among the Lee papers, where, to be sure, it would have been mis-sorted.

CHAPTER VIII

1 Letter of July 8, 1828. Kindly communicated by Professor Armistead Churchill Gordon, of the University of Virginia.
2 Lipscomb, vol. 4, p. 11, July 15, 1763.
3 The manuscript ledger of the *Virginia Gazette* lists as sold to Jefferson: "October 10, 1765, Shenstone's Works, 2 Vols., 8vo."
4 The same ledger shows that Jefferson bought this book on August 6, 1765.
5 William Shenstone, *Works* (2d edition), vol. 2, p. 25.
6 Lipscomb, vol. 5, pp. 436-37.
7 Jefferson's garden book, Coolidge Collection, Massachusetts Historical Society.
8 I am deeply grateful to Fiske Kimball for his kindness and generosity in having reviewed for me, in the light of this new material, his fundamental work, the great folio *Thomas Jefferson, Architect*, 1916.
9 Reproduced as Figs. 5 and 6 in Fiske Kimball, *Thomas Jefferson, Architect*, cited henceforth as "Kimball." A crude, square plan reproduced there as Fig. 4, already showing the loggia of Fig. 6, and doubtless preceding that, has notes by Jefferson for a Tuscan order and an estimate of the lead and nails required. It is signed by Dabney Minor, a Tidewater builder. This is doubtless the earliest of all sketches for Monticello.

10 Kimball, Fig. 119, there supposed to be a study for the plan of Brandon.
11 Pocket account book for 1767, Library of Congress.
12 Pocket account book for 1768, Library of Congress.
13 The edition Jefferson owned, as we know from the catalogue of his library, was one of the splendid ones with English translation, by Giacomo Leoni. He owned both the edition of 1715 and that of 1742 before he went abroad in 1784.
14 Book II, Chap. 12, quoted from Leoni's translation.
15 Kimball, Fig. 12.
16 *Ibid.*, Fig. 11.
17 *Ibid.*, Fig. 19.
18 Undated papers, Coolidge Collection, Massachusetts Historical Society.
19 Kimball, Fig. 68.
20 *Ibid.*, Fig. 23. As the entire order with pedestal here is of over 23 feet, this drawing was evidently made after Jefferson solicited the English estimates of stonework.
21 Pocket account book for 1767, unnumbered page containing notes dated 1769, Library of Congress.
22 Kimball, Fig. 79.
23 A sketch at the Huntington Library, HM9365, is embodied in a finished plan. *Cf.* Kimball, Fig. 10.
24 Pocket account book for 1769, p. 32, Library of Congress.
25 Letter of March 6, 1770, Coolidge Collection, Massachusetts Historical Society.
26 Ford, vol. 1, pp. 390-91.
27 Ford, vol. 1, p. 395.
28 Pocket account book for 1772, p. 10, Coolidge Collection, Massachusetts Historical Society.
29 We learn the time and terms of this contract from a later entry on August 22, 1773.
30 Kimball, Figs. 24 and 34.
31 A study for this, bearing the date of August 2, 1771, is in the Huntington Library, No. HM9365.
32 Kimball, Fig. 31.
33 Lipscomb, vol. 4, p. 24.
34 Account book for 1774, p. 16, Coolidge Collection, Massachusetts Historical Society.
35 Marquis de Chastellux, *Travels in North America*, vol. 2, pp. 41-42.
36 Lipscomb, vol. 17, p. 292.
37 T. A. Glenn, *Some Colonial Mansions*, 2d series, p. 65.

NOTES

38 The references in this paragraph are to Jefferson's pocket account books of 1768 and 1769, deposited in the Library of Congress by General Jefferson Randolph Kean.
39 Lipscomb, vol. 17, p. 236.
40 Whately, *Observations on Modern Gardening* (1771), p. 1.
41 *Ibid.*, p. 2.
42 Pocket account book for 1771, Coolidge Collection, Massachusetts Historical Society.
43 That Jefferson, at this early time, knew and admired the "Lantern of Demosthenes"—the monument of Lysicrates at Athens—was remarkably prophetic. Long before he owned his folio copies of Stuart and Revett's *Antiquities of Athens*, or LeRoy's *Ruins of Athens*, his keen eye had noted in Spon's *Voyages* this favorite model of the coming Greek revival.
44 Both quotations are from Jefferson's account book for 1771, Coolidge Collection, Massachusetts Historical Society.
45 Chastellux, *Travels in North America*, vol. 2, p. 49.
46 Whately, *Observations on Modern Gardening*, pp. 120 and 127-28.
47 *Cf.* Kimball, Fig. 90. Chamber's folio *Designs of Chinese Buildings* had appeared in 1757.
48 *Ibid.*, Figs. 38 and 39.
49 April 23, 1779. Kimball, p. 134.
50 A drawing for this is in the Huntington Library, HM9398. *Cf.* Kimball, Fig. 64.
51 Kimball, Figs. 62 and 63, especially.
52 Pocket account book for 1771, Coolidge Collection, Massachusetts Historical Society.

CHAPTER IX

1 A search of such eighteenth-century books as Algernon Sidney's *Essay on Love*, and others, has failed to reveal the source of these reflections. The presence of one word "ours" in the last line of the fourth paragraph leads to the supposition that they might have been written by a woman. However, the word may be a slip of the pen. Jefferson wrote "fell" for feel in the sixth paragraph.
2 Jefferson papers, Library of Congress.
3 Lipscomb, vol. 1, p. 21.
4 Lipscomb, vol. 1, p. 5.
5 *Cf.* Goochland Records, Book 29, p. 178.
6 *William and Mary Quarterly*, Series 1, vol. 7, pp. 148, 152; vol. 8, pp. 2, 5, 13, 14; vol. 14, p. 145.
7 *William and Mary Quarterly*, Series 2, vol. 1, p. 39.
8 *Ibid.*, vol. 4, p. 119.

9 Inventory and appraisement of the estate of Bathurst Skelton, deceased, in the county of Charles City. Charles City County Records, vol. 1766-74, p. 525.
10 A drawing for a later remodeling of Elk Hill, in the Huntington Library, shows it to have been a typical story and a half house, two rooms to a floor. The existing nineteenth-century house bears no relation to this.
11 The date of Skelton's death has been variously given as 1768 and 1771. The bursar's book of William and Mary notes in 1769, "he is since dead." Randall gives the former date, stating "we glean these details from records, lying before us, in the handwriting of Thomas Jefferson, and furnished by his family." (Vol. 1, p. 63, note). Skelton's will was proved September 4, 1771.
12 Will of Bathurst Skelton. Charles City County Records, vol. 1766-74, Virginia State Library. Published in Tyler's Quarterly, vol. 6, p. 268.
13 At the back of one of Jefferson's fee books, dated February 12, 1767-December, 1794, are four pages headed respectively "John Skelton, son of Bathurst, in acct. with Th. Jefferson, his guardian in right of Martha, his wife" and "The Distributee as of John Skelton dec^d in acct. with Th. Jefferson, adm. of J. Skelton in right of Martha his wife." There are a few notes on his inheritance, but no dates and no sums of money are mentioned. In Jefferson's account of the estate of John Wayles we find under date of February 26, 1772, an item of "goods imported for Mrs. Jefferson & J. Skelton from Cary & Co. £20-14-0." There is no later mention of the child. This document is in the Huntington Library.
14 William B. Reed, *Life and Correspondence of Joseph Reed*, vol. 2, pp. 260-72.
15 Reproduced through the courtesy of Miss Mary Perley of Charlottesville, Virginia. Another version of the letter, addressed to Frances Bland Randolph Tucker, is in the Tucker Papers, Library of Colonial Williamsburg.
16 *William and Mary Quarterly*, Series 2, vol. 10, p. 11.
17 It has been several times erroneously stated that Tabitha Wayles was married to Henry Skipwith. The latter married her sister, Ann Wayles, July 7, 1773. See their marriage bond, Charles City County Records, *Virginia Magazine*, vol. 23, p. 87. From the context of Robert Skipwith's letter, it is obvious he was married to Tabitha, or about to be.
18 Unpublished letter of Robert Skipwith to Thomas Jefferson. Coolidge Collection, Massachusetts Historical Society, vol. 1705-83.
19 Jefferson papers, Library of Congress.

NOTES

20 *Cf.* Mrs. Jefferson's accounts, Library of Congress.
21 Jefferson pocket account book for 1770, October 6. Deposited in the Library of Congress by General Jefferson R. Kean.
22 Lipscomb, vol. 4, p. 233.
23 *Ibid.*, p. 231.
24 *Ibid.*, pp. 235-36.
25 *Ibid.*, p. 240.
26 Undated Jefferson papers, Coolidge Collection, Massachusetts Historical Society.
27 The word "spinster" is crossed out and "widow" written above it.
28 Randall, vol. 1, p. 62, note.
29 Jefferson's pocket account book for 1772, Coolidge Collection, Massachusetts Historical Society.
30 *Idem.*
31 The seat of Colonel Edward Carter, near by. Lieutenant Anburey described it in 1779: "It stands on a lofty eminence, commanding a very extensive prospect. The present proprietor, Colonel Carter, possesses a most affluent fortune and has a variety of seats, in situations far surpassing this one, which he suffers to go to ruin."
32 Randall, vol. 1, p. 64.
33 Jefferson's garden book, Coolidge Collection, Massachusetts Historical Society.
34 Chastellux, *Travels in North America*, vol. 2, pp. 42-43.
35 *Thomas Jefferson Correspondence*, printed from the originals in the collection of William K. Bixby, pp. 11-12.
36 Lipscomb, vol. 1, p. 5.
37 Randall, vol. 1, p. 66. See also Jefferson's farm book, Coolidge Collection, Massachusetts Historical Society. There is likewise a summary of "Mr. Wayles lands," a "rough estimate of the land to be divided," and a "calculation of Mr. Jefferson's interest in Elk Island," at the back of Jefferson's account book for 1773. The Poplar Forest land was granted Wayles on December 21, 1764. See Coolidge Collection, vol. 1705-83, p. 11.
38 Randall, vol. 1, p. 65.
39 Quoted in Ford, vol. 1, p. 417.
40 Charles City County Records, vol. 1766-74, p. 461. Virginia State Library. Published in *Tyler's Quarterly*, vol. 6, pp. 268-70.
41 Will of Bathurst Skelton, Charles City County Records, vol. 1766-74. Printed in *Tyler's Quarterly*, vol. 6, p. 267.
42 Inventory and appraisement of the estate of Bathurst Skelton, Charles City County Records, 1766-74, p. 525.
43 *Ibid.*, p. 524.
44 *Idem.*

45 Jefferson manuscripts, Huntington Library.
46 *Virginia Magazine*, vol. 8, p. 14.
47 E. C. Burnett, *Letters of Members of the Continental Congress*, vol. 2, p. 28.
48 This draft is preserved in the Jefferson papers, Library of Congress, under that date. Jefferson may well have intended to say "solicitude" where he uses the word "decrepitude."
49 Lipscomb, vol. 4, pp. 192-93.
50 Ford, vol. 3, pp. 56-60. The sentences about Mrs. Jefferson's condition have been omitted from the Lipscomb edition.
51 Lipscomb, vol. 1, p. 90.
52 Undated Jefferson papers, Coolidge Collection, Massachusetts Historical Society.
53 Lipscomb, vol. 4, pp. 199-200.
54 These four lines, inscribed in Greek, are from the twenty-second book of the *Iliad*, in the apostrophe of Achilles to Patroclus over the dead body of Hector.

CHAPTER X

1 I. Finch, *Travels in the United States of America and Canada*, p. 254.
2 *Virginia Magazine*, vol. 43, p. 122.
3 Ford, vol. 9, p. 467.
4 *Ibid.*, p. 340.
5 *Ibid.*, p. 339.
6 *Ibid.*, p. 476.
7 *Ibid.*, p. 340.
8 *Ibid.*, p. 345.
9 *Ibid.*, p. 341. While President, Jefferson observed to a visitor, "Henry spoke wonderfully—call it oratory or what you please, but I never heard anything like it. He had more command over the passions than any man I ever knew... it was his profound knowledge of human nature and his manner of speaking more than the matter of his orations. After listening with the utmost attention, I sometimes endeavoured to recollect what he had been saying, but could never succeed." Finch, *Travels in the United States of America and Canada*, pp. 254-55.
10 William Wirt, *Life of Patrick Henry*, p. 40.
11 Ford, vol. 9, p. 339.
12 *Ibid.*, p. 466.
13 *Ibid.*, pp. 339-40.
14 Jefferson, quoted in Wirt, *Life of Patrick Henry*, p. 41.

NOTES 327

15 *Journals of the House of Burgesses,* vol. 1761-65, p. lix.
16 John Burk, *History of Virginia,* vol. 3, p. 305.
17 Ford, vol. 9, p. 340.
18 Burk, *History of Virginia,* vol. 3, p. 309. See also W. W. Henry, *Patrick Henry, Life, Correspondence and Speeches,* vol. 1, p. 86. There has been considerable divergence of opinion as to the exact wording of this speech. Henry's remarks were extempore and no written record was left, except, occasionally, the impressions of one of his hearers.
19 Ford, vol. 9, p. 473.
20 *Idem.*
21 *Cf.* John Adams's remarks in his *Works,* vol. 2, pp. 154-55.
22 Burk, *History of Virginia,* vol. 3, p. 331.
23 *Journals of the House of Burgesses of Virginia,* vol. 1766-69, pp. 181-92.
24 P. Toynbee, *Letters of Horace Walpole,* vol. 6, p. 50.
25 A. von Ruville, *William Pitt, Earl of Chatham,* vol. 3, pp. 237, 241.
26 "Meade Family History," *William and Mary Quarterly,* Series 1, vol. 13, p. 87.
27 *Idem.*
28 *Idem.*
29 *Virginia Gazette,* May 11, 1769.
30 *Journals of the House of Burgesses,* vol. 1766-69, p. 187.
31 *Ibid.,* p. 188.
32 *Ibid.,* p. 189.
33 Ford, vol. 9, p. 475.
34 *Journals of the House of Burgesses,* vol. 1766-69, p. 190.
35 *Ibid.,* pp. 189-90.
36 *Ibid.,* pp. 214-15.
37 *Ibid.,* pp. 215-16.
38 "Meade Family History," *William and Mary Quarterly,* Series 1, vol. 13, p. 86.
39 Proprietor of the Raleigh Tavern at this period.
40 *Virginia Gazette,* May 18, 1769.
41 F. N. Mason, *John Norton and Sons, Merchants of London and Virginia,* p. 94.
42 *Ibid.,* p. 103.
43 *Journals of the House of Burgesses,* vol. 1766-69, p. 227.
44 Lipscomb, vol. 1, p. 4.
45 *Journals of the House of Burgesses,* vol. 1766-69, p. 232.
46 *Ibid.,* p. 259.
47 Ford, vol. 9, p. 477.

CHAPTER XI

1 This bill has been preserved by the Virginia Historical Society.
2 *Massachusetts Gazette*, October 19, 1772.
3 *Virginia Gazette*, July 29, 1773, September 30, 1773.
4 *The Federalist*, edited by Paul Leicester Ford, p. vii.
5 *Ibid.*, p. 320.
6 *Idem.*
7 Lipscomb, vol. 8, p. 31.
8 *Ibid., vol.* 12, p. 414.
9 *Ibid.*, vol. 13, p. 13.
10 *Ibid.*, vol. 12, p. 407.
11 *Ibid.*, vol. 14, p. 120.
12 John Locke, *Two Treatises On Government*, Bk. II, Chap. 11, §141.
13 Lipscomb, vol. 8, p. 31.
14 Locke, *Two Treatises On Government*, Bk. 2, Chap. 2, pp. 339-40.
15 *Ibid.*, Bk. 2, Chap. 19, p. 472.
16 Lipscomb, vol. 4, p. 259.
17 *Ibid.*, vol. 1, p. 53.
18 *Ibid.*, vol. 2, pp. 217-18.
19 *Ibid.*, pp. 219-21.
20 *Ibid.*, vol. 1, p. 53.
21 *Ibid.*, p. 54.
22 *Idem.*
23 *Ibid.*, p. 55.
24 *Idem.*
25 *Ibid.*, p. 62.
26 *Ibid.*, pp. 62-63. Thomas Ludwell Lee is the "Mr. Lee."
27 *Ibid.*, p. 64.
28 *Idem.*
29 *Ibid.*, p. 65.
30 *Ibid.*, p. 66.
31 *Ibid.*, vol. 12, p. 300.
32 *Ibid.*, vol. 1, p. 66.
33 *Idem.*
34 *Ibid.*, pp. 59-60.
35 *Ibid.*, pp. 70-71.
36 *Ibid.*, p. 72.
37 *Idem.*
38 Ford, vol. 9, pp. 477-79.
39 Lipscomb, vol. 1, pp. 216-18.
40 *Ibid.*, vol. 2, pp. 218-19.

41 *Ibid.*, vol. 1, p. 58.
42 *Ibid.*, vol. 2, p. 221.
43 Bill for Establishing Religious Freedom.
44 Lipscomb, vol. 1, p. 67.
45 *Ibid.*, pp. 73-74.
46 *Ibid.*, pp. 60-61.
47 Letter to Dr. Benjamin Rush, Sept. 23, 1800. Ford, vol. 7, p. 460.

CHAPTER XII

1 Lipscomb, vol. 1, p. 6.
2 *Ibid.*, vol. 4, p. 235.
3 *William and Mary Quarterly*, Series 1, vol. 5, pp. 156 *ff*.
4 Edmund Randolph's Essay, *Virginia Magazine*, vol. 43, pp. 137-38.
5 Such a plan with an arcaded court is that of the Palazzo Thieni at Vicenza. Palladio, Bk. II, plate 9.
6 Letter to Lord Dartmouth, *Journals of the House of Burgesses*, vol. 1773-76, pp. ix *ff*.
7 Lipscomb, vol. 1, p. 7.
8 William Wirt, *Life of Patrick Henry*, pp. 90-91.
9 Lipscomb, vol. 1, p. 7.
10 *Ibid.*, vol. 14, p. 399.
11 Wirt, *Life of Patrick Henry*, p. 89.
12 *Journals of the House of Burgesses*, vol. 1773-76, p. 28.
13 *Idem.*
14 *Journals of the House of Burgesses*, 1773-76, p. 36.
15 Lipscomb, vol. 1, p. 9.
16 *Idem.*
17 *Journals of the House of Burgesses*, 1773-76, p. 124.
18 *Ibid.*, p. 132.
19 Lipscomb, vol. 1, p. 10.
20 *Idem.*
21 *Ibid.*, p. 182.
22 Peter Force, *American Archives*, 4th Series, vol. 1, p. 638.
23 *Idem.*
24 *Idem.*
25 Edmund Randolph's Essay, *Virginia Magazine*, vol. 43, pp. 216-17.
26 Jefferson's account book for 1774, Coolidge Collection, Massachusetts Historical Society.
27 *Ibid.*
28 Lipscomb, vol. 1, p. 183.
29 *Virginia Magazine*, vol. 43, p. 216.
30 Lipscomb, vol. 1, p. 183.
31 *Ibid.*, p. 11.

32 Ford, vol. 9, p. 474, note.
33 This entry appears in Washington's Ledger B, under date of August 6, 1774. *Cf.* John C. Fitzpatrick, *Diaries of George Washington*, vol. 2, p. 159.
34 James Wilson, *Considerations of the Nature and Extent of the Legislative Authority of the British Parliament*, p. 34.
35 *Ibid.*, p. 3.
36 Frances N. Mason, *John Norton and Sons*, p. 52.
37 Item No. 694 is an extract from Lord Kames's *Natural Religion*; No. 695 an extract from Warner's *History of Ireland*, which Jefferson acquired in December 1769.
38 The quotations from *The Summary View* are from Lipscomb, vol. 1, pp. 181-211.
39 *Ibid.*, p. 185.
40 *Ibid.*, p. 209.

CHAPTER XIII

1 John Adams, *Works*, vol. 2, p. 365. Carpenter's Hall at this time housed the books of the well-known Library Company of Philadelphia.
2 Edmund Randolph's Essay, *Virginia Magazine*, vol. 43, p. 216.
3 Adams, *Works*, vol. 2, p. 362.
4 Lipscomb, vol. 1, pp. 212-13.
5 *Ibid.*, p. 214.
6 Papers of Silas Deane, *New York Historical Society Collections*, vol. for 1886, pp. 19 and 26.
7 Adams, *Works*, vol. 2, pp. 366-67.
8 *Ibid.*, pp. 362-63.
9 Deane papers, p. 26.
10 John C. Fitzpatrick, *The Writings of George Washington*, vol. 3, pp. 246-47.
11 Adams, *Works*, vol. 10, p. 177.
12 *Idem.*
13 *Journals of Congress* (edition of 1777), vol. 1, p. 34.
14 *Ibid.*, p. 35.
15 John Burk, *History of Virginia*, vol. 4, pp. 6-7.
16 Lipscomb, vol. 4, pp. 23-26.
17 Jefferson's pocket account book for 1775, p. 17. Huntington Library.
18 Ford, vol. 1, p. 448.
19 Mrs. Carrington's account in William Meade, *Old Churches, Ministers and Families of Virginia*, vol. 1, p. 140.

20 *Virginia Magazine*, vol. 43, pp. 219-20. *Cf.* also Peter Force, *American Archives*, 4th Series, vol. 3, p. 167.
21 William Wirt, *Life of Patrick Henry*, pp. 116-17.
22 *Ibid.*, pp. 118-19.
23 Edmund Randolph's Essay, *Virginia Magazine*, vol. 43, p. 223.
24 Wirt, *Life of Patrick Henry*, pp. 121-23.
25 *Ibid.*, p. 124.
26 Edmund Randolph's Essay, *Virginia Magazine*, vol. 43, p. 222.
27 *Ibid.*, p. 223.
28 *Ibid.*, p. 228.
29 Jefferson's pocket account book for 1775, p. 6. Huntington Library.
30 Force, *American Archives*, 4th Series, vol. 2, p. 236.
31 Edmund Randolph's Essay, *Virginia Magazine*, vol. 43, p. 299.
32 *Ibid.*, p. 132.
33 Gilmer papers, *Virginia Historical Society Collections*, vol. 6, pp. 102-103.
34 The other members were Archibald Cary, Robert Carter Nicholas, Thomas Nelson, Jr., Dudley Digges, Robert Mumford of Mecklenburg County, James Mercer of Hampshire, and Joseph Jones of King George.
35 *Journals of the House of Burgesses*, 1773-76, p. 175.
36 Lipscomb, vol. 1, p. 14.
37 Edmund Randolph's Essay, *Virginia Magazine*, vol. 43, p. 294.
38 *Journals of the House of Burgesses*, vol. 1773-76, pp. 219-21.
39 William T. Read, *Life of George Reade*, p. 106.
40 Adams, *Works*, vol. 2, p. 511.
41 *Ibid.*, pp. 513-14.
42 Lipscomb, vol. 1, p. 16.
43 *Journals of Congress* (edition of 1777), vol. 1, pp. 143-48.
44 "Being disliked, it was recommitted, & Mr. Dickinson & T. Jefferson added to the committee. The latter being desired by the commee to draw up a new one, he prepared this paper. On a meeting of the commee J. Dickinson objected that it was too harsh, wanting softening etc. Whereupon the commee desired him to retouch it, which he did in the form which they reported July 6, which was adopted by Congress." (Ford, vol. 1, p. 463). Ford prints Jefferson's first, rough draft and the second, submitted to the Committee, with notes in the writing of Dickinson. There is nothing advanced in the argument of G. H. Moore, in connection with a reproduction of the declaration in Dickinson's hand, to convince the critical that this is anything more than a copy over which Dickinson worked and on which he made notes. *Cf.* C. J. Stillé, "Life and Times of John Dickinson" in *Memoirs of the Historical Society of Pennsylvania*, vol. 1, pp. 353-64.

45 *Journals of Congress* (1777), vol. 1, pp. 147-48.
46 *Warren-Adams Letters*, vol. 1, p. 74.
47 Force, *American Archives*, 4th Series, vol. 3, p. 369.
48 Published by kind permission of the Historical Society of Pennsylvania, Gratz Collection, case 1, box 19.
49 Lipscomb, vol. 1, p. 17.
50 *Journals of Congress* (1777), vol. 1, p. 191.
51 Lipscomb, vol. 4, pp. 28-31.
52 Deane papers, p. 52.
53 *Journals of Congress* (1777), pp. 267 and 268.
54 Lipscomb, vol. 4, pp. 245-46.
55 *Ibid.*, pp. 246 and 251.
56 Jefferson's account book for 1775, p. 21. Huntington Library.
57 *Summary View*, Lipscomb, vol. 1, p. 185.
58 Lipscomb, vol. 4, pp. 31-33.

CHAPTER XIV

1 *Journals of Congress* (edition of 1777), vol. 1, p. 292.
2 Lipscomb, vol. 4, p. 250.
3 Pocket account book for 1776, p. 4. Coolidge Collection, Massachusetts Historical Society.
4 Lipscomb, vol. 4, p. 253.
5 Jefferson papers, Library of Congress.
6 Thomas Paine, *Common Sense Addressed to the Inhabitants of America* (1776), pp. 1 and 17.
7 Thomas Paine, *The American Crisis*, No. I, p. 1.
8 Edmund Randolph's Essay, *Virginia Magazine*, vol. 43, pp. 306-307.
9 J. C. Ballagh, *The Letters of Richard Henry Lee*, vol. 1, p. 173.
10 W. B. Reed, *Life and Correspondence of Joseph Reed*, vol. 1, p. 158.
11 Charles Francis Adams, *Familiar Letters of John Adams*, p. 135.
12 *Warren-Adams Letters*, vol. 1, pp. 233-34.
13 Lipscomb, vol. 2, p. 166.
14 *Warren-Adams Letters*, vol. 1, p. 230.
15 Peter Force, *American Archives*, 4th Series, vol. 5, p. 863.
16 *Southern Literary Messenger*, vol. 27, p. 255.
17 *Ibid.*, p. 326.
18 *Warren-Adams Letters*, vol. 1, p. 219.
19 *Journal of the Provincial Congress of South Carolina*, 1776, p. 112.
20 *Warren-Adams Letters*, vol. 1, p. 232.
21 William L. Saunders, *Colonial Records of North Carolina*, vol. 10, p. 512.

NOTES

22 Ballagh, *The Letters of Richard Henry Lee*, vol. 1, p. 176.
23 Force, *American Archives*, 4th Series, vol. 6, p. 1524.
24 Edmund Randolph's Essay, *Virginia Magazine*, vol. 44, p. 42.
25 Adams, *Works*, vol. 9, p. 374.
26 Lipscomb, vol. 1, p. 17.
27 *Virginia Magazine*, vol. 43, pp. 43-44.
28 Jefferson ledger, Huntington Library.
29 Adams, *Works*, vol. 9, p. 391.
30 *Warren-Adams Letters*, vol. 1, p. 245.
31 *Journals of Congress* (1777), vol. 2, p. 166.
32 Lipscomb, vol. 4, pp. 253-56.
33 Force, *American Archives*, 4th Series, vol. 6, p. 1524.
34 *Notes on Virginia*, Lipscomb, vol. 2, p. 166.
35 Ford, vol. 2, pp. 7 ff.
36 Lipscomb, vol. 16, p. 116.
37 Both versions are printed in Ford, vol. 2, pp. 7-30.
38 Burk, *History of Virginia*, vol. 4, p. 151, note.
39 Lipscomb, vol. 16, p. 116.
40 *Warren-Adams Letters*, vol. 1, pp. 249-50.
41 Force, *American Archives*, 4th Series, vol. 6, p. 1700. The original manuscript in Lee's hand, is in the Library of Congress, Papers of the Continental Congress, No. 23, Vol. 11. On the back it is endorsed by Benjamin Franklin and Charles Thomson, as well as in another hand, believed to be R. Livingston's—"Resolved that it is the opinion of this committee that the first resolution be postponed to this day three weeks, and that in the meantime, least any time should be lost in case the Congress agree to this resolution, a committee be appointed to prepare a declaration to the effect of the first resolution."
42 H. P. Johnston, *Correspondence and Public Papers of John Jay*, vol. 1, p. 66, note.
43 *Journals of Congress* (1777), vol. 2, pp. 204-205.
44 Johnston, *Papers of John Jay*.
45 These notes were later embodied by Jefferson in his *Autobiography*. They are written on sheets of a different kind and size from the rest of the manuscript.
46 The quotations concerning this debate are from Jefferson's notes in Lipscomb, vol. 1, pp. 17-28.
47 *Ibid.*, p. 25.
48 *Journals of Congress* (1777), vol. 2, p. 206.
49 *Ibid.*, p. 207.
50 The quotations concerning this day are from the *Journals of Congress* (1777), vol. 2, pp. 236-37.

51 Gratz Collection, Historical Society of Pennsylvania. Quoted in John H. Hazleton, *The Declaration of Independence*, p. 139.
52 Lipscomb, vol. 1, p. 26.
53 *Ibid.*, pp. 17-28.
54 *Cf.* Lipscomb, vol. 1, p. 17, "In Congress, Friday, June 7," to p. 18. "Monday the 10th in debating on the subject," and p. 25, "it appearing in the course of these debates" to p. 28, "lest they should give them offence."
55 Adams, *Works*, vol. 2, pp. 512-15.
56 For a discussion of the drafting of the declaration, and the changes made by Adams, Franklin, and Congress, see Hazleton, *The Declaration of Independence*, pp. 141-156, also Carl Becker, *The Declaration of Independence*, pp. 135-194.
57 Lipscomb, vol. 15, p. 461.
58 Diary of Christopher Marshall, Historical Society of Pennsylvania.
59 Adams, *Works*, vol. 9, p. 414.
60 *Journals of Congress* (1777), vol. 2, p. 238.
61 Adams, *Works*, vol. 3, p. 54.
62 *Ibid.*, vol. 9, p. 415.
63 *Journals of Congress* (1777), vol. 2, p. 238.
64 Lipscomb, vol. 17, p. 148.
65 *Ibid.*, vol. 1, p. 27.
66 Adams, *Works*, vol. 9, p. 416.
67 *Ibid.*, vol. 9, pp. 418 and 420.
68 Lipscomb, vol. 1, p. 28.
69 Ford, vol. 10, p. 120, note.
70 *Idem.*
71 Lipscomb, vol. 15, p. 463.
72 Ford, vol. 9, pp. 377-78.
73 *Journals of Congress*, vol. 2, p. 241.
74 Ford, vol. 2, pp. 42-45. The text of the so-called "Rough Draught," as reported to Congress.
75 The similarity of form and ideas between the preamble of the Declaration and that of the Virginia Constitution has often been commented on. Edmund Pendleton well expressed the views of his contemporaries when he wrote Jefferson, "I expected you had in the Preamble to our form of Government, exhausted the subject of complaint against Geo. 3rd and was at a loss to discover what the Congress would do for one to their Declaration of Independence without copying, but find you have acquitted yourselves very well on that score."
76 Ford, vol. 2, pp. 57-58.

NOTES

77 Jefferson states in his *Autobiography* that the Declaration was signed on July 4 by "every member present except Mr. Dickinson." This was apparently not the case. For a discussion of the signing see Ford, vol. 1, pp. 28-29, note. Also Hazleton, *The Declaration of Independence*, pp. 193-220.
78 *Journals of Congress* (1777), vol. 2, p. 247.
79 Adams, *Works*, vol. 9, p. 420.
80 *Warren-Adams Letters*, vol. 1, p. 261.
81 J. C. Fitzpatrick, *Writings of George Washington*, vol. 5, p. 245.
82 Lipscomb, vol. 16, p. 121.
83 Ballagh, *Letters of Richard Henry Lee*, vol. 1, p. 210.
84 Jefferson papers, Library of Congress.
85 Lipscomb, vol. 15, p. 462.
86 *Ibid.*, vol. 16, p. 121.
87 *Ibid.*, vol. 15, p. 462.
88 *Ibid.*, vol. 16, pp. 117-19.
89 *Ibid.*, vol. 12, p. 297.
90 Adams, *Works*, vol. 9, p. 420.

INDEX

Account books, Jefferson's, 87, 102, 149, 150, 278, 284, 318, 324
Acrobats, 59-60
Adams, Henry, 4
———, John, 128, 251, 252, 253, 266, 268, 270, 281, 282, 283, 284, 286, 290, 291, 292, 294, 295-296, 297, 299, 300, 303, 305, 306, 334
———, Richard, 102
———, Samuel, 5, 266
———, Thomas, 101, 156, 174, 230
Addison, writings, 13
Aeolian harp, 163
Agriculture, 106, 149, 209; see also Tobacco
Akenside, writings, 87, 116
Aland, "Reports," 107
Albemarle County, 19-20; see also individual places and estates
Albemarle Resolutions, 237-238
Alberti, 54-55
Allegheny Mountains, 36, 194, 309
Allegre, William, 174
Alliances, 291-293
Alsop, 266
Ambler, Jacquelin, 69, 71
———, Rebecca Burwell, see Burwell
Amelia County, 309
"American Crisis," 280
Amherst County, 19, 135

Ampthill, 185
Anacreon, 110
Anburey, Thomas, quoted, 27
Andrews, George, "Reports," 87, 88
Anglomania, 213
Anglo-Saxon, 107-108, 224
Anglo-Saxons, 246
Annapolis, 88, 135, 136-137, 138, 265, 270
Anson, "Voyage around the World," 13
Antoninus, 115
Apollo room, see Williamsburg, Raleigh tavern
Appomattox County, 19
Architecture, in Virginia, 52, 138-139; 147-160; see also Houses
Aristotle, 306
Armistead family, 47
———, W., 69
Arms, coat of, 173
Army, 267, 273
Arnold, Benedict, 177
Assembly, Virginia, 8, 11, 36, 54, 60-61, 182, 187-209, 217, 229-237, 240, 261-265, 290; see also Council; and House of Burgesses
Associations, non-importation, 203-205, 229, 236-238, 251, 252, 254-256
Astronomy, 80, 110, 141, 169

INDEX

Athens, Monument of Lysicrates, 162, 322
"Attorney's Pocket Companion," 83
Augusta County, 36, 90, 141
"Autobiography," *see* Jefferson, Thomas, writings
Aylett, William, 282

Backgammon, 130
Bacon, Matthew, writings, 81
Baker, Dentist, 177
Ballenger's Creek, 310
Balls, *see* Dancing
Bartley, James, 28
Bartram, John, 15-16
——, William, 16
Bear Castle, 45
Beccaria, Cesare, writings, 224, 244
Beck, Will, 155
Bedford County, 173, 178
Belinda, *see* Burwell, Rebecca
Bellini, Charles, 154
Belmont, 24
Belvoir, 131, 142, 143, 144, 145
Belvoir Church, 35
Berkeley family, 196
——, Norborne, *see* Botetourt
Bermuda Hundred, 10, 15, 169
Bernard, John, 113
Beveridge, Albert J., 4
Beverley Town, 310
Bible, 13, 80, 106, 123-129
Bill of Rights, Virginia, 290
Billingsport, 294

Biswell, John, 21-22, 23
Blackstone, Sir William, "Commentaries," 76, 77, 79, 81, 106
Blackwater, 310
Blair, John, 200, 201, 202
——, cited, 61, 169
Bland family, 9
——, Edward, 47
——, Richard, 90, 193, 196, 199, 206, 230, 233, 238, 240, 241, 252, 254, 257, 270, 288, 305
——, Theodoric, 90
——, William, 132
Blenheim, 176
Blue Ridge Mountains, 7, 17, 18, 21, 37, 148, 163, 194, 309
Boccherini, Luigi, 57
Bold Branch, 310
Bolingbroke, Lord, writings, 105, 106, 113-114, 124, 243, 318
Bolling, Archibald, 47
——, Captain, 10
Boston, 195, 235, 266, 273, 279; Port Bill, 234-235, 253
Botany, 38, 79
Botetourt, Lord, 196-206, 211, 229, 230
Bourdaloue, Louis, "Sermons," 81
Bowling Green, 270
Bracton, Henry De, writings, 81
Branch family, 9
——, Christopher, 8
Brandon, 47
Braxton, Carter, 55, 196, 261
Bristol parish, 9
Broadnax, William, 47

INDEX   339

Brooke, Robert, 29
———, Thomas (the younger), 23, 29
Brown, student at William and Mary, 69
———, Dr., physician, 177
———, John, 76
———, Richard, 321
Brunswick County, 310
Buchanan, James, 256
Buckingham County, 19, 31
Building, *see* Architecture
Bullock, Archibald, 297
Bunker Hill, 281
Burgesses, House of, *see* House of Burgesses
Burk, John, "History of Virginia," 50, 51, 82, 195, 261
Burke, Edmund, writings, 105
Burlamaqui, Jean Jacques, writings, 210, 243, 244
Burlington, Lord, 147, 164
Burnaby, Andrew, cited, 74
Burr, Aaron, 142
Burwell, Col., 61
———, Fanny, 132
———, Lewis, 3d, 66
———, Lewis, 4th, 44, 47, 65, 90, 135, 196
———, Mary Willis, 66
———, Nathaniel, 122
———, Rebecca, 66-72, 111, 132, 147, 166
Byrd, Mrs., 277
———, William, 8, 10, 23, 51, 99, 103, 139, 211, 277, 308, 311

Cabinet-makers, 57
Cadell, T., 210
Caesar, 106
Caesar, ship, 35
Callender, Thomas, 5, 144-145
Camden, William, "Britannia," 246
Campbell, John, 189
Campbell County, 19
Campioni, 58
Canada, 273, 282
Capital punishment, 225
Caroline County, 198, 221, 254
Carr, Barbara Overton, 45
———, Dabney, 45-47, 115, 168, 185, 211, 231, 232-233
———, Dabney, Jr., 46
———, John, 45
———, Martha Jefferson, 168, 184
———, Peter, 115, 125
Carter, Edward, 187, 325
———, Landon, 54
———, Robert, 56-57, 136
Carter's Creek, 65
Carter's Grove, 139
Carter's Mountain, 164
Cary, Archibald, 198, 233, 255, 288, 331
Cary & Co., 159-160
Case register, Jefferson's, 90, 91
Castle Hill, 24, 25, 131
Cato, 25
Cedar Creek, 140
Celtic, 119
Celts, 245

340 INDEX

Chamber's, Sir William, "Designs of Chinese Buildings," 154
Chambone, 14
Chancery, 81, 83, 88, 89
Chapel Ridge, 21
Charles City County, 169, 176, 179, 180, 187, 196
Charlottesville, 123, 130, 206, 278, 311
Chase, Samuel, 266
Chastellux, Marquis de, 120, 159-160, 163-164, 177-178
Chatsworth, 39
Chelsea, 79
Cherokees, 19, 206
Chess, 104, 130, 141
Chesterfield County, 10, 198
Chew, Benjamin, 139
Chinese taste, 162, 164
Chipman, "Principles of Government," 82
Chippendale, 102, 138, 139
Chiswell, John, 133
——, Mary, 133
Christianity, a part of common law?, 95-96; see also Religion
Church, Anglican, 36-37, 95-96, 127-128, 188, 189-190, 217, 226
Church, Presbyterian, 217
Cicero, 111-112, 115, 306; "Offices," 80, 106; "Orations," 82; "Tusculan Disputations," 112, 319
Clavichord, 174
Clay, Henry, 74
——, Rev. Mr., 239
Clergy, 95, 127-128, 226; see also Parson's Cause

Clothing, 74, 172, 205-206
Coalter, John, 76
Cocke family, 9
——, Mr., 56, 61
——, Benjamin, 20
Cockfighting, 60
Coffeehouse, 134, 135
Coke, Sir Edward, "Institutes," 37, 66, 78, 79, 81, 87
Coles, Col., 143
——, Edward, 207
Colle, 171
Colleges, 222; see also individual names
Collinson, Peter, 15-16
Colonial policy, 247-249; see also Taxation, Trade, etc.; rights, 241, 245-246
Columbian Sentinel, 146
Committees of Safety, 253-256, 284
Commonplace books, Jefferson's, 81, 84-89, 94, 106, 110-116, 210-214, 224
Concerts, 134; see also Music
Condorcet, Marie-Jean-Antoine, "Esprit Humain," 80
Confederation, 291, 294
Congress, Continental, 103, 138, 159, 212, 216, 236, 238, 243, 246, 250-253, 256, 260, 262, 264, 265-271, 273-274, 277-205
Congreve, William, writings, 115
Conscience, freedom of, see Religious Freedom
Constitution, Virginia, 87-290, 334
Continental Congress, see Congress, Continental

Convention, Virginia, 256-259, 268, 270, 281, 283, 284, 285, 286-290, 291
Corbin, Alice, 64, 132
———, Colonel, 91
———, Richard, 261
Corcyra, 246
Corelli, 57, 88
Corinth, 246
Corneille, 122
Cornwallis, Lord, 170, 177
Correspondence, Committees of, 46, 200, 232-234, 236, 277
Cosway, Maria, 57, 142, 148
Cotton, "Virgil," 170
Coules, Mr., 29
Council, Virginia, 17, 32, 101
Courts, 91-93; organization of, 218; *see also* General Court
Coutts, Rev. Mr., 176
Coxendale, 9
Cox's Creek, 311
Craig, 240
Crane, William, 78
Cresswell, Nicholas, 61
Criminal law, 220, 224-226
Croft, Herbert, 107
Croke, "Reports," 88
Culpepper County, 133, 285
Cumberland, Duke of, 197
Cumberland County, 47, 179, 180, 310
Cunningham, "Law Dictionary," 106
Curles, 8, 15
Currency, depreciation, 178, 231

Dale, Sir Thomas, 8, 11
Dalrymple, "Feudal Property," 88
Dancing, 35, 53, 60-62, 130, 205, 240
Dandridge, Colonel, 39
———, Nathaniel, 188, 189
Danes, 241
Dangerfield, 68
Dargenville, "Jardinage," 148
Dartmouth, Lord, 274
Darwin, Erasmus, 45, 48
Davila, Enrico Caterino, writings, 106, 318
Davis, Rev. Mr., 176
Davis Creek, 309
Dawson, Thomas, 41
Deane, Silas, 252, 272
Declaration of Independence, 243, 276, 292-297, 299-306, 334, 335
Declaration of Rights, 254
"Declaration to be published by General Washington," 266-268
Declaratory Act, 194
Deer, 162, 163-164
Deism, 124
Delaplaine, Joseph, 107
Delaware, 291, 298
Delaware River, 294
"Della Istoria D'Italia," 106
De Lolme, "Constitution d'Angleterre," 82
Demosthenes, 82, 112
Denmark, 246
Descents, law of, **220**

"Determinations of the House of Commons," 210
Dewey, Stephen, 75
Dialogue of Head and Heart, 67
Dickinson, John, 266, 267, 268, 292, 297, 298, 305, 331; "Farmer's Letters," 242
Dictionaries, 13, 106, 169
Digges, Dudley, 233, 234, 331
Dinwiddie, Robert, 44, 91
Dissenters, 226
Divers, George, 37
Dixon, J., 103
Dodsley, Robert, "Description of the Leasowes," 148
"Don Quixote," 105
Douglas, Rev. William, 30-31
Dover Church, 31
Dover Creek, 28
Drummond, Mrs., 174-175
Dryden, John, writings, 105, 115, 122, 169
Duane, William, 214
Dudley, George, 155, 157
Dungeness, 3, 15, 47
Dunmore, Lady, 240
Dunmore, Lord, 230-231, 234, 236, 260, 262, 274, 279
Dutch Republic, 246
Duval, William, 78

Earthquake, 239
Ecclesiastical jurisdiction, 95
Eden, William, "Penal Law," 95-96
Edgehill, 4, 23, 70

Edgeworth, 35
———, Maria, 122
Edinburgh University, 138
Edmunds, J., 68
Education, reform of, 222-223
Electricity, 106
Elizabeth City County, 8, 75
Elk, 135, 162
Elk Creek, 311
Elk Hill, 170, 173, 251, 260, 270, 324
Elk Island, 169-170, 180, 181
Elk Run, 45
Ellis, "Tracts on Liberty," 210, 244
Elstob, "Anglo-Saxon Grammar," 108
Emancipation, 223-224
England, see Parliament and other topics
"English Prosody, Thoughts on," 118
Entail, 11, 219
Epictetus, 110
Epicurus, 110
Eppes family, 9
———, Captain, 10
———, Francis (Jefferson's brother-in-law), 47, 175, 179, 180, 274, 277
———, Francis (Jefferson's grandson), 113
———, John Wayles, 47, 122
Eppington, 184, 240
Equity, 81, 88-89
Essex County, 23, 29, 60
Euripides, 110-111

INDEX 343

Everand, Thomas, 56
Expatriation, right of, 247

Fairfax, Lord, 29, 90
Fairfield, 65, 70, 78, 86, 134, 135
Farm book, 17, 278, 309-311, 325
Farming, *see* Agriculture, Tobacco.
Fauquier, Francis, 36, 45, 48, 49-51, 76, 120, 125, 196, 211, 230
Fauquier County, 133, 285
Federalist, The, 212
Federalists, 142
Fee book, 90, 91, 96, 324
Fees, legal, 91
Fénélon, François, "Dialogues of the Dead," 106; "Télémaque," 170
Ferguson, Adam, "Civil Society," 210, 244
———, James, writings, 141, 169
Feudalism, 228, 245
Field family, 9
———, Judith, 10
———, Mary, 10
———, Peter, 10
Fielding, novels, 105
Fine Creek, 7, 11, 12, 13, 14, 28
Fitch, Col., 253
Fitzhugh, William, 136
Fleischer, F. G., 319
Fleming, William, 47, 70-72, 80
Flower de Hundred, 8
Flute, 57
Fluvanna County, 19
Fluvanna River, 32, 33, 310, 311

Fonblanque, Albany William, writings, 81
Fontaine, Peter, 36, 37
Fontainebleau, 34
Forest, The, 122, 156, 169, 172, 173, 174, 176, 177, 256
Fort Stanwix, New York, 140, 143
Fossils, 37
Fowey, ship, 262
Fox hunting, 63
France, 291, 292, 293
Franchise, 289
Frank, "Astronomy," 13
Franklin, Benjamin, 106, 270, 280, 294, 297, 299, 333, 334
Frederick County, 230
Fredericksburg, 220, 261, 265
Fredericksville parish, 34, 123, 251
Fredericktown, Maryland, 285
Free trade, 247
French, Jefferson's knowledge of, 31, 107
Frontier, 3, 8, 19
Fry, Joshua, 13, 17, 20, 22, 23-24

Galatians, 245
Galt, John, 315
Game, 162, 163-164
Gaming, 42, 43, 51, 63, 130
Garden book, 38, 46, 149, 176, 278
Gardeners, 57
Gardening, 53, 106, 148-149, 160-165, 175, 177
Garrick, David, 117

Gaspee incident, 231
Gates, William, 153
Gauls, 245
General Court, 85, 89, 90, 91, 92-93, 100-101, 317
Genlis, Madame de, 122
Geography, 80, 106, 169
George III, 192, 197, 200, 202-203, 204, 208, 233, 235, 242, 247-249, 250, 252, 257, 259, 260, 265, 266, 274, 275-276, 280, 285, 286, 289, 293, 302
Georgia, 291, 292, 298, 299
German, Jefferson's study of, 108-109
Germans, 245; see also Saxons
Gerry, Elbridge, 138
Gibbon, Edward, "Roman Empire," 82
Gibbs, James, "Designs," 164; "Rules for Drawing," 153
"Gil Blas," 105
Gilbert, Baron, writings, 81
Gilbreth, Frank B., 157
Gilmer, George, 137-138, 256, 261
——, George, Jr., 278, 284-285
——, Mrs., 185
Girardin, Louis H., "History of Virginia," 50, 255
Gleim, J. W., 319
Gloucester County, 8, 44, 47, 65, 134, 196, 240
Goethe, Johann Wolfgang von, 85, 109, 119
Goldsmith, Oliver, writings, 105
Goochland County, 7, 11, 14, 15, 16, 17, 18, 30, 31, 46, 47, 133, 134, 179, 180, 309

Goodall, lawyer, 137
Goodwin et al. vs. Lunan, 94-95
Gordon, "History of Parliaments," 210
Gordonsville, 35
Gothic architecture, 139, 164
Government, principles of, 209-228
Graaf, Mr., 285
Graves, Joshua, 24
Grayson, William, 140
Great Britain, see Parliament and other topics
Grecian taste, 162, 164
Greece, 245
Greek, Jefferson's knowledge of, 31, 106, 110-111
Greek revival, 322
Greenspring, 135
Grenville, George, 192
Grotius, Hugo, writings, 244
"Grounds and Rudiments of Law," 83
"Guardian," 13
Guitar, 58
Gunn, 70
Guthrie, William, "History of England," 246

Habington, "Edward IV," 82
Hale, Matthew, "Common Law," 88
Halifax, 36
Halifax, N. S., 195
Hallam, 59
Hamilton, Alexander, 14, 212

INDEX

Hampshire County, 331
Hancock, John, 5, 303
——, Robert, 10
Handel, George Frederick, 57
Hanover, 241
Hanover County, 34, 36, 39, 133, 135, 169, 188, 190, 261
Hardware River, 33
Harpsichord, 57, 58
Harris, B., 310
——, Joseph, 170
Harrison, "Chancery Practice," 83
Harrison, Col., 136, 172
——, Benjamin, 47, 90, 132, 136, 196, 199, 202, 233, 238, 252, 255, 257, 259, 266, 268, 270, 292, 297, 301
——, Carter Henry, 90
Harvie, John, 13, 17, 21, 23, 24, 33, 35, 39, 102, 317
Hatsell, "House of Commons," 82
Hawtry, Stephen, 49-50
Hay, Anthony, 203
Haydn, Franz Josef, 57
Head and Heart, Dialogue of, 67
Heidelberg, University of, 216
Helvetic Republic, 246
Helvétius, Claude Adrien, writings, 96, 213
Henderson, Bennet, 279
——, John, 279
Hening, William W., "Statutes at Large," 96
Hennings, Betty, 176, 180
Henrico County, 8, 9, 10, 11, 169, 196

Henry, Patrick, 36-37, 39, 46, 56, 84, 92, 140, 188-194, 202, 231, 232, 233, 234, 238, 240, 252-253, 257, 258-259, 261, 268, 283, 285, 288, 326, 327
Herder, Johann G., 119
Heresy, 218
Hermitage, *see* Monticello
Herring, 58
Herring Creek, 179
Highland County, 19
Hill, Edward, 308
——, Richard, 274
Hillsborough, Earl of, 205
Hiltzheiner, Jacob, 265
Hippocrates, 25
"History of Civil Wars," 244
Hobbes, Thomas, writings, 303
Hobs Hole, 60
Hogarth, William, "Analysis of Beauty," 105
Holliday, 238
Homer, 110-111, 118, 326; *see also* Pope, writings
Hopkins, Arthur, 16
Hopkinson, Francis, 294
Horace, 88, 113, 116
Horsemanden, Chief Justice, 230
Horsemanship, Jefferson's, 38, 134
Horse-racing, 11, 42, 60, 63, 130
House of Burgesses, 15, 19, 30, 46, 52, 53, 75, 96, 177, 187-209, 231-236, 238, 241, 257, 262-265, 266, 306
House of Delegates, 217, 218, 222, 225, 226

346 INDEX

Houses, Virginia, 14-15, 21, 22, 52, 65, 139, 147, 148; *see also* names of individual houses
Howard, S., 117
Howell *vs.* Netherland, 93-94, 216
"Humble Address," 202-203
"Humble Petition," 274
Hume, David, writings, 79, 104, 106, 107, 213-214
Humphreys, Charles, 299
Hunting, 38
Hutchinson, "Moral Philosophy," 80

Independence, Declaration of, *see* Jefferson, Thomas, writings; sentiment for, 279-306
Indians, 8, 19, 36, 206, 286
Industry, sloop, 210
Ingles, Mr., 35
Inoculation, 137, 165
"Instruction for Indians," 13
Inventories, 9, 12-13, 33-34, 172, 180-181
Ireland, 273
Irish, 194, 210
Isham family, 9
———, Henry, 15
Italian, study of, 106

Jacquelin, Martha, 205
Jamaica, 257
James I, 241
James City County, 196, 254
James, John, "Gardening," 148
James River, 4, 7, 8, 11, 13, 15, 16, 19, 47, 132, 168, 170, 179, 222, 309
Jamestown, 196
Jay, John, 266, 291
Jefferson, of Flower de Hundred, 8
———, Elizabeth, 26, 28, 239
———, Field, 12
———, Jane, sister of Thomas, 18, 28, 163
———, Jane Randolph, wife of Peter, 3, 4, 16, 18, 27, 32, 33, 277-278
———, Jane Randolph, daughter of Thomas, 273
———, John, 8
———, Judith Farrar, 12
———, Lucy Elizabeth, 181, 184
———, Martha, sister of Peter, 12
———, Martha, sister of Thomas, 168, 184
———, Martha, daughter of Thomas; *see* Randolph, Martha Jefferson
———, Martha Wayles, 58, 103, 120, 122, 156, 159, 165, 168-186; 216, 271, 274, 277
———, Mary, sister of Peter, 12
———, Mary, sister of Thomas, 18, 28
———, Mary (Maria), daughter of Thomas, 47, 181, 239
———, Mary Field, 10
———, Peter, 3, 7, 11, 12-14, 16-24, 28-30, 31-34; land holdings, 16-18, 32-33, 309-311; library, 13; will and inventory, 32-34
———, Randolph, 32, 33
———, Robert, 8
———, Thomas, of Henrico, great-grandfather of President Jefferson, 8-9

INDEX 347

Jefferson, Captain Thomas, Jun'r, grandfather of President Jefferson, 9-12, 14

——, Thomas, 3rd, 11

——, Thomas, ancestry, 3, 8-12; birth, 26; schooling, 27-28, 30-32, 34-38; at William and Mary College, 39-63; youthful attachment to Rebecca Burwell, 64-72; study of law, 73-89; practice of law, 89-96; literary tastes, 100-129; diversions, 130-146; building and planting, 147-165; courtship and marriage, 166-186; in House of Burgesses, 1769, 187-208; principles of government, 208-229; political activity, 1770-1775, 229-265; in Second Continental Congress, 265-306.

Writings: "Autobiography," 10, 12, 18, 27, 34, 47, 206, 224, 226, 228, 229, 263, 295, 333; "Bill for Establishing Religious Freedom," 123, 227; Declaration of Independence, 243, 276, 292-297, 299-306, 334, 335; "Declaration to be published by General Washington," 266-268; Dialogue of Head and Heart, 67; "Essay on the Anglo-Saxon Language," 108; "Life and Morals of Jesus of Nazareth," 128-129; "Manual of Parliamentary Practice, 97-99; "Notes on Virginia," 183-184, cited, 19, 37, 38, 99, 123, 139, 226, 282; Reply to Lord North's motion, 270; to Lord North's proposals, 263-265, 266; "Report of Cases," 85, 93-95, 172; "Summary View of the Rights of British America," 240-250; "Thoughts on English Prosody," 118

Papers, 4, 5, 307; account books, 87, 102; case register, 90, 91; commonplace books, 81, 84-89, 94, 106, 110-116, 210-214, 224; farm book, 17, 278, 309-311, 325; fee book, 90, 91, 96, 324; garden book, 38, 46, 149, 176, 278

Biographers, 3-5; books, 31, 80-82, 100-130, 148, *see also* under individual authors and titles; education, program of, 79-83; handwriting, 85-88, 129, 244-245; horsemanship, 64; land holdings, 17; languages, knowledge of, 31, 106-109; library, *see* books; philosophy, 111-113, 115-116, religion, 123-129; seal, 35; slaves, 32, 163, 173, 180, 278; travel, plans for, 68, 69, 135

Jefferson Bible, 128-129

Jeffrys, Thomas, 30

"Jesus of Nazareth, Life and Morals of," 128-129

Johnson, "Dictionary," 169

——, William, 56

Jones, Emanuel, 41, 261

——, Gabriel, 90

——, Hugh, 51, 60

——, Inigo, "Designs," 164

——, Joseph, 331

——, Walter, 43

Jouett, Jack, 5

Judiciary, 289

Kames, Lord, writings, 80, 81, 88, 89, 105, 106, 330

Kennon, Will, 10

Kent, William, "Designs," 164

King, *see* George III, etc.

King George County, 331

King and Queen County, 25, 34

King, rights of, 37

King William County, 34, 79, 196, 265, 282
King William parish, 31
King's Bounty, 313
King's College, 76
Kings, election of, 214, 245, 246
Kingship, or royal prerogative, 245-246
Kinloch, 131
Kirmovan, Chevalier de, 294
Knowlands, 285

Ladd, 311
Ladds, John and Noble, 32
Lancaster, Pennsylvania, 285
Land tenure, 248; *see also* Entail, Primogeniture, Feudalism
Landscape gardening, *see* Gardening
Langhorne, William, writings, 116, 246
Lantern of Demosthenes, 162, 322
Latin, Jefferson's knowledge of, 31, 107, 110-112, 141-142
Laws, Virginia, collection of, 97
Leasowes, The, Worcestershire, 116, 148-149, 160
Le Blond, Alexander, "Jardinage," 148
Lee, Edward, 90
———, Francis Lightfoot, 231, 271
———, Henry, Sr., 196, 288
———, Henry ("Light Horse Harry"), 4, 142-144
———, Henry (Son of "Light Horse Harry"), 305, 321
———, Richard Henry, 75, 90, 181, 196, 199, 202, 231, 232, 233, 234, 238, 253, 257, 258, 259, 266, 268, 270, 281, 282, 283, 284, 286, 287, 291, 292, 294, 297, 299, 304, 333
———, Thomas, 34
———, Thomas Ludwell, 76, 220, 288
Le Nôtre, André, 148
Leonard, Charles, 54
Leoni, Giacomo, 322
LeRoy, J. D., "Ruins of Athens," 322
Lewis, 75
———, Col., 60
———, Andrew, 90, 284
———, Charles, 284
———, John, 17
———, Mary, 171
———, Nicholas, 279
———, Thomas, 29-30
———, Warner, 43, 133, 134, 135
Lex talonis, 225
Lexington, battle of, 5, 261, 268
Libraries, 12-13, 24-25, 31, 46, 53, 102-103, 212, 251; *see also* Jefferson, Thomas, books
"Life and Morals of Jesus of Nazareth," 128-129
Lincoln, Levy, 145, 146
Lindsay, Mr., 37
Littlepage, James, 189
Livingston, Robert R., 292, 294, 333
———, William, 286
Livy, 106, 112, 125, 318
Locke, John, writings, 80, 82, 105, 210, 211, 214-215, 243, 244, 304, 306

INDEX

"London and Country Brewer," 13
Louis XV style, 138
Louisa County, 34, 35-38, 45, 46, 190, 232
"Lovely Peggy," 117
Lower Quarter, 28
Loyal Land Company, 17
Ludwell family, 135
Lunan, Patrick, 95

McAlister's town, Pennsylvania, 285
McCaul, Alexander, 165
McClurg, James, 43
McDowell, James, 159
McKean, Thomas, 253, 298
MacKenzie, Captain, 253
Macpherson, Charles, 119
———, James, 119-120
———, John, 139
Machiavelli, Niccolo, writings, 106
Madison, James, 79, 84, 212, 222, 296, 305
Mallet, David, writings, 116
———, P. H., "Histoire de Danemark," 246
Malthus, Thomas Robert, "Principles of Population," 82
Manakin Creek, 12, 13
Manakin Town, 31
"Manual of Parliamentary Practice," 97-99
Maps, 13, 29-30
Marbois, Barbé de, 183
Marcus Aurelius, *see* Antoninus

Marmontel, Jean François, writings, 105, 122, 215
Marriage bonds, 16, 175-176
Marshall, John, 4
Maryland, 266, 291, 293, 297, 298
Mason, George, 91, 204, 220, 228, 258, 285, 288, 290
———, Thompson, 199, 202
Massachusetts, 145, 194, 195, 196, 200, 233, 234, 235, 237, 253, 281, 283, 298
Massachusetts Gazette, cited, 212
Massillon, Jean-Baptiste, "Sermons," 81
Mathematics, 40, 80, 106, 110, 169
Matrimony, 131, 133, 166-168
Mattaponi River, 135
Maury, James, 13, 34-38, 188
———, M., 103
———, Mary Anne Fontaine, 34
———, Mary Walker, 34
———, Matthew, 34
Mayo, William, 29
Mazzei, Philip, 106, 154, 171, 239-240, 304
Meade, William, cited, 52
Mechanics, 169
Mecklenburg County, 331
Mercer, "Abridgement," 85, 86
Mercer, James, 92, 263, 337
Meriwether, Nicholas, 25
Middlesex County, 132
Migrations, 247
Militia, 10, 257, 259
Mill, Peter Jefferson's, 13, 21

INDEX

Millot, Claude-François, "Histoire Moderne," 82

Milton, John, writings, 88, 105, 107, 114-115, 169, 303

Ministers, *see* Clergy

Ministry, 281; *see also* Dartmouth, Hilsborough, North, Townshend

Minitree, David, 139

Minns & Young, 145

Minor, Dabney, 321

———, John, 79

Mitchell, Capt., 136

"Modus Tenendi Parliamentum," 210

Molesworth, Robert, "Account of Denmark," 246

Molière, 122

Monroe, James, 79, **182**

———, Spence, 30

Montalto, 164

Montesquieu, Charles Louis, writings, 82, 105, 113, 210, 211-213, 215, 224, 243, 244, 245, 304

Monticello, 4, 5, 17, 18, 45, 46, 55, 57, 104, 116, 120, 134, 135, 147-165, 166, 168, 169, 171, 172, 176, 177, 206, 217, 238, 239-240, 251, 271, 277-285, 309; building at, 135, 147-166, 206, 209, 255-256; graveyard, 46, 163; kitchen, 154, 155, 158; offices, 154-155, 157-158; orchard, 149, 160; outchambers, 149, 152, 156; park, 161, 163; planting, 148, 160-165; roundabouts, 155, 165; slave quarters, 155; stables, 154, 155, 158; stairs, 158; temples, 162, 163, 164; terraces, 152, 154, 157, 158; towers, 164; well, 155

Moore, Mr., 135, 150

———, Bernard, Sr., 131-132

———, Bernard, Jr., 79, 82, 116

———, Edward, writings, 116

———, Elizabeth (Betsey), 79, 131-132, 140-146; *see also* Walker, John

Moot court, 76

Morgan, John, 37

Morris, Robert, 298

———, Robert, "Select Architecture," 150, 151, 157

———, Roger, 139

Morven, Princeton, New Jersey, 160

Mount Malado, 10-11

Mount-My-Lady, 10

Mount Pleasant, 47

Mulattos, servitude, 94

Mumford, Robert, 331

Munford, Thomas, 150

Music, 51, 53-59, 65, 104, 123, 130, 172, 174, 176

Napoleon, 214

Natural Bridge, 139-140

Natural history, 37, 110; philosophy, 79, 106

Natural law, 94, 242, 244, 301; *see also* Burlamaqui, Puffendorf, Vattel; rights, 245-247, 301-302

Naturalization, 222

Nature, Jefferson's love of, 38

"Nature Displayed," 106

Negroes, *see* Slavery

Nelson County, 119

Nelson, Elizabeth Burwell, 67

INDEX 351

Nelson, "Office of A Justice," 13
——, Thomas, Sr., 47, 101, 155
——, Thomas, Jr., 47, 101, 196, 259, 270, 278, 286, 315, 331
——, William, 67, 229
New England, 31, 253, 292, 298; *see also* individual states
New England Palladium, 145
New Jersey, 291, 293, 298
New Kent County, 10, 133, 135
New Quarter, 21
New River, 310
New York, 88, 135, 137, 138, 139, 230, 248, 253, 266, 274, 291, 293-298
Nicholas, Robert Carter, 91, 193, 196, 199, 202, 212, 226, 231, 233, 234, 235, 254, 259, 263, 282, 283, 288, 331
Non-importation agreement, 203-205, 229, 237-238, 251, 252, 254-256
Norfolk, 196, 256, 279
North, Lord, 271; Proposals, 262-265; Motion, 270, 275
North Carolina, 23, 36, 90, 282, 283, 291, 298
North Mountain, *see* Allegheny Mountains
Northanna, *see* Rivanna River
Northern Neck, 29
Norton, John, & Sons, 205, 244
"Notes on Virginia," *see* Jefferson, Thomas, writings
Novels, Jefferson's opinion, 120-122

Ogilvie, "Description of America," 13

Ogilvie, James, 156, 173
Ogle, Cuthbert, 54
Ohio Company, 36
Ontasseté, 19
Orange County, 133, 285
Orchestra, 57
Organs, 54, 56-57
Osborne's, 10, 12
Osborne, Thomas, 9, 10
Ossian, 105, 119-120
Oswald, James, 117
Otis, James, 305
Otway, Thomas, writings, 115
Overseers, 17, 28, 194
Ovid, 88, 113
Owen, Goronwy, 42
Oxford University, 23, 76

Paca, Governor, 138
Page, John, 43, 44-45, 64-71, 86, 100, 101, 115, 132, 133, 134, 135, 136, 140, 147, 168, 169, 205, 206, 258, 282, 288, 304, 315
——, Mann, 44, 45
Paine, Thomas, 113, 305; "Common Sense," 275, 279-281, 282; "American Crisis," 280
Paintings, 154
Palladio, 151-153, 157, 231
Pamunkey River, 35, 135, 136
Pantops, 310
Paris, 58, 244, 292
Parks, Mr., 29
Parliament, 192, 194, 200, 204, 205, 206, 233, 234, 235, 237, 238,

242, 247-248, 252, 258, 263, 264, 268, 269, 274, 275, 279, 286, 292
Parliamentary practice, 82, 97-99
Parson's Cause, 36-37, 188, 189-190
Pasteur, Elizabeth Stith, 315
——, William, 55, 135, 315
Peachylorum, 131
Pelham, Peter, Jr., 54
Pelloutier, Simon, writings, 245
Pendleton, Edmund, 91, 92, 193, 196, 198-199, 219, 220, 221, 226, 232, 233
Penn, John, 139, 282
——, Richard, 274
Pennsylvania, 253, 291, 293, 294, 298
Pennsylvania Evening Post, 282
Pennsylvania Gazette, etc., 254
Percy, Thomas, "Reliques," 105
Pergolesi, G. B., 59
Perrault, "Vitruvius," 164
Peter's Creek, 23
Peter's Mountain, 35, 38
Peters, Richard, 139
Petersburg, 282
"Petits Jus Parliamentum," 210
Petty, Thomas, writings, 105, 153, 210, 244
Peyton, Craven, 20
Philadelphia, 88, 103, 128, 135, 137-139, 159, 181, 216, 236, 238, 240, 243, 251, 260, 265-274, 278, 279, 289
——, "Carpenters' Hall," 251
——, City Tavern (Smith's Tavern), 251, 265
——, Library Company, 212, 251

Philadelphia, State House, 138, 286, 303
Phillips, Major Gen., 177
Pianoforte, 174
Pickering, Timothy, 296, 305
Piedmont, 34, 38
Piganiol de la Force, "Description ... de Versailles," 53
Pitt, Sarah, 210
Pittsylvania County, 311
Plato, 110, 116
Platonists, 129
Plutarch, 106
Pockett, The, 311
Poetry, Jefferson's taste in, 116-120
Point of Fork, 19
Poland, 246
Pope, Alexander, writings, 86, 114, 116, 122, 170; garden, 160; translation of Homer, 88, 105, 111
Poplar Forest, 178, 325
Port Royal, 270
Port Tobacco, 265
Portobello, 309
Potomac River, 29, 285
Potter, Henry, 132
Potter, Susannah (Sukey), 64, 70, 132, 136, 315
Pouncey's, 310
Powder, 260, 262, 279
Powel, Samuel, 139
"Practice, King's Bench," 83
Prayer, Book of Common, 13
——, Day of Fast and, 234-235
"Preceptor, The," 169
Presbyterians, 217

"Present State of Great Britain," 13
Priestley, "Principles of Government," 81
Primogeniture, 220-221, 227
Prince George County, 75, 254
Prison, design of, 225
Puffendorf, Samuel, writings, 110, 212, 215-216, 244
Purcell, Henry, 57
Purdie & Dixon, 212

Quakers, 217
Quebec Bill, 253
Quintus Smyrnus, 110

Racine, Jean, 122
Raffles, 61-62
Randall, Henry S., 4-5, 20
Randolph family, 3, 9, 11, 15
———, Benjamin, 265, 273
———, Edmund, 96, 263, 288; cited, 84, 123, 124, 161, 187, 230, 234, 238, 240-241, 251, 252, 258, 259, 260, 261, 280, 285
———, Elizabeth, 133
———, Henry, 10
———, Isham, 3, 12, 15-16, 18, 308
———, Jane Rogers, 16
———, John, 55-56, 92, 93, 199, 270-272, 274-275
———, Sir John, 93
———, Judith, 26, 28
———, Maria Judith Page, 26
———, Martha Jefferson, 59, 176, 177, 181, 184, 185
———, Mary, 26, 28
———, Mary Isham, 15
———, Nancy, 132

Randolph, Peter, 39
———, Peyton, 62, 75, 91, 193, 196, 198-199, 203, 233, 234, 238, 240, 254, 259, 266, 270, 274
———, Priscilla, 26
———, Richard, 196
———, Thomas Jefferson, 62, 178
———, Thomas Mann, Jr., 23, 99
———, Thomas Mann, Sr., 26-27, 28
———, Virginia, 58
———, William, of Tuckahoe, 7, 16, 17, 24, 26-27, 28, 310
———, William of Turkey Island, 3, 15
Rapin, "History of England," 13
Rappahannock River, 28, 29
Rastall, "Statutes," 83
Raymond, "Reports," 87, 88
Read, George, 266, 299
Recorder, 144
Reed, Joseph, 281
Religion, Jefferson's views, 123-129
Religious freedom, 217, 225-227; statute for, 123, 227
Republicanism, 227, 258
Republics, size of, 213
Resolutions, against the Stamp Act, 193; against the Declaratory Act, 200-202
Resolutions, Albemarle, 237-238
Resolutions regarding Committees of Correspondence, 232-234
"Resolutions respecting Independency," 291-294, 297-299
Revenue laws, 192-193, 194-195, 201, 204, 253, 263
Revere, Paul, 5

Revisal of Virginia laws, 5, 92, 96, 220-222, 245
Revolution, American, 191, 194, 204, 216, 235, 257-306
Revolutions, 215
Rhode Island, 231
Rice, William, 159
Richardson, Samuel, writings, 25
Richmond, 13, 29, 76, 144, 145, 159, 171, 182, 222, 256-259, 260, 311
Rights, of citizens, 201, 233, 241-242, 245-246, 289, 290; natural, 245-247, 301
Ritchie, Mr., 78
Rivanna River, 4, 18, 21, 32, 170, 239, 309
Roan, Judge, 77
Robertson, William, writings, 82, 107, 245
Robinson, John, 190-191, 193, 199
Rock Castle Creek, 310
Rodney, Caesar, 266, 298
Rogers, Charles, 16
———, Jane Lilburn, 16
Rollin's "Ancient History," 169
Rosewell, 44, 102, 134, 135, 205
Round Top, 190
Rousseau, Jean Jacques, writings, 105
Rowanty, 104
Rowe, Nicholas, writings, 115
Royle, 103
Ruffin's Ferry, 265
Rush, Benjamin, 127, 128, 329
Russell, "Modern Europe," 82
Rutledge, Edward, 266, 291, 292, 298

Sador and Man, Bishop of, "Instructions for Indians," 13
Sailor's Creek, 309
St. Anne's parish, 123, 251
St. James' parish, 18, 20, 31
St. John's College, 138
Salkeld, William, "Reports," 87, 88, 89
Sallust, 112
Salmon, Thomas, "Modern History," 246
San Domingo, 224
Sandy Falls, 309
Savage, L., 90
Saxons, 241, 247; *see also* Anglo-Saxons
Say, "Economie politique," 82
Schobert, 59
Schools, elementary, 222
Schuyler, Philip, 286
Scott, Gustavus, 92
"Scrivener's Guide," 13
Sculpture, 154
"Secret History of Queen Anne's Ministers," 13
Secretary's Ford, 18, 309
Senate, U. S., 97, 99
Seneca, 115
Severn River, 133, 134
Shadwell, 17-23, 24, 26, 28, 30, 32, 46, 71, 78, 82, 134, 135, 142, 148, 187-193, 309, 310; fire at, 82, 100, 134, 154, 214
Shakespeare, 25, 59, 105, 115-116, 121, 122
Shells, 37

Shenstone, William, writings, 116, 148-149, 160, 161
Sheridan, "Elocution," 83
Sherman, Roger, 294
Sherrando, 309
Shooting, 130
Short, William, 110, 112, 128, 147
Sidney, Algernon, writings, 82, 215, 244, 304, 306, 322
Silver, 9, 33, 103, 180, 181
Singleton, Mr., 54
Skelton, Bathurst, 114, 169-170, 175, 180, 181, 324, 325
———, James, 169
———, Jane Meriwether, 169
———, John, 170, 181, 324
———, Reuben, 169
Skipwith, Ann Wayles, 324
———, Henry, 179
———, Robert, 103-105, 119, 121, 160, 172, 174, 215, 244, 245
Slavery, 89, 90, 204, 207, 223, 300
Small, William, 42, 47-50, 62, 124, 141, 211
Smallpox, 68, 137, 185
Smith, Charles, 13
———, J., 310, 311
———, Robert, 146
Smollett, Tobias George, writings, 105, 169
Socrates, 110, 115
Solomon, "State Trials," 13
Songs, owned by Jefferson, 58
Sorrels, Richard, 161
South Carolina, 282, 283, 291, 293, 298, 300

Southwest Mountains, 25, 34-35, 38, 309
Sovereignty, popular, 245-247
Spafford, Horatio, 128
Spain, 292, 293
Spanish, Jefferson's knowledge of, 107
Speaking, art of, 82, 83-84
"Spectator," 13, 170
Spence, Joseph, "Polymetis," 154
Spinet, 174
Spon, Jacques, "Voyages," 322
Spotswood, Alexander, 53, 131
———, Mrs., 189
———, Alexander (the younger), 265
Spotsylvania County, 75
Stafford County, 202
Stamp Act, 192-193, 194-195, 241, 254
Stanyan, Abraham, "Grecian History," 106, 246
Starke, Richard, 56
Statues, 154
Staunton, 29, 135
Steep Rock Creek, 23
Steptoe, James, 56
Sterne, Laurence, writings, 81, 104, 106, 116, 174
Stewart, Sir James, writings, 80, 210, 244
Stinson, Alexander, 17
Stith, P., 136
———, William, 29, 106, 107, 315
Stockton, Davis, 13
———, Richard, 160
Stoics, 112-113

INDEX

Stone-cutters, 57
Stuart, Sir James, "Political Œconomy," 105
Stuart and Revett, "Antiquities of Athens," 322
Sullivan, Francis S., writings, 245
"Summary View of the Rights of British America," 240-250
Surgery, 106
"Survey of Ireland," 244
Surveyors, 23-24, 28-30
Swan, Abraham, "British Architect," 138
Sweden, 246
Swift, Jonathan, writings, 25, 105, 113, 170
Switzer, 13
Switzerland, 246

"Table of the Bees," 170
Tacitus, 112, 125
Taliaferro, Jenny, 132
Tanistry, law of, 210
Tarleton, Banastre, 5
Tarrytown, Pennsylvania, 285
"Tatler," 13
Taverns, 42, 60; see also Williamsburg, Raleigh Tavern
Taxation, 192-193, 194-195, 201, 204, 206, 234, 235, 253, 263
Tea, tax on, 195, 204, 206, 234, 235, 253
Temple, Sir William, writings, 246
"Terence Delphini," 169
Theaters, 54, 59-60, 134, 135, 177
Thompson, Charles, 333

Thompson, student at William and Mary, 44
Thomson, James, "Seasons," 114, 122
"Thoughts on English Prosody," 118
Three Notch'd Road, 18
Thweatt, Archibald, 181
Tidewater Virginia, 3, 7, 11, 34, 38, 68, 139, 147, 156, 157, 159, 191, 239, 256, 321; see also individual places and houses
Tobacco, 8, 13, 28, 103, 131, 261
Tomahawk Creek, 310
Totier Creek, 311
Townshend, Charles, 195
Tracy, Destutt de, 213
Trade and Revenue, Act of, 195
Trade, restrictions on, 195, 234-235, 247, 263-264
Treason, Trials for, 201, 202, 231
Treasury, 277
Trist, Nicholas P., 316
Trumbull, John, 74
Tuckahoe, 14, 21, 27-28, 29, 31, 33, 176, 239
Tuckahoe Creek, 311
Tucker, Frances Bland Randolph, 324
Tucker, George, 4
———, St. George, 232
Tufton, 310
Turkey Hill, 131
Turkey Island, 3, 15, 133
Turpin, Thomas, 17, 23, 33, 310
Tutors, 28
"Two-penny Act," 36, 188
Tye River, 311

INDEX 357

Tyler, John, 77, 78
———, John, Sr., 190

Union of Utrecht, 246
University, 223
University of Pennsylvania, 137-138

Valley of Virginia, 194
Van Cortlandt, Frederick, 139
Vardill, John, 76
Varina, 10, 11
Vattel, Emeric, "Droit des Gens," 81, 244, 304
Vernon, Thomas, "Reports," 89
Vertot, René Aubert de, "Révolutions en Suède," 246
Vicenza, 329
Vice-Presidency, 98
Viewmont, 22, 23
Vignerons, 57
Violins, 54-56, 135, 271; see also Music
Virgil, 113, 119, 170
Virginia, see individual places and topics
Virginia Gazette, cited, 30, 36, 54, 60, 92, 170, 175, 179, 197, 203, 204, 205, 206, 210, 212; purchases from, 83, 87, 103, 106, 114, 209, 213, 316, 321
"Virginia Justice," 13
"Virginia Laws," 83
Vitruvius, 164
Vivaldi, 57
Voltaire, François M., writings, 95, 106

Wadham College, 23
Walker, James, 34
———, John, 25, 43, 45, 47, 68, 79, 115, 131-132, 140-145, 169, 237-238, 256-278
———, Mildred Thornton, 25
———, Thomas, 17, 24-25, 31, 33, 35, 36, 131, 140, 141, 187, 256; library of, 24-25
Wall paper, 154
Waller, Benjamin, 56
———, Thomas, 102, 104
Walpole, Horace, cited, 196
Walthoe, 90
———, Nathaniel, 197, 203
Ware River, 47, 134
Ware, The, 11
Warm Spring, 90
Warner Hall, 133, 134, 135
Warner, "History of Ireland," etc., 210, 244, 330
Warren, James, 268, 282, 283, 290, 303
Washington, George, 23, 39, 140, 159, 182, 199, 204, 238, 241, 253, 258, 259, 266, 268, 280, 286, 303
———, Martha, 171
Washington Federalist, 145
Watch paper, 66
Watermarks, 85-87
Watkins, D., 310
Watt, James, 48
Wayles, Elizabeth Lomax, 169
———, John, 168-170, 174, 178-179, 180, 324, 325

Wayles, Martha Eppes, 169, 179
——, Tabitha, 172
Weavers, 57
Webb, "Essay on Painting," 105
——, William, 41
Wells, Samuel Adams, 295
Westmoreland County, 30
Westover, 103, 139, 240
Westover Church, 36
West Point, 135
West Virginia, 19
Wetherburn, Henry, 18, 55
Whately, Thomas, "Observations on Gardening," 105, 161-162, 164
White Hall, 47, 134
Wilkinson, 12
William and Mary College, 13, 23, 28, 34, 39-52, 59, 65, 75, 76, 78, 140, 141, 147, 168, 169, 196-207, 231, 232
Williams, Peere, "Reports," 88, 89
Williamsburg, 14, 19, 29, 40-64, 68, 70, 72, 75, 78, 89, 90, 101, 102, 103, 130, 132, 134, 137, 139, 140, 147, 177, 187-209, 221, 222, 229-237, 238, 239-241, 251, 252, 254, 259-265, 268, 270, 271, 278, 284, 287
——, Bruton parish church, 52, 53, 196, 235
——, Capitol, 52, 53, 76, 169, 187, 196, 197, 284
——, Governor's Palace, 51, 52, 53, 120, 159, 206, 262
——, Raleigh tavern, 61, 70, 71, 202, 231, 235
Willing, Thomas, 299

Willis, Francis, 47, 69, 90, 134, 206
——, Miss, 68
Wilmington, 265
Wilson, James, 241, 292, 298, 305
Wilton, 132
Winslow, Captain, 29
Wirt, William, cited, 46, 84, 188, 193, 258-259
Woffington, Peg, 117
Wolff, Christian, "Droit de la nature et des gens," 110
Wood, Mr., 230
Woodward, Augustus B., 290
"World, The," 170
Worsham, Captain, 10
Writing, art of, 82
Wythe, George, 44, 47, 48, 55, 62, 73-78, 84, 90, 92, 94, 97, 98-99, 101, 125, 188, 193, 197, 209, 211, 220, 221, 228, 241, 244, 254, 261, 271, 288, 289, 292, 304

Xenophon, 115

Yardley, Sir Thomas, 8
Yates, Mr., 132
——, Betsey, 132
——, William, 41
Yeardley, George, 307
York, Pennsylvania, 285
York County, 196, 259, 286
York River, 134, 135, 260
Yorktown, 60, 67, 101, 134, 181, 206, 229, 240
Young, writings, 105, 115